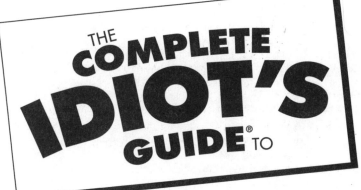

THE **COMPLETE IDIOT'S GUIDE** TO

The Confederacy

by J. Stephen Lang

ALPHA

A Pearson Education Company

International Standard Book Number: 0-02864383-6
Library of Congress Catalog Card Number: 2002111657

04   03   02   8   7   6   5   4   3   2   1

Interpretation of the printing code: The rightmost number of the first series of numbers is the year of the book's printing; the rightmost number of the second series of numbers is the number of the book's printing. For example, a printing code of 02-1 shows that the first printing occurred in 2002.

Printed in the United States of America

For marketing and publicity, please call: 317-581-3722

The publisher offers discounts on this book when ordered in quantity for bulk purchases and special sales.

For sales within the United States, please contact: Corporate and Government Sales, 1-800-382-3419 or corpsales@pearsontechgroup.com

Outside the United States, please contact: International Sales, 317-581-3793 or international@pearsontechgroup.com

Publisher: *Marie Butler-Knight*
Product Manager: *Phil Kitchel*
Managing Editor: *Jennifer Chisholm*
Acquisitions Editor: *Gary Goldstein*
Development Editor: *Jennifer Moore*
Production Editor: *Billy Fields*
Copy Editor: *Amy Borrelli*
Illustrator: *Chris Eliopoulos*
Cover/Book Designer: *Trina Wurst*
Indexer: *Tonya Heard*
Layout: *Ayanna Lacey*

Contents at a Glance

Contents

Contents

Foreword

There's something romantic about lost causes, and the Granddaddy of them all is the Confederacy. More good (and bad) novels and movies have been set in the Old South than just about anywhere else, and for good reason—it's difficult to imagine a more exciting time in American history.

But the real story of the Confederacy is better than anything you're likely to see on the big screen.

Did you know, for example, that the first submarine ever to sink an enemy ship was a Confederate vessel? Or that the course of the entire Civil War might have been different if a Yankee private hadn't found Robert E. Lee's grand battle plan, wrapped around three cigars, which was lost on the ground before the battle of Antietam?

These are the kinds of stories you'll find throughout this book, along with something else: a different point of view. Whatever you think you know about the Civil War, prepare to have it challenged. Think the war was about slavery? It was, but don't forget states' rights. Think the war started in 1861? It did, but the shooting began in Kansas long before Fort Sumter. And by the way, don't call it the Civil War—to Southerners, it's the *War Between the States*.

Even the battles have different names.

Antietam, for example, was *Sharpsburg* to the Confederates, and it was the site of the single bloodiest day in American wars. Nine times more soldiers were killed and wounded than in the D-Day invasion of World War II. The bloodshed shook both sides and led Abraham Lincoln to issue the Emancipation Proclamation.

While slavery was a cornerstone of the Old South (it was even spelled out in the Confederate Constitution), most Rebel soldiers were too poor to own slaves. While Southern aristocrats saw themselves in a chivalric fantasy right out of a Sir Walter Scott novel, the average Johnny Reb was coping with the reality of being underfed and outgunned.

The amazing thing about the Confederacy is not that it was so brief, but that it managed to hold out for so long against overwhelming odds.

In this book you'll not only learn about brilliant soldiers like J. E. B. Stuart and Stonewall Jackson, you'll hear the rattle of sabers and the thunder of cannons. You'll discover why the combination of improved weapons and outdated tactics produced such a heartbreaking body count.

And you'll understand why the Confederacy, which lasted only four short years, has cast such a controversial shadow over American history for more than a century. Author J. Stephen Lang has given us a fascinating insider's look at a lost way of life.

—Max McCoy

Max McCoy is an award-winning novelist and investigative reporter. His fiction debut, *The Sixth Rider*, was the winner of the prestigious Medicine Pipe Award for Best First Novel from the Western Writers of America. Until recently, he was an investigative reporter for the *Joplin* (Missouri) *Globe*.

Introduction

Let's begin with a fact: The Confederate government came to an end in spring 1865. Whether the Confederacy itself ended then is another matter. It appears the Confederacy is still with us. Consider a few recent news items:

In 2001, Georgia voted to remove the Confederate battle flag from its state flag—sort of. The new Georgia flag no longer features the Rebel flag in its upper left corner. But it does appear in a small band underneath the state seal on the flag.

The same year, Mississippi held a referendum: new flag, or keep the old flag with its Confederate battle emblem? The voters, two to one, opted for the old flag.

The year before, the Confederate battle flag was lowered, for the last time, from the dome of South Carolina's capitol building. But immediately afterward a Confederate flag was raised next to a Confederate monument on the capitol lawn. The state has found itself the target of a tourist boycott by those who protest the Confederate flag being displayed anywhere on the capitol grounds.

In Richmond, the capital of the Confederacy, a city park displayed a large mural showing General Robert E. Lee in his Confederate uniform. After loud protests, the city changed the mural, showing Lee in civilian dress.

Obviously, the Confederacy still has a hold on people's imaginations and emotions. Such symbols as the Confederate battle flag and the image of Robert E. Lee in uniform get a rise out of people, even though Lee died in 1870 and the Confederacy itself died in 1865. Why so? Is it purely a matter of race? Are people correct in assuming that the Confederate flag is a symbol of white supremacy? Are they correct in assuming that slavery and racism were the only reasons the Confederacy existed?

Well, let's face an inescapable fact: You can't discuss the Confederacy without discussing slavery and race. But you have to throw in a few other inescapable facts—such as the fact that most white Southerners didn't own slaves. So what motivated all those Southern boys in gray? Were they fighting and dying for slavery? For white supremacy? Hardly. Life, and history, are more complicated than that. So was the Old South.

Most Southerners were not itching for a war with the North, nor itching to secede. A handful of very loud and very influential writers and politicians in both North and South pushed the South into secession and war. When it came, Southern boys did what patriotic folk have done throughout history: They went off to fight the foe.

They lost. After four years of hard fighting, they endured 12 more years of humiliation known as Reconstruction. The Northern politicians who heaped insults on the "barbaric" South before the Civil War, took some delight in making things unpleasant after the war.

And yet, Confederates were hard to keep down. If you thumb through biographies of Confederate politicians and military leaders, you'll notice something interesting: Most of them rose to high positions later on. They became governors, legislators, college presidents, successful lawyers and businessmen. Quite a few served in the U.S. Congress. On the local level, plenty of Confederate privates and corporals later became mayors and town councilmen. And most of them made no apology for having served the Confederacy. Many of them proudly proclaimed that they were "unreconstructed."

That was true of the common people, too. Many a Southern home graced its walls with pictures of Robert E. Lee, Stonewall Jackson, and Jefferson Davis. "The Lost Cause" became almost a religion. And, as you can see from the news items mentioned at the start of this introduction, the religion hasn't died out. People still have an attachment to the Confederacy. How else do you explain the countless Civil War and Confederate websites, the flood of books, the reenactors who put on wool uniforms in the heat and humidity of summer? How else do you explain popular singing groups that call themselves Confederate Railroad and Dixie Chicks?

An obvious question: Do all the people waving the Rebel flag and singing "Dixie" really know much about the Confederacy? Maybe not. And maybe the people who protest the flag don't know enough, either. That is what this book is all about: explaining how the Confederacy came into existence, how it fought and lost a bloody war, and how it still makes its presence felt today.

Extras

In addition to the book's main narrative and illustrations, you'll also find "boxed" information throughout. Look for these four features:

RebeLingo
These are definitions of key words and phrases relating to the Confederacy.

Go See It!
The South is full to the brim with battlefields, monuments, museums, memorials, cemeteries, and other sites relating to the Confederacy. We'll tell you about some of the most interesting.

Voices from Then

Notable quotables from Confederates (or, sometimes, *about* them). These include snippets from songs, poems, speeches, and letters.

Did Y'all Know?

Some amusing trivia tidbits, anecdotes, and surprising facts.

Special Thanks to the Technical Reviewer

The Complete Idiot's Guide to the Confederacy was reviewed by an expert who double-checked the accuracy of what you'll learn here, to help us ensure that this book gives you everything you need to know about the Confederacy. Special thanks are extended to Max McCoy.

Trademarks

All terms mentioned in this book that are known to be or are suspected of being trademarks or service marks have been appropriately capitalized. Alpha Books and Pearson Education, Inc., cannot attest to the accuracy of this information. Use of a term in this book should not be regarded as affecting the validity of any trademark or service mark.

Part 1

Breaking Up Is Hard to Do

You might say the Confederacy began when a group of Englishmen settled at Jamestown, Virginia, in 1607. Or maybe it began with those Virginians who first purchased slaves for use on their farms. But maybe the real beginning was the date that the South began to realize it was different from the North. In the 1830s it suffered some shocks—a short but bloody slave revolt, and a steady stream of insults and sermons from abolitionists. Then, in the 1840s, the nation's churches began to divide over the issue of slavery. Political compromises kept the Union together—barely.

Even before Abraham Lincoln was elected president in 1860, many people in both North and South had come to feel that the Ohio River and the Mason-Dixon Line were really, really wide. Each section accused the other of not being genuinely American. Each section felt the other had betrayed the dreams of the Founding Fathers. All things considered, the North-South separation is a sad story. And sad stories always make for good reading.

Chapter 1

The Old South: Planters, Plain Folk, and Other Folk

In This Chapter

◆ The meaning of "planter" and "plantation"

◆ The plain folk of the Old South

◆ Slavery's effect on white solidarity

◆ The King Cotton mentality

Say the words "Southern plantation," and people think of *Gone with the Wind*—Scarlett O'Hara at Tara, the huge house with Greek columns, endless fields, and a swarm of contented and devoted slaves. If all white Southerners had lived that way before the Civil War, you could see why some still pine for the Old South.

Now, back to reality. Margaret Mitchell's Pulitzer Prize–winning novel shows a much wider picture of the Old South than the movie did. There were wealthy "planters" like Scarlett's father, but also "white trash," "crackers," "yeomen," and many other categories that don't quite fit the Tara image. Southern society, before and during the Civil War, was diverse—and fascinating.

Let's Define "Planter"

No, a planter isn't a brass pot for holding a palm tree. In the Old South a planter was a farmer who owned 20 or more slaves. This class of people probably made up about 5 percent of the total population of the South. That is a tiny minority, but what it lacked in numbers, it made up for in power, wealth, and land.

A planter lived on (surprise!) a plantation, which included the main house where the family lived, plus cabins for the slaves, perhaps a schoolhouse for the children, and maybe even a chapel for worship. There was a collection of outer buildings like the smokehouse (for meat), stables for horses, chicken houses, a barn for dairy cows, various sheds for storing tools, farm equipment, and grain, plus small buildings for making barrels, furniture, and cloth. In addition to the fields for growing the cash crop (cotton, in most plantations of the *Deep South*), gardens and orchards were cultivated for fruits, vegetables, and herbs.

RebeLingo

The Confederate South is usually divided into the **Deep (or Lower) South**, the **Upper South**, and the **border states**. The states of the Deep South are Alabama, Florida, Georgia, Louisiana, Mississippi, South Carolina, and Texas. The states of the Upper South are Arkansas, Tennessee, North Carolina, and Virginia. The border states are Delaware, Kentucky, Maryland, Missouri, and the District of Columbia.

For people so attached to their land, Southern planters had to be cosmopolitan when it came to furnishing the house. Pictures, tapestries, carpets, and china were generally from Europe or the North, not the South itself. The South didn't do much manufacturing—a fact Southerners would come to deeply regret during the Civil War.

In 1860, there were approximately 306,300 slaveholders in the United States, scattered over the huge territory from Virginia to Texas. Of those, 50,000 were planters. The rest—over 85 percent of the slaveholders—owned 19 or fewer slaves. The percentages break down as follows:

Slaveholders in the United States in 1860

Owners of 1–4 slaves:	139,718 (45.6%)
Owners of 5–19 slaves:	123,085 (40.2%)
Owners of 20–49 slaves:	32,882 (10.7%)
Owners of 50–99 slaves:	8,170 (2.7%)
Owners of 100–499 slaves:	2,251 (0.7%)
Owners of 500+ slaves:	14 (0.005%)
Total:	306,300

(Note: The percentages are of all the slave owners—not of the population at large.)

In one crucial way, the Old South didn't differ from any other human society: The people at the top set the standard. This is important to remember, because even though planters made up about 5 percent of the South's population, they were the 5 percent that most of the other 95 percent admired and tried to imitate if they could afford to. The South in 1860 was home to 60 percent of the nation's wealthiest men. However, average income was lower in the South than in the North.

As a rule, planters based their wealth on the growing of one cash crop. "King Cotton" was the main cash crop in the Deep South. Cotton requires a long, long growing season, so it doesn't do well in the Upper South. In Virginia, Maryland, North Carolina, and Kentucky, tobacco was still a profit maker. Ditto for rice in some of the coastal areas of South Carolina. The most labor-intensive (meaning hardest for the slaves) was sugar farming, mostly confined to Louisiana and part of Texas. None of these were low-maintenance crops, which is why whites with money preferred owning slaves who could do the grunt work.

Who's in Charge Here?

Clearly, a plantation was more like a community than a single-family home. In fact, it closely resembled a manor farm of the Middle Ages. The larger ones were spread out over hundreds of acres, with dozens—perhaps even hundreds—of people living on the land, not to mention the livestock. No wonder the man in charge of all this was proud of himself. He was part of a privileged elite. It will come·as no surprise that many (though not all) of the Southern politicians were planters. This was appropriate. They were accustomed to giving orders, seeing that they were carried out, settling disputes, overseeing large financial transactions, and (in their frequent role as host) being polite and tactful. Could you ask for better qualifications for a politician? (No worse than having a government dominated by lawyers, is it?)

> **Go See It!**
>
> You can visit plantation homes almost anywhere in the South. One of the grandest is the Nottoway plantation in White Castle, Louisiana. The 3-story, 64-room showplace somehow managed to escape damage during the Civil War. The house was the center of a 7,000-acre sugar plantation. On the "Wow!" scale, most visitors rate it a 10.

Just about every planter had a wife at his side. Contrary to what you may have heard, the average plantation mistress was no delicate little flower, put on a pedestal for the menfolk to admire. She probably worked as hard as, or harder than, her husband—and maybe even harder than some of the slaves. While many plantations had a white overseer in charge of the slaves, many didn't. This job usually fell to the mistress, who had to supervise the slaves' food, shelter, clothing, and health.

RebeLingo

The word **antebellum** literally means "prewar." When Americans use it, it means "before the Civil War." So an antebellum home is one built before 1861.

Did Y'all Know?

Some slaveholders thought slavery was efficient. Not all agreed. James Madison lamented that he knew of a 10-acre farm worked by paid labor that produced more than his own 2,000-acre plantation worked by slaves. He wasn't the only slaveholder who doubted whether slavery made good economic sense.

Besides her duties with the slaves, she had a multitude of tasks connected with her own family: sewing and knitting, growing and preserving fruits and vegetables, making candles, curing meats, and … well, if you thought they sat around all day looking pretty and fanning themselves and sniffing magnolia blossoms, it just wasn't so. (Plantation women did draw the line at working out in the sun. No freckles or moles on their hands and faces and shoulders, thank you.)

Southerners frequently sneered at Northerners' obsession with business, money, and numbers. Planters especially liked to speak of Yankees as "a bunch of shopkeepers." But of course, a plantation *was* a business, and someone had to monitor the business affairs. That was more often the mistress than the master. For some (not all) of the planters, engaging in commerce was beneath a master's dignity. (Keep this in mind, as we later learn about some of the Confederate treasury's woes.)

Obviously, planters were strongly pro-slavery. A few had misgivings about it; a few even freed their slaves. But most reacted with horror to the Northerners suggesting that all slaves should be freed. Planters were like most people at the top of society: They were pleased with themselves and believed they deserved to keep the things they possessed.

Planter = Secessionist

We already saw that the planters made up the political elite of the South. They also made up the vanguard of secessionists—those who wanted to break away from the Union. When secession came in 1860 and 1861, probably not 1 planter in 20 remained loyal to the United States.

Plain Folk, Yeomen, and Such

We have a pretty standard definition for planter (a man owning 20 or more slaves), but what do we call farmers owning fewer than 20 slaves?

"Plain folk" and "*yeomen*" are two terms used to refer to the South's rural middle class, farmers and herders who made enough to support themselves but not enough to become wealthy. Most plain folk didn't own slaves or "rent" them out from planters. If they owned slaves, they generally owned five or fewer.

Here is one of the most important pieces of data in this entire book: About 25 percent of Southern whites owned slaves. Flipping that number around, 75 percent lived in homes without slaves. Of the roughly 300,000 slave-holders, 45 percent of them owned fewer than 5 slaves. We mentioned earlier that planters—those who owned more than 20 slaves—were only 5 percent of the Southern population. This can't be overstated: *Most Southern whites did not own slaves.*

RebeLingo

The word **yeoman** is often used by historians to refer to middle-class Southerners. Most were farmers, but some were tradesmen and craftsmen. Unlike planters, yeomen didn't look down on, or shun, manual labor. **Cracker** has about the same meaning, though it suggests someone who is just barely above the level of "po' white."

Go See It!

You can see how Southern plain folks lived at Louisiana State University's Rural Life Museum near Baton Rouge. Old Alabama Town in Montgomery also has several buildings showing how nonplanters lived in the Old South.

Typically, the plain folks' homes were made of logs or planks, probably unpainted. Windows might, or might not, be glass. (If not, cloths had to keep out the weather.) Furniture was sparse and simple. Rugs, if there were any, were braided by hand at home. Generally, the house was one story, with perhaps some attic rooms where children would sleep (and bump their heads if they arose too quickly). In many homes a breezeway or "dog trot" separated rooms on either side—a bedroom and sitting room on one side, a kitchen with dining area on the other.

The plain folks' slaves sometimes slept under the same roof as the owners. In a home with only two or three slaves (and not too many rooms to go around), it was common for slave and master to eat at the same table. On small farms, master and slave worked side by side, toiling away in the fields. Some planters turned up their noses at manual labor, but the average Southern farmer took pride in working with his hands. Being a free man didn't mean "free from manual labor" so much as it meant "free from taking orders from someone else." ("My own boss" was an honored concept the plain-folk farmer shared with the richest planter.)

Living on a farm, plain folk ate pretty well—almost always food they had raised themselves. (They no doubt had fresher meat and produce than what you buy in your local supermarket.) As often happens in rural settings, they were as likely to barter with farm produce as to use money.

Plain folk shared the planter class's love of hospitality. They also, like the planters, thoroughly enjoyed their leisure time, even if they had less of it than the planters did. Pleasures were fairly simple: music courtesy of a fiddle or banjo (or piano, if they could afford one), dancing, storytelling, fishing and hunting, and perhaps drinking or gambling. (These were also the pleasures of the planters.) Plain folk generally attended church, though usually not the planters' Episcopal church. Their own churches—Methodist, Baptist, and Presbyterian, mostly—allowed for a little more emotion and feistier preaching (more hellfire) than the Episcopalians liked.

Did planters and plain folk get along? Mostly, yes. Planters had plain folk relatives, and blood was important in the Old South. Southerners have never been very tolerant of snobbishness, and planters who turned up their noses at plain folk were rare. Plain folk may have envied the planters' wealth (such is human nature), but they also admired them for it (such, too, is human nature). And if your neighbor down the road owned more slaves than you or had a grander house, so what? Maybe you could outshoot him or outfiddle him (or drink him under the table). Such was the plain folks' attitude.

> **Did Y'all Know?**
>
> In 1860, there were roughly 500,000 farms in the South. Of those, only 34 percent were more than 100 acres. The average plain-folk farmer, or yeoman, probably lived on a farm of between 20 and 50 acres.

As in most societies around the world, the upper class set the tone for society. Most Southern planters took great pride in their courtesy and hospitality. So did the plain folk. Travelers from Europe and the North commented often about manners in the Old South. Visitors also commented on Southerners' love of the land—something shared by all Southern whites.

How did plain folk feel about slavery? For the minority who owned slaves, the answer is obvious. But most didn't own slaves. Yet they were aware that the upper crust (the planters, that is) owned slaves and believed the practice was fine—ordained by God, in fact. Plain folk, if they had ambition, usually aspired to own more land—and slaves. Looking at the top of the social pyramid, they saw that the goal was to be someone with lots of land and as many slaves as possible.

But there were exceptions. In many rural areas of the South, planters were hard to find. In the hill country of east Tennessee, western Virginia, or northern Alabama, small farms with no slaves were the rule. Plain folk in those regions were no more fond of blacks than any other Southerners at the time, but in their daily lives, they had little contact with slaves or slave owners. These folks didn't want to abolish slavery, but neither did they wish to secede from the Union over the issue of slavery. They saw no particular reason to leave the Union and they were irritated that some of the rich planters seemed to be pushing for just that. When war finally came, these areas were home to many *Unionists*.

RebeLingo

Larger plantations had an **overseer,** usually a white man from the plain-folk class. (Many were Yankees.) They also had **slave drivers.** Contrary to what you might think, the drivers were not whites, but were slaves in the role of foremen, overseeing (and working alongside) a group of slaves ("gang") assigned to a task. Drivers, since they had extra responsibility, were rewarded with extra food and other privileges.

Remember, it was planters, not plain folk, who pushed for secession. But plain folk had a sense of honor no less than planters. They were aware, dimly, that some very loud-mouthed Northerners had been proclaiming that the South was barbaric and un-Christian (see Chapter 3). When secession did come, they were prepared, and they didn't flinch at the idea of killing Yankee invaders if it came to that.

RebeLingo

Unionists were Southerners who opposed secession. During the Civil War, Unionists often aided the invading Federal armies and helped Confederate deserters hide out.

The Bottom Rung, Sort Of

Just what constituted "white trash" or "po' whites"? No one has a technical definition. To be "poor" in the Old South generally meant you owned no land or property but had to hire out your services to someone else, usually a farmer. The majority of "po' whites" were tenant farmers, meaning they worked for a little bit of pay on land they didn't own. Others worked in factories, though there weren't many of these in the South.

Southerners, like most people in the 1800s, made a distinction between the "respectable poor" and the other kind. If you laid about all day and drank and gambled and whored all night, then you deserved to stay poor. If you were willing to work, there was no lack of labor that needed to be done (though you might still stay poor doing it).

The Color Line

One thing that poor whites shared with all other whites was … whiteness. Every Southern white, regardless of his wealth (or lack of it), believed himself to be superior to blacks—not only to black slaves, but to free blacks as well.

Naturally, there were plenty of upper-class whites who wouldn't be caught dead hobnobbing with po' whites. But the fact remains: With Southern slavery in place, every white person, even the poorest, could look at blacks with a feeling of superiority.

In theory, the very bottom rung was the slaves themselves—a huge chunk of the Southern population, and a chunk with very few legal rights. There was a class structure among the slaves. Field hands were at the bottom, house servants at the top. Naturally, the house servants dressed better and generally ate better than field hands. Many slaves were craftsmen—blacksmiths, barrelmakers, and so forth—and the more talented among these were sometimes hired out for wages and were allowed to keep a part of the wages for themselves. Some could, in time, earn enough to buy their own freedom.

That brings us to another small but important group: free blacks, often designated as "F.C.P" (free person of color) on census forms. They tended to cluster in the cities, though some worked as farmers. And, yes, there were free blacks who owned black slaves. Free blacks had, in theory, more legal rights than slaves, but they kept a low profile in a predominantly white society. When the Civil War came, it shocked many Northerners (and pleased most Southerners) that many free blacks supported the Confederacy. Some lighter-skinned free blacks passed themselves as white and fought as Rebel soldiers.

Were slaves loyal and contented, as most Southerners liked to believe? Or were they oppressed and bitter, as most abolitionists liked to believe? We can only say that not all slaves felt the same about their lot. Some dearly loved their white masters, and some despised them. When war came and many of the masters were away, many loyal slaves stayed on, but many more ran away. Slavery was a terrible thing, yet (much as abolitionists hated to admit it), there was often genuine affection between master and slave. Even in evil institutions, human compassion can manifest itself.

"Ole King Cotton"

Cotton had been grown in the 1700s in Georgia and South Carolina's Sea Islands. It didn't make much of a profit because the task of removing the seeds from the white fibers required so much time and labor. Most farmers found it more trouble than it was worth.

The "white gold," cotton, the labor-intensive crop that was the foundation of plantation wealth in the Deep South.

(Library of Congress)

Along came the inventive schoolteacher Eli Whitney. In 1793, Whitney, a New Englander living in Georgia, created an amazingly simple invention called the cotton gin, which quickly and efficiently removed the seeds from the fibers of the *boll*, the fluffy white part of the plant. It is hard to overstate the effect this machine had on agriculture, on the South, and on American history. Within a decade of the gin's invention, cotton production was eight times greater. Huge tracts of land in the Deep South were planted with this suddenly profitable crop. It didn't hurt that England's textile factories had a huge demand for cotton at the time.

If you had the will, and the land, you could make money quickly from cotton. A cotton plantation could be laid out and in full swing within two years. Of course, clearing out the woods in the Deep South was not a sweatless task. Southerners used slaves to clear the land, and to do the tilling, planting, weeding, picking, and ginning. Once ginned, cotton was compressed into large cubes called *bales*, then taken (usually by boat) to market.

To put it mildly, cotton farming is labor-intensive. It has a long growing season, with an early planting and even earlier prepping of the soil. Actual harvest was late September or even October in some areas.

Plenty of white people worked in the cotton fields. But in the booming cotton economy, the way to make the big profits was to purchase as much of the richest land as you could, then work it with slave labor. Southern plain folk might farm a few acres of cotton and make a small profit from it. But the plantation aristocrats made a killing, creating a new cotton aristocracy in the South. It created a need for more slaves, too. One of the great questions of history is this: What would have happened if Whitney's cotton gin hadn't been invented?

Cotton wasn't king everywhere in the South, however. The plant didn't grow in the Upper South. There were still plenty of tobacco planters in Virginia, North Carolina, and Kentucky. And there were rich people in the Deep South who didn't get their wealth from cotton. But Whitney's gin, and a lot of very sweaty slaves, had succeeded in making a select group of cotton growers very, very wealthy. No wonder David Christy gave the title *Cotton Is King* to his 1855 book. And no wonder there were a number of cotton aristocrats in the U.S. Congress—including a Mississippi planter named Jefferson Davis.

Wealth leads to arrogance. Cotton planters believed that the world market would always need Southern cotton. Textile plants in the United States and abroad were always crying out, "More cotton!" Small wonder that in 1858 a senator from South Carolina would write to an abolitionist senator from New York: "What would happen if no cotton was furnished for three years? England would topple headlong and carry the whole civilized world with her. No, you dare not make war on cotton! No power on earth dares make war upon it! Cotton is King."

Since you probably know which side won the Civil War, you can infer that the cotton planters were wrong. But the idea of "King Cotton" dominated Southern thinking long before the war began and even afterward. There were a few voices of reason around to give that advice that all financial advisers still give: Diversify your portfolio. No one paid much attention to them. After all, cotton was king.

The Least You Need to Know

- Slave owners were only a quarter of all white Southerners, and planters (owners of more than 20 slaves) only 5 percent.

- "Plain folk" made up the majority in a rural society mostly free of class conflicts.

- The presence of slavery in the South helped create solidarity among all classes of whites.

- Cotton farming helped transform the Deep South, creating wealth but also making it slave-dependent.

Chapter 2

The (True) Spirit of 1776

In This Chapter

◆ Southerners and the Founding Fathers

◆ Agrarian vs. industrial

◆ Jefferson, Calhoun, and nullification

◆ The tariff problem

Here's a question that pops up on quiz shows now and then: Which state is called the "Mother of Presidents"? Answer: Virginia. Virginia was the birthplace of Washington, Jefferson, Madison, Monroe, Harrison, Tyler, and Taylor—all of them born into slave-owning families. Of the 15 presidents before Abraham Lincoln, 7 were born into Virginia slaveholding families.

If it looks like I'm trying to draw some connection between Virginia, slavery, the Founding Fathers, and U.S. presidents, I am. That is exactly what Southerners before and during the Civil War liked to do. It made them feel very patriotic, very American.

A Distinguished Southern History

Let's look at the first 15 presidents again. Besides the seven men from Virginia, two others—Andrew Jackson and James K. Polk—were Southerners and slave owners. Two New Englanders, John Adams and son John Quincy, had little to say about slavery while they were president. (John Quincy became outspokenly anti-slavery, but only after leaving office.) Martin Van Buren was from New York but was the protégé of Andrew Jackson. Franklin Pierce and James Buchanan, the two Northern presidents just before 1860, were Democrats who had Southern slave owners in their cabinets and were sympathetic to Southerners and slavery. The one president left over, Millard Fillmore, disliked slavery but was willing to tolerate it.

Summing up: Prior to the election of 1860, Southerners seemed to have a lock on the U.S. presidency. Not only that, but the real stars among the presidents were Virginia plantation lords—Washington, Jefferson, and Madison, three of the Founding Fathers. There was a "Virginia mystique," something Southerners outside of Virginia felt was partly their own.

If you have ever visited Richmond, Virginia (which became the Confederate capital), you may have seen the capitol building. In Capitol Square stands a huge equestrian statue of George Washington. (Equestrian = he's seated on a horse.) That imposing piece of bronze is also on the city seal. When Jefferson Davis, president of the Confederacy, gave an inaugural speech in Richmond, he was standing at the base of the Washington statue—on February 22, Washington's birthday. This was no accident. And it was no accident that the same statue appeared on the Great Seal of the Confederacy.

All of this may seem like trivial information, but it wasn't seen that way by Southerners in the 1800s. The whole South was hearing some loud accusations from the North: *You are bad, immoral people. You are not good Americans.* The South could point with pride to Washington and other great Southern statesmen and say, *Ah, you are wrong. Look at the great men we've produced in the South. Not only did most of them own slaves, but they took no steps to abolish slavery in America. It is you meddlesome, intolerant Northerners who are bad Americans—telling us how to live our lives down here in the South.*

You might say that this was the whole issue behind the Confederacy and the Civil War: a fuss over what being good Americans was all about, who (or where) the true America really was.

Did Y'all Know?

Confederate president Jefferson Davis had been named for (of course) Thomas Jefferson. Davis's father was a Revolutionary War veteran.

Did Y'all Know? _____

The Founders on Slavery: a Summary

- ◆ Many of the Founding Fathers owned slaves (in some cases, *lots* of slaves).
- ◆ All the founders, including those who owned slaves, claimed they believed slavery was wrong. They also claimed it would eventually die out.
- ◆ The founders were aware that to unite the new nation, they had to keep the Southern states happy and allow them to keep slaves. This set a precedent: Compromise to keep the country together.
- ◆ They carefully kept the words "slave" and "slavery" out of the Constitution.
- ◆ They did not know what to do with slaves if they were freed. Some (James Madison was one) supported the idea of resettling them in Africa. Most of them doubted that a large free black population could exist peacefully with whites.
- ◆ They did not believe any government should abolish slavery without compensating the owners, but they had doubts about compensation ever being practical.
- ◆ None of them ever took any practical steps to abolish slavery.

The Great Tom J. Himself

Having lived in Virginia many years, I know which president Virginians truly honor: not Washington, but Thomas Jefferson. They admire Washington, but the multi-talented, brilliant, eloquent Jefferson utterly fascinates them. This is probably true of the country at large. One reason Jefferson fascinates is because he had his, er, contradictions. He penned those immortal words, "All men are created equal"—but he owned slaves, and never freed any of them. He claimed it was wrong to keep any people in a state of slavery—but in his eight years as president, he did nothing whatsoever to hinder slavery in America. Southerners took great comfort from that.

In Jefferson's writings, he says all sorts of negative things about blacks. He wrote that they "require less sleep" than whites, that they are "much inferior" in reason. He claimed their sex drive was "more ardent" but lacked the whites' "tender, delicate mixture of sentiment and sensation." None of this shocked his contemporaries.

RebeLingo _____

The word **agrarian** means "relating to farms and agriculture." The South had been an agrarian region since it was first settled by Europeans.

*Thomas Jefferson
(1743–1826), staunch
believer in a limited national
government and in an
agrarian society.*

(Library of Congress)

But Jefferson's toleration of slavery wasn't the only thing endearing him to the South. Jefferson, the plantation owner, was a great believer in the *agrarian* way of life. He distrusted industry, and he distrusted cities as well. The man who loved Paris didn't think a crowded city was healthy for human beings. He thought the luckiest man alive was the self-sufficient farmer, a man capable of producing most of his own goods. Jefferson died in 1826, and didn't live to see the new waves of European immigrants coming to America. He might have been pleased that few of them settled in the South, thus keeping the South from becoming crowded. They clustered in the Northeast, mostly in cities, where industry grew.

In short, the South had stayed much closer to Jefferson's ideal than the North had done. Northerners didn't mind. The North was booming. For a new immigrant with a lot of energy and ambition, the North offered more opportunities than the South. The South seemed happy to stay rural and agricultural. It was more *Jeffersonian*.

There was another Jeffersonian thing that Southerners loved: the Kentucky Resolutions. These were written from 1798 to 1799 and dealt with the power of the federal government. According to Jefferson, the government was formed by a "compact" among the states. It was to be a limited government, possessing only a few specific powers. If it attempted to exercise any other powers, its acts were "unauthoritative, void, and of no force." The individual states were to decide when and whether the federal government had committed "unauthoritative" (and unconstitutional) acts. A state legislature could have the state "nullify" an act of the federal government. Nullification, Jefferson said, is the "rightful remedy" for a federal government that oversteps its authority.

If your eyes are glazing over at this point, let me summarize: In 1798, Jefferson wrote that the federal government has limited power, and that state governments must watch it carefully and call its hand when it tries to do more than it should. He was laying the foundation for what are called states' rights. This was at the heart of the American Revolution: Don't let some big, faraway government tell you how to live your life. The American colonists had gotten free from the English king's government in London. They should not turn around now and submit to tyranny from Washington, D.C. (If you think such ideas have died out, you haven't listened to talk radio lately.)

> **Voices from Then**
>
> The power not delegated to the United States by the Constitution, nor prohibited by it to the States, are reserved to the States respectively, or to the people.
>
> —United States Constitution, Amendment X

State and local governments are (usually) more in tune with local people's wants and needs than the federal government is. They are usually easier to monitor than federal authority is, too. You might never meet your senator, a Supreme Court justice, or the president, but you might meet—and even scold—your city councilman or county commissioner.

Of Jefferson's admirers, one stands out from the crowd, one who Southerners liked to put on a pedestal, as high as or higher than Jefferson himself.

The "Stately" Mr. Calhoun

When someone called Confederate president Jefferson Davis "the Calhoun of Mississippi," no higher compliment could have been paid. For Southerners, especially those of the planter class, John C. Calhoun was one of the godlike men.

Ironically, he was not plantation-born. Calhoun was a frontier boy, son of a barely literate Indian fighter. But he had looks and, even better, brains. In a few years he went from shooting panthers in the South Carolina wilds to graduating from Yale, marrying a plantation heiress, and serving in Congress. His dissertation at Yale was titled "The Qualifications Necessary to Make a Statesman."

Calhoun was 6-foot-2, strikingly handsome, a model of courtesy, and brilliant. If you ever saw the portrait of him in his younger days, you would understand why he made a strong impression on his peers.

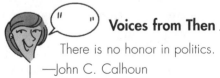

> **Voices from Then**
>
> There is no honor in politics.
> —John C. Calhoun

Two future Confederate notables—Robert E. Lee and Jefferson Davis—owed their appointments to West Point to Secretary of War John C. Calhoun.

He dedicated his life to solving a problem America has dealt with since the very beginning: How do you maintain a balance between the central government's power and the need of people to control their own lives? Calhoun, master of a plantation and many slaves, didn't believe Americans in general hated slavery. (He was right.) He believed certain interest groups pressured the federal government to squeeze the South economically. In other words, he believed in political forces that we would today call "special interests." Squeaky wheels get the grease, as Calhoun knew, but he didn't believe these squeaky wheels represented America at large.

Calhoun was proud of himself and his accomplishments. He had the right to be, as he had been a distinguished lawyer, senator, secretary of war, and U.S. vice president. He looked at the positive side of slavery: It allowed intelligent, eloquent men like himself to have the time to devote to public affairs. He saw slavery the way the ancient Greeks and Romans saw it: It gave aristocrats time for leisure and politics, leaving the grunt work to people whom they believed could do nothing else. Calhoun was aware that the Founding Fathers liked to depict themselves as "neoclassical," the spiritual descendants of the Greeks and Romans. It is no accident that many American buildings from the 1700s were built in neoclassical style.

It's easy for us to sit in judgment on Calhoun, Jefferson, and other slaveholders. To us, they were all hypocrites, ranting about "democracy" and "freedom" while keeping people in bondage. But you can't really understand—or enjoy—history unless you try to get inside the skin of people in the past. We think of slavery today as an issue, something we can discuss and pass judgment on. It wasn't just an issue for these men. Slaves were part of their daily lives. Most of them had grown up believing it was perfectly normal—and right—for blacks to do what whites told them. And in return, whites were totally responsible for the welfare of their slaves. Calhoun, and almost all plantation owners, honestly believed that if their slaves were suddenly free, they would be exploited by unscrupulous whites.

Calhoun looked at America as a great experiment in tolerance. It could be, he said, the land where people from different social and economic backgrounds could dwell together in harmony. Each group could live as it wished—so long as it didn't violate the rights and privileges of any other group. This was what freedom was all about. And as far as he could tell, there was danger of the South losing that freedom to the tyranny of the Northern majority.

Old Hickory, Union Man

The face on the $20 bill is the face of a real powerhouse in American politics: Andrew Jackson, Old Hickory, Indian fighter, War of 1812 hero. Like Calhoun, Jackson was from the Carolina backcountry, a frontier boy, tough as nails, tall and handsome, and with the manners of a prince. He became a politician and a plantation owner. He had no interest whatsoever in interfering with slavery.

Sounds like Jackson and Calhoun were practically clones of each other, right? Not so. When he was on his deathbed, Jackson facetiously remarked that he regretted he hadn't executed Calhoun. Why didn't these two Southern gentlemen plantation patriarchs like each other?

The key word was *Union*. Jackson shared Jefferson's and Calhoun's beliefs in small government and states' rights. But he also had a powerful belief in keeping the United States together, no matter what. Here he and Calhoun parted company. Calhoun was a great believer in nullification, the idea (think back to Thomas Jefferson) that a state can nullify a federal act whenever the federal government oversteps its boundaries.

Jackson happened to be the U.S. president when a state decided to see if nullification would actually work. Hold tight here, because as background we have to talk about (yawn) economic matters.

Go See It!
You can tour Andrew Jackson's beautiful plantation home, the Hermitage, near Nashville, Tennessee. He and his wife, Rachel, are buried there.

The Tariff Terror

The South was, from its very beginning, an exporting region. Virginia's first settlers raised tobacco, mostly to send to Europe. In the 1800s, cotton and tobacco were both major export crops for the South. So naturally, Southerners favored a low tariff (tax, that is) on exported goods. The North had a different view: It was building up new industries, industries geared to producing goods for American use. Low tariffs meant they had to compete with foreign industries. So the North preferred high tariffs. Underline this: *North and South feuded over tariffs before they feuded over slavery.*

In 1816, Congress passed a high tariff act—or more accurately, Northern congressmen voted for a high tariff, with Southern congressmen voting against it, but losing. Congress tried to pass an even higher one in 1827. The vice president at the time was John C. Calhoun. He presided over the Senate, and when the Senate vote tied over the tariff bill, Calhoun voted against it. (You might recall from civics class that the U.S. vice president can only vote in the Senate when there is a tie.)

But in 1828 Congress enacted a higher tariff—one the South referred to as the "Tariff of Abominations." Southern planters were horrified—and with good reason. A piece of federal legislation was affecting their economy in a dramatic way. The rich state of South Carolina feared becoming poor.

In the 1820s and 1830s, it was becoming more and more noticeable that the country seemed to be dividing into North and South. The two sections seemed to have goals that were at odds with each other. It may seem boring to talk about tariffs and such, but you can't really understand the North-South split unless you grasp some of the economic realities.

Calhoun was convinced that the tariff was a matter of the South having to subsidize the North. He penned the widely read *Exposition and Protest*. Essentially, he restated what Jefferson had said years earlier: States join together to form the United States, and thus the states are the final judges of whether the U.S. government is acting according to the Constitution. When it isn't, states can nullify a federal law, making it void within that state.

Jackson took office the year after the Tariff of Abominations passed. Southerners were hopeful: Surely this Southern president, a plantation owner and a states' rights man, would do something to reduce the tariff. He did, in fact. The 1832 Tariff Act was an improvement over the Tariff of Abominations.

But Calhoun and his followers still saw it as a federal act that helped the North and hurt the South. In his home state, the South Carolina legislature passed an ordinance of nullification in 1832. It stated that the tariff acts of 1828 and 1832 were null and void in their state and would not be enforced after February 1, 1833.

Jackson was a Union man all the way. Much as he loved the South, he saw an obvious danger in states being able to ignore federal laws they didn't like. He sent Federal troops to Charleston harbor and to parts of North Carolina near the South Carolina border. (A former general, he knew how to use force when necessary.) He had the troops, and he had a proclamation that didn't mince words: "I consider the power to annul a law of the United States, assumed by one state, incompatible with the existence of the Union." Calhoun had claimed nullification was rooted in the Constitution. Jackson's proclamation declared that it was "contradicted expressly by the letter of the Constitution, unauthorized by its spirit, inconsistent with every principle on which it was founded."

Jackson had the backing of Congress. It passed a force bill, authorizing the president to use Federal troops in such situations. So, who blinked first? South Carolina did. No other state openly took her side in the dispute. Slightly embarrassed but unrepentant, South Carolina repealed its ordinance of nullification.

Did Y'all Know?

Some historians believe that the tariff issue would have eventually led to the Civil War even if there had been no slavery issue. Obviously we can't know this for certain. We do know that as soon as the Southern states pulled out of the Union in 1861, the Northern-dominated Congress passed a high tariff, raising it again in 1862, and even higher in 1864.

The lowdown on the nullification controversy: The federal government had won—sort of. It had forced South Carolina to shut up and accept a federal law, but it also lowered the tariff to appease the state. A pattern was set for the next three decades: Southern states used the threat of nullification—and secession—as political leverage.

Selling Out the Founders

At the time of the tariff tiffs, the United States was still a very young country—well under 100 years old. There were still people around who could vividly recall—because they had lived through it—the reasons for the American Revolution. Southerners were beginning to feel like it was up to them to keep the Spirit of '76 alive by getting rid of yet another tyrannical government. They had broken away from England. Couldn't they break away from Washington, D.C., if it became tyrannical too?

The Least You Need to Know

- There were many slaveholding Southerners among the Founding Fathers, which made Southerners proud.

- Thomas Jefferson, with his beliefs about limited government and agrarian life, was an idol of Southerners.

- Southern statesman John C. Calhoun refined the theories of states' rights and nullification.

- The nullification controversy of 1832 to 1833 was a preview of the Civil War.

- Confederates believed they were true to the ideals of the American Revolution.

Abolitionists and the Sin Issue

In This Chapter

- Garrison and the very loud abolitionists
- Harriet Beecher Stowe's fictional slave world
- Anti-slavery, anti-South voices in Congress
- The Supreme Court and Dred Scott
- John Brown, liberator or terrorist?

Southerners not only had to put up with what they thought were unreasonable tariffs, they had to deal with a growing number of loud-mouthed Northerners, called *abolitionists*, telling them they should free their slaves.

To understand the abolitionists, you have to see slavery as they saw it. Slavery wasn't a political or social issue—it was a religious one. It was a sin, and God wanted it abolished. The majority of abolitionists considered themselves to be faithful Christians. The flip side: those who opposed them were evil. As you read this chapter, hang on to that word *sin*, because you can't understand the abolitionists—and the people they hated—without understanding sin.

The Bald and Holy Mr. Garrison

Abraham Lincoln gets the credit for issuing the Emancipation Proclamation, forever ending slavery in America. Well, with all due respect to Lincoln, abolitionists had done much of the spadework for the cause 30 years before the Civil War. Of course, the abolitionists are much less likable than the folksy, log-cabin boy Lincoln. They were that painful phenomenon we meet often within the world: people who are morally right but who are so downright irritating to people who don't agree with them. Perhaps they irritate because the line between righteous and holier-than-thou is so thin.

One of the abolitionist luminaries was William Lloyd Garrison, whose portrait tells so much: intense, humorless, probably no fun at all at a party or picnic. In 1831, Garrison founded his famous Boston newspaper *The Liberator*, in which he declared, "On this subject I do not wish to think, or speak, or write, with moderation … I will be harsh as truth and as uncompromising as justice …. I am in earnest—I will not equivocate—I will not excuse—I will not retreat a single inch. And I will be heard."

This sounds about as subtle as an Old Testament prophet—and America has never been completely comfortable with such people. Granted, the revival preacher calling individuals to repent of their sin was (and still is) part of the American scene. But Garrison and his fellow abolitionists condemned a whole *section* of the nation (the South). For abolitionists, America's "original sin" was slavery. While the Bible taught that "the Kingdom of God is within you," abolitionists taught that the Kingdom of Evil was in the South.

The gospel of abolition was centered in Massachusetts, Garrison's birthplace. The old Puritan fire there had never died out, it just burned in a different form. The Puritans of the 1600s had emphasized individual sin and redemption and divided the world into the righteous and the damned. The neo-Puritans of the 1800s divided the world into the abolitionists and the damned. Rather than depicting hell as the final fate of slave owners, the abolitionists foresaw a violent, horrible end in this lifetime—a revolt of slaves, perhaps, or even a civil war (hell in this world instead of afterward). They got the war they had hoped for.

RebeLingo

The **abolitionists** got their name because they wished to *abolish* slavery.

Did Y'all Know?

The more radical abolitionists would sometimes interrupt church services and cry out that it was a crime for Christians to condone slavery. Many churches in the North as well as the South objected to these tirades, often delivered by people they didn't even know.

Back to 1831: The year Garrison launched
The Liberator was also the year of Nat
Turner's bloody slave rebellion in Virginia.
Garrison approved of that bloodbath, in
which Turner, a slave and lay preacher, led a
small band of slaves in a brief but bloody war
against whites, brutally mutilating some of
them. Turner and his cohorts were captured
and executed, and, not surprisingly, Southern

Voices from Then

Abolitionism is nothing but
perfidious interference in the
rights of other men.
—Jefferson Davis, speaking in
the U.S. Senate

whites feared that unless slaves were closely monitored, more violence would occur.
It's hard to overestimate the effect the Turner revolt had on Southern whites. And, to
make things worse, Christians like Garrison claimed they approved of the violence.
So the year 1831 drove two messages home to Southerners, particularly slave owners:
Slaves can be easily provoked to kill their masters, and when they do, these meddle-
some abolitionists (who probably egged on the slaves in the first place) will applaud it.
Many abolitionists did applaud Turner's murderous spree. Those who didn't applaud
at least approved of it.

Slave owners and the politicians who kowtowed to them were called the "Slave
Power" by abolitionists. The Slave Power was Garrison's favorite target, and although
the South worked to keep *The Liberator* from circulating there, Southern newspapers
loved to quote Garrison's venomous anti-slavery harangues, holding them up as examples of Yankee extremism. Some abolitionists who called themselves Christians
claimed that they would abolish slavery not through violence but through "the power
of love" and "moral suasion." But you will not find much evidence of "love power" in
Garrison's anti-South tirades.

Garrison called for the North to secede from the United States and free itself from
the corruption of slavery. Did he really mean it? Probably not. He was trying to make
a point with one of his operatic tantrums.
The point: We can't go on as one nation
as long as we are divided over this issue.
(The Southern reply: *Why not? We've been
divided over it for years.*)

Did Y'all Know?

Some radical anti-slavery
authors claimed that since the
word *slavery* never appeared
in the Constitution, the Founding Fathers hadn't given it their
blessing. The truth is, the Constitutional Convention deliberately
avoided using the words *slave* or
slavery because they knew the
issue was controversial.

Garrison's newspaper was one among
hundreds of anti-slavery publications—papers,
tracts, pamphlets, and sociological studies. But
what really caused a shift in public opinion was
a novel by a dowdy New England woman.

Mrs. Stowe's Book, by God

Harriet Beecher Stowe couldn't avoid being a Christian and a reformer. It was in the blood. Her dad was the famous revival preacher Lyman Beecher. Stowe found fame of her own by writing the world's great anti-slavery novel, *Uncle Tom's Cabin*.

She didn't exactly do hardball investigative journalism to research the book. Other than a short visit to Kentucky, she had spent practically no time in the South, so she had little firsthand knowledge of slavery. She gleaned most of her "facts" about slavery from the abolitionist literature she loved to read. Anyway, she had good intentions. She wished to acquaint the world with the life of slaves on a Southern plantation. So in 1851 and 1852, she dashed off 40 installments of a novel that were published in an abolitionist newspaper. When it appeared in book form, *Uncle Tom's Cabin* sold 300,000 copies in its first year, and one million before the Civil War began. Several popular plays were based on the book. It was also the basis for songs, toys, games, handkerchiefs, and tableware.

Corny, sentimental, and melodramatic, the book was a smash hit. In England it sold 1.2 million copies in a single year. The English enjoyed looking down on backward Americans. When Stowe visited England in 1853, she was treated like a goddess. Historians suspect the book's immense popularity in England played a role in England never taking the Confederacy's side.

What did it tell the world about slavery in the South? Slaves are stripped naked and beaten. Slave women are the sexual playthings of their masters. Slave owners frequently father children by slaves. Slaves can be beaten to death without the owner batting an eye. Truth? Exaggeration? Probably a bit of both, but it didn't matter. Stowe's novel was a global opinion-shaper.

Voices from Then

At the time of *Uncle Tom's Cabin*'s popularity, the *New York Tribune* supported its images of slavery by stating that plantations were "little else than Negro harems." It also claimed that respected presidents like Washington, Jefferson, Madison, and Monroe had left broods of mixed-race children.

Southerners despised the book, for obvious reasons. The best-seller had insulted an entire region of country. But they understood the book's appeal. Southerners saw it as giving Northerners an excuse to strike a moral pose. They read the book, cried, sided with the slaves, and booed and hissed the slaveholders. It was a painless way for Northerners to make themselves feel superior to Southerners. It involved no real sacrifice on Northerners' part. Many Southerners believed that Mrs. Stowe and the other abolitionists overlooked an obvious fact: Liberating the slaves would have involved major sacrifices for the South. It would have meant loss of their property. It would have meant a dramatic (maybe dangerous) change in race relations. It would have meant social and economic upheaval in the South—while the abolitionists in the North would be barely affected. Mrs. Stowe and the other abolitionists were saying "Abolish this immoral institution." The Southern reply was, "Sure, that's easy for *you* to say!"

Saintly Sumner of the Senate

All the abolitionist literature in the world was of no use if it didn't cause a change in the laws. For that to happen, you had to have politicians who would turn anti-slavery attitudes into anti-slavery laws. One who hoped to do this was Charles Sumner, who was (surprise!) a New Englander.

Charles Sumner was one of the Puritan descendants, Boston-born, of course, who never once showed evidence of a sense of humor. Of course, politicians *should* be serious—but human, too. The first Puritans hated sin and the devil. Sumner, their descendant, hated Southern slave owners and the South in general.

Sumner graduated from (where else?) Harvard Law School, becoming a Boston lawyer and, most significantly, an extreme anti-slavery spokesman. "Mr. Abolition" was elected to the Senate in 1851 and became Congress's most vocal opponent of slavery. He claimed he dealt not in politics but in morals. (He certainly would have sneered at today's belief that you can't legislate morality.)

In May 1856, Sumner delivered his famous "Crime Against Kansas" speech. He denounced the Kansas-Nebraska Act (the brainchild of Sen. Stephen Douglas of Illinois), which he saw as an immoral compromise with the slave power. More personally, he denounced Sen. Andrew Butler of South Carolina, whom he accused of having a "mistress … the harlot, slavery." Sumner delivered his speech to a packed Senate chamber. "My soul is wrung with the outrage, and I shall pour it forth." His wrath on Senator Butler was unfair, since Butler was not present. (A true gentleman did not make a derogatory speech when the person was not there to defend himself.)

The deliberately inflammatory speech naturally annoyed Southerners. One who was supremely irked was U.S. Rep. Preston Brooks, who happened to be the nephew of Sen. Butler. Brooks was aware of the double meaning of Sumner's phrase "the harlot slavery." Abolitionists constantly accused

Did Y'all Know?

To fully understand the Brooks-Sumner Affair, you have to understand the Southern code of honor. A gentleman would challenge an *equal* to a duel. But an *inferior* would receive a beating. Brooks didn't challenge Sumner to a duel but simply thrashed him. Southerners understood, and mostly approved.

slaveholders of fornicating with their slaves. Brooks took his cane and beat Sumner senseless on the Senate floor.

The so-called Brooks-Sumner Affair helped solidify Northern opposition to slavery. The people of Massachusetts naturally reelected Sumner, their beaten icon, to the Senate.

Mary Chesnut's Civil War diary has some insightful comments on Sumner and his fellow abolitionists, who lived "in nice New England homes—clean, clear, sweet-smelling—shut up in libraries, writing books which ease their hearts of their bitterness to us …. What self-denial do they practice? It is the cheapest philanthropy trade in the world—easy. Easy as setting John Brown to come down here and cut our throats in Christ's name."

Northerners Weren't So Nice to Blacks, Either

Slave owners were quick to point out to the abolitionists that life for blacks in the *North* was no picnic. Sure, they were free, but they certainly weren't treated as equals. A few choice examples:

- ◆ Indiana and Ohio required any black person entering the state to post $500 bond as a guarantee of good behavior.

- ◆ In New York State, any person who paid taxes could vote—any *white* person, that is.

- ◆ Pennsylvania allowed all adult males—*white* males—to vote.

- ◆ Many Northern trade unions would not admit blacks.

The Few, the Loud, the Brave

Uncle Tom's Cabin was a popular book, but don't let that blind you to a key fact: Abolitionists weren't popular in the North. It's safe to say that the average Northerner didn't feel strongly about slavery. Most Northerners, if they thought about it at all, probably believed slavery would just melt away gradually, over time. They generally resented abolitionists as loud-mouthed meddlers trying to tell Southerners how to mind their affairs. Certainly the average Northerner wasn't terribly concerned with the welfare of slaves.

But here is something you learn from world history, and from American history in particular: A tiny minority of people can do amazing things if they persist. In the 30 years between Garrison launching *The Liberator* and the beginning of the Civil War, the "slavery is bad" message had taken root in many people's minds. A younger generation of Northerners had grown up hearing this message. Some shrugged it off, but not all did. "Slavery is bad" had sunk in, although "blacks are equal to whites" had not.

With all this anti-slavery stuff floating around, are you wondering whether it affected Southerners? It did, but not in the way the abolitionists hoped.

> **Voices from Then**
>
> The people of the North were, indeed, opposed to slavery, but merely because they thought it stood in the way of their struggle for empire. I think it safe to affirm that if the question of slavery had stood upon moral and religious grounds alone, the institution would never have been interfered with.
>
> —Adm. Raphael Semmes, Confederate Navy

The Southern Reaction

As Northern abolitionists grew louder, Southern ones grew quieter—or moved to the North. They certainly weren't welcome in most Southern communities. After about 1850, it became literally dangerous for abolitionists to speak openly in the South or distribute anti-slavery literature there. Southern postmasters did what they could to censor out abolitionist literature and books. Maybe it didn't really matter, because Southerners were painfully aware that Northerners thought Southerners were scum.

> **Voices from Then**
>
> An entire new generation had come upon the stage in the South, in the midst of the slavery agitation. They had grown up amid assaults upon their rights, and attacks from the North upon the domestic institution inherited from their fathers. Their post offices had been perverted for the circulation of incendiary pictures and publications intended to excite the slaves to servile insurrection. In the North, the press, state legislatures, anti-slavery societies, abolition lecturers, and above all the Christian pulpit, had been persistently employed in denouncing slavery as a sin, and rendering slaveholders odious.
>
> —Former president James Buchanan, on the causes of the war

Following Nat Turner's grisly slave revolt, a professor at the College of William and Mary in Virginia began writing articles defending slavery. His name was Thomas R. Dew, and his writings were widely read by Southerners (especially the younger men) in the 30 years between Turner's revolt and the Civil War. Dew based his arguments on logic, the Bible (which does not condemn slavery), and the Greek and Roman classics. In the years before the war, many sons of plantation masters had absorbed

Dew's writings, as well as the writings of Plato and other ancient philosophers, who (alas) approved of slavery. Accustomed to being bitterly attacked, young Southerners were bitter in return.

The Dreaded Dred Scott Issue

It so happened that in the 1850s the head man on the Supreme Court (chief justice, that is) was a Southerner sympathetic to slavery. His name was Roger Taney (pronounced *tawny*). Taney's chief claim to fame is the infamous Dred Scott decision of 1857, in which the Supreme Court, with Taney at the helm, decided that blacks were not citizens—period. It sounds perfectly barbaric to us, as it did to many people in 1857 as well—but at the time it made perfect sense to a lot of other people, certainly to slave-owning Southerners, and certainly to the pro-Southern Taney himself, who didn't see himself as a racist but simply as a wise judge using logic and common sense to reach a decision.

Dred Scott, a Missouri slave, had been taken by his master into the free states of Illinois and Wisconsin. Scott sued for his freedom on the ground that he was in a territory where he was no longer a slave. Could he, the Supreme Court was asked, legally sue for his freedom? The nine justices each wrote a separate opinion in the case, but Taney spoke for the majority when he wrote that a slave was not a U.S. citizen and thus could not sue in federal court, and that residing in a free state did not automatically free a slave.

Taney specifically noted that the Declaration of Independence had stated "all men are created equal." Taney noted that these words "would seem to embrace the whole human family .... But it is too clear for discussion that the enslaved African race were not intended to be included." (Ouch!) The *Dred Scott* decision made the South happy but sent Northern abolitionists into a tailspin.

Despite the North's assumption that Taney was pro-slavery, he in fact had freed the slaves he inherited. When he wrote his decision in the Dred Scott case, he was not writing as a white supremacist (though it certainly impresses us that way now) but as a lawyer. He thought he was protecting the legitimate interests of a minority (Southerners) against the majority (Northerners)—a valid idea, except that another minority (blacks) counted for nothing.

Bloody Mr. Brown

The Connecticut-born abolitionist agitator John Brown is one of the more controversial figures in U.S. history. One glimpse at a picture of the stern, craggy-faced Brown will convince you that this was not a politician or a peacemaker. Brown had one driving motivation in life: Free the slaves. God willed it. That was all there was to it.

Brown and his followers were key reasons why Kansas was known as "Bleeding Kansas" in the 1850s. In a nutshell, here is what happened: Anti-slavery forces and pro-slavery forces both wished to occupy Kansas, claiming it for their own side. So these early settlers of Kansas weren't exactly soft-spoken moderates. They tended to be rabidly anti-slavery or rabidly pro-slavery, and throwing these groups together didn't prove to be healthy.

A pro-slavery crowd sacked the Kansas town of Lawrence, blew up the largest hotel with cannons, and burned the governor's house. The anti-slavery crowd countered, led by John Brown. Brown and his gang slaughtered a number of pro-slavery settlers, and a detailed account of it can still turn stomachs. Brown's band led a farmer named Doyle and his sons down a road, then hacked the boys to death. One boy had his head sliced open and both arms cut off. Brown shot Doyle square in the forehead. Yet, proper Bostonians adored Brown as an angel of righteousness.

After his murderous spree in Kansas, the abolitionist saint concocted a plan to free the slaves throughout the South. It had as much chance as a snowball in Key West of succeeding, but Brown, like all fanatics, was never put off by reality. In October 1859, he made a place for himself in the history books by using an "army" of 21 men to raid the federal armory at Harper's Ferry, Virginia, hoping to arm slaves with the weapons. (Not one slave actually joined up with Brown.) U.S. Marines under the command of a colonel named Robert E. Lee nipped the plan in the bud. Brown was tried for treason and went calmly to his death by hanging.

Abolitionists were ecstatic: They had a martyr. The poet Henry Wadsworth Longfellow, typical of Yankee intellectuals, wrote in his diary that Brown's execution was "the date of a new

Did Y'all Know?

Gradual emancipation was always an option, though hard-liners like Brown didn't consider it. Great Britain had abolished slavery in 1833—but slaves were not liberated immediately. They had to undergo a seven-year apprenticeship, working for their former masters for three fourths of each day. In 1858, Portugal passed a law freeing its slaves—*over a 20-year period.* The Dutch began gradual emancipation in 1863.

Did Y'all Know?

At least 200 people died in Kansas in conflicts over slavery in the years leading up to the Civil War. No state's settlement was ever accompanied by such violence and hatred. So much for Stephen Douglas's "compromise." Some historians have stated that the Civil War really started in Kansas in 1856.

> **Go See It!**
>
> Harper's Ferry National Historical Park in West Virginia has the John Brown Fort, the old brick armory where Brown and his followers holed up before his capture.

revolution, quite as much needed as the old one." Put yourself in the Southerners' place: The most notable authors and intellectuals of the time were not only anti-slavery, but were singing the praises of an anti-slavery and anti-Southern terrorist.

Southerners feared that someone more organized and more level-headed than Brown would attempt the same kind of thing—and with success. Many Southerners who considered themselves good Union men began to reconsider. Brown's Harper's Ferry raid convinced many Southerners that the North was the enemy.

The abolitionists had a hero. The Southerners had a villain. Everyone was wondering if political compromise could keep the nation united while fanatics like John Brown were waiting to slit Southern throats.

The Least You Need to Know

- ◆ William Lloyd Garrison and most abolitionists were regarded as extremists in both the North and South.

- ◆ The best-selling novel *Uncle Tom's Cabin* helped the abolitionist side, in spite of its author's lack of familiarity with the South.

- ◆ The Supreme Court's decision in the Dred Scott case enraged abolitionists and gave them more reason to fight.

- ◆ The raid of violent abolitionist John Brown terrified Southerners and intensified their hatred of abolitionists.

Chapter 4

Doughfaces, Compromisers, and Fire-Eaters

In This Chapter

- ◆ Some South-loving Northern presidents
- ◆ A few nation-saving compromises
- ◆ An early glimpse of Jefferson Davis
- ◆ The most committed secessionists

Politics is, so an old proverb says, "the art of the possible." It is fine to have ideals and morals, but in the political world you face reality, meaning you have to cut deals with people you disagree with. This isn't always easy, and certainly it wasn't easy in the antebellum period when slavery had become a wedge issue in the country. Nonetheless, there were some crafty compromisers and appeasers in those years.

There was also a very uncompromising group, the Southern counterpart to the abolitionists: the secessionists. Like the abolitionists, some of these were real characters. Like the abolitionists, they helped bring the country to war.

Peopling the Purchase

The Louisiana Purchase was one of the greatest investments the U.S. government ever made. Maybe you recall from history class that this enormous territory was purchased from France in 1803 while Thomas Jefferson was president. This is one of history's great ironies: Jefferson, the man who was so obsessed with not giving too much power to the federal government, was president when that government did something that he wasn't even sure was legal. (Regarding the purchase, he said, "The less said about the constitutional difficulties, the better.") But hardly anyone regretted the purchase. Everyone expected that within a short time the vast territory would be settled, and that new states would be carved out of it.

The big question was: free states or slave states?

A line had already been drawn—the famous Mason-Dixon Line, that is. Surveyed back in the 1760s, it was the state boundary between Maryland and Pennsylvania. That line, and the Ohio River, were the unofficial (but later official) boundaries between slave states and free states. The Louisiana Purchase raised a new question: In this new territory far away from the Mason-Dixon Line and the Ohio River, what was the boundary between slave states and free states?

The state of Louisiana had already entered the Union, and it had plenty of slaves. North of Louisiana, the territory of Missouri was asking Congress to let it become a state. This was in 1819. At that time there were exactly 11 slave states and 11 free states. Missouri had 10,000 slaves already and was bringing in more. No one doubted that it would be a slave state. This upset many Northerners: If Missouri came in, there would be more slave states than free states.

Did Y'all Know?

Time now for a little refresher course on what your teachers taught you (or should have) in civics class. Remember that the U.S. House of Representatives is composed of people elected on the basis of population. So at the time of the Missouri Compromise, there were more Northerners than Southerners in the House. The Senate is different, since there are exactly two senators from each state. For Congress to pass a law, it has to be approved by both House and Senate. As long as there was the same number of Northerners and Southerners in the Senate, there was no danger from the House. Even if the entire House tried to ram through strict laws against slavery, they would never pass through the Senate. So for the slave states, the Senate balance was important—*very* important.

A slick political operator by the name of Henry Clay happened to be a powerhouse in Congress. Under his guidance, the House and Senate put forward a neat compromise: Admit Missouri as a slave state, and at the same time admit Maine as a free state. This would maintain the balance in the Senate. The House (barely) approved this in March 1820. It is known to history as the Missouri Compromise. For almost 30 years it kept Northern and Southern politicians happy—or if not happy, at least kept them from killing each other.

Voices from Then

If the Union must be dissolved, slavery is precisely the question on which it ought to break.

—John Quincy Adams, secretary of state at the time of the Missouri Compromise

The compromise didn't open up the entire Louisiana Purchase to slavery (much as Southern politicians would have liked that). The dividing line was 36°30'. North of that latitude, no slavery. But that still left plenty of acreage that could, in time, become slave states.

The Kentucky Wonder Boy

Henry Clay probably had more influence on American politics than several of the presidents in the 1800s. Clay was born in Virginia into a family that owned slaves. He claimed that slavery was "a great evil" and that if the country could start over again, slavery would have to be prohibited. But he didn't free his own slaves, and he was realistic enough to know that most slave owners weren't going to free theirs.

When he was fairly young, Clay went west to the new state of Kentucky, where he became a prominent lawyer. He was elected to the U.S. House in 1810 and within one year was elected its speaker. Remember that the Congress was still relatively new then, still establishing traditions. Clay established one of his own: He made the post of speaker into one of leadership, controlling the majority party and making himself darn near as powerful as the president.

Clay was a realist and a compromiser. He looked at a nation in which there were a lot of slaves and lot of very powerful slave owners. And he assumed the obvious: We ought to keep them appeased. (Remember, he owned slaves himself.) At the same time, he knew it also was wise to keep the North appeased. Here was the task, something like walking on eggs. He was good at it. We have to wonder what might have happened to America if there had been more Clays and fewer abolitionists and secessionists.

The Senate Balancing Act, Still Dizzy

The Senate had managed to maintain its balance—an equal number of senators from slave states and free states. Following the Missouri Compromise, more new states were carved out of the Louisiana Purchase (Arkansas and Iowa), two from what we today call the Midwest (Michigan and Wisconsin), and two from territories formerly belonging to Spain (Texas and Florida). Of those six, three were slave and three were free. Politically speaking, everything seemed hunky-dory.

But the culture wasn't sitting still. Abolitionists were loud and active, Christian denominations were splitting over the issue of slavery, and attitudes were hardening. While most people in the country at large did not have strong feelings about the slavery issue, some "squeaky wheels" in the South and North did. Somewhere down the line, everyone knew, Congress was going to face another slave-or-free crisis. There was no question of if, but merely a matter of when.

Blame it on California. Or blame it on greed, since it was the wild lust for gold that turned California practically overnight from a barren desert to a boomtown (or boom territory, rather). The territory had enough people to apply for statehood. And it wished to enter the Union as a *free* state.

The president at that time (1849) was Zachary Taylor—a Southern slave owner. It surprised many people when Taylor threw his support to letting California in. He did something even more surprising: He encouraged creating another new free state, New Mexico.

Southern slave owners were not pleased, to put it mildly. They organized a convention in Nashville, Tennessee, scheduled for June 1850. Whose idea was this? None other than Sen. John C. Calhoun of South Carolina. The South had to show some unity, he said, otherwise that large chunk of Western territory that the United States had added as a result of the Mexican War might become several new free states.

More about the Nashville Convention in a moment. In the meantime, the Great Compromiser, Sen. Henry Clay, was busy as a bee. He introduced a package of bills which would (he hoped) satisfy both pro-slavery and anti-slavery groups.

Here was Clay's package, which is known today as the Compromise of 1850:

1. Admit California as a free state.

2. Organize the territories of New Mexico and Utah without specifying whether they were slave or free.

3. Prohibit slave trade in the District of Columbia.

4. Pass a rigorous new law for the return of runaway slaves.

Points 1 and 3 pleased the anti-slavery folks. Point 4 pleased the pro-slavers. Point 2 pleased (in theory) everybody by not mandating whether some new territories might be slave or free.

Oh, if only there had been C-SPAN in those days, because Clay's proposals sparked one of the great debates in Senate history. Calhoun had a lot to say, of course, taking his usual position that the North was infringing on the rights of the South. Calhoun himself didn't deliver his speeches, however. He was ailing and frail (and old) at this point, so his eloquent speeches were delivered by James Mason of Virginia. (More on him later: He was a biggie in the Confederacy.) Calhoun's speeches contained the usual threat: If the South couldn't feel secure about being allowed to continue holding slaves, it could not remain part of the Union.

Sen. Daniel Webster of Massachusetts supported Clay's package. Webster advanced his theory that slavery could not prosper in the Far West. Sen. Stephen Douglas of Illinois also supported the bills. The visitors' galleries in the Senate were packed. Here was a golden opportunity to hear some of the greatest orators and statesmen of the century—all eloquent and all very passionate about what they were saying.

The compromise faced a major obstacle, however. President Taylor stated he would veto it, and there were not enough votes to pass it over his veto. The compromise seemed dead. But then, quite unexpectedly, Taylor was dead. The tough old general had overindulged himself at a Fourth of July celebration. He literally bust a gut, and died on July 9, 1850. (Cause of death: acute gastroenteritis.) The nation went into mourning, all the time wondering what might happen to the Compromise of 1850 now.

The new man in the White House was Millard Fillmore. Poor Millard is usually written off as a nonentity, a do-nothing president. That isn't quite true. He actually served longer as president than Taylor had. Fillmore was an extremely well-read, intelligent man. He was even intelligent enough to sign the Compromise of 1850, which Taylor had refused to do. Though he disliked slavery, Fillmore didn't wish to see the country split over it, and he thought the compromise would prevent that.

Compromisers and moderates applauded the compromise. In spite of Calhoun's not-so-veiled threats about secession, the South was appeased for another 10 years. Still, when California entered the Union, Congress from that point on had a free-state majority in both House and Senate. Don't think the Southerners weren't aware of it.

Did Y'all Know?

Millard Fillmore was the last president from the Whig Party. In 1856, he ran for president again, but lost to James Buchanan.

Meanwhile, Back in Nashville

Remember that Calhoun had called for a convention of Southern delegates to meet and discuss secession. They assembled in Nashville in June 1850—before Zachary Taylor died, and before anyone knew what the fate of the Compromise of 1850 would be. Only 9 of the 15 slave states sent delegates. Out of 175 delegates, 102 were from Tennessee, so the convention hardly represented all the slave states.

Even so, some hotheaded delegates from South Carolina called for immediate secession of the Southern states. Fortunately, the hotheads—"fire-eaters," as the radical secessionists were called—were not in control, and cooler heads prevailed. The convention passed several resolutions (what else do conventions do?). One important resolution called for the federal government to open all territories to slavery. The convention adjourned, with the big question remaining: Would Henry Clay's compromise pass?

It did, and Millard Fillmore signed it. In November that year, the Nashville delegates reassembled to denounce the compromise and to reassert their right to secede. But as we already said, most moderates in both North and South were satisfied with the Compromise of 1850.

Did Y'all Know?

Part of the Compromise of 1850 was the Fugitive Slave Act. Under this law, Northern authorities were required to return runaway slaves to their owners. Anyone assisting a runaway could get six months in prison and a stiff fine, plus would have to reimburse the owner for the slave's value. One reason that some Southerners didn't accept the Compromise of 1850 was the suspicion that the Fugitive Slave Act would be frequently disregarded—a "scofflaw" that Northerners would ignore more often than enforce. They were correct.

But hotheads enjoy each other's company, and the Nashville Convention—Part 1 and Part 2—gave the gung-ho secessionists a chance to mix, mingle, and spew out their hatred for the North in each other's presence. The 1850 convention was a kind of preview or rehearsal for what was to happen 10 years later.

Not to Be Confused with "Doughboys"

"Doughface" was the name some Northerners used to describe Northern politicians sympathetic to the South. Just before the Civil War, the United States had two doughface presidents. Both of them are usually considered failures as presidents. But that doesn't mean their two terms were in any way boring. A lot was going on, particularly in regard to maintaining the North-South harmony.

The first doughface was "Handsome Frank" Pierce, a Mexican War veteran, a New Hampshire lawyer, and an old buddy of the novelist Nathaniel Hawthorne (author of *The Scarlet Letter*, and also author of Pierce's official campaign biography). He wasn't terribly bright but, fortunately, he wasn't terribly opinionated either, and he made a fairly competent senator from New Hampshire. In 1852, the Democratic Convention couldn't decide on a presidential candidate until the delegates from Virginia put forward Pierce's name. His running mate was William R. D. King of Alabama. Put all this together and you figure out that Pierce definitely appealed to Southern voters.

Did Y'all Know?

The Democrats used the campaign slogan "We Polked You in 1844, We Shall Pierce You in 1852." (James K. Polk was their 1844 candidate.)

In 1852 Pierce swept the election. He proceeded to stock his cabinet with several Southerners. One of these was an old Senate buddy, a man named Jefferson Davis. Pierce made him secretary of war, and it was a good choice, for Davis was a West Point grad and had sparkled during the Mexican War.

In Pierce's inaugural address, he asked the people to put aside their differences and work together. (What an original idea for an inaugural address!) He stated that he wished to maintain the Compromise of 1850 and try to bury the slavery controversy. Fat chance.

The slavery issue didn't go away, and Pierce's chance of getting elected to a second term pretty much died because of something called the Kansas-Nebraska Act.

Undoing the Missouri Compromise

Pierce's secretary of war, Jefferson Davis, had an idea: Purchase some land in the northern part of Mexico. That way, the United States could build a transcontinental railway through the southern part of the country. The territory that was acquired in 1853 was known as the Gadsden Purchase. The land eventually became a chunk of Arizona. It wasn't all that Davis had wanted. He tried to finagle a purchase of several of Mexico's northern states, including the whole of Baja California. The Senate knew very well that Davis was hoping to get more slave states into the Union.

Sen. Stephen Douglas of Illinois had helped put together the Compromise of 1850. Now he had another compromise in mind. Congress would create two new territories in the west, Nebraska and Kansas. The settlers there would have *popular*

RebeLingo

Popular sovereignty referred to allowing people in a given territory to vote on key issues. Specifically, before the Civil War it applied to the practice of allowing citizens in U.S. territories or states to decide for themselves if they would allow slavery.

sovereignty—that is, they could vote on whether to become slave or free states. This sounded like something that would please everyone, North and South. But there was one hitch. The Missouri Compromise in 1820 had banned slavery north of latitude 36°30'. Kansas and Nebraska were both north of that. So by giving those territories the option of having slavery, Douglas's Kansas-Nebraska Bill in effect repealed the Missouri Compromise. Some Northerners were horrified, because they thought of the 36°30' rule as practically sacred.

Even so, the controversial Kansas-Nebraska Act passed in 1854. Pierce backed it. He had good intentions, but neither he nor anyone else expected the wide-open territory of Kansas to turn quickly into "Bleeding Kansas" (see Chapter 3).

Doughface II, "Old Buck"

Doughface I, Franklin Pierce, had come from New England, the hotbed of the abolitionists, even though he didn't have an abolitionist bone in his body. (He referred to abolitionists as "reckless fanatics.") Doughface II, James Buchanan, came from Pennsylvania, land of the Quakers, land of the Underground Railroad and lots of anti-slavery sentiment—but he was no more anti-slavery than Pierce. In the 1856 election, he beat the first Republican presidential candidate, John C. Fremont.

Like Pierce, "Old Buck" had wanted to add new territory to the United States, and he didn't mind if that territory was turned into slave states. Like Pierce, he hoped to buy Cuba to add more slave states to the Union. Spain wanted $150 million for it, and the Republicans in Congress squelched the purchase.

Even though Buchanan was pro-Southern, he couldn't control the Congress, which by now was tilted in favor of the North. In 1858, it admitted a new free state, Minnesota, then in 1859 another one, Oregon. The South was outvoted in the Senate 36–30. In the House it was 147–90.

Voices from Then

Buchanan stated that the United States was "providentially entitled" to possess all of "the North American Continent," including Mexico and Central America.

Buchanan did what he could to get the blood-spattered territory of Kansas admitted as a slave state, but this was not to be. It wasn't until January 1861, shortly before Buchanan left office, that Kansas became a state—a *free* state.

The Fire-Eaters

The abolitionists most definitely did *not* like compromise. We will now meet their Southern counterparts, the diehard secessionists, known as "fire-eaters." On the scale of Human Beings Who Took Themselves Very Seriously, the abolitionists and secessionists both rated a 10.

As you read the following paragraphs, keep in mind the great Southern politician from Chapter 2, John C. Calhoun. Most of the fire-eaters honored him as a god. Mr. Calhoun had emphasized the right of states to nullify federal laws and, if necessary, to secede. The fire-eaters were disciples of their master and quoted him often. Calhoun happened to die in 1850, the year of the famous compromise. Unlike most Southern moderates, the fire-eaters were not pleased with the compromise, and they worked to put Calhoun's ideas into action.

Grave, Golden-Tongued Mr. Yancey

William L. Yancey of Alabama was one of the most noted fire-eaters, those obsessive anti-North, anti-abolitionist, pro-slavery, pro-South, anti-federal politicians, editors, and speakers who formed the opposition to the just-as-fanatical abolitionists of the North. Fanatics and obsessives help bring about revolutions—consider Patrick Henry and Samuel Adams in the 1770s. But once the revolution is underway, and once a new nation is being formed, they prove to be pretty useless. This was certainly true in Yancey's case, as we shall see in a few chapters.

Yancey was an orator in an age that prized passionate, eloquent speakers. Everyone, even his enemies, agreed that Yancey had a beautiful, even *sweet*, speaking voice. He was one of those lucky men who could speak very loudly without seeming to bellow. And the one theme he loved to speak on was the South—that is, a South left alone by meddlesome abolitionists, a South that had slaves and (if things went as Yancey hoped) always would. Yancey himself owned many, largely thanks to his wealthy wife. He had painful memories of his self-righteous stepfather, a preacher who became a never-quiet abolitionist.

Yancey served briefly in Congress but never liked it. He lacked the tact and willingness to compromise that make good (or at least successful) politicians. He came to hate political parties in general, and (like the South's idol, John C. Calhoun) urged Southerners to avoid party labels and pursue an independent pro-Southern course.

One observer described his speeches as "seasoned with the salt of argument, the vinegar of sarcasm, the pepper of wit, and the genuine champagne of eloquence." He learned to contain his notorious temper and channel it into eloquence. And he sometimes made sense. He claimed that the sole function of government was "the greatest

WHO DEFINES "GOOD" THOUGH?

good for the greatest number, consistent with the inalienable rights of the minority." (The "minority" he had in mind was, of course, Southerners—Southern planters in particular.)

Voices from Then

No national party can save us; no sectional party can do it. But if we do as our fathers did, organize "Committees of Safety" all over the Cotton States, we shall fire the Southern heart—instruct the Southern mind—give courage to each other, and at the proper moment, by one organized concerted action, we can precipitate the Cotton States into a revolution.

—William L. Yancey, in a letter to a group called the League of United Southerners

---

Yancey had a knack for hobnobbing at commercial conventions, evangelizing men with his gospel of secession. Most people considered him an extremist, but he made some converts. As Yankees grew louder in their anti-South rhetoric, Southerners were more receptive to Yancey. We will meet Mr. Yancey again in Chapter 6.

Call Him "Tex"

Twenty-five years before secession came, Louis T. Wigfall was pushing for it. His home state of South Carolina was, of course, the land of John C. Calhoun, hotbed of pro-secession and anti-federal sentiment. But Wigfall had a rough time on his home turf. His reputation as a duelist hung over his head, and the man was constantly in debt, having quickly run through his sizable inheritance. He saw greener pastures in that new state, Texas, where he started a law practice and, in 1859, was chosen as a senator by the Texas legislature. He was elected in the wake of the hanging of John Brown, so Texas was whipped up into an anti-Northern, pro-secession frenzy. The openly secessionist Wigfall seemed the right choice.

Go See It!

You can visit the grave of the fire-eaters' idol, John C. Calhoun, in Charleston, South Carolina. His impressive tomb is in the cemetery of St. Philip's Episcopal Church.

Wigfall and the other fire-eaters may have been fanatics, but they weren't always wrong. One thing they never let Southerners forget about was the Fugitive Slave Law. It had been passed (as part of the Compromise of 1850) to appease the slave states, and it hadn't, for the simple reason that Northerners delighted in breaking it. It had become a scofflaw—a law on the books, but more often broken than observed. There was enough abolitionist sentiment in the North that runaway slaves, once they entered a free state, could probably count on staying free. The Yanks were very unlikely to turn them in to the authorities. Wigfall and many other Southerners (particularly any with runaway slaves!) realized the Fugitive Slave Act had been a political joke played on the South.

Mr. Wigfall will show up again in later chapters. Like the other fire-eaters, he became mostly an irritation once the Confederacy was formed.

Ruffin, His Gray Eminence

Edmund Ruffin was the long-silver-haired patriarch of secession. The Virginian began life as a Tidewater plantation lad, his family rooted in the Old Dominion's soil since 1666. Edmund, intelligent and well read, was one planter who took a genuine interest in the welfare of his family, his lands, even, yes, his slaves. And Ruffin was one of the few people in the 1800s to try to approach farming scientifically. He saw that tobacco farming was wearing out Virginia's soil. Reading everything he could get his hands on, he concluded that a substance called *marl* (lime-rich silt or clay) was the best way to rejuvenate his lands. It worked, and by the 1840s, most Tidewater farmers had adopted his methods. He gave one of his prosperous plantations the appropriate name "Marlbourne."

Ruffin might have gone down in history as an agricultural reformer, but like most men of celebrity status in those days, he felt compelled to take a stand politically. (That still happens, in case you haven't noticed.) To no one's surprise, the successful plantation master took a pro-states' rights, pro-South, anti-abolition stand.

Ruffin devoted his energy to his magazines, the *Southern Review* and others. Under the pen name "A Virginian," he also contributed some widely read pro-secession articles to newspapers in Richmond and Charleston. When he was made Virginia's state agricultural commissioner, he used his "bully pulpit" to address audiences not only on farming but (surprise!) on politics.

Some nation-shaking events made Ruffin want to do more than lecture. When abolitionist John Brown was captured at Harper's Ferry in 1859, Ruffin rushed to the scene, hoping a war would begin when abolitionists came to rescue Brown. He arrived to find himself a Southern celebrity, and he joined with a company of Virginia Military Institute cadets on guard at Brown's hanging. It was a win-win situation:

Did Y'all Know?

Ruffin was a rarity in that he didn't hire white overseers for his slaves but gave the reins to Jem Sykes, a trusted slave who had keys to every building on his plantation.

The abolitionists would precipitate a war when they showed up to rescue Brown, or the villain Brown would be hanged. Brown was hanged. Later Ruffin embarked on a speaking tour, showing audiences the fearsome-looking pikes that John Brown's army intended to use on slave owners. (A holdover from medieval times, pikes were long poles with sharp metal ends—sort of heavy-duty spears.) One of the pikes became part of Ruffin's look in public. His message was clear: These abolitionists are blood-thirsty, mania-driven fanatics, and the sooner we are out of the Union, the better.

Seeing war on the horizon, Ruffin put his writing talents to work on *Anticipations of the Future*, a novel depicting the events following Southern secession. As you might imagine, things didn't turn out exactly as he predicted. He certainly didn't predict, for example, that the Yankees would sack his plantation and use tobacco spit to write "you ruffinly son of bitch" on his walls. He didn't predict he would commit suicide at war's end, either.

Watch for Ruffin's name throughout this book, because the old patriarch had a Forrest Gump way of showing up at critical moments in history.

The Least You Need to Know

♦ Presidents Pierce and Buchanan were pro-Southern and accommodating to slave owners.

♦ Thanks to Henry Clay and other moderates, the Missouri Compromise and the Compromise of 1850 kept the nation from dividing over the slavery issue—for a while.

♦ The Kansas-Nebraska Act led to serious bloodshed in Kansas, a preview of the Civil War.

♦ Fire-eaters, the most extreme Southern secessionists, seemed determined to take the Southern states out of the Union.

5

1860: Fasten Your Seat Belts

In This Chapter

- ◆ War preview: The churches split
- ◆ The "Black Republicans"
- ◆ Dumb politics, 1860 style
- ◆ The underestimated power of myth

So far, so good—the nation is still one. In spite of the fuss over slavery, in spite of abolitionists and secessionists spewing out a lot of hate, somehow the States were still United. Moderates and compromisers had smoothed things over—barely.

But extremists North and South weren't happy. Inevitably something was going to snap. And that something might be the new kid on the political block, the Republican Party—not so affectionately known to Southerners as "Black Republicans."

Before we get to that painful political split, we'll look at a spiritual split that the history books often neglect.

Sneak Preview: Splitting the Steeples

In the 1800s, most Americans took Christianity, and the Bible, seriously. There were a handful of Jews, and very few outright atheists, but most

Did Y'all Know? _____

At the time of the Civil War, 262 of 288 American college presidents were clergy. A little more than one third of the faculty were ministers.

people identified (more or less) with Christianity. Christians all read the same Bible. You might say the Bible was the one thing that united people of every region, every class, and every age.

The biggest Christian groups were Methodists, Baptists, Presbyterians, Episcopalians, Lutherans, and Catholics. The first three of those grew tremendously during the spiritual movements known as the First and Second Great Awakenings. The Episcopalians were, in large part, people of the elite, the upper crust. The Catholics and Lutherans were concentrated among new European immigrants, mostly in the Northeast and Midwest. Keeping things as simple as possible, we can say that the average American in the pre–Civil War period was most likely to be a Methodist, Baptist, or Presbyterian.

The movement to abolish slavery in the United States was spearheaded by Christians, especially by ministers. The more moderate abolitionist Christians had a sensible idea: If they could convince their fellow Christians that slavery was wrong, then their Southern neighbors would emancipate the slaves of their own free will. If every so-called Christian in the South freed his slaves, slavery would soon disappear.

But not all Christians jumped on the anti-slavery bandwagon. Some pointed out a painful fact: The Bible, which is supposed to be the foundation of Christian behavior, doesn't condemn slavery. Jesus never said one word about it. The apostle Paul, who wrote a good chunk of the New Testament, told slaves to stay in their place and do their duty. (He also commanded Christian masters to treat their slaves kindly.) When Christianity was first being spread, many of the first Christians were slaves. There was no revolt among them, so, strictly speaking, you couldn't base abolition on the Bible.

So both abolitionists and anti-abolitionists were basing their beliefs on the Bible and religion. They could either settle the dispute amicably, live with the dispute and continue to fight, or divide. And divide they did.

Divorcing Churches

The Methodists officially divided in 1844. The wedge issue was a Methodist bishop who owned slaves. The Methodists' General Conference ordered the bishop to cease performing his official duties. Southern Methodists found this offensive and broke away to form a new denomination. Probably about 25,000 Methodist laymen and 1,200 Methodist ministers owned slaves.

Here was a first in America: A large Christian denomination had split over slaveholding. This doesn't sound too earth-shaking to us today, but in the 1840s it was dead serious. Not counting the federal government, the Methodist church was the largest organization in the United States. And it had split apart over the issue of slavery.

The Baptists? Prior to 1844, Baptists in the United States all cooperated in sending missionaries abroad. But the missionary agency, called the General Convention for Foreign Missions, decided in 1845 not to license missionaries who owned slaves. Baptists in the South split off and formed the Southern Baptist Convention.

The Presbyterians? In 1837 they experienced a theological split into Old School and New School. It wasn't precisely a North-South split of the Presbyterians, but generally the New School was sympathetic to abolitionists, while the Old School wasn't. It prepared the way for the real split that came with the war.

The Episcopalians, as already mentioned, tended to be upper-class folk. That meant that Southern Episcopalians were likely to be slave owners, and many were. Not many Northern Episcopalians were anti-slavery, and wealthy Northern Episcopalians were fairly tolerant of Southern Episcopalians owning slaves. So the denomination didn't actually split until the war forced it to. But the bigger denominations—Methodist, Baptists, and Presbyterians—had already come to the point where regional differences couldn't be tolerated.

> **Did Y'all Know?**
>
> The Northern and Southern Methodists reunited—finally—in 1939. Northern and Southern Presbyterians didn't reunite until 1983. Southern Baptists never reunited with the Northern Baptists. The slavery issue is long dead, but given the theological differences, reunion is very unlikely.

> **Voices from Then**
>
> John C. Calhoun observed that the various religious denominations had been a "strong cord that held the Union together." He believed (correctly) that their splitting was an omen of something worse.

About 95 percent of Southern churches were Methodist, Baptist, or Presbyterian. So the vast majority of people in the South had already been affected by a North-South split before the Civil War began. Most Southerners had, spiritually speaking, seceded from the North. They were tired of being told that they were not true Christians because of their tolerance of slavery.

A disturbing question was in the air: If the churches couldn't find a peaceful way to settle the slavery issue, what hope was there?

Flipping the Whigs

For most of the years we've been looking at, there were two major political parties: Democrats and Whigs. The Whigs pretty much died out in the late 1850s, to be replaced in a hurry by the new kids on the block, the Republicans, also called the *Black Republicans*. The Republicans ran their first presidential candidate, John C. Fremont, in 1856. He lost, but a lot of Republicans made their way into Congress, and more of them entered the political arena in the 1858 elections.

Were the Republicans an anti-slavery party? Sort of. The Republicans claimed to oppose only the *extension* of slavery. That is, they wanted to keep it from expanding into new U.S. territories. They didn't (so they claimed) wish to abolish it in the slave states. The Republicans were aware that Northerners in general weren't comfortable with extremists. Even so, the 1856 Republican platform did describe slavery as "a relic of barbarism."

But here is something curious about the Republican Party in those days: It made no attempt whatsoever to appeal to Southerners. It was the first time in American history that a party with its eyes on the White House (and control of Congress) simply dismissed a huge section of the country. The old Whig party had been national; the Republicans weren't. That in itself made Southerners nervous. They had endured many years of Northerners looking down on them, depicting them as barbaric, uncivilized, un-Christian, people who beat their slave men and bedded their slave women. But for a party with presidential aspirations to completely ignore the South was, to put it mildly, a slap in the face.

RebeLingo

From the very beginning, Republicans were called **Black Republicans** by many Southerners. *Black* had a double meaning—it meant "pro-Negro" and also "just plain bad."

The Abe Preview, 1858

In a book about the Confederacy, we really can't avoid talking about Abraham Lincoln. Interestingly, the Confederacy's favorite villain was born in a slave state (Kentucky, and not far from where Jefferson Davis was born). Both his parents were from another slave state (Virginia). But Lincoln had seen slaves being sold in the market, and he found the practice disgusting. Curiously enough, like a lot of anti-slavery people, he didn't believe freed slaves would be able to coexist with whites in America. He played with several notions of resettling them in Africa, the Caribbean, or Central America.

Lincoln, the wily lawyer with his treasury of amusing stories, had very limited political experience. He had served a term as a Whig congressman from Illinois. And in 1856, he gave a mesmerizing speech at a convention of the Illinois Republican Party. He spoke about the "big issue"—slavery—and stated he had heard

> **Go See It!**
>
> The Illinois State Capitol in Springfield has statues of both Stephen Douglas and Abraham Lincoln on the grounds.

Southerners say that slavery was actually good for the blacks. If that is so, Lincoln said, then logically we should make slaves of whites also. The Republicans saw his wisdom and remembered Lincoln as a man of homespun eloquence.

He was to say much more about slavery in his famous Senate race against Stephen Douglas in 1858. As the Republican candidate for the seat, Lincoln made his famous "House Divided" speech. It has been quoted to death, but we're going to quote from it again anyway:

> A house divided against itself cannot stand. I believe this government cannot endure half slave and half free. I do not expect the Union to be dissolved. I do not expect the House to fall. But I do expect it will cease to be divided. It will become all one thing, or all the other.

Lovely words, aren't they? Lincoln was an avid Bible-reader (though not a churchgoer), and he borrowed the line "a house divided against itself cannot stand" from a good source: Jesus. (Speeches from the 1800s are full of quotations from the Bible. Listeners expected that.) Lovely as the words are and sensible as they sound, were they true? He wasn't the first person to say that the country could not go on half-slave and half-free—but it had been doing just that since 1776. The Founding Fathers had managed to sweep the issue under the rug, and whenever it became an issue (which was usually whenever new states were being created), clever compromisers like Clay and Douglas were there to keep everyone happy, more or less. Was it absolutely certain, as Lincoln said, that compromise wouldn't work anymore?

The easygoing Lincoln, who didn't hate many people, came darn close to hating Douglas. He thought Douglas was too much of a compromiser (is there such a thing?) and perhaps a dangerous man for the country.

Their seven famous debates were held in August through October 1858. They drew huge crowds, and they lasted a long time.

Voices from Then

Despite being anti-slavery, Lincoln always had doubts about abolition, too. He went on record as saying, "I think no wise man has yet perceived how it could be at once eradicated without producing a greater evil even to the cause of human liberty itself."

Douglas made his listeners aware of where Lincoln was headed: The belief that the country could no longer endure half-slave and half-free could, Douglas said, lead to civil war. He was correct. Lincoln claimed during the debates that the South knew in its heart that slavery was really wrong. True? Hard to say. Politicians have a habit of claiming that people "know in their hearts" that a certain behavior is wrong. It may be wishful thinking.

Lincoln lost the Senate race to Stephen Douglas. But the exposure he got from debating the famous Douglas gave the one-term congressman a shot at the White House.

Whose Democratic Party, Exactly?

At the 1860 Republican Convention, Lincoln got a lot of mileage out of his debates with Douglas—and his image as the rail-splitter. Deciding they liked Lincoln's beliefs—and his homespun image—the Republicans nominated him as their presidential candidate.

Remember that the previous two presidents were Democrats (Pierce and Buchanan). Democrats were strong nationwide and had a lock on the South. The Republicans knew they had not a ghost of chance of getting a single electoral vote from the South. Summing up, Lincoln's chances didn't look good. All the Democrats had to do was what they had done the previous two elections: run a Northerner who would be acceptable to the South.

Enter some extremists.

The Democrats held their convention in Charleston, South Carolina. This may not have been a wise choice. The idea of secession had been floating around in South Carolina's air for 30 years. No state represented Southern extremism more than South Carolina, and Charleston was Secession City.

One of the South's key players at the 1860 convention was William L. Yancey—not exactly a moderate. He and some fellow fire-eaters pushed for a Southern platform, insisting that any Democratic candidate for president *must* be openly pro-slavery. (More specifically, the platform had to pledge Congress and the president to protect slave property in the territories.) The platform was rejected. Northern Democrats had grown accustomed to *tolerating* slavery (it had helped them win the White House more than once). But they balked at openly *embracing* it. Yancey literally stomped out of the gathering, followed by several other Southern delegates. Yancey had put himself in a win-win situation: either his Southern platform passed (it didn't), or he would split the Democratic party (bingo!).

Did Y'all Know? _____

In the 1860 election, the Republican Party was the only one without a Southerner on the ticket. Lincoln was from Illinois, and his vice presidential running mate, Hannibal Hamlin, was from Maine. Stephen Douglas of Illinois had Herschel V. Johnson of Georgia as his running mate. The two Southern presidential candidates aimed for balance, too: John C. Breckinridge of Kentucky had Joseph Lane of Oregon, and John Bell of Tennessee had Edward Everett of Massachusetts.

With so many Southern delegates gone, the convention couldn't nominate anyone and had to adjourn. It reconvened at Baltimore in June and nominated the great compromiser himself, Stephen Douglas. The breakaway Southern Democrats nominated the current vice president, John C. Breckinridge of Kentucky. Poor Breckinridge reluctantly accepted the nomination, even though he didn't expect to win. He tried his darndest to present himself as pro-Union, but there was a feeling in the country that "pro-Union" and "Southern" no longer went together.

John C. Breckinridge (1821–1875), vice president under James Buchanan, reluctant 1860 presidential candidate, and later Confederate general and secretary of war.

(Library of Congress)

What were the *Southern* Democrats thinking? If they had gone along with the nomination of Douglas, there was the likelihood that Douglas would have won, and Douglas had never been an enemy of slavery. Yancey and his ilk were throwing away the chance of keeping in power the one national party that protected slavery.

But Yancey and his cohorts were itching to start their own nation, even though the majority of Southerners weren't. Yancey and his cronies may have hoped to bend the Democratic Convention to their will. That failed. By nominating Breckinridge, they may have hoped Douglas and the Northern Democrats would cave in and adopt the Southern platform, at which time Breckinridge would politely withdraw. That didn't happen either.

Just to Confuse You, Another Party

Here is the rundown so far. Republican candidate, Abraham Lincoln. Northern Democratic candidate, Stephen Douglas. Southern Democratic candidate, John C. Breckinridge. Now here's a *fourth* name for the mix: John Bell, Constitutional Union candidate.

Where did Bell come from? From that great American urge (which we've seen in some recent elections) for an alternative party. The Constitutional Union party was launched in February 1860 by some moderate-minded folks who weren't happy with either the Republicans or Democrats. (Does any of this sound familiar?) The founders of the party believed (correctly) that the public at large was burned out on the slavery issue. Their solution: Keep quiet about it. ("Can't we all just get along?")

Bell, a Tennessean, was a slave owner but had never been a secessionist. His running mate was (for balance) a Northerner, Edward Everett of Massachusetts. The party convention declared that the real issue of the day was preserving the Union.

Did Y'all Know?

John Bell had served as Speaker of the House under President Andrew Jackson and as secretary of war under President John Tyler.

The party did have some appeal, because many Americans were put off by the Republicans (too new, too anti-slavery) and by the Democrats (too divided, stupid enough to run two candidates instead of one). The party's platform was "the Union, the Constitution, and the enforcement of the laws." Translated: Let's all stay together in the Union, and we'll work to enforce the laws—specifically, the Fugitive Slave Law, which Northerners had broken so often that the law was a joke.

John Bell had a very sensible message the South needed to hear: *If you stay in the Union, you may be able to keep slavery. If you leave the Union, you will definitely have to give it up.* A wise and prophetic man.

Drum Roll, Major Suspense

A lot of folks were certain that Lincoln would win, including Sen. Jefferson Davis of Mississippi. He wanted, like John Bell, to keep the South in the Union if at all possible. He feared what the secessionists would do if Lincoln won. So he tried to use his considerable charm on three of the presidential candidates: Breckinridge, Douglas, and Bell. Would they please, he asked, be willing to step aside in favor of a compromise candidate? Breckinridge and Bell said yes, they would. Douglas would not. The little egomaniac had been nursing his ambition to be president for years. For once, the great compromiser couldn't be budged.

Here are the national totals, in case you're curious:

Candidate	Popular votes	Percent	Electoral votes
Lincoln	1,865,908	39.82	180
Douglas	1,380,202	29.46	12
Breckinridge	848,019	18.09	72
Bell	590,901	12.61	39

The Secession Door Wide Open

As you may already know, or will find out in Part 2, the signal for secession to begin was the election of Abraham Lincoln in November 1860. Now is a good time to pause and ask that question Americans have asked ever since 1860: Was the break-up (or breakdown) of the Union inevitable? Could it have been stopped? Or delayed? No one knows for certain, of course (we aren't God), but there are so many might-have-beens and what-ifs in the story. For example, what if the Southern Democrats hadn't peevishly broken away in the summer of 1860? You can look at the numbers in the table and do the math: Lincoln got more electoral votes than the other three candidates combined. If the only opponent had been Douglas, would Lincoln have won?

What if the secessionists had been more willing to compromise? What if the abolitionists had not been so judgmental? What if Mrs. Stowe hadn't written *Uncle Tom's Cabin?* What if Southerners hadn't made an idol out of John C. Calhoun and his beliefs about nullification? What if the North hadn't tried to impose a high tariff on the South? What if the South had encouraged more industry and less dependence on agriculture? What if Eli Whitney had never invented his cotton gin? What if American colonists had never purchased African slaves?

Here's the biggest what-if of all: What if Americans in 1860 had taken a deep breath, put their prejudices aside a moment, and looked at the many, many things that tied all the parts of the country together? For all the rattling on about sectional differences, the people of the Union had a *lot* in common. They shared laws, a basic moral framework, a Judeo-Christian spiritual heritage, a rich literary heritage, a respect for hard work, a belief in the common people having dignity, a contempt for pomp, a devotion to the Founding Fathers, and ....

Well, in all the excitement of 1860, people forgot about how much they shared. And no wonder. We should never underestimate the power of myth.

Voices from Then

The South—the poor South.
—John C. Calhoun, on his deathbed, 1850

Myth Understanding

Between roughly 1830 and 1860, Northerners (especially abolitionists) had constructed a myth about the South. It was the "land of the lash," where slave owners beat slaves and begat children by them. Southerners were hypocrites, attending church but keeping blacks in bondage. The South was a backward, backwater land: crude, uncivilized, with no respect for education or industry or progress. Its people were both ignorant and immoral.

The South had its counter-myth. The North was a land of money-grubbing, materialistic, rude people, with no sense of courtesy or hospitality. They lived for the dollar. Instead of making money through honest farming, many Northerners chose speculation and extortion. They ran factories where men, women, and children toiled away for a pittance in grimy conditions for long hours. Then Northerners were hypocritical enough to condemn Southerners as "slave drivers." They despised blacks and excluded them from their social world, while Southerners lived among blacks and looked after them.

Southerners had a myth about themselves, too. While they were realistic enough to know that not every Southerner lived on a plantation with a swarm of slaves (only a minority did), the politeness and the hospitality of the plantation owners was the possession of every white person. Southerners were courteous, hospitable to all, loyal to their kin, devout, and kind to the slaves. They gained their daily bread by honest toil on their farms (Thomas Jefferson would have approved). Here was a world that was not in a mad rush, a mellow place where courtesy and kindness still mattered.

In a time when the average person didn't travel very widely, it was easy to assume that those people hundreds of miles away weren't very nice people. It was easy to forget the things all Americans shared and to focus on the differences. It was easy to believe those people in the other part of the country weren't just *different*—they were *bad*. For too long South and North had not been talking *to* each other, but *at* each other, and finally *past* each other. So they were ready for a separation.

The Least You Need to Know

- The North-South split in the major churches was a preview of the Civil War.

- The rise of the "North-only" Republican Party frightened many Southerners.

- The North-South split in the Democratic Party in 1860 helped elect the anti-slavery Republican, Abraham Lincoln.

- South and North had both developed hateful stereotypes about each other, making separation easier.

Part 2

Nation-Making—or Rebellion?

You probably think it all began with the firing on Fort Sumter, right? Nope. There were lots of things going on *politically* before anything happened *militarily*. Following Lincoln's election in 1860, secessionists saw their golden opportunity: Pull out of the Union, and get a brand new nation started before Lincoln even took office. A tall order—particularly when you remember that only a minority of people truly wanted to leave the Union.

We'll definitely look at Fort Sumter in this part. But we'll also look at some political maneuvering that is just as interesting—maybe more so—as anything that happened on the Civil War battlefields. If you think politics is boring, wait till you meet the Southern boys of 1861.

Chapter 6

Departing in a Southern Huff

In This Chapter

- The "who will secede first?" dance
- Compromisers feeling extremely frustrated
- Meet me in Montgomery
- Mr. Davis and the Southern jubilation

Lincoln, a "Black Republican," had been elected in November 1860. Obviously, the Republicans were happy. So was that tiny but loud Southern group known as the fire-eaters. Here was a great excuse to make the daring leap from threatening to secede to really seceding.

It didn't happen overnight—but it did happen pretty darn fast. The secessionists imposed a tight deadline on themselves: Get out of the Union and get a new Southern nation started before the Black Republican Lincoln took office in March 1861. By gum, they did it.

First, South Carolina (Naturally)

If you have been paying attention, you know that South Carolina was the hub of the secession movement. The mighty John C. Calhoun, vice president and senator, was South Carolina's pride and joy. He died in 1850, but

Did Y'all Know? ____

South Carolina had been threatening secession for 30 years. Its population had the highest percentage of slaves (57.2 percent) in the nation. It was the only state left in which the legislature, not the voters themselves, voted for the electors in presidential races. It was unique—unashamedly so.

Voices from Then ____

We separated from the North because of incompatibility of temper; we are divorced, North from South, because we have hated each other so.

—From the diary of Mary Chesnut of South Carolina

his spirit lived on. Not every South Carolinian wished to secede, of course, but enough people among the elite did. These included a character who had known Calhoun and adored him: Robert Barnwell Rhett, who had served in both House and Senate. He owned a newspaper, the *Charleston Mercury*. His son, Robert Jr., was editor, and Bob Sr. contributed articles. He was hot for secession, so much so that history has dubbed him "Father of Secession."

Rhett had been working for secession since the nullification crisis back in the 1830s (see Chapter 2). He knew one state seceding by itself would be ridiculous—it would have to be joined by others, preferably all the other slave states. Naturally, he wanted his beloved South Carolina to go first.

Rhett and the other fire-eaters had been howling for years about "resistance or submission" to the hated North. Now that Lincoln was president-elect, did they really expect horrible things to happen the day he took office? Probably not. The more intelligent secessionists knew that one Black Republican couldn't turn the country upside down. Republicans didn't control Congress or the Supreme Court. Like every president of every party, Lincoln would have to cooperate somehow with Democrats (and Southerners). In spite of their fears of the Republicans' anti-slavery stance, secessionists really had no idea what the first Republican president might do. They feared he was such a bumpkin that he would be under the control of hard-line abolitionist Republicans like William Seward of New York. Also, in spite of the fact that the Republican Party platform only opposed the *extension* of slavery to new states, Southerners were aware of how easily platforms could be forgotten after elections.

They knew that the lame-duck president, James Buchanan, would probably do nothing whatsoever to stop secession. They were right. (At his last public reception as president, Buchanan heard the band play both "Yankee Doodle" and "Dixie.") Lincoln wouldn't take office till March 1861. So rather than wait, South Carolina chose a preemptive strike. On November 10, the state legislature (which happened to be in session when Lincoln's victory was announced) gave the go-ahead to a state convention to decide "future relations between the State and the Union."

The fire-eaters were in their glory. They went out to the smaller towns in the state, trying to whip the people into an anti-Lincoln frenzy. They did their job well. The delegates to the state convention were overwhelmingly secessionists. People who had considered themselves good Unionists (that is, true blue Americans) in

Go See It!

You can see South Carolina's Ordinance of Secession on display at the State House (capitol, that is) in Columbia.

the past found themselves voting for secessionists. Their pride wouldn't let them be branded "submissionists." The Spirit of '76 got mentioned more than once. (The secessionists were definitely better organized and more energetic than the submissionists.) The sad thing about this swift secession movement is that very sane, sensible, level-headed folk got stuck with the submissionist label—which caused many of them to either support secession or shut up.

The December convention at Charleston's St. Andrew's Hall wasn't just a gathering of delegates. Fire-eaters from other Southern states came to South Carolina to nudge the delegates along (not that they needed much nudging). The pattern would be repeated in the other states' secession conventions. The convention voted—*unanimously*—on December 20 to take South Carolina out of the United States. It issued its famous Ordinance of Secession. Its equally famous "Declaration of Immediate Causes" was issued on Christmas Eve—a nice Christmas present for the fire-eaters. In between the convention's speeches, a band played (what else?) "Dixie." Charleston was wild with excitement, bells ringing, cannon firing, military parades, and so on, showing that people were glad to be citizens of "South Carolina, an independent commonwealth."

Rhett's newspaper, the *Charleston Mercury*, came out with a special edition, and a blunt four-word headline: "The Union Is Dissolved!" (The special edition was off the press within 15 minutes of the convention adjourning.) Rhett was happy as a lark. Strange enough, it wasn't Rhett or any other fire-eater who penned the Declaration of Immediate Causes. That task went to Christopher Memminger, a German-born Charlestonian who wasn't an extremist about anything. The fire-eaters had to rely on these calm, methodical types to get things done. In the coming weeks, much to the fire-eaters' surprise, it would be the South's Memmingers, not its Rhetts, who were given high posts in the new government.

Voices from Then

South Carolina's Ordinance of Secession, passed on December 20, 1860:

> An Ordinance to dissolve the union between the state of South Carolina and other states united with her under the compact entitled 'The Constitution of the United States of America.' ... The union now subsisting between South Carolina and the other States under the name of 'The United States of America' is hereby dissolved.

Declaration of the Immediate Causes of Secession, Charleston, South Carolina, December 24, 1860:

> In April 1852, South Carolina had declared that the U.S.'s "encroachments upon the reserved rights of the States fully justified this State in their withdrawal from the Federal Union .... Since that time these encroachments have continued to increase, and further forbearance ceases to be a virtue. And now the State of South Carolina having resumed her separate and equal place among nations ..." [It goes on to speak of Britain, the Declaration of Independence, 1776, and all that.]
>
> The ends for which this Government was instituted have been defeated, and the Government itself has been destructive of them by the action of the non-slaveholding States.
>
> Sectional interest and animosity will deepen the irritation; and all hope of remedy is rendered vain, by the fact that the public opinion at the North has invested a great political error with the sanctions of a more erroneous religious belief [abolitionism, that is].

The ordinance ends by "appealing to the Supreme Judge of the world for the rectitude of our intentions."

Follow Us, Southern Sisters

The states that had promised to follow South Carolina's lead in the secession movement kept their promises. Mississippi's convention voted to secede on January 9, 1861. (The state had not heeded Jefferson Davis's advice to "move slowly.") Florida followed on January 10, Alabama on January 11. (Alabama's secession ordinance was written by noted fire-eater William L. Yancey.) Georgia followed on January 19, Louisiana on January 26. Texas withdrew from the Union on February 1, adding a huge chunk of territory to the seceders. (Texas also was the gateway to the Southwest, which secessionists had their eyes on. Read on.) Very impressive work, and all

Did Y'all Know? _____

Some secessionists were so confident that all 15 slave states would secede that someone designed a flag with 15 stars.

done swiftly. In less than two months, the entire Deep South was gone from the Union.

Listing only the dates and names of the seceding states leaves out some important details. One is this: There was no unanimous move to secede in any state. Every state, even South Carolina, had huge numbers of people

Voices from Then

I must say that I am one of those dull creatures that cannot see the good of secession.
–Col. Robert E. Lee of Virginia

who opposed secession, or at least didn't support it. Many people who later became leaders in the Confederacy were among those dragging their feet about secession.

In a time when people often change their state of residence, it's hard to explain the grip that "home state" had on people's minds in the mid-1800s. Not everyone lived in the state he was born in, true, but most people *settled* somewhere and felt a deep loyalty to that state. Southerners certainly did, and if they owned farms, they felt a literal attachment to the land. And so many people who thought of themselves as good Union people opposed secession—but, once their state had seceded, they accepted it and were prepared to live with the consequences.

On his last night in Washington, Sen. Jefferson Davis of Mississippi, who had just resigned his post because his state had seceded, prayed this prayer: "May God have us in His holy keeping, and grant that before it is too late peaceful councils may prevail."

Be Wise (and Compromise)

Think back to Chapter 5: Lincoln didn't win a majority of the votes in 1860—he only got 39 percent of the popular vote. Not only had he received practically no votes in the South, but most *Northerners* had voted against him, too. Besides that, his party, the Republicans, didn't have a majority in the House or Senate. Couple that with the fact that he could (and likely would) be voted out in four years, and prospects for the South looked good.

We saw in Chapter 2 that Southerners had a lot of political clout in the early days of the country—several presidents, numerous Congressional powerhouses, Southern (or pro-Southern) Supreme Court justices. The two presidents before Lincoln had been "doughfaces"—Northerners sympathetic to the

RebeLingo

Cooperationists was the name applied to Southerners who opposed immediate secession. Some cooperationists suggested an obvious political move: Let each state hold a referendum on secession. That is, don't secede unless a majority of voters in the state wish to do so. The fire-eaters were smart enough to know that unless secession happened swiftly, it probably would never happen.

South. So the secessionists' reaction to Lincoln was almost juvenile—something like, "Well, if we can't run things like we're used to doing, we'll just leave!"

By a funny coincidence, on December 20, South Carolina's secession day, the U.S. Senate, hoping some compromise could be worked out, appointed the Committee of Thirteen. That committee happened to include three Southern powerhouses that were known as the "Southern Triumvirate"—Jefferson Davis of Mississippi, Robert Toombs of Georgia, and Robert M. T. Hunter of Virginia. The chairman was sweet-tempered John Crittenden of Kentucky, admirer of Mr. Compromise himself, Henry Clay. Crittenden had come up with six proposals known as the Crittenden Compromise.

The committee's six proposals essentially gave Southerners assurance that the federal government would not encroach on slavery, so long as it was kept below the long-established 36°30′ line of latitude. That was the old Missouri Compromise line. Crittenden was hoping it would keep everybody happy. It certainly didn't please the Republicans on the committee. (Lincoln, not yet sworn in as president, had let the Republicans on the committee know that he didn't support the compromise, either.) So Crittenden's masterpiece of moderation died in committee. The sad report of the Committee of Thirteen included the statement that it was unable "to agree upon any general plan of adjustment."

The House had a similar committee, its Committee of Thirty-Three. It fared better, coming up with a Constitutional amendment guaranteeing no interference with slavery in the states where it already existed. Curiously enough, both House and Senate passed this and submitted it to the states as the Thirteenth Amendment. But in politics, timing is everything; the Confederacy had already been formed, so the committee's labors came to nothing.

War? No Way!

After states began to secede, newspaper mogul Horace Greeley wrote in his *New York Tribune*, "We hope never to live in a republic whereof one section is pinned to the residue by bayonets."

Greeley was overlooking something crucial: Young men *like* a fight—political or military or both. They had proven this already in the secession process. Secession was the young and radical view of things. Older, wealthy slave owners weren't all pro-secession, since they tended to be conservative and wanted to keep things as they were. (Many of them had business and banking connections with the North, too.)

Some of them realized, correctly, that staying in the Union was a more likely way to preserve slavery than seceding. They probably hoped the younger men would either grow up or simmer down.

But youth must have its fling. For the younger men, Unionism meant continuing the same old same old. It meant staying in the Union and constantly fretting over the abolitionists and their power in the North. Secession at least meant *change*. And they had a handful of middle-aged fire-eaters to remind them they were doing right. The South Carolina convention, in its secession ordinance, had claimed the South stood "exactly in the same position toward the Northern states that our ancestors in the Colonies did toward Great Britain." In other words, the holy cause of the American Revolution was being repeated. The states' secession ordinances all had words to the effect that the federal government had trampled on the states' rights, done terrible unconstitutional things, insulted the Southern people, and tried to incite slaves to rebel, for example.

Young bucks may have hankered for a war, but most of their elders did not. Even gung-ho secessionists like Robert Barnwell Rhett hoped there would be no bloodshed. Rhett said he would personally eat the bodies of all the people slain if a war occurred. One saying making the rounds at the time was "A lady's thimble will hold all the blood that will be shed."

Did Southerners really believe this? It was widely believed that Yankees were basically a bunch of money-grubbing cowards. One joke was that if a Yank pulled a gun on you, all you had to do was offer to buy it from him, and he would sell and walk away. If you study history a while, you learn that human beings everywhere assume that their enemies are cowards. Four years later, the belief had changed from "Yanks are cowards" to "Yanks are butchers."

Did Y'all Know?

Before and after the secession season, some Southerners resurrected the old "Don't Tread on Me" flag from Revolutionary days. You might recall from U.S. history class that the flag showed a rattlesnake—representing the American colonies in the 1770s, but in 1861 representing the newly seceded states.

Voices from Then

People who are anxious for war don't know what they are bargaining for; they don't see all the horrors that must accompany such an event. I feel satisfied that the Northern people love the Union more than they do their peculiar notions of slavery.

—Maj. Thomas J. Jackson, later known as "Stonewall"

Secession Party!

Even though seven states had seceded, no Confederacy had been formed yet. It was probably inevitable, but for a few weeks the seceded states got a bang out of being totally independent. So there was a Republic of Alabama and a Republic of Georgia, and people enjoyed that. All of John C. Calhoun's preaching about states' rights was finally bearing fruit. Each state was (temporarily) its own sovereign nation.

The newly sovereign states celebrated that winter of 1861 by lighting bonfires, ringing church bells, firing cannons, parading down main streets, and lighting up the winter nights with fireworks. But it couldn't last, of course. Southerners knew they had to unite, just as the 13 colonies had done in the 1770s. Right after South Carolina seceded, Robert Barnwell Rhett suggested Montgomery, Alabama, as a good meeting place for a Southern convention. It was the capital of Alabama, the home state of his fellow fire-eater William L. Yancey, who had worked so effectively to split the Democrats in the 1860 election. (Yancey owned a house in Montgomery, and his plantation was nearby.) Rhett saw himself and Yancey setting up a Southern government that would never be coaxed or forced back into the Union.

The Lincoln Deadline

The Black Republican Abraham Lincoln would be inaugurated on March 4. Not knowing what he might do, the seceded states thought it wise to unite before then. Poor old lame duck James Buchanan had stated it was illegal for the Southern states to secede—but also said it was illegal for him to force them back. The Southerners thought they better do something fast while this doughface was still in the White House.

The Montgomery meeting was called for February 4—exactly one month before Lincoln's inauguration. Create a new nation in a *month*? Fasten your seat belt, dear reader—it happened.

Remember that the South pictured itself as the true keeper of the American Revolution's ideals. So, on the one hand, it was *revolutionary*. On the other hand, it was *conservative*, sticking to American ideals of the past. The new nation was based on a *conservative revolution*. The South's leaders wanted to show the Union—and other nations of the world—that nothing wacky or radical was happening (like the

French Revolution in 1789). No, just American business as usual—respect for liberty, property rights, and other red, white, and blue ideals.

Naturally, the fire-eaters who had helped bring about this second American Revolution expected to be rewarded for their services. Rhett, Yancey, and Wigfall were counting on holding high posts in the new nation. Radicals, however, are better at nation-breaking than nation-making. To their credit, the Southerners who gathered in Montgomery in February 1861 realized that.

You might say the Confederacy's first president was Howell Cobb of Georgia. That is, the convention chose him to preside over the proceedings. Cobb had been secretary of the treasury under Buchanan, so he had the aura of having held a cabinet post under the Union. He had also been Speaker of the House at one time. Cobb was no radical. A very portly planter, he was moderate and reserved—having neither the demeanor nor the brain of a radical. He probably had a lot of experience managing people, since he personally owned more than a thousand slaves.

Both the provisional constitution (put together in a mere four days) and the permanent constitution were closely modeled on the old U.S. Constitution. The 12-man committee included fire-eater Robert Barnwell Rhett and the "James Madison of the Confederacy," Thomas R. R. Cobb of Georgia. The brother of Howell Cobb, he was the South's legal whiz kid, probably more responsible than any other member for retaining what Southerners considered good in the old Constitution.

Ditto for the presidency. The chief executive would have powers (and limits) like the U.S. president. He would (big surprise here!) be pro-slavery (best to be safe and select a slave owner, of course). If it was someone with experience in state and national government, good. It needed to be a name Northerners (and foreigners, too) would respect.

Choosing the Chieftain

Robert Barnwell Rhett may have been the Father of Secession. But he had served only briefly in the House and Senate, and his career as a pro-slavery journalist was fine as far as it went—which wasn't far. People who write editorials may have wonderful ideas, but politics involves collaboration and compromise. Fire-eaters like Rhett and Yancey weren't noted for either compromise or tact.

Fire-eater Louis Wigfall of Texas had years of government service under his belt, but he was still too radical (and too hot-tempered) to be president of the new nation. Even if he had been more of a moderate, he was too combative for most people's taste. Plus, he was from Texas—a fairly new and sparsely populated state.

Did Y'all Know? _____

Historians have puzzled over why William L. Yancey did not try harder for the presidency, since he had worked so hard for secession. One explanation is that the new nation badly wanted Virginia to join—and there was a fear that Virginians would probably see Yancey and the other fire-eaters as too radical to be good politicians.

That left three tantalizing choices: the Southern Triumvirate of Davis, Toombs, and Hunter.

Robert Toombs, senator from Georgia, was both a successful lawyer and a wealthy planter. Following Lincoln's election, Toombs gave his farewell speech in the U.S. Senate, proclaiming, "The Union, sir, is dissolved." When delegates met in Montgomery, Alabama, to form the Confederacy, Bob Toombs was on the "short list" for president.

Toombs had been known as a moderate in the Senate. He claimed he dearly loved the Union (and probably meant it). But he was tiring of Northern politicians who no longer seemed willing to compromise with the South. After South Carolina seceded, Toombs used his considerable speaking skills to push Georgia to "reconquer liberty and independence."

Unfortunately, big Bob was noted as being "fond of the grape." The boozy man was foolish enough to become "tight every day at dinner" in Montgomery, and shortly before the election became *very* drunk. Toombs had a major role (several, actually) in the Confederacy, but president wasn't it.

Robert M. T. Hunter, the senator from Virginia, was a more sober (in more ways than one) character than Toombs. He had been Speaker of the House in his younger days and had nursed ambitions for the U.S. presidency. But the obvious reason he wasn't given serious consideration for Confederate president was that Virginia had not seceded yet.

That left an interesting and fateful choice: the Mississippi senator, Mexican War hero, and former secretary of war, Jefferson Davis.

Jefferson the First (and Last)

The Confederacy's one and only president had an odd middle name—*Finis*, the Latin word for "last." He was the last of his family's large brood of children. Aside from being named for Thomas Jefferson, Davis had another connection to the American Revolution: His father was a cavalryman in the Revolutionary War.

Davis was a Kentucky boy—just like Abraham Lincoln, and in fact born fewer than a hundred miles from the cabin where Lincoln was born eight months later. Like Lincoln, he made his fame in another state—Mississippi, the home state of his second wife, the devoted Varina. (Davis's first wife, who died three months after their marriage, was the daughter of General—and later president—Zachary Taylor.)

Jefferson Davis (1808–1889), planter, Mexican War hero, U.S. secretary of war, senator from Mississippi, and the Confederacy's only president.

(Library of Congress)

Except for his West Point education and a stint in the Mexican War (which brought him glory), Davis was never anything but a planter-politician, a role he loved. He served as a congressman, then senator, then as secretary of war under President Franklin Pierce. Davis was genuinely good in his cabinet post, certainly a more energetic figure than the vacuous Pierce. His one long-term legacy to the U.S. Army (and later the Confederate Army) was the ankle-high "Jeff Davis boot." He also formed a short-lived (but very sensible) camel corps in the U.S. Southwest.

After serving in the army, Davis returned to the Senate and became an outspoken champion of Southern rights. He was never a fire-eater, but he came around, slowly, to believing that compromise was no longer possible: "If the folly and fanaticism and pride and hate and corruption of the day are to destroy the peace and prosperity of the Union, let the sections part like the patriarchs of old and let peace and good will subsist among their descendants." (This was not going to happen, but Davis was an optimist.) Davis was painfully aware that the days of the noble compromisers like Henry Clay were gone.

Mississippi seceded from the Union, and Davis made his valediction speech in the U.S. Senate. Davis was such an eloquent speaker that many people in the Senate's visitors' gallery wept. To the senators remaining, Davis said, "I am sure I feel no hostility to you. There is not one of you to whom I cannot say now, in the presence of my God, I wish you well. And such, I am sure, is the feeling of the people whom I represent toward those whom you represent. I hope, and

Did Y'all Know?

In his first term in Congress, Davis was part of the seven-man committee deciding on the use of a huge sum of money given to the United States by James Smithson. Davis agreed it should fund an institution, not a national university. Whenever you visit the Smithsonian Institution, you can thank Jefferson Davis.

they hope, for peaceful relations with you, though we must part."

Howell Cobb and the other delegates in Montgomery never got the Founding Fathers out of their minds. They recalled that the new republic had not fought over who would be president but had been unanimous in putting George Washington in the slot. So, to many people's surprise, there wasn't much bickering in Montgomery, either. (Considering all the ego-trippers there, this really was amazing.)

Alexander Hamilton Stephens was chosen as Davis's vice president. The scrawny, often ailing little Georgia congressman was a bachelor who never weighed more than 90 pounds. Stephens had opposed secession, but he followed his home state out of the Union. Like many politicians then and now, Stephens had been a lawyer. Specifically, his area was *constitutional* law—so the new nation was placing at its top tier a man obsessed with adhering to the Constitution. (As we shall soon see, Stephens' obsessive nature was to cause major problems for the country.) The Montgomery delegates apparently made him vice president because of his intelligence and eloquence—plus his Unionism sent the world the message that the new nation was not being managed by radicals like Yancey and Wigfall. (And sure, the delegates were aware that Alexander Hamilton Stephens, like Jefferson Davis, had been named for one of the Founding Fathers.)

Stephens was already in Montgomery, and on February 11 he was inaugurated. Jefferson Davis had not been present at the convention. He was at home in Mississippi at his Brierfield plantation. In a moment that would have been great on video, he and his wife were pruning rosebushes when a messenger arrived with the fateful news. The message had been signed by Davis's former senate colleague, Bob Toombs.

Davis's long train trip to Montgomery was good—and bad. It was good because the train stopped frequently and gave a lot of Southerners a chance to see their new president. It also gave Davis a look at a huge chunk of the South. (He got a very warm welcome in Tennessee—which had not even seceded yet.) The bad part: The long train trip was a painful reminder that the South was sadly lacking in good rail connections. Davis's plantation near the Mississippi River was not that far from Montgomery. But to get there, he had to go north to Memphis, then east to Chattanooga, then south to Atlanta, and finally to Montgomery. Putting it in numbers, he traveled 850 miles to get to a spot less than 300 miles away. The South's railroad problem would prove to be a biggie in the coming years.

But people were in a festive mood. Davis gave more than 20 speeches during the trip. He shook a lot of hands, saw a lot of bonfires, and probably kissed a few babies, too. Even though he arrived at Montgomery in the late evening, a cheering crowd met him at the station.

> ### Go See It!
>
> Alabama's white marble capitol building is worth touring. On the capitol lawn, a statue of Jefferson Davis commemorates his inauguration as Confederacy president. Inside the capitol, the Old Senate Chamber has been restored to look just as it did when delegates from the seceding states organized the Confederacy there.

Yancey was present at that crucial moment in Montgomery: He made a welcoming speech at Montgomery's Exchange Hotel and introduced Davis with one of the most famous quotes in U.S. history: "The man and the hour have met. We may now hope that prosperity, honor, and victory, await his administration." Davis gave a brief speech and went to bed, probably feeling a mix of happiness and terror over what lay ahead.

On February 18, Davis rode with Stephens and Cobb in a carriage drawn by six gray horses. A band played "Dixie" (what else?). For February, the weather was gorgeous, warm and sunny (an omen?). Davis proceeded up the low hill to the Alabama Capitol—which was also, for the time being, the Confederate Capitol.

When Davis took office, the 5,000 onlookers saw a stately man in his early 50s, very slim, with a sometimes noticeable facial tic. In the days before TV and sound bites, people didn't expect warm and cuddly politicians. They wanted their statesmen reserved and unshakable. Davis was all that. Like George Washington, he was a class act. The Confederates were quite aware that he looked more impressive than the "ape" Lincoln that the foolish Northerners had elected.

Davis was a superb speaker. (If only we possessed recordings of some of these amazing orators of the 1860s!) His speech was perfect. It reminded Southerners that they weren't radicals or traitors, but true Americans, faithful to

> ### Voices from Then
>
> We have changed the constituent parts, but not the system of government .... The impartial and enlightened verdict of mankind will vindicate the rectitude of our conduct; and He who knows the hearts of men will judge of the sincerity with which we have labored to preserve the government of our fathers in its spirit ....
>
> —Excerpts from Jefferson Davis's inaugural address

the Founding Fathers. The "system of government" was not being changed at all. Davis had assured them that "the Constitution framed by our Fathers is that of these Confederate States." But he made it clear that "a reunion with the states which we have separated from is neither practicable nor desirable." And if the North tried to interfere in the new nation's affairs, "a terrible responsibility would rest upon it, and the suffering of millions will bear testimony to the folly and wickedness of our aggressors."

He was a prophet.

The Least You Need to Know

♦ Secessionists in South Carolina and the Deep South states quickly organized secession conventions after Lincoln's election.

♦ Committees in both the House and Senate tried to avert secession, but their compromise measures failed.

♦ The Montgomery convention in February 1861 quickly organized a new government of the seceded states but bypassed the fire-eaters for the executive posts.

♦ Jefferson Davis of Mississippi, a respected and fairly moderate statesman, was sworn in as the first Confederate president amid much rejoicing (and a few doubts).

Chapter **7**

The House That Jeff Built

In This Chapter

- ◆ Imitating (mostly) the old Constitution
- ◆ Stars and Bars, and other symbolic things
- ◆ Whistling "Dixie"
- ◆ Queen Varina of Montgomery

If seven is a lucky number, things looked good for Jefferson Davis. The new nation, which was formed in Montgomery, Alabama, had seven states. It wanted more, and Confederates were still anxious for the other slave states to join up. In the meantime, the seven that had already left the Union had to give some thought to some political matters—a constitution, a flag, advisers to the president, and so on. This would show the world they meant business about making a new nation.

The model for the new government was … the old government of the United States. If you want to truly understand the Confederacy, pay attention to the ways the Southerners imitated—and sometimes discarded—the patterns of the U.S. government. Also pay attention to how many high-ranking U.S. officials quickly turned into high-ranking Confederate officials.

Montgomery Law Men

Things were moving fast down South. The seven seceded states had a president and vice president, and a *provisional* constitution. With the attitude of "so long as we're here …," the Montgomery Convention proceeded to revise the provisional constitution into the permanent constitution. The work was done by March 11, just seven days after Lincoln took office.

RebeLingo

The word **provisional** was attached to darn near everything in the Confederacy's earliest days. It meant "for the time being." So there was a Provisional Constitution, Provisional Congress, and so on.

The U.S. Constitution made its way—often word for word—into the Confederate Constitution. A few differences are worth noting. For one, the U.S. Constitution never mentions God. The Confederate one refers in its preamble to "Almighty God." (Meaning what? That Southerners were more spiritual than Northerners? Or did they want to make it appear that God had blessed secession? Maybe both.)

Another difference: President and vice president were limited to only one term—but of *six* years, not four. The president had something that U.S. presidents always wanted but got only in the 1990s: the line-item veto—that is, power to veto separate items in any spending bill that Congress passed.

U.S. cabinet members have never had seats in Congress. Under the Confederate Constitution, they did. More specifically, they could be present in Congress when it discussed matters that concerned their departments. They could not vote, however. (More about Davis's cabinet in Chapter 17.) One item worth noting here: Bob Toombs, who had been on the short list for president, was given a consolation prize by Davis—the post of secretary of state.

Speaking of Congress, it could not make appropriations without a two-thirds majority. It could not impose a protective tariff. It could not provide money for internal improvements. In short, the Confederate Congress could not do the things Southerners had hated about the U.S. Congress.

Did Y'all Know?

The Confederate Constitution stated that all laws of the United States still applied unless they specifically conflicted with the new laws.

And now the dreaded *S* words: *slave* and *slavery*. You might remember from Chapter 2 that our Founding Fathers (many of them slaveholders) chose not to use those awkward words in the Constitution. The Montgomery Convention was not so coy.

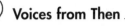 **Voices from Then** _____

We, the people of the Confederate States, each State acting in its sovereign and independent character, in order to form a permanent government, establish justice, insure domestic tranquility, and secure the blessings of liberty to ourselves and our posterity—invoking the favor and guidance of Almighty God—do ordain and establish this Constitution for the Confederate States of America.

—Preamble to the Confederate Constitution

Notice in the Preamble (quoted in the preceding sidebar) the mention of "each State acting in its sovereign and independent character." Obviously a Southern nation was going to have to show some reverence for states' rights. Hold that thought in your mind, because you will see shortly how states' rights and the needs of a new national government were in almost constant conflict.

Aside from these key differences, the Montgomery guys proudly adopted the U.S. Constitution, including its Bill of Rights. Former U.S. Senator Benjamin H. Hill of Georgia claimed that "we hugged that Constitution to our bosoms and carried it with us."

As with the U.S. Constitution, the states had to ratify it. This was done by either the state's secession convention (some were still sitting) or the state legislature. As with secession, there was no referendum.

You're a Grand New Flag

They had a president, a vice president, and a Constitution—and all before the inauguration of the hated Lincoln. Someone asked the obvious question: Shouldn't a new nation have a flag? Even before Davis was made president, the Montgomery Convention was taking suggestions for a new flag. Some of the designs were pretty bizarre. Most were some variation on the familiar old Stars and Stripes of the United States. While a few fire-eaters said they detested the American flag ("symbol of a hostile government"), most Southerners wanted something that reminded them of their old national flag. Obviously, the only colors to use were red, white, and blue.

Did the South have its own Betsy Ross? Sort of. Nichola Marschall, an Austrian, was an art teacher living in Alabama. The stories about him differ, but it is generally agreed he came up with the design for the first Confederate flag, the "Stars and Bars." Instead of 13 red and white narrow stripes, it had three broad ones (red, white, and red, that is). The canton (the upper left portion of the flag) was blue like the U.S. flag. It had, of course, seven stars—one for each (so far) Confederate state.

The Stars and Bars, the Confederacy's first national flag, adopted on March 4, 1861. Designed by Nichola Marschall, its seven stars represented the seven states that had seceded at that time.

The first Confederate flag was raised over the capitol dome in Montgomery on March 4—the day Lincoln was inaugurated in Washington. It was hoisted by the granddaughter of John Tyler, who was the only former president living in the Confederacy. A seven-gun salute was fired, and bands played. (It was a big day. You know you are a *real* nation when you have your own flag.)

The Confederacy never had an official national anthem, but certainly "Dixie" was widely loved. You may already know that its author was Ohio-born Dan Emmett, who wrote the song in 1859 in New York City, for use by his minstrel troupe. Minstrel shows, popular all over the nation in those days, featured white men in "blackface" and outlandish costumes, playing the roles of jolly, wise-cracking plantation slaves. "I Wish I Was in Dixie's Land" (Emmett's original title for the song) caught on, and before long people North and South were whistling the tune. It was played (though not sung) at Davis's inauguration, and after the war began, some eloquent Southerners penned some new (and patriotic) verses for the song. (Northerners countered with their various anti-Confederate versions of "Union Dixie.")

Sealing the Deal

A nation also needs an official seal.

The provisional government in Montgomery came up with one in a hurry. It was stark and simple: a scroll with the word "Constitution" above it and "Liberty" below it. This was only "provisional," and, as with the flag, the new government was glutted with suggestions about a permanent seal for the nation. One suggestion from the Deep South was the live oak tree—a nice symbol, since the tree is not only sturdy but evergreen to boot. The eagle was out, since that was too much associated with the United States.

It wasn't until 1863 that the Confederacy finally approved a permanent design for the seal. What the Congress approved was something they saw every day outside the Capitol (the Richmond Capitol, not the Montgomery Capitol—we'll take about that move in a moment). The familiar sight was an enormous statue of the great George Washington on horseback. The image of Washington was flanked by a wreath of the South's various crops—cotton (of course!), tobacco, sugar cane, corn, rice, and wheat.

And with every seal goes a national motto. In this case, the motto was the Latin words *Deo Vindice*—"God vindicates." (Loosely translated, "God approves what we've done" or "God will approve" or "God makes it right.")

C.S.A. and Other Options

It bears repeating: The seceded states thought of themselves as true Americans. Most didn't wish to throw away the beloved name "America." Since "United" was already spoken for, the Constitution-makers in Montgomery substituted "Confederate," and so we have C.S.A. standing for Confederate States of America. (If you see C.S.A. in military use, it also meant Confederate States Army.)

Still, before Confederate States of America got set in stone, all kinds of options were floated around. Thomas R. R. Cobb suggested the Republic of Washington. (Again, that Southern affection for the Founding Fathers.) At least one person suggested Southern United States of America. And how about these: Alleghania, Appalachia, Chicora, and Panola. And what about Southland?

States' rights had been a driving force behind secession. So some Southerners objected to calling it "Confederate States." Why not "League of Nations"? Or how about "Allied Republics" or "Allied Nations"? (Remember that in the days between secession and the Confederacy, the seceded states referred to themselves as independent republics.)

Still, when the dust finally settled, the name was Confederate States of America—or, for short, the Confederacy.

> **Voices from Then**
>
> A few sneering Northerners suggested the obvious name for the new country was Secessia. Southerners never objected to being called secessionists, and they wore the name with pride. Being a mouthful, "secessionist" was often cut down to simply "secesh" (as in, "Oh, that cousin of mine is a secesh").

A typical poem from the Confederacy's early days:

> Yes, call them rebels! 'Tis the name
> Their patriot fathers bore,
> And by such deeds they'll hallow it,
> As they have done before!

Here's another:

> Washington a rebel was,
> Jefferson a traitor—
> But their treason won success
> And made their glory greater.

How 'Bout Them Rebs?

Even before war broke out, the word *Rebel* was being used to refer to people in the seceded states. Did Southerners mind? No way! Hadn't George Washington been a rebel against tyrannical Britain? And also Thomas Jefferson, James Madison, and the other founders?

Southerners harked back to earlier rebels. How about religious leader Martin Luther in the 1500s? Most Americans (the Protestants, anyway) admired Luther, and there were plenty of Christians in North and South who named their sons after Martin Luther and John Calvin, both rebels against the Catholic Church in the 1500s.

Happy at Home

The Confederacy had only one First Lady. She wasn't perfect, but she was, like her husband, a "class act." If Confederates could have chosen their own queen, Varina Davis wouldn't have been a bad choice.

Varina Howell of Natchez, Mississippi, was 17 when she first met 35-year-old Jefferson Davis in 1843. She was a tall, statuesque brunette, not beautiful, but serene-looking, with striking eyes. She was dark in complexion, which in those days of idealized ivory-skinned gentlewomen was a minus, not a plus. Varina was devout, but also witty and well educated, tutored in the Greek and Latin classics. Davis was a wealthy widower, his first wife being the daughter of Zachary Taylor. (This was Sarah Knox Taylor, Davis's beloved "Knoxie.")

Varina (pronounced *"var-EE-nuh"* by her family, though almost everyone else says *"var-EYE-nuh"*) found Davis a bit arrogant and chilly, but also handsome and polished. She also thought (as did many people) that he had the loveliest voice she had ever heard. Davis was a man who appreciated an intelligent woman who enjoyed discussing politics, even though he and Varina were of different parties (she was a Whig, he was a Democrat). Her home was known as the Briers, his was a plantation known as Brierfield.

Did Y'all Know?

Like many Southern belles of that era, Varina had been sent to a finishing school in the North. Her family was originally from New Jersey.

The woman he called "sweet Winnie" made the adjustment to her Democratic husband and, when he went to Congress, became a model political wife, a gracious hostess, and a vivacious talker of politics. Considering she was only 19 when he became a congressman, she was a remarkable woman and a fast learner. In her days as a Washington political wife, Varina met the great John C. Calhoun. He said she was one of the most charming women he'd ever met.

Varina opposed secession and believed (correctly) that a separate Southern nation could never survive on its own. Even so, the Confederacy did form, and Varina wrote that "we felt blood in the air." Varina became the Confederacy's only First Lady, and in the (second) capital, Richmond, she spent what she later called the worst years of her life. But she was loving and supportive to the man she called by the nickname "Banny."

One reason we know a great deal about the First Lady is that one of her bosom friends was Mary Chesnut, keeper of the most famous Civil War diary. Both women had been "Washington wives," and both were (briefly) "Montgomery wives" and then "Richmond wives." We know from the Chesnut diary that the life of Jefferson and Varina Davis was never boring.

The Least You Need to Know

- The new government formed in Montgomery quickly wrote a constitution, based very closely on that of the United States (but different in some key areas, too).

- The Confederacy adopted its own flag, the Stars and Bars, first flown on the day the Union inaugurated Abraham Lincoln.

- Southerners *and* Northerners whistled "Dixie," although each side had its preferred lyrics for the song.

- The Confederacy's First Lady was the intelligent and politically astute Varina Davis.

Chapter 8

If at First You Don't Secede ...

In This Chapter

- ◆ That little Fort Sumter problem
- ◆ The new Creole hero
- ◆ The Upper South in anti-Lincoln mode
- ◆ Neutrality with a lot of blood

You already know about Phase I of secession. Seven slaveholding Southern states had thumbed their noses at the United States and gone their own way. Their timing was impeccable, because they had seceded and set up their new government before the man they feared and hated (Abe Lincoln) took office. You might say Lincoln's election and inauguration were the start and stop dates for Confederacy-making.

But the Confederacy, although pleased with itself, wanted the other slave states to join it. Several were hesitating. Jefferson Davis and Abraham Lincoln both wanted to nudge them (or shove them) off the fence. What started things moving (and, incidentally, started the Civil War) was a nagging question: What will the Confederate states do with federal property on their turf? This would lead to Phase II of secession.

Go Forth for the Forts

Every U.S. state today has acreage belonging to the federal government. (In the spacious case of Alaska, more than half the land is Fed-owned.) In 1861, this was less true. The most obvious (and potentially dangerous) pieces of federal property were military bases—or "forts," as they were called at the time.

Did Y'all Know? _____

Louisiana didn't stop with seizing federal forts. It also seized the U.S. mint in New Orleans. This proved to be a useful asset.

Go See It!

Fort Sumter National Monument is a definite must-see for anyone interested in American history. Since it sits on a small sandy island off Charleston, South Carolina, you have to get there by boat—either from the Patriot's Point park or from Fort Moultrie.

It made no sense for a new nation (or independent states) to have Federal soldiers stationed on their soil. So just after secession (and even before, in a few cases), the seceding states proceeded to take over the Federal forts. Most of these forts weren't of crucial importance, and they were taken with no bloodshed. The only holdouts were Florida's Fort Pickens and that sandy little island outside Charleston that is still being talked about. We're speaking of Fort Sumter, of course.

Everyone seems to know that the whole thing began with the firing on Fort Sumter. What everyone forgets is that the uncompleted pile of rock wasn't all that important in itself. But it happened to be a piece of federal property that lay offshore from Secession City itself, Charleston, South Carolina. The secessionist hotheads couldn't tolerate a Union military post staring at them from the Charleston bay, so poor Maj. Robert Anderson, the Union commander of the fort, had the fortune—or misfortune—to be the North's man of the hour, the first Yankee hero of the war. Why exactly the North treated him as a hero when he surrendered the fort is one of those peculiar puzzles of fame, timing, and the public's odd need to idolize someone.

Anderson was Kentucky-born, a former slave owner, a man who had no real beef against slavery or secession. In one of the war's delightful ironies, the Southern boy happened to be commanding the Union fort that the newly formed Confederacy insisted on having.

Anderson and his men had first been stationed at the mainland Fort Moultrie. But in December 1860, South Carolina seceded, and the locals were making Anderson and his Feds feel very uneasy at Fort Moultrie. So one night Anderson's men quietly moved to Fort Sumter on its man-made island—safer, but sitting on a powder keg.

As of March 4, 1861, President Buchanan was gone (much to his own relief) and the Black Republican, Lincoln, was in office. The Confederate Congress had already resolved that "immediate steps should be taken to obtain possession of Forts Sumter and Pickens ... either by negotiation or by force." Jefferson Davis proved he was keeping both options open: He sent three Confederate commissioners to Washington (negotiation), but also sent P. G. T. Beauregard to Charleston to take charge of the military there (force).

Introducing the Grand Creole

Who was this Beauregard fellow? General Pierre Gustave Toutant Beauregard was a short man, 5-foot-7, with an oversized ego. He was of old *Creole* stock, born on a sugar planta- tion south of New Orleans. He spoke French before he learned English (which he probably did not speak before age 12). He was a wor- shipper of Napoleon and disciple of military theorist Henri de Jomini.

Beauregard was second in his West Point class of 1838. During the Mexican War (prep school for the future Civil War officers), he served as an engineer under Gen. Winfield Scott, whom he impressed by his service in the war. General Scott referred to him as a "bulldog with his ears pinned back." Beauregard saw him- self as life's only child, and his vanity was breathtaking. He believed he was America's Napoleon, and everyone else was his inferior.

RebeLingo

Creole refers to a per- son descended from the early French settlers of the Gulf states (Louisiana in particular). The Louisiana Creoles had, and still have, a distinctive culture. General Beauregard was proud of his Creole ancestry (and proud of being *French*, of course), and he was certainly the most famous Creole in the Confederacy (and perhaps the vainest as well).

After Mexico, he pulled some family strings (his wife's sister's husband was Sen. John Slidell) and was appointed to head West Point—but served only five days when it was learned he was pro-secession. When Louisiana seceded, he scurried home, expecting a commission as commander of the state's military. Slidell recommended Beauregard to Confederate President Davis, who made him a brigadier general and placed him in a fateful position: Charleston. (Beauregard was reputed to be an expert gunner. The world would soon find out.)

Lincoln would not meet with the three Rebel commissioners that Davis sent to nego- tiate, and neither would his secretary of state, William Seward. But Seward did use two federal judges as go-betweens in communicating with the Confederates. Seward promised to do nothing to change the situation at Sumter. One of the Reb commis- sioners called this "masterly inactivity."

In Montgomery, Alabama, Jefferson Davis and his cabinet debated the Sumter issue nervously. The boozy but sometimes sensible secretary of state, Robert Toombs, paced the room and predicted—correctly—that "the firing upon that fort will inaugurate a civil war ... it is suicide, murder, and will lose us every friend in the North .... It is unnecessary, it puts us in the wrong, it is fatal." All true—but the cabinet voted to take the fort anyway. A message was sent to feisty General Beauregard in Charleston: Demand surrender of the fort; if refused, "reduce it."

Reducing Sumter

On April 11, 1861, Beauregard sent his aides to Anderson—the former West Point artillery instructor who had been Beauregard's favorite teacher there. The aides demanded surrender; Anderson refused. He also made a practical observation: Their food was running out. His men, Anderson said, would be "starved out in a few days." This news went, via Beauregard, to the cabinet, which then ordered Beauregard to avoid bloodshed if possible. But negotiations between Anderson and the Rebs broke down, partly because Anderson said he would willingly evacuate in three days—*unless he received additional supplies*. The cabinet plainly told Beauregard he must not allow Anderson to receive provisions. So Anderson was informed at 3:30 on the morning of April 12, 1861, that firing would commence in one hour. The deeply spiritual man said to the Confederate agents, "If we never meet in this world again, God grant that we may meet in the next."

" " Voices from Then

Twenty years after Fort Sumter, Jefferson Davis defended his actions and denied that the Confederacy had drawn first blood: "He who makes the assault is not necessarily he who strikes the first blow or fires the first gun."

The firing commenced and continued for 34 hours. There is some debate over just who fired the first shot. Credit is often given to gray-haired Virginia secessionist Edmund Ruffin. He was definitely on the scene, joining the much younger men of the Palmetto Guards, who had been selected to fire the first shots at Sumter. The Guards, so we are told, gave old Ruffin the honor. The shell he fired struck Sumter, and the Civil War began. (Tradition has it that the Union's first return shot was fired by Anderson's second in command, Abner Doubleday, who is credited—incorrectly—with inventing baseball.)

Cannon balls battered the fort's brick walls, and "hot shot" set fire to the wooden buildings inside. Anderson's men were suffering from smoke inhalation. Fires blazed out of control inside the fort, and around 1:00 on the afternoon of April 13, Anderson surrendered, minutes after the Union flag was shot down.

In April 1861, Beauregard the fame-seeker found what he wanted: In directing the Confederate bombardment of Fort Sumter, he touched off the Civil War and made himself the first hero of the Confederacy. Southern newspapers couldn't say enough good things about "Old Bory."

Did Y'all Know?

Not a soul was killed during the bombardment of Sumter. The 84 soldiers and 43 workers at the fort all survived. Two men were killed because of an ammunition dump explosion at the surrender ceremony, however.

"Join Up, You Hesitaters!"

Like secession, the bombing of Fort Sumter was a relief. Something had been done (whew!). What the Confederacy hoped, of course, was that the event would nudge (or shove) the remaining slave states toward secession. That didn't happen—not exactly. What really affected the slave states still in the Union was Abraham Lincoln's fateful act on April 15, two days after Sumter surrendered.

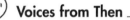

Voices from Then

The Star-Spangled Banner has been shot down by Southern troops.
—Lincoln, after the firing on Sumter

Lincoln called for 75,000 troops. Specifically, he called for 90-day volunteers to suppress "a combination too powerful to be suppressed by the ordinary course of traditional proceedings." This was not, technically, a declaration of war. He stated the troops might be needed for repossessing "the forts, places, and property" which had been seized by the Confederacy. But practically everyone saw that it was a declaration of war. To be specific, Lincoln was asking Americans to make war on other Americans. Plenty of Northerners were willing. But residents of the slave states still in the Union were not.

For a lot of reasons—fewer slaves than the Deep South, closer economic ties to the North, and so on—the states of the Upper South had remained loyal to the Union. And why not? This new thing, this Confederate States of America, might fizzle out quickly. Or its leaders might fall out among themselves (as had happened in so many South American countries). Or Lincoln might not turn out to be such a bad president ....

Oops. Scratch that last item from the list. Lincoln *was* bad. He was asking for Southerners to fight Southerners. The Confederates had been right after all. It was time to un-Union.

Did Y'all Know? _____

The Order of Secession

- ◆ South Carolina—December 20, 1860
- ◆ Mississippi—January 9, 1861
- ◆ Florida—January 10, 1861
- ◆ Alabama—January 11, 1861
- ◆ Georgia—January 19, 1861
- ◆ Louisiana—January 26, 1861
- ◆ Texas—February 1, 1861
- ◆ Virginia—April 17, 1861
- ◆ Arkansas—May 6, 1861
- ◆ Tennessee—May 6, 1861
- ◆ North Carolina—May 20, 1861

Not one governor of a slave state responded affirmatively to Lincoln's call for troops after Fort Sumter.

The Old Dominion Strikes Back

Ah, sweet Virginia, the Mother of Presidents. Where the Confederacy was concerned, no greater addition could have been made to the new nation than the Old Dominion. It would bring with it all the patriotic associations of Washington, Jefferson, Madison, and the other founders.

The governor of Virginia in April 1861 was John Letcher, who was pro-slavery but also pro-Union. Letcher was aware that some in his state were itching for secession even before the Fort Sumter incident. Some staged a celebration at Richmond's Tredegar Iron Works, which had produced the cannons that fired on Sumter. Some secessionists even hoisted the Stars and Bars—the Confederate flag—over the capitol dome.

Voices from Then

The time for war has not yet come, but it will come, and that soon. And when it does come, my advice is to draw the sword and throw away the scabbard.

—Maj. Thomas J. Jackson, professor at Virginia Military Institute (later better known as "Stonewall")

It wasn't this post-Sumter party that changed Letcher's position on secession. It was Lincoln's call for troops. Suddenly Governor Unionist changed to Governor Secessionist. Letcher publicly proclaimed that Lincoln had "chosen to inaugurate civil war." But, the governor said, Lincoln would get no troops from Virginia.

On April 17, Virginia's secession convention, which had been hesitating, acted. The Old Dominion was out of the Union. Letcher naturally took the steps of seizing the Federal arsenal at Harper's Ferry and the navy yard at Norfolk.

Not all Virginians were pleased by this move. Residents in the state's mountainous western counties had an old beef against Richmond and the rich planters in the eastern part of the state. The mountains had few slaves or slaveholders, but plenty of Unionists. So strong was sentiment against secession that Unionist delegates convened at Wheeling in June 1861, nullified Virginia's secession ordinance, and elected a pro-Union governor. Virginia had seceded from the Union—so why couldn't the western counties secede from the state? In 1863, the "loyal" counties entered the Union as the new state of West Virginia. Ironically, one of the Confederacy's best-known generals, Thomas "Stonewall" Jackson, was born in the area.

The Other Hesitaters Follow

Arkansas, sparsely settled, had hesitated even more about secession than Virginia had. The state's secession convention had already voted no. But once Lincoln had issued his call for troops, things changed. Governor Henry Rector issued a quotable reply to Lincoln: "The people of this Commonwealth are freemen, not slaves, and will defend to the last extremity their honor, lives, and property against Northern mendacity and usurpation." On May 6, the state's secession convention changed their vote to yes.

In North Carolina, Lincoln's call for troops had gotten the citizens worked up, too. Governor John Ellis proclaimed his state would "be no party to this wicked violation of the laws of the country, and to this war upon the liberties of a free people." Ellis seized the federal forts in the state and, even further, called for 30,000 volunteers. Things moved fast in the Tarheel State. On May 1, the state legislature called for a secession convention. It was elected on May 13, and it voted for secession on May 20.

Perched on the northern borders of Georgia, Alabama, and Mississippi was Tennessee. Tennessee had few slaves in its mountainous east, more in the middle, and lots of them in the western flatlands. Sentiment for the Confederacy varied, naturally, according to how many slaveholders were present. Eastern Tennessee, like western Virginia, was never strong for the Confederacy.

After Lincoln's call for troops, secessionist Governor Isham Harris sprang into action. He announced to Lincoln (and the world) that Tennessee would "furnish not a single man for purposes of coercion, but 50,000, if necessary, for the defense of our rights and those of our Southern brothers." On May 6, the legislature declared the state to be independent of the Union, and on May 7, it allied itself with the Confederacy. On June 8, the people of the state got to vote on it, and they approved it by a large majority.

Did Y'all Know? _____

One Tennessean who very publicly opposed secession was a future U.S. president: Andrew Johnson. A resident of east Tennessee, Johnson was typical of the people in that region, middle-class farmers and laborers who owned no slaves and who resented the rich slaveholding planters of middle and west Tennessee. He stood out as the only Southern senator who didn't leave the Senate after his state seceded.

Tennessee faced a situation similar to Virginia's: Residents of its mountain counties were pro-Union and had no desire to be part of the Confederacy. There was talk of seceding from Tennessee and forming a new "State of Franklin." This never materialized, and in fact the eastern part of Tennessee stayed in Confederate hands longer than middle and west Tennessee did. Curiously, when the Civil War ended, the president of the United States was an east Tennessee Unionist—Andrew Johnson.

The Confederacy.

CONFEDERATE STATES of AMERICA

Straddling a Painful Fence

Did Lincoln know his call for troops would have the effect of creating four new Confederate states? Did he have any idea that the four remaining slave states would *not* join the Confederacy?

We give the name "Border States" to the four slave states that didn't leave the Union. In 1861, of course, no one was sure whether those states would stay in or leave.

Tiny Delaware was a slave state, but its population was small, and slaves were only about 2 percent of the total. Some of the state's slaveholders were rattled by Lincoln's call for troops, but the state as a whole yawned through the whole thing. No secession convention was called, and the legislature never really debated the possibility of joining the Confederacy.

Location was a crucial factor for Delaware. It shared a border with Pennsylvania and an even longer border with Maryland. Pennsylvania was a free state (and full of anti-slavery Quakers to boot). Even had Delaware wanted to secede, it could never have done so if Maryland stayed in the Union.

Maryland was, and considered itself to be, a Southern state. Maryland probably would have thrown in its lot with the Confederacy except for one crucial geographical fact: The U.S. capital was surrounded by Maryland and Virginia. The federal government hadn't stopped Virginia from seceding, but it sure wasn't going to let Maryland do the same.

Maryland's governor at the time was Thomas Hicks, who was irked by Lincoln's call for troops but not irked enough to secede. Hicks hoped to keep the state neutral. Lincoln's main concern was to keep Maryland from seceding. He had enough troubles without sitting in a capital city surrounded by Confederate states.

Maryland didn't stay neutral for long, however. Just a few days after Fort Sumter, troops from Massachusetts passed through Baltimore on the way to D.C. Baltimore was notoriously pro-Southern; ditto for its main newspaper, the *Sun*. The troops quickly learned they weren't welcome guests in Baltimore. At 10:30 on the morning of April 19, the 6th Massachusetts Infantry arrived at a Baltimore train station from Philadelphia. They were scheduled to march from there to another station and travel on to Washington. A crowd of locals (estimated at maybe 10,000) gathered, first shouting, then throwing stones and bricks. The soldiers fired into the mob. By 12:45 most of the regiment had left on a train. But 4 of the soldiers had been killed, 39 wounded. The mayor of Baltimore claimed that 12 civilians were killed and dozens more wounded.

More violence followed. The locals were determined not to let any more Union troops pass through. The night following the riot, police and militiamen burned railroad bridges on the city's north side. The governor and mayor both sent the same request to Lincoln: No more Union troops passing through Baltimore, please. The following day, Lincoln wisely suspended troop movements through Baltimore.

Here was an interesting situation: A state that had not seceded nor joined the Confederacy was demonstrating, at the grassroots level, some serious hatred for Lincoln and his government. Seeing the Union had no friends in Baltimore, Lincoln

RebeLingo

Habeas corpus—refers to the legal principle against holding a person prisoner without charging him or her with a specific crime. In the United States, this has always been considered a sacred right of citizens, but in times of emergency it may be suspended. Abraham Lincoln suspended it often; Jefferson Davis did sparingly.

Voices from Then

We may well rejoice that we have forever severed our connection with a government that thus tramples on all the principles of constitutional liberty.

—Jefferson Davis, on Lincoln's suspending habeas corpus

did the obvious thing. Within a month of the riot, Federal troops occupied Baltimore and treated it as enemy territory for the remainder of the war.

The Federals didn't stop with Baltimore; troops took up positions throughout the state. And Lincoln began something that horrified people in both North and South: He suspended the writ of *habeas corpus* and swiftly arrested Southern sympathizers throughout Maryland. This included 19 members of the Maryland legislature. Baltimore's mayor was thrown into jail. Hundreds of Maryland citizens found themselves under lock and key.

For the South, it was a heaven-sent piece of propaganda. As Southerners had been saying for 30 years, the federal government was tyrannical, with no real respect for human rights. Just as the seceded states had suspected, the Black Republican president was proving to be a tyrant with no respect for civil liberties. James Ryder Randall, a Marylander living in Louisiana, penned a patriotic poem, "My Maryland." Someone fit it to the old German tune "O Tannenbaum" ("O Christmas Tree"), and the result was the song "Maryland, My Maryland." It is still Maryland's state song, and it was often sung by Confederates during the Civil War, having some powerfully anti-tyrant (meaning "anti-Lincoln") words.

Plenty of Marylanders must have shared Ryder's sentiments, for 20,000 Maryland men fought for the Confederacy.

Bluegrass Neutrals

Like the governors of Virginia, Tennessee, North Carolina, and Arkansas, Governor Beriah Magoffin of Kentucky issued a combative reply to Lincoln's call for troops: "I say, emphatically, Kentucky will furnish no troops for the wicked purpose of subduing her sister Southern states." That sounds pro-Confederate, and Magoffin was. Acting cautiously, on May 20, 1861, the governor officially proclaimed his state neutral—meaning that neither Confederate nor Union troops would enter the state.

It was one thing for Kentucky to say it was neutral. It was another thing to keep army recruiters from both sides out of the state. Both Davis and Lincoln badly wanted the state on their side. Davis was willing to observe Kentucky's neutral status—but he also approved setting up recruiting stations smack on the state's southern border.

Technically, Confederate troops entered the state first, giving Kentucky Unionists an excuse to call in Federal troops. They came in droves and occupied half the state. In November, a convention of 200 pro-secessionist delegates met in Russellville. They declared the state to be independent (due to "natural right resting upon the law of God"), then passed a secession ordinance. The convention set up its own government, with a governor and council. It was a kind of "government-on-standby," since it could not do much as long as all the Union troops were around. What it did do, however, was join (on paper) the Confederacy. On December 10, 1861, Kentucky became (technically) the twelfth Confederate state. That is definitely not the end of the story, however. The war was not going to be very kind to Kentucky.

Lucky Number 13?

An interesting possibility was in the air: There were 12 Confederate states. Imagine if there were 13—the same number as the original United States? The Confederates had always positioned themselves as the true heirs of the American Revolution. Wouldn't it be wonderful to have, as the Republic had at the beginning, 13 states?

Could Missouri be lucky number 13? Its governor, Claiborne Jackson, was a secessionist. In the 1860 election, Missouri gave few votes to Lincoln. As early as January 1861, Jackson and the state legislature called for a convention to discuss secession. To Jackson's surprise and regret, the convention didn't pass a secession ordinance, and in March it adjourned.

But then there followed Fort Sumter and Lincoln's call for troops. Like several other governors already mentioned, Jackson got very eloquent when responding to Lincoln: "Your requisition is illegal, unconstitutional, revolutionary, inhuman, diabolical, and cannot be complied with." In short: No dice, Abe.

It happened that in May 1861 Jackson assembled the state militia on the outskirts of St. Louis. The abolitionist, pro-Union Nathaniel Lyon, head of the Federal arsenal, scoped out the militia. (He was disguised in women's clothing at the time—meaning he had to hide his flaming red beard under a shawl and bonnet. He must have been a sight.) Using 7,000 Federal soldiers, he captured the 700

Did Y'all Know?

Missouri could have been easily moved to join the Confederacy had it not been for a large immigrant population (mostly Germans) in the St. Louis area. German immigrants tended to be strongly pro-Union and anti-slavery.

militiamen. This did not go unnoticed. Locals started a riot in St. Louis, and Lyon's troops killed 15 civilians.

We will say more later about the nastiness that followed in Missouri. For now, it is worth noting that Governor Jackson and his supporters fled the state capital (Jefferson City) and in the town of Neosho set themselves up as the "real" Missouri legislature. They voted to secede from the Union and join the Confederacy. So here was that thirteenth state and the thirteenth star in the Confederate battle flag. Jackson's "government in exile" never had any real power. The Federals had their hands full during the war, maintaining order in a state with plenty of violent extremists on both sides of the slavery issue. Even more than Kentucky, Missouri was the scene of its own hellacious civil war.

Worth remembering: Although Kentucky and Missouri were "disputed" states during the war, the Federal government never recognized them as having seceded. The states would benefit from this when the war ended, for, unlike the 11 states that were indisputably part of the Confederacy, Kentucky and Missouri did not have to undergo the horrors of Reconstruction.

The Least You Need to Know

- After much hesitating and dallying, Confederate forces under General Beauregard fired on Fort Sumter on April 12, 1861, which is considered the start of the Civil War.

- After the Sumter incident, Abraham Lincoln called for all Union states to supply troops to put down the rebellion.

- Lincoln's call for troops horrified the slave states that were still in the Union, and four of them joined the Confederacy.

- Unionists in western Virginia opposed secession and broke away to form their own state.

- After Lincoln's call for troops, violence erupted in the divided states of Maryland, Kentucky, and Missouri.

What the South Had (and Hadn't)

In This Chapter

- ◆ A general lack (of things in general)
- ◆ Lack of arms (and the arms that hold them)
- ◆ The white gold illusion
- ◆ The "American Rome" and the founders

A new beginning is exciting—and frightening, too. The 11 states that took themselves out of the Union in early 1861 witnessed parades, peppy speeches, fireworks, the whole nine yards. The fire-eaters were overjoyed: The new Southern nation they had wanted for years had come into being. But once the parades were over, reality had to set in. The new nation existed, but could it endure? The Confederacy had a lot going for it. It was certainly not what we would today call a Third World country, mired in poverty. In spite of all the Northern sneers concerning Southern barbarity, many people found the South to be a pretty civilized and appealing place to live. But you can't start a new nation—and also fight a war—without looking at the negatives as well as the positives.

More Demands Than Supplies

In a well-received speech in the Confederacy's early days, Vice President Stephens pointed out that the new Confederacy was by no means a small or weak nation. He pointed out that it was much larger than either France or Austria, and also much larger than the original 13 states of the United States. The speech was a "pep talk" to the new nation, reminding them they had great resources and a bright future ahead—and overlooking the *lack* of many resources.

Southerners had been boasting that the South would do just fine on its own, thank you. Northerners were quite sure they would get along fine without the South—not that the South would ever be stupid enough to *really* secede, mind you.

Who had the most right to be arrogant? Putting it in purely material terms, the North did. It had, frankly, more of everything—except slaves and cotton.

Some Comparisons, April 1861

Asset	Confederacy	Union
White population	5.4 million	21.2 million
Real and personal wealth	$6.7 million	$12.2 million
Railroad miles	9,000	22,000
Banks	221	1,400

And Some Ratios of Assets, North:South

Factory production	10:1
Firearms production	32:1
Textile production	14:1
Coal	38:1
Corn	2:1
Wheat	412:1
Cotton	1:24
Farm acreage	3:1

The one crucial area where the South led the North was cotton, and we've already talked about the King Cotton mentality. The South was proud of its most famous crop. It depended on it—overly so, as we shall see.

The North often sneered at the South as an agrarian backwater. We've already seen that *agrarian* could be a term of pride. Hadn't the wise plantation master (and slaveholder) Thomas Jefferson claimed that farmers were the "chosen people" of the earth? The North was (so the South liked to claim) a mob of grimy factory workers, while Southerners were hardy men of the soil.

Did Y'all Know?

At the beginning of the Civil War, the value of goods manufactured in New York state alone was four times that of goods manufactured in the Confederacy.

Northerners saw their factories as symbols of progress. One reason they looked down on the South was that Southerners didn't share this obsession with progress and industry. Most Southerners *liked* the Southern lifestyle, and Northerners interpreted that as just another sign of Southern backwardness. They never could grasp Southerners' love of land, nor understand that Southerners detested factory work because it involved being cooped up inside all the time, working according to a clock instead of by the sun and seasons ("clock time" versus "God time"). But now there was a problem: The agrarian South was at war, and a nation at war *needed factories*.

Jeff the Realist

The Confederate president had a long career in Washington, and he had traveled in the North. He was no bumpkin, and he was painfully aware that the North was outrunning the South in certain areas. He had no desire to give up slavery, but he did believe the South could learn a few things from the North. While in Congress, he had urged Southerners to diversify the economy. Agriculture was fine, but it would be even better if the South would use its homegrown cotton to make its own textiles. Certainly the South, with its long tradition of military honor, needed to manufacture its own weaponry—or at least begin stockpiling it in case (gulp) civil war ever came.

Did Y'all Know?

Davis was aware that the Confederacy possessed only $25 million in gold bullion—and no prospects of getting more. No wonder he and other Confederates focused so much on the "white gold," cotton.

Davis in his pre-Confederate days lamented that so few Southerners tried to set up factories. Why didn't they? Probably the fear that industrializing might mean the end of slavery. There was also a fear of too many immigrants. The North had been inundated with Irish after Ireland's potato famines in the 1840s. Most of the Irish were hardworking and respectable enough, but there were enough troublemakers and row-dies that Northern newspaper editors were always wailing about "the Irish troubles." The South could ask an obvious question: If this is what industrialization leads to, why do it?

You Can't Get There from Here

Davis became painfully aware of the South's transportation problems on his long and nondirect journey from his Mississippi plantation to Montgomery, Alabama. Recall that this 300-mile journey ("as the crow flies") involved 850 miles over Southern railroads. This didn't bode well for a Confederacy in which transporting troops and supplies would be a major concern.

The 9,000 miles of railway in the South hadn't been laid with a view toward civil war. The main purpose was transporting cotton from the fields to the coast, where it would be shipped on to Europe or the northern United States. Various small private companies had laid the tracks, and they hadn't bothered to coordinate their efforts. Why would they? They got the cotton to market, and that was their only goal.

> **Go See It!**
>
> You can see the types of trains used in Civil War days at several museums, including the Kennesaw Civil War Museum in Kennesaw, Georgia.

There was also the standardization problem: Railways were not all the same gauge (width, that is). No national or state agencies existed to enforce a particular standard, so the private companies did as they liked. A train coming into Richmond, Virginia, might be rolling on a track of one gauge. Stopping in Richmond, its freight would have to be unloaded and loaded onto another train, which would move on a track of another gauge to the final destination.

Had there been no war, the South might have done just fine with inadequate railroads. But, as every book on the Civil War will tell you, this was the first major war in which railroads played a key role. A major technological change had occurred in the world: A nation could transport troops and supplies over long distances, with no need for horses or rivers. Whoever could use that technology to their best advantage definitely had the upper hand. And we know which side that was.

Well, We Won't Starve, Anyway

You might already know enough Civil War history to know that the Confederacy experienced serious food shortages during the war. Considering how the South prided itself on its agriculture, isn't that kind of odd?

Farmers themselves knew the basics of getting food: plant seeds, keep the weeds and animals away, harvest it, and you have something to eat. We saw in an earlier chapter that larger plantations could be darn-near self-sufficient villages, growing every conceivable type of vegetable and fruit, plus cattle, hogs, and chickens. Even the "cotton barons" devoted some of their vast acreage to raising edible crops. Small farmers did the same. And even the preacher or teacher in a rural area would probably maintain a kitchen garden.

The South's long growing season meant Southerners could feast on practically every plant that grew in the North, plus such hot-weather items as okra and, in the farthest South, citrus fruits. It's no doubt true that both before and during the war a Yankee factory worker probably had blander fare than a Southern "po' white." So how could the South face a famine?

One major problem (as we shall see shortly) was that the invading Yankees were predators—stealing goods or, even worse, setting fire to crops in the fields and barns, and driving off (or killing) the livestock. Unfortunately, the Confederate soldiers might do the same—not out of spite, necessarily, but due to their own hunger.

And that brings us to the main problem: Food is no good if you can't transport it to those who need it. At the war's end, when Robert E. Lee's ragged soldiers were hearing their bellies rumbling, it did them no good at all that Texas was full of beef cattle, or that Georgia (even after Sherman's Yankee boys had marched through) had fruits and vegetables to spare.

Cannon Fodder

In 1860, the 11 states that would form the Confederacy had about 5.4 million white residents. The 19 Union states had about 21.2 million. During the war, immigration added another million to the North, with about 400,000 of those serving in the Union army. (Most of these were Irish, German, and Scandinavian.) The immigration number is important, because it meant that even as Yankee boys were dying on the battlefields, there was a seemingly endless supply of replacements. So not only did the North begin the war with a larger population, but its population was actually increasing while the South's was declining.

Looked at as a ratio, for white males aged 18 to 60, the North had a 4.4:1 advantage over the South. When you fight a war, you need young

Did Y'all Know?

In spite of having 13 stars in the Confederate battle flag, and in spite of Kentucky and Missouri sending men to Congress, most Confederates thought of their nation as having 11 states. Davis in his speeches referred to 11 states, never to 13.

men who will hurt people and break things. The Union had more—*lots* more—of those men.

Not all the men were soldiers, of course. That was another advantage the North had: While thousands of Yankee boys were on the march, plenty of others were left to run the farms, factories, banks, and schools. The South didn't have this luxury. If Johnny Reb was off marching and fighting, he wasn't at home farming.

How 'Bout Them Forts?

The South had long prided itself on being the land where every boy (and quite a few girls) learned how to shoot at an early age. But the Confederacy learned when the war began that not every Rebel volunteer had his own gun. (He might not be willing to bring it with him anyway, since he certainly wouldn't leave his family at home without protection of their own.) The various states owned guns—some of them usable, many of them not. Some were muskets dating from the colonial period. Some were shotguns. Whatever they were, it became apparent early in the war that the South (much to its own surprise) didn't have enough weapons. Even worse, it wasn't set up to manufacture them.

Summing up the weapons situation: At the beginning of the war, the Confederacy was lacking in both arms and arms manufacture. In 1860, only 3 percent of the firearms made in the United States were made in the South. Although the South started off with a major weapons handicap, this was one key area where Confederates used efficiency and business smarts to transform a lagging industry. (More about that in the next chapter.)

The White Gold Fantasy

Before the Civil War began, the South was the source of two thirds of the world's supply of cotton. So a lot of hope was fastened on that one magic word: *cotton*. King Cotton. White gold. Didn't the North need it? Didn't all those busy textile plants in England have to have it?

Voices from Then

They assume that the British crown rests on a cotton bale.

—A correspondent for the *London Times* in Charleston, 1861

The years 1859 and 1860 had seen bumper crops of the white fluffy stuff. A whopping 3.6 million bales were harvested in 1860—even more the previous year. And the mills abroad weren't slowing down any. They were calling for more all the time. You don't have to be an economics whiz to know that high demand is good news for the supplier.

The bad news: Cotton is a good "keeper." Unlike edible crops, it won't rot if it sits in a warehouse. And in 1861, that's what a lot of cotton was doing—sitting in European warehouses, until the mills would need it. Naturally, that supply wouldn't last forever, and Europe would be calling for more. But how soon? And what if they found Southern cotton so hard to procure in wartime that they bought it elsewhere? (One relief to the South was that the North couldn't grow its own cotton, nor could Europe buy it from the North.) Timing was everything. Hold out long enough against the Union, and the need for Southern cotton would be felt. But it was not felt in 1861, and no one could predict when the "cotton famine" would strike the North or Europe.

The Old Dominion Calls

For all its lack of resources (and people), the Confederacy had the Old Dominion—Virginia, that is. All those Virginia ties to the American Revolution made it inevitable that the government would move there. Anyway, politicians like to be comfortable. It is one of the perks of holding office. As you probably noticed, many of the first wave of Confederate brass had been Washington brass. Davis had been a senator; ditto for Toombs. Cobb had been secretary of the treasury, and on and on. The fact that they organized the Confederacy in charming (but small) Montgomery, Alabama, didn't mean they were committed to staying there. The little city on the Alabama River lacked the space and amenities for a national government.

In fact, the Constitution Committee gave the Confederate Congress the power to designate a capital district of not more than 10 square miles. Like the District of Columbia, it could be land donated by one or more states. As you might imagine, there was a kind of bidding war, with various locales hoping to become the site of the permanent Confederate capital. But the city that seemed the best was, of course, Richmond, Virginia.

A Wide River, Hills, and Charm

When the colonial Virginians chose the site of Richmond for their permanent capital, they probably couldn't have done better. Situated on the wide James River, the city (founded in 1737) is hilly, with its famous capitol situated nicely on one of the hilltops. Richmond (originally named Nonesuch) grew from a frontier tobacco market into a rather charming city, with about 40,000 residents in 1860, about one third of them black.

Go See It!

You *must* visit the Virginia Capitol in Richmond. Besides the famous old equestrian statue of Washington, there's an impressive statue of Stonewall Jackson, a bronze statue of Lee, and … well, visit the Capitol.

Its capitol building was impressive. In 1785, two Richmond officials asked Thomas Jefferson, America's minister (ambassador, that is) to France, to design a capitol that would "unite economy with elegance and utility." Jefferson, like the other founders, was fascinated by everything Roman, and he found his model for the Virginia Capitol in a Roman temple, the Maison Carrée in Nimes, France.

Richmond had the South's largest iron manufactory (the famous Tredegar Iron Works), the *world's* largest flour mill (Gallego), and good rail connections in all directions. True to its history, the city was also the world's largest tobacco market. And though it was almost 100 miles from salt water, its location on the James River made it Virginia's largest port.

Richmond was near the Confederacy's northern border—and since war was now inevitable, it made sense (to some people, not to everyone) to have the Confederacy's commander in chief near the military action.

With all the concern about the Founding Fathers and the "Second American Revolution," it was a good public relations move to have the capital in Richmond. This was the city where fiery orator Patrick Henry delivered his "Give me liberty or give me death" speech. Looking out from the capitol building designed by Thomas Jefferson, Confederate lawmakers would see the tall equestrian statue of George Washington on the grounds. You might say that being in Richmond was the next best thing to being in Washington. Better, in fact—no South-hating Yankees to deal with! Symbolically, for people so concerned to show the world that they were walking in the footsteps of George Washington and the other founders, Richmond was the place to be.

Go See It!

The White House of the Confederacy is definitely worth a visit. It is located next to, and run by, the Museum of the Confederacy, at 1201 W. Clay Street in Richmond, Virginia. It has been restored to its appearance when the Davises lived there.

Welcome, and Get to Work

President Jefferson Davis arrived in the city at 7 o'clock in the morning on May 29. When he stepped off the train in Richmond, he was greeted by the governor and mayor, who took him on a leisurely carriage ride through the city, where the citizens were bursting with patriotic fervor.

The city of Richmond presented him with a lovely three-story house not far from the capitol. It was made of stucco-covered brick, painted gray (the "White House of the Confederacy" was *not* white). It had a columned balcony overlooking a walled garden in the rear.

The capitol, attractive and historic, wasn't large enough for the government's business (since it was sharing space with the state bureaucrats), so the former U.S. Custom House served as a Confederate office building. Davis's executive office was in the Custom House, as were the offices of most of his cabinet members.

Changing "Provisional" to "Permanent"

So far everything in the Confederate government had been "provisional"—even the president. The Montgomery Convention had rushed everything through, with the understanding that the delegates acted on behalf of the states they represented (and that other states would probably join later). Popular vote hadn't been involved in anything—yet. Davis and the other top officials knew this was all rather undemocratic, so they scheduled elections for November of that year. It was assumed (and hoped) that the people would approve the choices that had already been made for president and vice president.

They did. There was still a powerful feeling that the new nation should appear to the world to be united. So the ballots in November 1861 had the names Jefferson Davis and Alexander Stephens on them; there were no alternate candidates.

That may sound like what occurred in the former Soviet Union: elections with no choices. That wasn't the case at all. In the states and various Congressional districts, voters had choices. But no one really wanted, at this point, to unseat Davis and Stephens. The country was new, and it would have seemed unpatriotic.

One thing notably lacking in the 1861 elections: *parties*. The Congress was made up of both Whigs and Democrats, labels that no longer applied. (There were no *Republicans*, of course!) Not surprisingly, many of the senators and congressmen who had served in Washington were elected to serve in Richmond. They were doing what they had done before, in a location 100 miles farther South—and with no blasted Yankees to rant about slavery!

RebeLingo

Unicameral means "one chamber" and refers to a legislative body that comprises only one unit. The original Confederate Congress set up in Montgomery was unicameral. Beginning on July 20, 1861, the Congress was **bicameral,** having two chambers, the House and Senate, like the U.S. Congress.

Church bells tolled on July 20, 1861, announcing the official opening of the Confederate Congress. Unlike the Congress that met in Montgomery, this one was *bicameral*. That is, it had both a House of Representatives and a Senate, exactly what everyone was used to (and including many of the same faces everyone was used to).

You might say the bells announced something else: Richmond was about to change, swiftly and dramatically, from a tidy Southern commercial town to a large, cramped, overpriced government-bureaucracy town.

Hot Southern Blood

Stating the obvious, Fort Sumter, followed by Lincoln's call for troops in the North, electrified the South. There was no need for the Confederate government to post "Uncle Jeff Wants You!" placards. The news was the best recruiter. The Southern blood was on fire. After decades of wanting to whip some arrogant Yankees, it was now legal to do so. Better than just legal—it was an honorable task, for that vulgar barbarian Lincoln had called on the Yankees to invade Southern soil. Enthusiasm was so high that the government was in the enviable position of having to turn away some volunteers. Secretary of War Leroy Walker had to refuse 200,000 men due to lack of weapons. Having an oversupply of eager men gave the Confederacy a nice option: Sign up only the long-termers, the ones who would enlist for the duration of the war.

In the spring of 1861, darn near every Southern man was thinking (and probably saying), "I can whip the Yankees!" And why not? Southerners were aware that most Northerners considered them a bunch of uncivilized barbarians. Well, let the Yanks find out (the hard way!) how hard a bunch of barbarians can fight.

It must have been a glorious time to be a Confederate.

The Least You Need to Know

- Except in agriculture, the Confederacy had vastly fewer resources than the Union, particularly lacking in railroads and manpower.

- A serious problem was the Confederacy's misguided belief that the world's need for Southern cotton would overcome all obstacles.

- The Confederacy moved its capital from Montgomery to Richmond in May 1861, mostly to be near the war front.

- Richmond had industry, space for government offices, and historic connections with the Founding Fathers.

Part 3

Johnnies and Generals

You've probably been itching to get to this part—military men, cannons, rifles, the Rebel yell, death, and gore. Well, you may have noticed that the United States delayed it as long as possible. When it did come, there was relief (no more wondering), then the joy of arming to fight the foe, the South's expectation of beating the Yanks, some early victories, then ... harsh reality, boredom and deprivation, marching shoeless, and living without soap or salt. The old saying is true: Bad luck makes good stories.

You'll encounter some familiar names and faces here—Lee, Jackson, and other colorful generals. You'll also get an up-close and personal look at that faceless, anonymous soul who combined grit, griping, grunt work, and grace under fire—Johnny Reb, the Confederate soldier.

10

Skimming Off West Point's Cream

In This Chapter

- ◆ Winfield Scott's many sons
- ◆ R. E. Lee and some painful decisions
- ◆ Southern Yanks, and Yankee Southerners
- ◆ We happy few, we band of ex-brothers

When Fort Sumter was fired upon, the U.S. Army had 1,098 officers and 15,304 enlisted men. Most of those officers were West Point men. And a whopping one third of them would resign their U.S. Army commissions and throw in their lot with the new kid on the block, the Confederate States Army. Not all those who did so were native-born Southerners. In early 1861, there was a noticeable "migration" to the South.

You may have heard the statement, "The South had the best generals." Did it? It certainly had some devoted ones, for they risked being branded as traitors for siding with the Confederacy. The same was true of a handful of Southern officers who sided with the Union. Making the choice wasn't a pleasant task, especially since it wasn't the army men themselves who caused the war.

In a Word, *Lee*

Robert Edward Lee was well aware that his birthplace, Stratford Hall, was only a few miles downriver from the birthplace of the big man himself, George Washington. Lee's father, the wayward but gallant "Light Horse Harry" Lee, had counted it his crowning honor that he was a friend of Washington. Young Robert grew up with Washington as his role model.

Robert E. Lee (1807–1870), also known as "Uncle Robert," "Marse Robert," and "the Marble Man," probably the Confederacy's most admired man world-wide.

Voices from Then

It was "Light Horse Harry," Robert E. Lee's father, who described George Washington in these immortal words: "First in war, first in peace, first in the hearts of his countrymen."

The Washington connection became even closer when he married Mary Custis, great-granddaughter of Martha Washington. The heiress brought several estates to the marriage, including America's best-known and most visited plantation, Arlington. He and Mary produced 7 children in 14 years. They named their oldest son George Washington Custis Lee (calling him Custis). In short, Robert E. Lee was the closest thing the South had to a son of George Washington (who was the Father of His Country, but not the father of any biological children).

Like his father, and like Washington, Lee was destined to be a soldier. He was second in his class at West Point. (There seems to be some curse of anonymity on whoever is first in his West Point class. The second-place men have always fared better than the first.) Lee had zero demerits on his record. In his days there, West Point wasn't exactly a hotbed of scholarship—the library was only open two hours a week. Too much reading was considered unsoldierly. Lee was highly intelligent, but he always preferred people to books.

Like most of the key players in the Civil War, Lee had the Mexican War as an internship. He distinguished himself in Mexico and served on the staff of the formidable Winfield Scott. Scott later referred to Lee as "the best soldier I ever saw in the field." Lee won some glory, but saw the dark side of the military, too. From Mexico he wrote his son Custis, "You have no idea what a horrible sight a field of battle is." (Custis, who became a Confederate general himself, would learn in time.)

Lee wanted no part of secession. He himself never owned more than a half-dozen slaves, all of them either inherited or given to him by his father-in-law. In 1859, he was sent to Harper's Ferry with the Marines to capture abolitionist-terrorist John Brown. The South was in an uproar. In 1861, Lee watched in agony, wondering if his beloved Virginia would secede as other Southern states had done.

> **Go See It!**
>
> Lee's and Washington's birthplaces are within a few miles of each other, so you can check out both on the same trip. Lee's, Stratford Hall, is off Virginia's SR 214 in Westmoreland County. The Washington Birthplace National Monument off SR 3 has the graves of several Washington ancestors, though the home itself is no longer standing.

Decision Agony

After the firing on Fort Sumter, the Union's commanding general, obese old Mexican War hero Winfield Scott, ordered Lee to report to him in Washington. Scott had already expressed his hope that one day Lee would take his place as general in chief. The two Virginians met for three hours in Scott's office. No one knows exactly what passed between them, except that Scott wanted Lee to command the Union army, and Lee declined. Did Scott seriously expect the Virginia-loving Lee to fight against the South? We don't know. What Scott might have hoped—maybe—was that Lee would head an army so formidable that there might never be a war. When Lee declined the offer, Scott told him, "You have made the greatest mistake of your life, but I feared it would be so."

The next day, April 19, Lee learned that Virginia had seceded. He called it "the beginning of sorrows." Lee resigned from the army the following day and returned to Virginia. He wrote to Scott: "I shall carry to the grave the most grateful recollections of your kind consideration, and your name and fame will always be dear to me." Regarding his refusal of the Union's offer, Lee later wrote, "Though opposed to secession and deprecating war, I could take no part in an invasion of the Southern states."

Voices from Then

What a cruel thing is war, to separate and destroy families and friends, and mar the purest joys and happiness God has granted us in this world; to fill our hearts with hatred instead of love for our neighbors, and to devastate the fair face of this beautiful world.

—Robert E. Lee

Sometime in mid-March—before Fort Sumter, and before Virginia seceded—Confederate Secretary of War Leroy Walker sent Lee a letter, with an offer to make him a brigadier general. Lee made no answer to Walker at the time. But after Virginia seceded (though before it technically joined the Confederacy), Lee said yes to Vice President Alexander Stephens's request for an "immediate military alliance" between Virginia and the Confederate States of America.

In April 1861, Robert Edward Lee didn't yet look like the gray-bearded patriarch in the familiar pictures. He had a mustache, but no beard. His dark hair was only just beginning to gray. He had intense, but kind, eyes. Most people thought he was one of the handsomest men they ever met. Standing 5 foot 11 and well proportioned, Lee carried himself like a prince, and looked even more impressive on horseback.

People were impressed by Lee's character as much as—or more than—by his looks. If any Southerner could have melted the abolitionists' ice, Lee could have done so. Yes, his family owned slaves. But he was the most courteous man in the world, always thinking of others. He neither drank nor smoked, but neither did he impress people as a stuffy Puritan. He belonged to the aristocrats' church, the Episcopalians, and was one of those rare individuals who took the New Testament as a guide to conduct. He had a strong hand, a quiet tongue, and a gentle heart. People would soon learn whether he could be so saintly under pressure.

Loyalty ... or Self-Interest?

If you sympathize with the Confederacy, you probably believe that Lee and other U.S. Army officers who sided with the South were right. Many of them, like Lee, agonized over the choice. Their West Point education had been provided at government expense, they were federal employees, and most of them had a deep devotion to the Union. (Lincoln griped about Southern West Point grads who "proved false to the land which pampered them.") By siding against it in the war, they were risking their futures. They would be branded as traitors by the North and, should the North win, they could expect the worst. (And some of them got it.)

Did Y'all Know?

Of the Confederacy's 425 generals, 146 were West Pointers. In all, the Confederacy had 304 officers who were West Pointers.

However, if Southern-bred army men sided with the Union (as some did), they would face the malice of their families, friends, and neighbors. No Southern man wanted his kin turned against him. If he took the Union side, there was a good chance his property in the South would be sold or confiscated. When Lee threw in his lot with Virginia, he was aware that his Potomac-front property might be seized by the Federals (it was), but also aware that the Confederacy might have seized it if he had sided with the Union.

Were Southerners Better?

No soothsayer in 1861 could have foreseen how difficult it was for the Union to find some really good fighting generals. And yet, it wasn't really a surprise, either—not to Southerners, anyway. The South had a reputation—which Southerners loved to flaunt—of being the breeding ground for military heroes. Look at the Southern presidents who had been military leaders: Washington, Jackson, W. H. Harrison, Taylor. And in 1861, the head honcho of the Union army (Scott) was himself a Southerner. The South's men saw themselves as a race of warriors, and they had the data to back up the brag.

Not all these Southern warriors were West Point–trained. The South had several state-supported military colleges. (Two of them, the Virginia Military Institute and The Citadel in South Carolina, are still going strong.) While West Point cranked out its career army men, the state military schools prepared a host of "citizen soldiers," men who went into civilian careers but who could strap on their swords and uniforms if duty called.

Voices from Then

There are a good many officers of the regular army who have not yet entirely lost the West Point idea of Southern superiority. That sometimes accounts for an otherwise unaccountable slowness of attack.

—A Union officer

spine

Southern Yankees, or Yankee Southerners?

Not all the South's West Point men were secessionists; in fact, practically none of them were. Lee, as we already saw, opposed it. Jubal Early, at Virginia's secession convention, voted against it. Braxton Bragg said secession had been brought about by "political hacks" and "barroom bullies." (Southern military men as a whole left politics to the politicians.) Nonetheless, when push came to shove, these and many other soldiers sided with their native South and served its armies as faithfully as they could.

Did Y'all Know?

There were about 50 Northern-born generals in the Confederate Army.

Then there were the non-native Southerners, the Yanks who, for various reasons, settled in the South, loved it, and took its side. Some of these were army men who had been stationed at Southern forts and rather liked the region. Some married Southern women and, once children came into the picture, accepted that their roots were now planted in Southern soil. Instead of sneering at slavery and the "backwardness" of Southerners, many Northerners learned to love the South—loved it enough to fight against troops from their home states, in fact. We will say more about one of these transplants, John Pemberton, in Chapter 24.

Frankly, the North didn't provide the South with any really good fighting generals. (Perhaps this pleased some Southerners, since it supported the theory that native Southerners were better fighters.) For the Confederacy, the best thing to come out of the North wasn't a fighter but the man who proved to be the "Wizard of Arms," Pennsylvania-born Josiah Gorgas. Of Dutch descent, Gorgas was stationed at Alabama's Mount Vernon Arsenal. He met the daughter of a former Alabama governor, married her, then resettled the family in Pennsylvania. In 1861, after some hesitation, he sided with his wife's homeland. Gorgas somehow managed to turn the nonindustrial South into a war machine—in both manufacturing its own arms and procuring them from abroad. (The South sometimes found that Yankee efficiency and industriousness were useful things. Gorgas had both.)

Most Southern officers in the U.S. Army sided with the Confederacy. This says a lot about the hold the South had on its children. The fact that a number of Yanks joined up with the Southern side says a lot, too. If the South was as horrible a place as the abolitionists said, the army men must not have noticed it.

Didn't We Used to Be Friends?

The young West Point men doing their deeds of valor in Mexico in the 1840s didn't know they would one day be enemies. They probably were aware of the abolitionists and secessionists causing a ruckus in Congress. But the army had (and still has) the power to throw together people from different places and classes and make them work together. There was no regional segregation during the Mexican War. Men from North and South were on the same team. When that changed in 1861, the men in uniform weren't too happy about it.

We mentioned earlier that Jefferson Davis in his Senate days was close friends with Sen. William Seward of New York—a noted anti-slavery politician, a Black Republican who served in Lincoln's cabinet and actively worked against the Confederacy. Can we assume that former friends regretted having to oppose each other? Sure. Politicians are human. So are military men. The sad thing about the military split caused by the war is that most of the army's officers had nothing to do with bringing on secession or war.

The Least You Need to Know

- In 1861, most West Point–trained officers shared the common experience of the Mexican War and the patronage of Gen. Winfield Scott.

- The Union made Robert E. Lee the offer of commanding its armies, but he cast his lot with the South.

- One third of the United States' officers (some of them Northern-born) resigned and joined the Confederacy.

- Friendships and other personal ties bound the Confederate generals to their counterparts in the Union forces.

Meet Johnny Reb

In This Chapter

- ◆ Johnny the slaveless
- ◆ Travel plus Yankee-killing
- ◆ Companies, regiments, and all that
- ◆ Why some stayed home
- ◆ Women as recruiters

Military men today sometimes visit Civil War battlefields and puzzle at the willingness of the Johnny Rebs and Billy Yanks to give all. Vietnam was (so the vets say) a war of survival—the U.S. soldier putting in his time and hoping to get out alive. That definitely wasn't true of most of the Johnny Rebs. Although they wanted to get out alive (who doesn't?), that wasn't the main goal. Most of them had notions of duty and honor that we in the twenty-first century can't fully comprehend. This is one of the pleasures of history: putting yourself inside the skin of people who looked at the world differently.   *or trying to!*

The terrorist attacks on September 11, 2001, may have changed our perspective a bit. Suddenly those words the Southern boys of 1861 repeated—"attacked on our own soil"—seemed more real.

Not Fighting for the S Word

Let's repeat something that bears repeating: *Most white Southerners didn't own slaves* (less than a fourth did, in fact). Let's now add something else: Most Southern soldiers were not fighting in order to maintain slavery.

Was it on the soldiers' minds at all, even faintly? Probably—but not much. We do have a rich source of data on why Johnny Rebs fought: their letters to and from home. There are thousands of them, as well as hundreds of diaries from this period. If you knew nothing whatsoever about what led to the Civil War, you could read hundreds of these letters and not learn that slavery had been a key issue.

Voices from Then

I am not fond of the army. Indeed many things in it are hateful to me, but nothing so much so as the invader of my native soil.

—letter from a Confederate soldier to his wife

What you would find mentioned—often and with deep emotion—is that basic human desire: Defend the home. This is one key difference between Johnny Reb's letters and Billy Yank's. Billy's letters talked of "preserving the Union," but Johnny wasn't thinking about something as abstract as the Union. He was thinking of Alabama, Tennessee, Virginia, Georgia ... more particularly, his own little slice of land.

One of the things you notice in almost all letters from Confederate soldiers is that they were chronically homesick. Here was a tragic irony of the war: In fighting to defend the homes they loved, they had to leave them. Writing home to wife, sweetheart, mother, father, or children, the Rebs clearly missed their family circles.

Don't Show Me the Money

Johnny Reb had several motivations for joining up. Money was most assuredly not one of them. The idea of a career in the military with decent pay, education, veterans' benefits, pension, and so on, never occurred to these boys. The war would be over in a few months (ha), and normal life would resume, free from Yankee interference.

The pay was (in theory) $11 monthly for infantry, $12 for cavalry. Even by 1861 standards, it was paltry pay, and as the war progressed, the astronomical inflation in the Confederacy made $11 even more laughable. There was also the lamentable fact that, quite often, the boys simply didn't get paid.

We mentioned earlier that at the very beginning of the war, the Confederacy saw a mad rush of boys willing to sign up. You don't have to be a veteran to understand that an all-volunteer army is much more desirable than an army of grumbling draftees.

The first wave of Rebs was eager to fight, willing to face a few weeks or (at most, they thought) a few months of unpleasant conditions, all for the purpose of driving out the Union thugs. This first wave chose to go, and so morale was high. If Johnny was lacking in many ways, his commanders at least knew he was there because he wanted to be there.

Voices from Then

We are a band of brothers, and native to the soil,
Fighting for the property we gained by honest toil.
And when our rights were threatened, the cry rose near and far,
Hurrah for the Bonnie Blue Flag that bears a single star!
Hurrah! Hurrah! For Southern rights, hurrah!
Hurrah for the Bonnie Blue Flag
That bears a single star!

—"The Bonnie Blue Flag," by Harry Macarthy

The Confederacy never had an official national anthem. Probably the first unofficial one was "The Bonnie Blue Flag." It referred to the blue flag with the single star that was the "pre-Confederate" flag before the new nation had designed itself an official one. Its author, Harry Macarthy, set the song to a lively old tune, "The Irish Jaunting Car." One of the bounciest Confederate songs, this one catches the buoyant spirit of the first wave of Southern volunteers.

Vacation off the Farm

The South's workforce, made up largely of farmers, was now called upon to defend the soil the men labored in. And when war first came, it sounded like a grand way to take a vacation from that soil—temporarily, of course. Johnny Reb in the field behind a pair of mules and a plow probably was satisfied enough with life, but the call to drive out the Yankee invader offered a respite. Johnny didn't know the blasted war would last four years, so the prospect of a few exciting months (or even better, weeks) away from the fields didn't sound so bad.

Did Y'all Know?

Of all Confederate soldiers, approximately two thirds were farmers.

Ditto for the schoolteacher, the store clerk, even the lawyer in the county courthouse. They had all been listening for years to the Yanks' insults, all the chatter about those slave-beating, slave-raping, backward, ignorant, uncivilized Southerners.

Cocky, naive, or both? These two young Florida volunteers typified the Southern boys who rushed to enlist when the war first began. Within a short time, the boys were thinner (if they survived) and uniforms were shabbier.

(Florida State Archives)

To give you an idea of the various occupations of the volunteers in a Confederate regiment, the following is a breakdown of the 19th Virginia Infantry:

Farmers: 302	Blacksmiths: 4
Laborers: 80	"Gentlemen": 4
Machinists: 56	Artists: 2
Students: 24	Distiller: 1
Teachers: 14	Well digger: 1
Lawyers: 10	Dentist: 1

For all of them, the war was an opportunity to take a break from the routine, take a long train ride to Virginia or Kentucky or some other far-flung place, whip the hypocritical stooges of Lincoln, then return home, still healthy and young, and a hero to boot. Wars throughout the centuries have turned farmers and clerks and blacksmiths into heroes. The brief Rebel-Yankee war of 1861 would (so they thought) do the same.

One thing Southern boys shared with Northern boys: None of them had traveled much. In 1861, the world was pre-automobile, pre-jet, pre-everything. Trains were still relatively new, and commonly you got around by horse or, more often, by foot. If you were 18 years old and had never set foot out of your county, you weren't in the minority. One reason Yanks and Rebs could detest each other was that they really knew so little of each other. Career officers like Joe Johnston and Robert E. Lee had traveled the United States, even traveled to other countries. Not so the average civilian in 1861. The south Alabama boy toiling in his papa's cotton fields had heard about Virginia but probably had never seen it. Why not go have a look at it, and repel the hirelings of Abe Lincoln in the process?

Pressures: Peer, Female, and Time

Human beings are often like lemmings, those peculiar rodents that occasionally mass together and hurl themselves off cliffs. That is, we do things (sometimes very dumb things) because everyone else is doing it. This definitely happened to a lot of Southern boys in 1861. We have no statistics on motivations, of course. We know that some of the boys were chomping at the bit, eager to fight even before their states seceded. Others were a little slower making the decision, but as they saw their peers running off to join the regiments, they didn't want to be left out of the action—or be called cowards, obviously. There were people like Missouri boy Sam Clemens (later known to the world as author Mark Twain), who spent a few weeks soldiering for the Confederacy—not out of any deep conviction that the South was right and needed defending, but just for a little adventure, and the fact that he knew so many people, including his older brother, who had joined up already.

> **Did Y'all Know?**
>
> Approximately 36 percent of Rebel soldiers were married. This was a little higher than the percentage of the Union army—probably because the Confederacy needed more men (which meant drafting a lot of married men who probably had no wish to serve). The Union army had a much larger population to draw from, so fewer married men felt the call to arms in the North.

Then there were the women. If you were married, there was a good chance your wife would *not* want you to go, particularly if there were small children at home. Some households had knock-down-drag-out fights over the issue. Husbands appealed to those powerful words *duty* and *honor*. (Translated, "Honey, I must defend our land, and I won't have people calling me a coward.") In some homes it was the wife who urged her husband to volunteer, but this wasn't common. Wives, especially young ones with small children at home, weren't particularly eager to see their husbands (and breadwinners) killed or disabled. (During the war, one distraught North Carolina wife wrote, "I don't think that he is fighting for anything, only for his family to starve.")

Voices from Then _____

A poem printed in a Charleston newspaper caught some of the feeling of the time—men leaving their normal jobs, women cheering them on:

The wayside mill is still,
And the wheel drips all alone,
For the miller's brother and son and sire,
And the miller's self have gone.
And their wives and daughters tarrying still,
With smiles and tears about the mill,
Wave, wave their heroes on!

Young single women were another matter altogether. Johnny Reb didn't want his male friends calling him a coward, but even more unbearable would be if his sweetheart—or a girl he *hoped* would be his sweetheart—believed he had no backbone. If Janie Reb was flirting with both Johnny and Joe, you can bet that if Johnny enlisted, Joe would, too. The old cliché about women loving a man in uniform is based on fact. And the old question "Do you love me enough to fight for me?" packed a lot of punch. Plenty of Southern boys went off to war with the promise—or at least the hope—that some lovely belle back home would save herself for him.

The volunteers were anxious in another way: They wanted to have it out, finally, with the Yankees. The South had been putting up with Yankee insults for decades. The Northern press heaped scorn on the South. Yankee congressmen loved to make long speeches in Washington, denouncing Southerners and their "crime" of slavery. Now, on the field of battle, there would be no more fighting with words. They would do it man to man, the way it should be done.

Why Some Johnnies Stayed Home

Your author's great-great-great-grandfather, William J. McCluskey of Tennessee, is a good example of a Southern man who stayed at home—not because he didn't love the Confederacy (or hate Yankees), but for the most practical reason of all: He was needed more at home than in the army. When the war began, William was 28, married, with very young sons at home. William owned a very small cotton farm in middle Tennessee. He owned no slaves. If he toyed with the idea of volunteering, we can assume his wife, Nancy, would have worked to dissuade him. The boys were too young to take over William's farm chores while he was away, and if he were killed or disabled, what then?

Single men with no dependents could afford to be more cavalier about life and limbs. William McCluskey and his counterparts throughout the South may have been true-blue patriots, but duty for them might involve farming, not fighting. (I'll tell you more about William later, when we talk about the Confederate draft laws.)

Two other groups failed to volunteer: the Unionists (we already talked about them) and the very small number of Christian pacifists, such as the Mennonites. In the early months of the war, these folks did the obvious thing: They kept a low profile. When the draft came (more about that in Chapter 19), this wasn't so easy.

Minutemen, Southern Style

Once more, think of 1776; Southerners certainly remembered the American Revolution, with its minutemen—citizen soldiers, ready to grab their guns at a moment's notice and run to fight the foe. Hadn't those gallant defenders of their homeland won the war against those well-drilled redcoats of the British army? Couldn't that happen again? Weren't the Southern states already well stocked with minutemen—their militias, that is?

Militias have gotten a bad rap in recent years, but they were highly regarded at the time the Civil War began. In your typical Southern locale, all able-bodied men between 18 and 45 would muster at the county seat every so often—meaning, once or twice per year. The gatherings were as much social as military, but they did give Southern civilians a taste of army-style organization. It wasn't unusual for local bigwigs to be known as "colonel" or "major," purely on the basis of their social prominence and a little militia experience. Still, it's safe to say that Johnny Reb had more military experience than most American civilians today.

Typically, militia uniforms were gray in color—usually called "cadet gray." When the war began, gray wasn't yet the official color of the Confederate uniform, although it became that very quickly, as we shall soon see.

The 1800s were not years when gun control crossed anyone's mind. Most families probably kept at least one gun in the house, probably several. The average Southern man (and quite a few Southern women) felt comfortable firing a weapon. A gun, an anti-Yankee attitude, and a smidgen of militia experience aren't enough to make a soldier, but it's a start.

Voices from Then

If they beat us in the field, we'll take to the woods, and shoot them down like squirrels.

—A Southern soldier, regarding Yankees

Rich Men's Playthings

Not all the militia units were public. Some were like elite clubs, with members actually being elected. Sons of wealthy planters might form units that were more like snooty fraternities than actual fighting units. Officers would be elected by the members, meaning that the captain of a company was the most popular, not necessarily the one with military ability.

One element of the Southern armies that puzzles people today is the curious habit of a wealthy individual "raising" his own company, organizing it, and clothing it. In theory, it's a wonderful idea—a patriotic citizen using his own funds and time to organize a company or regiment to fight for the Confederacy. And some of these sponsored units were excellent. Filthy-rich South Carolina planter Wade Hampton was no West Point grad, but he was a physically powerful man, handsome and charismatic, and a patriot to boot. The Hampton *Legion* was an example of what a wealthy planter could do for the cause.

RebeLingo

Legion is a military unit that was kind of a mini-army, with its own infantry, artillery, and cavalry. There were 10 legions in the Confederate Army.

But not every backer of his own company was a Wade Hampton. Too often these units were extensions of their sponsors' vanity. If Jonathan Planter organized Planter's Legion, naturally Planter would be its chief officer—even if he wasn't a good leader or fighter. As anyone with military training can tell you, managing a plantation and managing soldiers under fire aren't the same thing, though a number of planters assumed they were.

William H. Russell, the opinionated and readable correspondent for the *London Times*, wrote approvingly of the number of rich men joining up. Not all did, but there were enough in the ranks that the phrase "a rich man's war and a poor man's fight" wasn't completely true.

Basic (Non) Training

The Confederacy had strict rules about enlisting: You had to be breathing. This is an exaggeration, but not much. In fact, volunteers were supposed to be over 18 and in good health. Plenty were under 18 and willing to lie about it, and no one tried hard to catch the liars. Medical science was primitive by today's standards (as we shall see in a later chapter), so extensive medical testing of volunteers wasn't possible. If you possessed all your limbs in working condition (more or less) and weren't blind or deaf, you could be a soldier.

You had probably already received a minimal exposure to marching and drilling, thanks to your militia experience. When you volunteered, you joined a local company or regiment, probably headed by a man who was both popular and prominent. The men in your company would likely be people you knew, not (as in the army today) a pack of total strangers from all over the United States. With this group, whether you were forced to do any further marching or drilling was up to your commander—who, since he was probably *elected* by you and the other men, wasn't going to overstress his volunteers too much. The good news: Soldiers would serve more happily under an officer they had elected. The bad news: An elected officer might be lax in discipline and totally inept as a field commander. Electing officers proved to be a major problem as the war progressed, and measures were taken to end the practice.

Did Y'all Know?

One reason historians have trouble counting the precise number of Confederate soldiers is that records listed *enlistments*, not *individuals*. If you reenlisted, you were two people, as far as the records were concerned.

You might or might not be issued a weapon. They were in short supply, even after the Southern states seized the various Federal arsenals in the South. Some Rebs brought their own weapons, some preferred to leave them at home. Needless to say, weaponry was a high priority for the Confederate government, which moved quickly to procure arms abroad and to begin manufacturing them.

Part of training involved the obvious: obeying commands quickly and without question. This didn't come easily to many of the recruits. Sure, they had the will to fight, and they were young and (usually) healthy. But anyone with military experience knows this basic rule: In the middle of battle, you do what the commander tells you—for the good of the unit, not just because you feel like doing it at the time. Southerners were rather proud of their individualism, especially the wealthier boys,

Voices from Then

Robert E. Lee claimed Southern soldiers were "invincible if they could be properly organized and officered. There never were such men in an army before. They will go anywhere and do anything if properly led."

who weren't accustomed to being bossed around. They weren't too accustomed to doing any activities as a unit, either, so drilling as a unit was a necessary (and painful) part of training. Johnny Reb may already have known how to fire a gun, but he didn't know much about firing in unison—or doing anything else in unison, for that matter.

Home Away from Home

This is as good a place as any to give the basics of military structure, moving from the smallest unit to the largest:

- **Squad**—composed of 10 to 25 men, commanded by a sergeant or corporal.

- **Company**—composed of 50 to 100 men (usually 4 squads), commanded by a captain. Most were designated by a letter (e.g., Company E), but many companies had an unofficial name (e.g., Railroad Guards). Generally the Confederate soldier identified with his company, as in "Private McCluskey, Co. K, 8th Tennessee Infantry."

- **Regiment**—composed of roughly 10 companies, commanded by a colonel. Confederate regiments were usually designated by a number, as in 9th Alabama Infantry. A regiment almost always was made up of men from the same state, usually from the same county. Usually the colonel was from the same area. There were 642 Confederate infantry regiments in all.

- **Brigade**—composed of four to six regiments, commanded by a brigadier general. A brigade was usually made up of regiments from the same state. Often the brigade bore the name of its commander, e.g., the Stonewall Brigade or Hood's Texas Brigade. Most often the commander was from the same state as its men.

- **Division**—composed of two or more brigades, commanded by a major general.

- **Corps**—composed of two or more divisions, commanded by a lieutenant general.

Unless you were an officer, you probably had only a vague awareness of brigades, divisions, and corps. You knew by name your squad sergeant, your company captain, and your regiment's colonel. Your regiment would (in theory) have a regimental staff with the following people: colonel, lieutenant colonel, adjutant, quartermaster, surgeon and assistant surgeon, sergeant major, commissary sergeant, quartermaster sergeant, hospital steward, and two musicians. Some regiments had bands.

The regiment was your little world most of the time—the people you drilled and marched and ate and slept and griped with. Your regiment's colonel was probably from the same state as you; ditto for your company's captain, who was most likely from your county or town. On a daily basis, the most important (and perhaps most irritating) person in your world would be your company's first sergeant.

Early in the game, names of the armies weren't yet set in stone. Civil War buffs know of the Army of Northern Virginia, the Army of Tennessee, and so on. Those names didn't just grow up overnight, and when Rebs met Yanks for the first battles in the summer of 1861, about the only thing most Rebs were aware of was "us versus them." If you were a soldier from Alabama, you were likely aware that there were Florida and Arkansas boys nearby. And you probably knew of this new thing called the Confederacy. But mostly you were aware of the contest being South versus North—our people versus the Yankee invaders.

Uniforms Weren't

Uniforms weren't uniform—that is, not in the beginning, anyway. As a militia member, you might or might not have had a uniform, and the Confederacy in its earliest stages had more important things to worry about. At the very beginning, Secretary of War Leroy Walker in Montgomery issued instructions that "volunteers shall furnish their own clothes." This was called commutation—meaning that instead of the Confederate government supplying you with togs, you were given a $50 allowance for BYOC ("bring your own clothing").

It would be several months before regulation uniforms, including *kepis*, were common. If your company was backed by a local planter with money to spare, he might arrange for tailors or seamstresses to outfit the unit. One regiment from Savannah, Georgia, was well dressed, its sponsors having spent $25,000 on some fine uniforms.

Most Southern women at this period were handy with a needle, and the voluntary sewing clubs and knitting societies rendered a valuable service throughout the war. Since the Confederacy spent four years in a prolonged clothing famine, the women at home never ran out of something they could do for the boys in uniform.

RebeLingo

Kepi was the name given to the generic Civil War cap with the leather visor and flat round crown slanted forward. It was the regulation cap of Union enlisted men and also (in theory) for the Confederacy. Some Confederate soldiers wore kepis, while others wore whatever was available. The wide-brimmed "slouch hat" was more common than the kepi.

The next time you look at a contemporary piece of Civil War art, look closely at the uniforms. The men in dark blue were, of course, the Yankees. The men in gray were the Confederates. Whether any actual battle scene resembled those works of art is doubtful, for the real Confederates may or may not have had gray uniforms, much less any standard headgear. For a variety of reasons, the Rebs' appearance was pretty individualistic. Considering the Southern mind and the whole background of the

Civil War, this was fitting—Southern individualists in a wide variety of uniforms versus Yankee boys all in blue, all alike, determined to make Americans all alike. Thus did the Southern boys perceive the fight.

In Gear

Supposedly, every soldier would pack his gear in a backpack, or knapsack, as they were usually called then. These proved not to be popular. Instead, Johnny preferred to roll up his sleeping blanket in oilcloth (if he was lucky enough to have an oilcloth), loop it over his left shoulder, and tie the blanket's ends at his right hip. This was the "horseshoe roll." It was expandable, so you could roll up clothing and other items inside it—a cheap and flexible set of luggage, composed entirely of a blanket and a piece of rope.

Did Y'all Know?

Bayonets, like bowie knives, did double duty as tools and weapons. Oddly, most Confederate soldiers didn't like bayonets, finding them heavy and cumbersome.

As a Confederate soldier, you probably also had a haversack, a waterproof canvas bag about a foot square. This was for the day's rations and for the few (*very* few) personal articles you were willing to carry. Over the haversack would hang your canteen. You would probably carry the familiar friend of the Southern boy, the bowie knife, which did double duty as both tool and weapon. In all, you would be marching with about 40 pounds of gear.

It wasn't much, but boys of the plain-folk class weren't spoiled at home anyway. Expecting the whole thing to end soon, it was all a lark, a kind of extended Boy Scout jamboree, roughing it but meeting good companions, getting away from the normal grind, doing your patriotic chore, making the home folks proud, impressing the ladies, and feeling like more of a man.

Johnny Got His Gun

Soon after Jefferson Davis took office, he sent agents scurrying off to buy firearms—Caleb Huse to Europe, Raphael Semmes to New York. Northern-born Josiah Gorgas was made chief of Confederate ordnance and set to work so that the Confederacy could produce its own weapons. But none of these sources would bring the Confederacy anything until fall 1861. It was already summer, and there was a pressure-cooker feeling: Something had to blow—a major battle had to take place, and soon.

In summer 1861, the Confederacy possessed a total of about 150,000 shoulder arms. (Maybe we need to clarify and say *functional* shoulder arms, since there were also a lot of creaky old antiques around.) Of the 150,000, about 20,000 were rifles; the rest were smoothbore muskets.

We stated in the previous chapter that there was no lack of eager young volunteers—but they outnumbered the available weapons. Contrary to what one boastful Southern speaker had said, the Rebs couldn't defeat the Yanks with popguns. Each volunteer needed a usable weapon. Plenty were on order, but that didn't mean much. But the weapon shortage did give the Rebel soldiers an added incentive to whip the Yankees—they needed the Yankees' rifles for their armless comrades, as the following war ditty illustrates:

> Want a weapon? Capture one!
> Every Doodle has got a gun,
> Belt and bayonet, bright and new,
> Kill a Doodle, and capture two!

There was no regulation rifle for the Confederate Army. As with uniforms, Johnny Reb shot whatever was available, and there might be a dozen different arms in use by his company. During the first year, probably the most common weapon was the .69-caliber smoothbore musket. This packed a wallop, but its effective range was pretty short. The .54-caliber Mississippi rifle and the .58-caliber Springfield rifle were both popular, certainly preferred to the smoothbores. Some Rebs went into battle armed with muzzle-loading shotguns—fine for close-up fighting, not good for distance. None of them was particularly fast by our standards. The Springfield rifle, for example, could fire about two rounds per minute—which in 1861 was considered pretty fast.

All these were muzzle-loaded—meaning the shot had to be packed in at the firing end. Breech-loaded, the standard for all firearms today, means loaded at the breech end, nearest your hand. There were a few of these in Civil War days, but not many. Most Confederate rifles fired the standard Minie ball—not really a ball, but a bullet. The Minie bullet and powder were wrapped in a paper cartridge, which the soldier tore open—sometimes with fingers but more often with his teeth. Following a battle, the soldier's mouth was likely to be smeared with black gunpowder.

It's probably worth mentioning here that the vast majority of Southern men served in the infantry—that is, as foot soldiers. There were far fewer men in the cavalry, artillery, engineers, or ordnance. When you hear the generic term "Confederate soldier," you can assume it probably refers to an infantryman.

Fair Belles, Flags, and Kisses

No one has yet come up with a name for Johnny Reb's female counterpart. For now, let's call her Janie Reb. When a company was formed and readying to travel, Janie (probably a girl with a Johnny sweetheart in the company) would present a lovingly sewn battle flag to the company. At a dress parade, a dinner, or even a church meeting, local brass (a mayor, banker, or planter, or all three) would make a patriotic speech, followed by lots of applause and cheers, then Janie would ceremoniously present the flag to the captain of the company. Janie would have carefully rehearsed her presentation speech; ditto for the captain.

History is always repeating itself: Men go off to war, with a big emotional send-off by fair young maidens. It isn't hard to imagine medieval knights being plopped down in a Southern county-seat town in 1861 and fully comprehending what was happening. Brave young men, off to fight the foe. Sent forth thinking of the flowers of womanhood. Sent forth with rousing speeches like those "we happy few, we band of brothers" lines from Shakespeare's *Henry V*.

Now that we've met Johnny Reb, let's watch him fight.

The Least You Need to Know

- ◆ Most Confederate soldiers were not slaveholders and were not fighting to preserve slavery.

- ◆ Most were motivated by the desire to drive out the Yankee invaders and to have a brief adventure.

- ◆ Many of the military units raised in the beginning were private affairs, financed and headed by wealthy men.

- ◆ Southern boys' individualism and independence often worked against discipline and organization.

- ◆ Many wives persuaded husbands not to fight, while the approval of single women was a key factor in single men joining the army.

Chapter **12**

Beginner's Luck, and Other Illusions

In This Chapter

- ◆ The illusion of a quickie separation
- ◆ Manassas, battle of the amateurs
- ◆ Turning the South into a fool's paradise

The South had two things in large supply: cotton and courage. Both were, so Southerners believed, real assets that would accomplish great things. Lacking so many other resources, the South believed its cotton would support it economically, while its courage would support it militarily and politically. As one noted writer of those days said, they had "a knack of hoping." Some might say it was a knack for being out of touch with reality.

One hope was that the Yankees would go home after one or two quick, decisive Rebel victories. Most Confederates believed that, deep down, the Yankees didn't have the will or courage to force the South back into the Union. When they saw how fiercely Southern boys could fight, they would scurry back north again.

Hopes and dreams always have to bump up against hard reality. The Rebs were about to fight, whether leading to fame or shame.

The Amicable Divorce Illusion

We look at the whole war with the benefit of hindsight. We know it lasted four years. We also know that a handful of wise people (such as Lee) knew it wouldn't be over quickly. (Lee thought it might last 10 years.) Given all the fighting and killing and deprivation, it all seems inevitable. The young bucks who went off to war in a jolly party mood were fools and dreamers, right?

Maybe not. Maybe they were just being Southern gentlemen, and believed their opponents (even if they were Yankees) might be gentlemen, too. The Yanks wouldn't really try to force them back into the Union, would they? Politicians like Jefferson Davis could look back on friendships with abolitionist politicians like William Seward, who was now Lincoln's secretary of state. Davis knew that Seward really wanted peace, as did Stephen Douglas, the foremost Democratic politician in the North. More importantly, so did most private citizens in the North.

Old Winfield Scott, commander of the Union's armies when the war began, claimed he detested secessionists, but he also claimed the North should let its "wayward sisters depart in peace." But Lincoln had no intention of letting that happen.

The Calm Before the Storm

Here's as good a place as any to take a quick look at what Johnny Reb faced on the day of battle. We can't reproduce the tension, anxiety, glee, diarrhea, or other sensations of the day, but we can try.

You would be given about 50 rounds of ammunition, a round being a bullet and enough gunpowder for a single shot. Each round was wrapped in a twist of paper, which you tore apart with your teeth. (You would have "black mouth" after firing several rounds.) Powder and ball went into the muzzle of the gun, to be exploded when you pulled the trigger. Bullets, powder, and the necessary "percussion caps" were stowed in your leather or metal cartridge box, which you kept on your belt, in your pockets, or in your haversack.

Your other gear—blanket, cup, and so on—were left with your unit's quartermaster. If you were wise (and many soldiers weren't), you would take your full canteen. Extra weight, true, but water in the heat of battle was more of a necessity than a luxury.

Military men know what the "long roll" is—the call to arms, beat on the snare drum. You and your comrades would form in lines, getting a final inspection from your officers. Typically this would take place at dawn, if not earlier.

One generic rule: Waste no ammunition. This didn't mean "Don't fire," but rather, "Choose your target carefully." There was no point in firing at a target too far away to injure.

Your unit's musicians are playing fifes and drums. The regiment's colors are waving in the breeze. Is someone going to yell "Charge!"? (Yes, that really happened.) An officer would wave his saber, and if you had the guts, you would move forward, perhaps hollering out the Rebel yell with your brothers in arms.

Forward, men, and mix with 'em.

> **Did Y'all Know?**
>
> Anyone who was ever within earshot of a battlefield remembered a familiar cry, "Water! Water!" Common sense and experience would teach you to arm yourself with bullets—and a full canteen.

Manassas, Bull Run, Take Your Pick

What was the first battle of the war? Most people don't really count Fort Sumter. Some do count Big Bethel, a minor battle, or "engagement," on Virginia's Peninsula, fought on June 10 that barely lasted an hour. It was a Rebel victory, and it gave the green Southern boys a shot of courage.

They would need it, for a real battle was gearing up, and inevitably it would take place somewhere between Washington and Richmond. It was going to be a battle of amateurs, since both sides were stocked with boys who were literally just off the farm. Some of them were excited that the hero of Fort Sumter had arrived, and the words "Old Bory's come!" were repeated around the Rebel camps. Cocky little P. G. T. Beauregard was still glowing over what happened at Fort Sumter, and he intended to wage a battle in Virginia that would further polish his Confederate halo.

Irvin McDowell was in command in the North. By an odd coincidence, he and Beauregard were not only the same age but members of the same West Point class (1838). McDowell had his good points, but he probably wasn't the right man to lead the inexperienced Federals at this time. (He freely admitted this. McDowell was one of the least vain generals.) He was fated to confront the Confederates at Manassas Junction, Virginia, an important railroad center barely 30 miles southwest of Washington. Nearby was a sluggish stream known as Bull Run. (Now you know why the battle is referred to as both *Manassas* and *Bull Run*.) McDowell knew his boys weren't prepared for a major battle, but the Northern newspapers had been screaming "On to Richmond!" and Lincoln bowed to public pressure.

RebeLingo _____

If you haven't heard this before, take note: Many Civil War battles have dual names, based on the South and North calling them by different monikers. As a general rule, the Yanks tended to name battles for nearby bodies of water or a hill, while Rebs tended to name them for the nearest town or building. Thus the Rebs referred to the **Battle of Manassas,** while the Yanks called it **Battle of Bull Run.** A few key battles, such as Gettysburg, had names that everyone agreed on.

Richmond knew McDowell was headed toward Manassas. The widow Rose Greenhow of Washington, one of the Civil War's cleverest spies, had wheedled the information out of some politicians and passed it on to the Confederacy. Her messages prompted Beauregard to telegraph Jefferson Davis in Richmond, urgently requesting reinforcements. Davis ordered Joe Johnston's newly named Army of the Shenandoah to head toward Manassas to reinforce Beauregard. Part of Johnston's troops' long trip was made by train. (War was entering the modern world. Generals could telegraph each other with vital information, and troop movements were quickened by railroads.) Johnston, an old Virginia soldier, wasn't too optimistic about his undisciplined volunteers, but they were certainly in a buoyant mood.

One of Johnston's brigades was commanded by an odd professor from the Virginia Military Institute, Thomas J. Jackson. This Jackson feared God, but he feared neither man nor devil. If McDowell commanded the largest force on American soil, what did that matter?

Johnston had about 10,000 men in his so-called Army of the Shenandoah. Beauregard had about 20,000 in what he called, for now, the Army of the Potomac. (The more famous name "Army of Northern Virginia" would come later.) Both men were egotistical as all get-out, and Johnston had checked with Jefferson Davis to confirm that he (Johnston) was the senior officer on the scene. But Johnston had arrived later, and Beauregard, who knew the lay of the land better, had already devised a battle plan, which Johnston approved. The vain and pompous Old Bory was pretending to be a new Napoleon, a field marshal with an experienced staff and troops, though they were anything but.

Not Waterloo, but Exciting

It was July 21, 1861. The Union's Irvin McDowell was in command of 33,000, the largest army yet assembled on American soil. At first it appeared the Union boys were winning, and the Reb boys could see that the enemy was "thick as wheat in a field." One of the Rebel generals was Barnard Bee of South Carolina, who at one low point in the battle rode up to his fellow cadet from West Point, Thomas J. Jackson. "General," Bee shouted, "they're beating us back!" Jackson answered sternly, "Sir, we'll give them the bayonet!"

Bee turned to his demoralized men and uttered probably the most-quoted words from the Civil War: "There stands Jackson like a stone wall! Rally around the Virginians! Let us determine to die here, and we will conquer!" Bee's men rallied. Bee himself, alas, was wounded within an hour. He died the following day, and the South lost a fine general. No one forgot his words about Jackson, however.

Jackson himself was wounded slightly, a bullet striking his left hand. He held his hand high to check the bleeding while he watched his brigade of green recruits transform itself into the Stonewall Brigade. Tight-lipped though he was, he ordered his men at Manassas, "Charge men, and yell like furies!" They did. They were beginning to appreciate the humorless professor.

Go See It!

The Manassas National Battlefield Park in northern Virginia is a must-see, particularly since not one but two major battles took place there. You'll find a very striking equestrian statue of Thomas J. Jackson on Henry Hill, where he stood "like a stone wall." Before the site was given to the National Park Service, it had been purchased by the Sons of Confederate Veterans as a Confederate Memorial Park. When the Sons turned over the park to the government, they insisted that a monument to Stonewall be erected.

Several officers besides Jackson performed gallantly that day. A jaunty Virginia boy named James Ewell Brown Stuart (known as Jeb) arrived with his cavalry. Florida-born Edmund Kirby Smith arrived late, but his troops performed well. A. P. Hill's 13th Virginia Regiment did admirably, and Hill would go on to greater glory. Ditto for cranky, foul-mouthed Jubal Early, the former Unionist who fought well for the South.

Something happened that day that everyone present remarked on: Some of the Confederates emitted a screeching wail that was quickly dubbed the "Rebel yell." Since no one ever recorded it, we will never be sure exactly what it sounded like.

It has been described as a screech, whoop, and many other things, and some men who had fought against Indians said it resembled their war cries. It became a standard feature of any Confederate attack, and if it was intended to strike terror in Yankee hearts, it often succeeded.

Historians talk of the "rout" of the Federals at Manassas. Apparently there was a sort of panic, with Federal troops scurrying back north toward Washington—along with the civilian sightseers. Being so near Washington, the battle had attracted a number of D.C. notables, who apparently treated it as a spectator sport. Some brought food and drink with them, which led to First Manassas being called the "picnic battle." Manassas wasn't a particularly bloody battle. Approximately 500 Union men and 380 Confederates were killed. By the standard of some later battles, this was pocket change.

Gray-haired Virginia secessionist Edmund Ruffin was also present at the battle. He had, so tradition says, fired the first shot at Fort Sumter. At Manassas he supposedly fired a cannon at a bridge, leading to the Yankees' panic.

> **Did Y'all Know?**
>
> No one knew in July 1861 that there would be another crucial battle near Manassas the following year. The 1861 battle is now known as First Manassas (or First Bull Run), while the 1862 battle is known as Second Manassas.

Prizes for Everyone

If the Grand Creole, Beauregard, expected a reward for what happened, he got it. Jefferson Davis arrived at Manassas and made him a full general (four stars) the day after the battle. He did the same for Joe Johnston. In truth, the two short, egotistical generals had performed well, as had their undisciplined but brave Southern boys. For all Beauregard knew, the battle had been what he'd hoped: the Waterloo that would settle everything.

Party! Then the Big Lull

While a surgeon dressed his wounded finger, Thomas J. "Stonewall" Jackson said, "Give me ten thousand men, and I will be in Washington tomorrow." This was typical Jackson—not pompous boasting, but sheer gutsiness. The newly decorated Beauregard and Johnston weren't feeling so gutsy, however. Davis urged a pursuit northward, but Bory and Johnston didn't support this. (Heavy rains and muddy roads the next day made it a moot point anyway.) In any case, the South had won its first big battle. Maybe, if they were lucky, it would be the last battle as well. They were still hoping that the North didn't really wish to coerce the Confederacy back into the Union.

Lincoln was not discouraged by the loss. If anything, it increased his determination. He issued another call: The Union needed 500,000, 3-year volunteers. Lincoln gave up his original line about trying to "hold, occupy, and possess the property and places belonging to the government." He was going to bring the South back into the Union fold, whether it liked it or not.

Some generals, like Jackson, knew they should have pursued the Federals. The bureaucrats in D.C. could have been easily panicked by advancing Confederate troops, just as the sightseers at Manassas had panicked. The South would have done well to follow Jackson's favorite line: "Press on! Press on!" Certainly there was no point in waiting for the Union's 500,000 new soldiers to be mustered and trained.

But the post-Manassas days were the Big Lull, militarily speaking. True, there was excitement in the air. Since the Feds fled so quickly, the Rebs found themselves in possession of 4,000 muskets, 29 artillery pieces, tons of ammo, horses, caissons, the works. Richmond ladies fussed over wounded soldiers, treating them like demigods. Veterans of the battle were wined and dined. Writers poured out praises of the Rebel generals and troops, mocked the disorganized and cowardly Yankees, and predicted a glorious future for the South.

We know better now, of course. So did a few people then. Mary Chesnut in her famous diary wrote that the victory had sent the South "off in a fool's paradise of conceit." At least one Richmond newspaper insisted that the Rebs must press on to Washington: "There can be no peace until that nest of Yankees and traitors is exterminated." We have to wonder: What would have happened in July 1861 if the Confederacy had pursued the Federals all the way to Washington?

Other than an engagement at Ball's Bluff on the Potomac on October 21, there were no large battles in Virginia for the rest of 1861. Things were not so quiet in the rest of the Confederacy, as we shall see in a later chapter.

Gray Matters

Beauregard, now a full general, had other things to do besides admire the new stars on his shoulders. The Rebs had won the battle, true, but there was some serious confusion. The lack of uniform uniforms had led to more than one case of Reb shooting Reb and Yank shooting Yank. Something had to be done.

The Union's 7th New York Regiment was outfitted in gray at Manassas. So were many of the Rebels. We said earlier that many militia uniforms were cadet gray, so since gray was the militia color, it was also considered the states' rights color. It made sense that the Confederacy, with its obsession with states' rights, should adopt gray for its uniforms—all its uniforms, if possible.

Union officials were discussing the issue also. Following Manassas, the Union mandated that blue would be the only official color for uniforms, thus leaving gray as the Confederate color. Henceforth, all Union boys were in blue. (On the occasions later in the war when the Confederate wore blue, the expected thing happened—being fired upon by fellow Rebs.) Whatever else Manassas accomplished, it set up the blue-gray scheme for the duration of the war.

RebeLingo _____

Southern Cross refers to the Confederate battle flag that is most familiar to people today.

The Battle of Manassas also made field commanders aware of the Confederate flag's inadequacy. The Stars and Bars, unless unfurled by the wind, looked too much like the Stars and Stripes. Accounts of the design change differ, but supposedly the Confederate battle flag, the *Southern Cross,* was designed by Congressman William Porcher Miles of South Carolina. This was the now-familiar blue X on a red field, with 13 stars on the X. (In flag terminology, an X is a "St. Andrew's cross.") The Stars and Bars remained the national flag (it would change later), while the Southern Cross became one of several used by the Confederates. In solemn ceremonies on November 28, 1861, Confederate troops saw the first display of the new battle flag.

Thanks to the clout of Beauregard and Johnston, the Southern Cross became standard in most of the eastern Confederacy. Further west, commanders were their individualistic Southern selves and used a wide variety of flags.

The Least You Need to Know

- Most Confederates clung to the belief that the Union would not fight a long war.

- The First Battle of Manassas, Virginia, was a Confederate victory that led to overconfidence in the South.

- The two Rebel commanders at Manassas, P. G. T. Beauregard and Joe Johnston, were the South's first heroes.

- Confusion at Manassas led to some new regulations about battle flags and uniforms.

Chapter 13

The Unlovely Reality of War

In This Chapter

- ◆ Salt horse, ironclad possum, and other dainties
- ◆ Lack of threads (and soap)
- ◆ Some seriously primitive medicine
- ◆ Cowards of the country

After the jubilation of the First Manassas victory, reality came a-calling, and the drudgery of war life set in.

But that was okay. After all, part of the fun of being a soldier is grumbling and griping. And Lord knows they had ample reasons to gripe: bad food (or, even worse, *no* food), ragged clothing, no soap, lots of cooties, diseases, cowardly comrades, and … well, it's a sad story with frequent reminders that Johnny Rebs mostly stayed optimistic, even if they were less naive than before.

Gray Boys and Growling Guts

The old proverb says that an army marches on its stomach. This must not be true, for if it was, many of the Johnny Rebs would never have marched at all. Food—or lack of food, rather—was often the biggest concern of the

Confederate soldier. If he was aware of the Yankee invader, he was probably more aware, hour to hour, of a chronic shortage of food.

How could this be? Wasn't the South an *agrarian* region? Didn't its soil produce bushels of edible things? Indeed. But connecting the food to the eater became a major problem.

It wasn't this way at the very beginning. When the Rebs descended upon Manassas, Virginia, in 1861, they were well fed. They had been sent off from their home counties with a round of parties, cakes, punch, wine, whiskey, and pretty much whatever their bellies desired. Once they were in the army life, they were usually restricted to their rations, but those were the same rations issued by the U.S. Army at that time, which in March of 1861 were:

¾ lbs. of pork or bacon, *or*

1¼ lbs. of fresh or salt beef

18 oz. of bread or flour, *or*

12 oz. of hard bread, *or*

1¼ cups of cornmeal

Plus: coffee, sugar, salt, peas, beans, and rice

Those weren't bad. Soldiers writing home in the early months generally spoke well of their rations—fresh bread, good-quality beef, coffee to spare, plenty of fresh vegetables. Some of the poorer boys found themselves eating better than they did at home. If the war had lasted only a few months, as so many had hoped, the veterans would have gone home without many memories of deprivation.

But pretty soon the official rations became a joke. Not long after the victory at Manassas, both soldiers and generals were complaining about food shortages. Some of the basics of the Southern boy's fare—sugar, bacon, milk—seemed to be in short supply.

"Foraging" referred to finding food outside the camp. Often it was a polite term for stealing, since foraging from a farmer's chicken coop was illegal. But foraging also included searching around for nature's bounty—nuts, berries, persimmons, and so on. Most Southerners hated to beg, but hunger can cut into pride pretty quickly. It wasn't rare for soldiers to visit a local home, asking for handouts of eggs, milk, or whatever people could spare. Most civilians obliged, if they had enough left after feeding their own families.

The Rebel soldier was, in theory, supposed to leave civilian property alone. But a regiment of hungry soldiers passing by an apple or peach orchard found they could quickly forget about "Thou shalt not steal." Fruits and vegetables are fairly easy to steal while on the march, and so are eggs and chickens. But beef and flour are a different matter. Every time Johnny turned around, he found his daily rations of meat and bread had been cut back again. So some soldiers did the obvious thing: Hunt for wild game, including *ironclad possums*.

The army frowned on this, since ammunition was also in short supply. You were supposed to save your Minie bullets for Yankees, not possums. But hunger had a way of overriding army restrictions. The Southern forests and fields abounded with deer, turkeys, squirrels, rabbits, and other game. If you were hungry enough, possums, raccoons, groundhogs, and other critters would do. Small songbirds like robins and meadowlarks weren't normally considered game birds, but with hunger in charge, even the smallest birds were fair game.

> **RebeLingo**
>
> Armadillos, found in the most southerly parts of the Confederacy, were referred to as **ironclad possums**. The creatures are ugly as all get-out, but also dumb and easily caught, and soldiers found that they were edible, once their "armor" was removed. (Regular nonarmored possums were eaten too, of course.)

Fishing had an advantage over hunting—no wasting of ammo. The problem with fish was that they couldn't be preserved and taken on the march. And much as Rebels may have enjoyed fish, they still preferred red meat, and they missed it when it wasn't available, which was often.

What? No Coffee?

The greatest lack, of course, was coffee. Here was an item that grew nowhere in the United States; it had to be imported, meaning it had to make its way past the Union blockade of Southern ports (more about that nasty thing later), and it seldom did. In all the letters and diaries of Rebel soldiers, no item gets mentioned more often than coffee. It was one of the first items to disappear from the list of official rations, and soldiers never stopped griping. Johnny Reb loved his coffee. Aside from missing something familiar, the lack of caffeine obviously had its effects on former coffee addicts.

Naturally it irked the Rebs that they went underfed while Yankees didn't. This made victory in battle even sweeter, for if you whipped the Yanks, chances were good you could raid their supply wagons. "Retreating Yankees!" was another way of saying "Food, glorious food!" Even on the battlefields, Rebs might pause to raid the bodies of fallen Yanks, looking for hardtack, bacon, or anything they could scavenge. On the occasions when Rebels could capture a supply train full of Yankee goods, all heaven broke loose—food, coffee, rifles, ammunition ... praise the Lord!

Southerners have always been fond of cornbread, but as the war continued, wheat flour became harder and harder to get, meaning cornbread was the *only* bread, and Rebs grew tired of it. At times they were lucky if they had corn in the form of bread, because circumstances didn't always allow for baking it; you therefore did what you could with a bag of cornmeal—mixing it with lard, bacon grease, water, or whatever was available.

RebeLingo

Salt horse was soldier slang for salt beef, beef preserved in brine. It was, as you might gather from the name, not a favorite item on the menu. Some soldiers referred to it as "blue beef."

Some of the inventive cooking would be familiar to Boy Scouts. Potatoes could be baked in their skins underneath the coals of a fire. Fresh corn on the cob could be roasted in its husk. Bread batter could even be wrapped in a corn husk and baked in the fire. But the Rebs had some tricks beyond Boy Scout capacities: They sometimes wrapped wheat dough around a heated ramrod.

Nasty Mr. Northrop

One of the most detested men in Confederate history is Lucius B. Northrop, a South Carolina man, West Point grad, and successful doctor. He also happened to be a longtime friend of Jefferson Davis, which explains why Davis made him commissary general of the Confederacy. It was one of the worst appointments Davis ever made, one that he—and every soldier and officer in the Rebel army—lived to regret.

Granted, commissary general was not a post anyone could have done well in. Supplying the Confederate armies was, in effect, asking the impossible. We've already looked at the South's inadequate transportation network, and the blasted Union blockade of Southern ports complicated things further. Still, having said that, it does appear Northrop was pretty darned incompetent. He was also a thoroughly unlikable character, which made it easy to hate him and blame him (and to pass on some of the hate to the man who appointed him). Northrop was stubborn, condescending, and opinionated, making him less than tolerant of the many suggestions people had for running his much-criticized department.

Did Y'all Know?

Northrop almost got his comeuppance after the war. He was arrested by Union authorities for having willfully starved Union prisoners of war. Much to the regret of Northerners (and many Southerners as well), Northrop was quickly released.

Northrop had a knack for issuing suggestions that irked the soldiers—such as recommending they add to their meat supply by including necks and hooves of cattle. Supposedly Northrop was a vegetarian, and some of his many critics believed he hoped to convert others to the practice. There were jokes about how the lack of meat must be the fault of the vegetarian doctor in Richmond.

> **Voices from Then**
>
> Diary keeper Mary Chesnut wrote that Northrop was "the most cussed and vilified man in the Confederacy." She was probably right. General Beauregard claimed that, thanks to Northrop, the Rebel troops would either die from starvation or "strangulation with red tape."

Southern Naturists

The Union blockade affected the South's supply of pretty much everything, including gray dye for Confederate uniforms. For a nation in wartime, dye was not the highest priority, so the generals threw aside the idea of standard uniforms and learned to make do with boys wearing whatever color they had. Except *blue*, that is. Johnny Reb in a worn-out jacket might be pleased to find a dead Billy Yank with a jacket his size, but a Rebel soldier in a blue coat was asking for trouble. More than a few Johnny Rebs ended up dead or wounded after making this mistake. But that didn't mean that blue jackets weren't usable. The solution: Dye them another color. Since regular dyes were unavailable, Rebs got creative in changing blue to nonblue, including using *butternut*. And if your Rebel uniform had holes in it, you would do the obvious thing: Patch the holes with blue cloth from a dead Yankee.

Another of the many shortages was soap. Soldiers went for days and even weeks without bathing. While they may have grown accustomed to each other's body odor, grimy sweaty skin didn't help the clothing last longer. Occasional washing would have doubled or tripled the life of coats and pants, but opportunities were few. If time and weather permitted, Rebs might locate a pond or creek and use it for cleaning both body and clothing—but likely as not this might mean just getting wet, not soaping up. Since a soldier was lucky just to have one change of clothes, rinsing them out in water required sitting around buck naked till everything dried. This wasn't always possible, and thus Johnny Reb and his clothing became home to the "soldier's friends," lice.

Sick of the Army

You may have heard this factoid before, but it bears repeating: For every soldier who died as a result of battle, three died from disease. Medicine was still pretty primitive

RebeLingo

Butternut is a name for the homemade yellow-brown dye made from walnut shells used for Confederate uniforms after regular dye became scarce. Soldiers wearing uniforms of this color were also called butternuts. As the months went on, there were more and more boys in butternuts and fewer and fewer in gray. If the Confederacy's official color was gray, its unofficial color was butternut.

Voices from Then

It gets mitey cold at nite here, me and Jamie have to bed down togethur and yet we still shivur. we have not seen sope in months so I ekspect we dont smell too pritty. when I get home to you I will take a long hot bath before I come to bed, you can count on it.

—Letter from an Alabama private to his wife

in those days, with no antibiotics, few anesthetics, and little of the medical equipment we take for granted these days. The Rebel soldiers fared even worse than their counterparts in the Union army, partly because they were underfed and partly because the Union blockade kept needed medicine from reaching the men.

Aside from bad food and lack of food, there was also lack of shelter. When it rained, soldiers got wet, and if you were the typical soldier, you didn't have a raincoat. When you stopped for the night, chances are you didn't have a tent or canopy of any kind (except trees, that is). Yankee soldiers generally had a rubber groundsheet underneath their blankets, but few Rebel boys did, unless they were fortunate enough to acquire one from a dead Yank.

There wasn't an oversupply of blankets among the Rebs, either. In theory you would have one blanket under you, another on top. In practice, you coped with the nights' cold by putting one blanket on the ground (which might be wet) and doubling up with a buddy under his blanket. Sleeping in a wet uniform on muddy ground is not the way to health. Some soldiers preferred to sit all night by the campfire, sometimes falling asleep in a seated position.

We already mentioned the infamous body louse, a familiar but hated companion of the soldier. These weren't the only irritants. The South had a bountiful supply of flies, mosquitoes, fleas, and those irritating skin-infesters called chiggers. Aside from being a major nuisance, insects were also disease transmitters, most notably the malaria-carrying mosquitoes. No one in those days made the connection between "gallinippers" (mosquitoes, that is) and malaria, though they were correct in linking malaria with swamps, which also happened to be mosquitoes' breeding ground.

When soldiers wrote home, they almost inevitably mentioned the *graybacks*. They were also likely to mention *Virginia quick-step*, a.k.a. diarrhea. This sounds to us like a minor complaint, but chronic diarrhea can take its toll on health. Diarrhea had its obvious causes: bad food (including green fruit, which they had no business eating) and bad water. Rebs couldn't always get to pure springs, and in those days none of them understood that the rivers, ponds, and even ditches where they got their drinking water contained all sorts of nasty microscopic creatures.

Diarrhea's nastier second cousin was dysentery, caused by a variety of tiny parasites in the intestines. Dysentery was basically diarrhea with a vengeance, involving severe intestinal pain and passing of blood. Dysentery immobilized many soldiers, and killed many others.

Some diseases that were almost wiped out in the twentieth century were major killers in the 1860s. Probably a fourth of the deaths from disease among Rebel soldiers were from

RebeLingo

Confederate soldiers were extremely creative with names for body lice: **graybacks, rebels, tigers,** and **Bragg's bodyguards.** This last name came from soldiers in the Army of Tennessee, commanded by Gen. Braxton Bragg. But lice were everywhere, not just among Bragg's boys. **Popping corn** referred to getting rid of lice by singeing one's clothes over an open fire. **Fighting under the black flag** referred to killing lice.

typhoid fever. A major epidemic began among troops in late summer 1861, followed by another epidemic a year later. It was no coincidence that both waves followed new inductions of soldiers. Measles today is a fairly minor disease of childhood, but this wasn't so in those days. Many of the young men who joined the army had never had it, and they soon learned that for adults, measles was serious, and sometimes fatal.

Call the Witch Doctor

When you read that people in the 1860s believed that malaria was caused by swamp mists, this gives you some idea of the state of medicine. This notion of malaria's cause is as wrongheaded as the various "cures" for diseases. It is a testimony to the ability of the body to heal itself that soldiers somehow survived not only diseases, but also the misguided attempts to cure them.

We could fill this entire book with a list of the various folk cures for diseases. One all-curing item was, of course, alcohol. Nine tenths of the so-called "medicines" were mostly alcoholic. Medicinally speaking, alcohol was no cure for anything, and probably made some conditions worse. Still, it served as a pain reliever, and it certainly helped many a sick soldier drop off to sleep, which sick folk need a lot of.

One bit of folk wisdom held that wearing the beard long was a way of keeping the chill off throat and neck. Obviously, this was true. It involved no sacrifice on the part of the men, for often they were in circumstances where they couldn't have shaved even if they'd wanted to. When you see photographs of Confederate soldiers and notice the profusion of beards, don't assume this was the style. Chalk it up to lack of hot water, lack of razors, and (maybe) the need for a neck-warmer.

Dr. Death

If you read some of the accounts of Civil War doctors, you will understand why many servicemen had a low opinion of army doctors. A noble few were genuinely wise and genuinely dedicated. "Wise" is a relative term, for even the smartest doctors then were unaware of many of the causes and cures of disease. But for every great physician there were 10 or 20 near-quacks, who probably worked through intuition and blind luck.

Doctors, good or bad, faced drug shortages caused by the blockade. Opium, the best pain reliever of those days, was difficult to get. So was quinine, the usual cure for malaria. Confederate doctors used turpentine and willow-bark extracts as quinine substitutes, and they were at least partially effective.

Out of a Limb

Doctors performed amputations by the thousands, and few were the men who had the luxury of an anesthetic. Amputations were, alas, the most common operations in hospitals and on battlefields. Many a wife or sweetheart saw her Southern boy off to the fields of glory, only to see him return home minus an arm or leg.

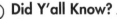

Did Y'all Know?

When Gen. William Bate was wounded at the Battle of Shiloh, doctors insisted on amputating his left leg. How did Bate respond? He drew a pistol on them. They didn't amputate the leg.

Amputations are rare in our day because we can easily treat infected tissue. This wasn't so in the 1860s, when there was a good chance that infected or gangrenous tissue would spread far beyond the wounded area. Surgeons, even the better ones, worked by the rule "When in doubt, throw it out." In the many cases of compound fracture (where a bone is protruding through the skin), amputation was inevitable and immediate.

When a Rebel soldier fired his Minie bullets at the Yanks, he made himself a target for the Yanks' return shots. The Minie bullets might seem primitive by the standards of twenty-first century ballistics, but they were serious killers in those days. The little lead cones picked up bits of skin and clothing before they penetrated the flesh. This was usually skin and clothing that hadn't been washed in many days—in other words, the bullet passed through a couple of layers of germs. If the bullet made its way through the body, it would leave a nasty gaping exit wound (bigger than you would ever guess from looking at a Minie bullet). The bullet inevitably shattered any bone it struck.

If you were wounded, there was a good chance you would bleed to death. If you didn't, there was a good chance you would loose a limb. If you didn't, there was a good chance your wound would result in "hospital gangrene," a bacterial infection that was almost always fatal, or blood poisoning, which also was almost always fatal. Nice, eh?

Still, more Southern soldiers survived the war than died in it. Attribute it to luck, God, folk medicine, a few good surgeons, or whatever. Attribute it to action, too. It sounds illogical, but soldiers and visitors to the camps generally agreed on it: There was more sickness when the men were bored in their camps than when they were actively on the march or in battle.

"Hospital Rats" and Other Cowards

We who are descendants of Confederate soldiers would love to believe they were all heroes. But every army is a mix of heroes, cowards, and in-betweeners. Historians who try hard to be objective generally render this verdict: The South had some of the finest fighting men who ever lived. Having said that, let's look at some of the other guys.

Every regiment had its "Company Q"—meaning the sick list. Men who were frequently on it were known as "hospital rats," though they were called other things we won't bother to print here. One of the problems of medicine in those days was that fakery was harder to detect. If a soldier said he was sick and acted sick, doctors assumed he was being honest. His comrades often knew better. He was "playing old soldier," and they resented it.

Not everyone has the makings of a soldier. At First Manassas, celebrated though the victory was, many Rebs (and Yanks, too) hightailed it to the woods when the guns began firing. No battle in the war was fought without men on both sides hiding out in the woods, in ditches, behind buildings, even in hollow trees.

Sometimes the timid could be shamed or otherwise intimidated by an officer yelling at them; sometimes, but not always. There were times when a pack of cowards didn't mind being called a pack of cowards. Sometimes the

Voices from Then

A panic which I had never before witnessed seemed to have seized upon officers and men, and each seemed to be struggling for his personal safety, regardless of his duty or his character.

—Report of Gen. Braxton Bragg on the Battle of Missionary Ridge, Tennessee

RebeLingo _____

Bucking and gagging was a common punishment of a court-martial. The offender was seated on the ground, hands bound, feet bound, knees drawn up between his arms, with a rod inserted under the knees and over the arms. The "gag" was a stick or bayonet bound sideways into his mouth. He might be forced to sit in this trussed-up pose for several hours. Sound uncomfortable? That was the whole idea.

lemming mentality took hold; if half your regiment was running to the rear, you wouldn't feel much shame in joining the herd.

Cowardice could be as dangerous as facing the enemy. Company and regimental commanders didn't smile upon cowards, and if you ran to the rear, you risked being whacked with the colonel's saber, threatened with being shot—or being shot. Or, following the battle, you were subject to court-martial, which led to some thoroughly degrading punishments such as civilians never endured.

A few other examples of punishment for cowardice: being branded with a red-hot iron on the cheek, hip, or palm with the letter *C*, having one's head shaved (or only half shaved), *bucking and gagging*, being forced to wear a barrel shirt, being shackled with a ball and chain, wearing a placard painted with the word *Coward*, having reduced rations, or forfeiting several months' pay.

Perhaps even worse, your comrades who did *not* flee would make your life a living hell. In a battle where men in your company bled to death on the field, or bled to death afterward, or suffered amputations, or were blinded or maimed, wouldn't the survivors look askance at the cowardly scum who ran and hid?

We have no statistics on such matters, but we do have the assurance of some historians who have studied the matter closely: Cowards were definitely in the minority in the Confederate Army.

The Least You Need to Know

- Food shortages affected Rebel soldiers almost from the beginning of the war, but soldiers became creative cooks.

- Lucius Northrop, in charge of supplying the Confederate Army, became one of the chief villains of the Confederacy.

- Many more soldiers died from disease than battle, mostly due to the primitive state of medicine in those days.

- Unpleasant conditions inevitably led to cowards who fled the battlefield, but these were a minority among Rebel troops.

Chapter 14

Johnny Reb Playing and Praying

In This Chapter

- ◆ The postal lifeline home
- ◆ Creative playtime in the Rebel camps
- ◆ Singing the blue (soldiers) away
- ◆ The naughtier side of soldiering
- ◆ Buckling on the Bible belt

Soldiers spend most of their time not fighting, which saves a lot of blood but also leads to boredom. The better officers could see to it that the men didn't run out of things to do. Drilling was always a useful (if tedious) activity. Latrines and trenches had to be dug, along with all the other grunt work that goes with soldiering. Still, there was time left over, and thousands of young Southern men had more free time than they expected when they joined up.

Farm boys found themselves engaged in that old agricultural pursuit of sowing wild oats. Some of it was good clean fun, some of it was best kept hidden from the folks back home. Some of it was downright dangerous. All of it showed that a war and a bunch of Yankees weren't going to stop

Southern boys from having a jolly old time. (On the other hand, war wouldn't stop them from praying, either.)

The Envelope, Please

One obvious way to pass the time was letter writing, something the officer encouraged and which most soldiers gladly did, for many were homesick. The Confederate government was kind in this matter: Soldiers could send their letters out for free, provided the envelope showed their name, company, and regiment. (The postage wasn't totally free—the recipient had to pay it when he or she got the letter.)

Letters are probably our best source of knowledge about the Rebel soldiers. Most of them had no idea that anyone in the twenty-first century would be reading their letters, so they let their hair down, admitting to their homesickness, airing their grievances about camp life, arrogant officers, and so on. There was always the chance that a fellow soldier would grab a letter from home, read it aloud, and cause some embarrassment—particularly a letter from a sweetheart.

Voices from Then

My dearest Nancy, be careful what you write me in your next letter, becauze Cpl. Norris has a habit of reading things out loud to our whole company, and your last letter made me blush a lot, especially after Norris read it several times to the boys. They have been teasing me something fierce and calling me Romeo and asking me why it is that you and me dont have a hundred younguns already.

—A Georgia soldier to his wife

Not all the Rebel soldiers were practiced at letter writing. Part of the pleasure of reading their letters are the misspellings and fractured grammar. Some of the less literate boys would have a friend write letters for them—and read aloud the responses when they arrived. The less literate among the soldiers' letters are a pleasure in themselves, since we know the writers were being so direct—not using words to impress, but just to communicate at the most basic level.

At the beginning of the war, Johnny Reb wasn't yet worn down or complaining excessively. He was the "accidental tourist," sent to a place far from his home, seeing new sights, meeting new people (some of them with guns pointed at him)—in short, full of tales to tell the folks back home. Many of the letters betray a certain amount of traveler vanity—the worldly soldier speaking of new things to the less traveled family back in the sticks.

Griping was an essential feature, however. Whatever the soldier griped about in camp, he had plenty of fellow gripers among his mess mates. But there was something special about sharing complaints with Mama and Papa and the Missus. Johnny Reb liked to get things off his chest, which made him feel better and assured the home folks that he wasn't just away on a shooting vacation.

Voices from Then

We wuz marchin down a durt rode yestiddy when we herd some shootin and we figgered the yankees wuz about to git us but it wudnt nuthin but a farmer out shootin some duvs fer hiz supper. I am sorry I hav nuthin to tell you about a battel yet but when there is wun I will hav lots to tell if I liv threw it.
—A soldier from Tennessee

Johnny relied on letters from home to keep him informed, not only of news of the village but news of the world, too. And aside from getting news, the main point was: Please let me know you're thinking about me while I'm away. (If you think the term "sensitive men" was invented in the last few years, you'll change your mind when you read the emotional letters of these boys.)

Other Things to Read

With so many farm boys making up the troops, you might assume Johnny Reb wasn't much of a reader. It's true there weren't many real bookworms among the soldiers, but Johnny did like to read, and not just letters from home. Newspapers were eagerly looked for in the camps, and there was a good chance its pages would be literally worn apart by the time it got passed around.

Books were popular, though soldiers on the march weren't too eager to weight themselves down with too much baggage. Aside from the Bible, and maybe some religious tracts, the average Johnny carried no books with him. But it wasn't unusual for someone in the company to carry a novel for reading aloud to a group. Typically this was not heavy or demanding stuff—for soldiers, escapist literature seemed just right. French author Victor Hugo's new novel *Les Miserables*, was popular, and the title morphed into a slang term for Southern soldiers: Lee's Miserables.

Particularly popular were the historical novels of Sir Walter Scott, who wrote *Ivanhoe* and other classics. Many Southerners, especially the aristocrats, saw themselves as the gallant knights of Scott's tales—chivalrous and courtly, nothing like the boorish, crude, small-minded Yankee scum. It was from Scott's novels that Southerners borrowed the name *Southron*, which meant "Southerners."

Games Rebels Play

In our age of computer games, we forget how important card playing was to earlier times. It certainly was a feature of camp life. Considering the low pay of soldiers, there was a fair amount of playing for fun, since there wasn't much money to gamble with. (But people are creative when it comes to gambling, of course. They gambled for tobacco, food, ink, whatever.) Besides using the standard deck of cards, there were new Confederate decks, with the kings being Jefferson Davis and some of the high-ranking generals. (When cards became scarcer during the war, an obvious source for a new deck was the Yankee you just shot.)

Rebel soldiers played baseball, or at least a version of it, early in the war. Soldiers also played "townball," a sort of two-base baseball. There was no regulation equipment to be had, of course. For a bat, any board (or fence rail stolen from a farmer) would do. The ball might be whatever was remotely spherical in shape, such as a nut or peach pit wrapped up in thread.

Bowling, usually called by its old name of ten-pins, was fairly common. Again, there was no regulation equipment, but a lot of improvising. The ball was typically a cannonball. (No point in letting them go to waste if there was no battle, right?) Pins were whatever was at hand—bottles, tree limbs whittled to the right shape—or, instead of aiming at pins, aiming at a hole dug in the ground.

Some of mankind's oldest games require no equipment at all. Rebs engaged in plenty of these—foot races, wrestling, boxing, swimming races, and so on.

Singin' the Blues Away

In theory, every regiment had its own band. In fact, few did. A regiment considered itself lucky to have a bugler and a drummer, and they were for use in battle, not for entertainment. Still, humans are musical by nature, and inevitably there was music in the Confederate camps, and even while marching.

Anyone who ever attended summer camp knows that campfires and singing go together. Much of the singing was unaccompanied, which was fine. If the regiment was lucky, it might have a fiddler or banjo player. These were probably the two most popular instruments, and a fiddle-banjo duet was considered ideal. (The guitar was still relatively new in America, and not widely used.)

Whether there was musical accompaniment or not, Rebel soldiers sang—at night around the campfires, while digging trenches, or while marching. After the war, veterans said that "The Yellow Rose of Texas" was probably the favorite marching song, but there were a hundred others to lighten the burden of a march. Some were old favorites—after all, war makes people nostalgic for happier days. But the war put Southerners in a lyrical mood, and some of the songs bear witness to man's ability to make light of a bad situation.

Did Y'all Know?

I don't believe we can have an army without music.

—Robert E. Lee

For example, the song "I Can Whip the Scoundrel":

> The Yankees took me prisoner, and if I get paroled,
> I'll go right back and fight 'em—I will upon my soul!
> So lay ten dollars down—or twenty if you choose—
> For I can whip the Yankee that stole ole Abner's shoes.

Shoe stealing was a common practice of both Rebels and Yanks. A dead soldier has no need of shoes, and if your own shoes were wearing out, why not? The song's words are kind of ironic, because it was the Rebels who were more hard up for shoes than the Yanks. The song implies that the Yankee stole poor Abner's shoes just for spite, not because they were needed. This is "gallows humor," of course—there is nothing funny about being captured or seeing one's soldier buddy killed (and robbed after the killing). But people need such songs to help them survive. If you laugh at death and prison, some of the fear subsides.

Not all the Rebel songs were bouncy spirit lifters. Homesickness and fear of death were never far from the Southerners' minds, even if the lighter songs made them forget, temporarily. One of the most popular songs in that vein was "Just Before the Battle, Mother," by Yankee songwriter George F. Root. The song contains no direct references to Rebs or Yanks, so both sides sang it.

> Just before the battle, Mother,
> I am thinking most of you,
> While upon the field we're watching
> With the enemy in view.
> Comrades brave round me lying,
> Filled with thoughts of home and God
> For well they know that on the morrow
> Some will sleep beneath the sod.

"Far from home" often meant "far from women." Not surprisingly, some of the most popular songs involved pining away for one's wife or sweetheart. Probably the most popular song of the Rebel soldier was the slow but melodic "Lorena," a lament about separation and a hope for a future together "up there." Such songs might have reminded Johnny Reb that he took his women for granted while he was back home. It probably wasn't unusual for a Johnny to sing "Lorena" by the fireside, get a little teary-eyed, then scribble off a letter to his darling before going to sleep.

Bad, Bad Boys

Not all of Johnny Reb's pastimes were G-rated. Take young men away from the watchful eye of parents, wives, and pastors, and they will misbehave a little—or a lot.

The average soldier had little money to gamble with, but that didn't stop it from happening. Gambling is, for some, a painful addiction, and some gamblers would stoop to stealing from fellow soldiers to finance their habit. Soldiers would gamble not only for money but for watches, knives, even articles of clothing. The generals frequently issued prohibitions against gambling, but these were about as effective as speed limits are today.

> **Did Y'all Know?**
>
> The old joke about drinking "for medicinal purposes" wasn't a joke in the 1860s. People had no pain-relieving medications as we do today, so drinking wasn't always for the purpose of getting a buzz, but for dulling pain.

During the Big Lull that followed the Manassas victory, officers noticed an increase of drinking. (Quite a few officers were notorious boozers themselves.) Boredom and drinking go together. Many soldiers who had been teetotalers or moderate drinkers in civilian life found themselves drinking more in the camps. Prohibitions against drunkenness were about as effective as those against gambling.

In spite of the war department's frequent complaints about drunkenness, the army actually did ration whiskey to soldiers—in small amounts, of course.

"The delightful weed" so loved by the soldiers was tobacco. Johnny Reb usually chewed his 'backy or smoked a pipe (cigars being expensive, and cigarettes being an odd new item). These were days before surgeon generals and fretting about lung cancer and heart disease, so smoking and chewing were guilt-free pastimes. As the war dragged on, soldiers chronically complained about the scarcity of tobacco, which was rationed by the army. The rationed tobacco of 1864 was so bad that soldiers complained that a goat wouldn't chew it. This was rather ironic, considering that almost all American tobacco was grown in the South. (Chalk it up to the chronic transportation problem: plenty of tobacco in North Carolina and Virginia, but lousy transport to the boys in Georgia and Texas.)

The Army's Female Buzzards

One Richmond newspaper compared prostitutes to buzzards and vultures—creatures that followed armies around. The difference was that the prostitutes were looking for *live* bodies.

Where there are soldiers, there will be prostitutes. This was certainly true in the cities, and especially so in Richmond, since so many soldiers were stationed nearby. (Richmond was also full of politicians, so we can assume it wasn't just the soldiers who kept the whores in business.)

The South had been the Bible Belt for a long time, and most Southern boys had probably been taught a pretty conservative moral code. It's probably safe to assume that in 1861 the average Southern boy was a virgin when he married (ditto for the bride). But soldiering did nothing to encourage the morality taught by Maw and Paw and the preacher, and more than a few soldiers took advantage of the situation, enjoying what was called "horizontal refreshment."

Troops could enjoy pleasures of the flesh even when they were far from any city, however. A nearby prostitute might ply her trade in her own tent or in an abandoned house. And every regiment had its camp followers, including women who were paid to do such chores as laundry or sewing. But many of the "laundresses" and "seamstresses" were prostitutes, and officers began to be concerned about their effects on the men.

There was serious concern about venereal diseases, which were not easily cured in those days. A host of diseases afflicted Johnny Reb, and everyone knew that venereal disease could be controlled ("Just say no!"). There was also the money problem: Men not only wasted their pay on prostitutes, but resorted to stealing to pay for it as well.

> **Voices from Then**
>
> Go on the Capitol Square any afternoon and you may see these women promenading up and down the shady walks, jostling respectable ladies into the gutters.
>
> —The mayor of Richmond, 1864

The Regiment That Prays Together

Johnny Reb may have loosened up his Bible belt, but he didn't discard it. Even without parent or pastor nearby, most of them had the feeling that somebody (God, maybe?) was watching, both in the positive sense (protection) and the negative (keeping account of sins). Most of the boys probably left their homes with a Bible—either one they'd owned for years, or one thoughtfully provided by mother, girlfriend, or church. Whether they read it might depend on their homesickness or the nearness of battle.

It's an old truism that there are no atheists in foxholes—or "rifle pits," as they were called in those days. Faith has a way of declining when things are going smoothly, thriving when things are not. In the first year of war, visitors to Rebel encampments commented on the soldiers' swearing, drunkenness, and gambling—behavior that the

same boys would likely not have engaged in had they been home. (Visitors would have commented on the prostitution, too, had they been aware of it.) Who was there to remind the Johnny Rebs to behave themselves—for their own spiritual welfare, and for the good of the cause they were fighting for?

As of May 1861, Jefferson Davis had the authority to appoint military chaplains, to be paid $85 per month (but quickly modified to $50 per month, then back to $80 in a few months). Since the typical preacher of those days was married with children (often several), leaving home to play chaplain might mean deprivation for his family. Some ministers served a while as chaplains, then were forced by finances to return home.

The chaplains didn't have an easy life (not that they expected one). They ate the same rations as the soldiers. They had a mix of duties: preaching, consoling the dying or wounded, writing to families of the sick or dead, and writing letters for barely literate soldiers. If there was fighting, the chaplain aided the wounded—or, in some cases, he fought.

Johnny Reb coped with camp life in different ways. He engaged in some good clean foolishness and horseplay, and he engaged in some seamier capers that might have made him blush in his prewar days. He also, at times, prayed and read his Bible. The playing and praying didn't necessarily contradict each other. Both were ways of coping with a life away from hearth and home, and with a war that grew steadily longer and nastier. To survive, he needed both faith and fellowship.

The Least You Need to Know

◆ Letter writing was a prime pastime of soldiers, and also our best source of information about them.

◆ Soldiers were creative in coming up with games, songs, and other pastimes in the camp.

◆ Drunkenness, gambling, and prostitution were common enough to gain the attention of the government in Richmond.

◆ Chaplains worked to provide spiritual guidance and lift up both morale and morals.

Chapter 15

Seeking the Military Messiah

In This Chapter

- ◆ Beauregard's falling star
- ◆ Davis's ideal general
- ◆ Retreatin' Joe meets Virginia Creeper
- ◆ Lee called to life
- ◆ The odd, amazing Jackson fellow

The jubilation over the Manassas victory of July 1861 had faded. It was clear that Lincoln and the Yankee masses weren't going to just give up and go away. As 1861 turned into 1862, the Rebels knew that the Federal army was creating a massive war machine, a machine with more human fuel than the Confederacy could hope to possess. Was it still possible to whip the Yankees hard enough to make them retreat northward for good? Many Southerners still thought so.

After all, the South still had some fine fighting men—not just the officers, but the Johnny Rebs themselves, who, despite getting discouraged now and then, still had the will to whip the Yanks good. And what about those generals? Was there one among them—or several—who could be the South's military Messiah?

What Became of Bory?

Old Bory, the Grand Creole, Gen. P. G. T. Beauregard, was the hero of Fort Sumter *and* the hero of Manassas. Soldiers idolized him; women showered him with letters, flowers, and clothing. (After the war, when Federal agents were combing through Bory's personal papers, they were amazed at the huge stash of letters from female admirers.) In the fall of 1861, if people had predicted who the Great Confederate Hero would be, many would have picked Beauregard. We now know this wasn't so. What happened to the Louisiana plantation snob to dim his star?

Beauregard was a legend in his own mind. He looked down on most people, and that included Jefferson Davis. In between Fort Sumter and Manassas, Davis had made a request of Bory: Since you were so good at booting the Federals out of Fort Sumter, go to Florida and boot them out of Fort Pickens. Old Bory didn't like the idea and said so. Davis never liked egomaniacs, particularly insubordinate ones, but he didn't punish Beauregard—yet.

> **Voices from Then**
>
> File this Beauregard quote under "Hypocrisy" or "Serious Self-Delusion":
>
> I have my faults and my deficiencies, but, thank God, selfishness and ambition form no part of my nature.

Even earlier, in the aftermath of his Manassas victory, Bory overstepped himself. Reporting on the battle to the Confederate Congress, he claimed that the president had scotched his plan for following up Manassas with an assault on Washington. (This wasn't so. Davis had urged the pursuit, but both Bory and Joe Johnston said no.) Davis countered, publicly, that Bory was trying to exalt himself at Davis's expense. This didn't bode well for Bory's future. Davis chose to slap the wrist of the little egotist by sending him west and putting him under the command of a less vain (and more Davis-friendly) general, Albert Sidney Johnston.

Had Bory used a bit more tact with the Confederate commander in chief, perhaps he would have fared better. As it is, history remembers him as a pretty competent general who happened to be on the scene at two key points in American history: Fort Sumter and First Manassas. And unlike several generals in both South and North, Old Bory really did like to fight.

Named for "The Liberator"

Old Bory wasn't sent west just as punishment. The western regions—Kentucky and Tennessee, to be specific—needed some aggressive generals, for the Yanks were pressing hard in this area.

Simon Bolivar Buckner was a Kentucky boy, a West Point graduate, and, like so many Civil War generals, a Mexican War veteran. He owned no slaves and hoped to keep Kentucky neutral when war erupted in 1861, but this was not to be. Buckner refused a commission in the U.S. Army *and* the Confederate Army. What prompted him to shift out of neutral was Kentucky's Unionist-dominated legislature's order to expel all Confederate troops from the state. Buckner happened to be head of the Kentucky militia. He asked Kentuckians to "defend their homes against the invasion of the North." Under suspicion of being a traitor, he fled south, where the Confederacy made him a brigadier general. Much of the Kentucky militia, being pro-Southern, went with Buckner, a package deal that pleased the Confederacy.

Did Y'all Know? _____

Simón Bolívar, the South American freedom fighter known as the Liberator, was widely admired in the United States, and Buckner was one of many sons named in his honor.

Did Y'all Know? _____

Kentucky being "neutral" really meant "divided." Henry Clay, the Great Compromiser in Congress, had seven grandsons in Kentucky. Four sided with the South, three with the North.

At West Point, one of Buckner's pals had been U. S. Grant. Between West Point and the Civil War, Buckner had encountered a boozy, depressed (and broke) Grant living in a dingy San Francisco hotel called the What Cheer House. Buckner gave his old buddy money to pay for his hotel room. They were to meet again in Tennessee in 1862, with Grant paying back the debt in a memorable fashion.

In 1862, no one expected much from Grant, but he surprised quite a few people when he advanced on the vital riverfront Forts Henry and Donelson in Tennessee. The 2 forts—Henry on the Tennessee River, Donelson on the Cumberland River—were only 11 miles apart, both of them guarding the water routes into Kentucky, Tennessee, and north Alabama. They were a gateway into the mid-South. Grant took Fort Henry without much resistance, and he expected little from Donelson, for he knew its commander, General John Floyd, and considered him an imbecile (as did many other people). Grant also knew Gideon Pillow, Floyd's second in command, and he knew both men were political generals with not much will to fight. When Grant was on the verge of capturing Fort Donelson, Floyd chose to flee, passing on the command of the fort to Pillow, who also opted to flee and passed the command on to … Simon Bolivar Buckner.

Buckner, the third in command now elevated to top banana, sent a message to Grant, requesting a parley to lay out terms for surrendering the fort. Grant gained his famous nickname when he demanded "no terms except unconditional and immediate surrender." No doubt peeved that his past kindness was cutting no ice with Grant, Buckner sent a message that conditions "compel me to accept the ungenerous and unchivalrous terms which you propose." U. S. Grant was now Unconditional Surrender Grant.

Consider the exchange between Buckner and Grant. Grant spoke of "unconditional surrender." Buckner then accused Grant of being "ungenerous and unchivalrous."

> **Go See It!**
>
> Fort Donelson National Battlefield near Dover, Tennessee, is definitely worth a visit. You can see the fort itself and also the Dover Hotel, where Buckner surrendered to Grant.

Buckner was right. At Fort Sumter, Beauregard had treated the Federals with the utmost courtesy. But the old standards of gentlemanly warfare were slipping away. You could no longer assume that a fellow American soldier—and an old friend to boot—would negotiate with you gentleman to gentleman. Buckner had hit the nail on the head, and the Union's generals and tactics would grow progressively more ungenerous and unchivalrous.

Forts Donelson and Henry guarded the Cumberland and Tennessee Rivers. With the two forts captured by the Union, Federal gunboats could now make their way into middle and west Tennessee. The result: Kentucky and much of Tennessee were under the Union's thumb. It would be just a matter of days before Nashville, Tennessee's capital and a thriving industrial and transportation hub, was occupied. There was jubilation in the North at the Union's first major victory in the war.

The Other Johnston

We've already met Gen. Joe Johnston of Virginia in Chapter 12. Now let's meet another high-ranking Johnston.

Albert Sidney Johnston fit everyone's idea of what a general looked like. He was a big man, over 6 feet tall, more than 200 pounds, solidly built, and well proportioned. Like all good Southern gentleman, he was also perfectly charming and courteous, and (not so common among generals) he even had a sense of humor.

He also had military experience—more than any other Confederate general, in fact. He had been a revolutionary general in Texas and (when Texas was its own republic for a while) was its secretary of war under Texas president Sam Houston. He was a distinguished colonel in the Mexican War (Robert E. Lee was his second in command), and the formidable Gen. Winfield Scott called him "a Godsend to the army and to his country."

Johnston, like Davis, was Kentucky-born, but he fell in love with Texas and adopted the Lone Star state as his home. When Texas seceded in 1861, he (like Lee) declined an offer of high rank in the Union army. He happened to be in California, and, along with a band of 30 other Southern-sympathizing officers, he trekked across the vast Southwest to get to Confederate soil. In Richmond, Davis, eager to see him, made him a full general (one of the first in the Confederacy) and offered him the command of the Confederate west. Johnston had the awesome task of defending a line running from Kentucky across Arkansas into Indian Territory, crossed by the Mississippi, Tennessee, and Cumberland Rivers. ("West" in the Confederacy referred to Alabama, Mississippi, and west Tennessee—and everything west of that.)

> **Voices from Then**
>
> In postwar days, Jefferson Davis recalled, "I hoped and expected that I had others who would prove generals, but I knew I had one, and that was Sidney Johnston." On the other hand, some Confederate generals thought Davis seriously overrated his friend. Cranky, outspoken Gen. Dick Ewell stated that Davis's "infatuation" for Johnston was "of the blindest and most unaccountable nature."

U. S. Grant's successes in Tennessee were sledgehammer blows to Confederate morale, and there was an outcry in the South, demanding that Jefferson Davis sack Johnston. But Davis stood by his old friend and believed there was no better man to put in his place at that time. Shortly after in Tennessee, Johnston encountered Grant at a fateful two-day battle called Shiloh, fought April 6 and 7, 1862, and named for a small log church at the battle site.

At a peach orchard at Shiloh, Johnston gave his men a hearty pep talk. The beefy man rose in his stirrups, waved his hat, and cheered them forward with "I will lead you!" The Rebs drove the Yanks out of the orchard. Johnston came riding back, all smiles, but bystanders noticed his pants leg and one boot had been ripped by bullets. Then he reeled in his saddle. One of his aides, Tennessee's governor Isham Harris, rushed to him and asked, "General, are you hurt?" Johnston replied, "Yes, and I fear seriously."

Harris saw that the general's right boot was full of blood. A bullet had pierced his knee and severed the large and vital femoral artery. Johnston's own staff doctor was not at hand, for Johnston had sent him to look after some wounded among the captured: "These men were our enemies a moment ago. They are our prisoners now. Take care of them." The general died, and very quickly. His compassion for his

Did Y'all Know? _____

Johnston was the Confederacy's only full general (four stars, that is) to die in battle. The Texans apparently thought well of him, since his grave in the Texas State Cemetery in Austin is one of the most elaborate tombs of any Confederate.

Did Y'all Know? _____

Shiloh was the first battle in America involving 100,000 men.

Go See It!

Albert Sidney Johnston's son, Col. William Preston Johnston, joined with other Civil War veterans to help establish the national battlefield and cemetery at Shiloh, the site where his father died. Shiloh National Military Park is 10 miles southwest of Savannah, Tennessee. Visitors can see "Bloody Pond" at the battlefield (stained with dye, not real blood, of course).

wounded enemies had led to his own death. Johnston has gone down in history as a great what-if, since no one knows how the Confederacy might have fared if he had lived.

With Johnston dead, command passed to Beauregard. Old Bory wired Richmond that Shiloh was a Rebel victory—an exaggeration, to say the least. (It was really a draw, though it is usually listed as a Union victory.) Formerly the South's darling and the hero of Southern newspapers, Bory found himself mocked regarding his "victory" at Shiloh. One paper carried the ditty, "Here's to General Beauregard / Who for the truth has no regard." The Confederacy's first military hero had slipped. In her famous diary, Mary Chesnut wrote that "Cock Robin is as dead as he will ever be now."

Davis blamed Beauregard for not pursuing the Federals. Bory's order for his frazzled troops to rest instead of pursuing the Yankees was perhaps the most fateful order of his life, for it permanently soured Davis. But Bory had good reason to rest the men: They had fought almost 12 hours nonstop and were almost out of ammo. Still, since Bory had survived the battle while Johnston had died, Bory got the blame. Johnston's postmortem reputation soared, while Bory's sank. Not long after the battle, Beauregard took a leave of absence due to a chronic throat ailment. Davis took advantage of this, turning the western army over to Braxton Bragg. (More about the luckless Bragg later.)

More was lost at Shiloh than General Johnston. Of the 100,000 soldiers engaged in the 2-day bloodbath, almost 24,000 were dead, wounded, or missing. The Union lost about 13,000, the Confederacy about 11,000. It was the bloodiest battle of the war up till then. Wounded Rebs and Yanks crawled to a small pond for a drink, dyeing the water red with their blood. Civilians in the area got their first look at war gore, with hotels, schools, and churches swiftly converted into hospitals, and dead or dying soldiers laid out on porches and depot platforms. Piles of amputated arms and legs horrified people who expected the war would be quickly fought and relatively bloodless. Reality was beginning to sink in.

Shiloh had been a valiant attempt by Johnston and his Rebs to drive the Yankees from middle and west Tennessee, areas they had held since capturing Forts Donelson and Henry. The Rebs failed, though they would be back for more fights. Shiloh, the battle the Yanks called Pittsburg Landing, was a major blow to Southern morale.

Retreatin' Joe

Back to the other Johnston, Joseph E. Recall that he and Beauregard were both heroes after Manassas. Joe Johnston, at his best, looked every inch a military commander, the distinguished Uncle Joe—small in size, but plucky, ready to fight. Too bad for the Confederacy that he wasn't much of a fighter. One of his soldiers claimed after the war that, under Joe's care, "We never missed a meal and never fought a battle." It's an exaggeration, but has some truth at its core.

Johnston had been a good friend of Lee. The friendship was an inheritance, for Johnston's father had served under Lee's father, "Light Horse Harry" Lee, in the Revolution. Joseph E. and Robert E. graduated in the same West Point class, its only two Virginians. The historians enjoy speculating that, though the two were friends, Johnston was jealous of Lee.

The Manassas victory garnered him much praise. It led to President Jefferson Davis making him a full general, along with four others. Joe ranked fourth among the five—after Lee, of course. Uncle Joe wouldn't let the matter lie. He exchanged catty letters with Davis and other Confederate officials. Why, he asked, did Lee and Albert Sidney Johnston outrank him, when "neither has yet struck a blow for this Confederacy"? (Considering that Davis practically worshipped A. S. Johnston, Uncle Joe's criticism of him was rash.) Johnston became the hub of the widening circle of people who had a beef against Jefferson Davis.

Voices from Then

In her readable, gossippy diary, Mary Chesnut referred to Joe Johnston as the "polar star" of the anti-Davis clique. She described him as "such a good hater, it is a pity he had not elected to hate somebody else than the president of our country."

War reality intervened in a dramatic way: Uncle Joe was seriously wounded at Seven Pines, Virginia. (More about that later.) With him out of commission for several months—and with Lee chalking up one victory after another—the question of who outranked whom was easy to answer.

Did Lee Disappear?

Did you think we'd forgotten about Robert E. Lee? No chance. The man who could have had command of the Union armies wasn't going to go unused by the Confederacy. But for the first few months of the war, Lee was probably *under*used. For months he worked in Richmond as Jefferson Davis's informal military adviser. Some time would pass before he became "Marse Robert," the gray god.

Early in the war he made little impression as a field commander. He was forced to abandon western Virginia to the Federals, and he took some criticism for it. But it was during this sojourn in the western counties that he grew his famous beard, which came in gray, adding a distinguished, patriarchal touch to the handsome man.

Skeptics called him "Granny Lee" and claimed he was riding on the Lee name and his classy appearance, not on his abilities as a fighter. He was reputed to be a mere paper shuffler in the Confederate bureaucracy.

Still, the classy, well-mannered, sweet-natured man didn't fail to impress. Richmonders loved him. The observant diarist Mary Chesnut heard him called the "first gentleman of Virginia," and she concurred. But she said she doubted anyone really knew the handsome, dignified Robert E. Lee, "so cold, quiet, and grand." Perhaps it didn't matter if anyone "knew" him. He was someone to admire deeply, and there are never enough of those in the world.

During the time Joe Johnston was in command of the primary Confederate Army in Virginia, Lee played the needed role of mediator between the high-strung Johnston and the high-strung Davis. Lee probably wondered if the two were more concerned about winning the war or fondling their own egos. Lee managed to keep his mind on the main goal: keeping a high-strung Yankee egotist, George McClellan, from capturing Richmond.

Did Y'all Know?

Not everyone was impressed by Lee. Col. Thomas R. R. Cobb of Georgia described Lee as "haughty and boorish and supercilious in his bearing and is particularly so to me." But Cobb was notoriously hypersensitive, and he eventually became an admirer of Lee.

Little Mac Attack

At age 34, George B. McClellan was commander of the Union's armies. Thanks to Lincoln's call for thousands upon thousands of men, "Little Mac" had plenty of material to work with. By early 1862, he had whipped an army into shape, making thousands of green recruits look like real soldiers. Many of his men were proud to be part of what they called "McClellan's Army." But it was *not* apparent that he would ever make his soldiers fight. Lincoln grew fidgety, and in January 1862 issued his notorious President's General War Orders No. 1, announcing that as of February, the Union army would actually attack Confederates in Virginia.

Little Mac was noted for dawdling (which gained him another nickname, the "Virginia Creeper"). Historians suspect that if Mac had been more of a fighter than a drill instructor, the Union armies could have triumphed in 1862 instead of 1865—a shorter war, less loss of life and property, less time in healing the nation.

The North was cheering Mac on with the cry "On to Richmond!" But the Creeper's attitude seemed to be "I'll get there when I'm damn good and ready!"—and he usually wasn't ready. Mac seemed so afraid of charging in half-cocked that he seldom charged in at all.

> **Voices from Then**
>
> A notable quote from Lincoln, regarding McClellan: "If the general is through marching the army around, I'd like to borrow it for awhile."

> **RebeLingo**
>
> The **Peninsula** is that part of eastern Virginia lying between the James and Rappahannock rivers. The various battles between McClellan's troops and the Rebels between March and August 1862 are known as the **Peninsula Campaign**.

He did have a sound and simple plan: Ship his blue-clad masses (about 105,000 of them) to Federal-held Fort Monroe at the tip of the Virginia *Peninsula*, where there were only 17,000 Confederate soldiers. March the Yanks up the Peninsula, capture Richmond—voilà!—end of war, glory for Mac. Like every plan, it sounded wonderful.

But Little Mac always believed the enemy was stronger than it appeared. He believed the vastly inflated reports of Confederate strength sent to him by the Union's spy chief, Allan Pinkerton. (The phrase "vastly superior numbers," used to refer to the Confederates, crops up more than once in his dispatches.) The Rebs used this to their advantage. On the Peninsula, the Confederates under Gen. John Magruder numbered only about 17,000. But Magruder used "Quaker guns" (logs painted to look like cannons) to fool Little Mac (with over 105,000 men) into thinking the Rebels numbered 100,000.

Standing in the way of "Paranoid Mac" was "Retreatin' Joe" Johnston, both of them men who apparently preferred that war be bloodless. Johnston began withdrawing the Rebels up the Peninsula, leaving much of the Tidewater region to be occupied by

McClellan's Union troops. In late May 1862, Johnston's troops were near the outskirts of Richmond, and Richmonders went into a tizzy. The politicians proved how brave they were by adjourning Congress and buying tickets on southbound trains.

Then God, or nature, or both, seemed to smile on the Confederacy: Torrential spring rains had washed away some river bridges, isolating two Union corps, giving Johnston a grand opportunity to strike hard. He did, and in what was called the Battle of Seven Pines (May 31 to June 1), Johnston himself was wounded. It was one of the most fateful wounds in Confederate history, for he was replaced with Robert E. Lee.

Did Y'all Know? _____

Robert E. Lee's favorite horse was the magnificent Traveller—probably the best-known horse of the Civil War. Traveller's original name was very political: "Jeff Davis."

Little Mac himself was rattled at all the bloodshed, and Seven Pines apparently strengthened his resolve to avoid battle if at all possible. He would not be able to, for Lee was quite a different man from Retreatin' Joe Johnston.

Lee took charge of all the Confederate forces around Richmond, which took the name of the Army of Northern Virginia. (The old name, Army of the Potomac, got dropped because George McClellan's Union forces also happened to be called Army of the Potomac.) Needing the best men he could find to keep McClellan away from Richmond, he called upon that quirky, devout, and very aggressive general who had made a name for himself at Manassas, Thomas "Stonewall" Jackson.

Tom Fool

February 1862 was not kind to the Confederacy. The Federals captured Forts Henry and Donelson in Tennessee, as we already noted, and on February 25 they occupied Nashville, the first Confederate capital to fall to the Union. Earlier, on the Atlantic coast, they captured North Carolina's Roanoke Island—notable because it was an amphibious assault involving 100 ships and 15,000 Union men. It was a small victory, but together with the gains in Tennessee it raised Northern morale and set Southerners to groaning.

One who did not groan was the former professor at Virginia Military Institute, Thomas J. "Stonewall" Jackson. It was not his style to groan or gripe. After all, God was in control of everything. His favorite Bible verse was Romans 8:28: "We know that all things work together for good to them that love God." Believing that wholeheartedly, Jackson, a deacon at the Lexington Presbyterian Church, didn't worry. He only did his duty, which was fighting Yankees. "Duty is ours, consequences are God's," as he said.

Jackson took the Sabbath seriously and announced that Sunday was off-limits for fighting—although he could be persuaded to fight "more ordinary battles" on Sunday. ("I always try to keep the Sabbath, if the enemy will let me.") His fellow Virginia general A. P. Hill—the two men had a longstanding feud—called him "that crazy old Presbyterian fool," but he admitted the fool could fight.

The people who knew him didn't believe he was odd because of his faith. There were plenty of other praying, Bible-reading, nondrinking, nonswearing men in the Southern army. But

> ### Go See It!
>
> Lexington, Virginia, is "Stonewall" land. You can visit his home, his gravesite, the Lexington Presbyterian Church (where the pew where he sat is marked), and the Virginia Military Institute (VMI), which has several Jackson artifacts in its museum, including his horse (stuffed, that is). A statue of Jackson stands on VMI's parade ground.

Jackson had other qualities that struck people as peculiar. He was obsessive about diet and exercise at a time when no one else was. He frustrated hostesses by showing up at dinner parties with his own food—usually plain bread. Or, he would dine at home on his own boring fare, then show up for dinner and only drink water. The hypochondriac was convinced that practically every sort of food gave him dyspepsia (the generic name in the 1800s for stomach troubles). He told one hostess, "The moment a grain of black pepper touches my tongue, I lose all strength in my right leg." He would have fit in well with today's food-and-fitness fanatics.

Thomas J. Jackson (1824–1863), "Old Jack," "Tom Fool," but better known as "Stonewall."

His VMI cadets had found him amusing or detestable, or both. "Tom Fool" was one of the more polite nicknames the VMI cadets bestowed on him. One student tried (but failed) to drop a brick on Jackson's head. Another challenged Jackson to a duel, but the duel never materialized. In one of the war's many ironies, that student later fought under Jackson and became one of his ardent admirers. Professor Jackson did become more animated when teaching his favorite subject, artillery, which happened to be the one subject he was genuinely qualified to teach.

> **Voices from Then**
>
> He was the most tender, affectionate and demonstrative man at home that I ever saw. His heart was as soft as a woman's.
>
> —Mary Anna Jackson, wife of "Stonewall"

His cadets never knew the *other* Jackson, the doting husband who turned into a bowl of mush around his wife, Anna (a preacher's daughter, as was his first wife, who had died). He referred to her as "my sunshine" and "my little pet dove." He adored children and loved to romp with them. Jackson, orphaned at an early age, wanted nothing more than a stable home life. He had only a short time of it in Lexington before the war began.

Jackson, like so many other Civil War generals, was a Mexican War vet. He had fallen in love with Mexico, developing a taste for tropical fruits that he never lost. He attended fiestas, danced, even toyed with the idea of becoming a Catholic. And he developed a fondness for Spanish, considering it the most romantic language, which is why he used it often in letters to his wife. He read the Bible in Spanish and French as well as English.

A Ball of Contradictions

Jackson was a multifaceted character, which is why he continues to fascinate people. Some have puzzled over how such a stern, disciplined, demanding character could also take pains to see that his men were comfortable and well fed. (Jackson said, "I never wish to fare better than my men," and he meant it.) They have puzzled over how a devout Christian could be so aggressive in battle.

> **Did Y'all Know?**
>
> After the war, his wife recalled that "nothing was so certain to him as that a protracted struggle would wear the South out. He believed that we had but one hope, and that was to press the Federals at every point, blindly, furiously, madly."

Aggressive he was, to the hilt. Remember that after Manassas he wanted to press on to Washington. ("An army routed, if hotly pursued, becomes panic-stricken, and can then be destroyed by half their number.") In fact, "Press on, press on!" became his military motto, as many of his soldiers remembered after the war. Jackson had his oddities, but he sized up the South's situation pretty well. He knew it was outmanned and outresourced. But it could still win its independence: "We must give the enemy no time to think. We must bewilder them and keep them bewildered. Our fighting must be sharp, impetuous, continuous. We cannot stand a long war."

This was not the stance of the Davis administration, however. Davis had said in his first inaugural address that the South only wished to be left alone. Following this line of thought, he tried to get the South to fight a *defensive* war. He had his reasons for such an approach, one being to convince other nations that the South was just defending itself. But Jackson knew it was a losing strategy.

When Lee ordered him to Richmond in June 1862, Jackson had just completed a stellar "diversionary operation" known as the Shenandoah Valley Campaign. In barely a month the man the soldiers had come to refer to as "Old Jack" had caught the world's attention. Jackson's aim had been to tie up Union forces in Virginia's Shenandoah Valley and thus keep them away from Richmond. He did so with a vengeance, marching his infantrymen so swiftly that they became known as the "foot cavalry," marching 400 miles in 6 weeks, fighting 5 major battles, and driving 3 Union generals crazy.

Jackson's habit of keeping his plans to himself drove his subordinates to distraction. Richard Ewell—"Bald Dick"—swore time and time again that Jackson was "mad as a March hare." But Ewell changed his tune as the men won battle after battle. Jackson had said that "mystery, mystery is the secret of success."

Maybe there was another secret: He had no vanity. Showered with gifts and kisses from the Valley residents who were calling him "Savior," Jackson blushed, but his ego didn't inflate. His modesty was part of his "look," and people learned to like it. Slouchy uniform, oversized feet, his visor pulled down so low his eyes were barely visible—quirkiness that was tolerable because he won battles. No pettiness, no vanity, just a lot of fight, a lot of brilliant battle plans, and a lot of praying.

The Least You Need to Know

- In early 1862, an enlarged and well-trained Union army menaced the Confederacy in both Tennessee and Virginia.

- The loss of Forts Donelson and Henry in Tennessee was a major blow to Southern morale.

- The bloody Battle of Shiloh in Tennessee caused the death of Albert Sidney Johnston and a major blow to P. G. T. Beauregard's reputation.

- ◆ Richmond was threatened by Union armies led by the slow-moving George McClellan, facing troops commanded by Joe Johnston, then the more competent Robert E. Lee.

- ◆ Lee called to his aid the brilliant Stonewall Jackson, who had become a hero thanks to his military success in Virginia's Shenandoah Valley.

Chapter 16

Rebs Ahoy!

In This Chapter

- The Confederates' quest for a sea monster
- C.S.S. *Virginia*, not *Merrimack*
- Torpedoes, and other infernal machines
- Subs, rams, and other floating things
- The rakish Raphael, "Terror of the Seas"

Confederate sailors? Were there such things? Yes, indeed. It couldn't have been otherwise, since something had to be done about that nasty Union blockade of the South's ports. Somehow Jefferson Davis and his short, pudgy (but forward-thinking) Navy Secretary Stephen Mallory had to come up with some clever ideas in regard to protecting the Confederacy's coast and doing the Union as much harm as possible.

Some of what happened in the Navy Department proved the South wasn't as tradition-bound as people think. In this chapter, you'll learn about Confederate submarines (yes, really) and also learn the truth about that famous *Monitor-Merrimack* battle (such as the real names of the ships).

We're Farmers, Not Sailors

The South had a long coastline—but almost no navy to speak of. The North didn't have much of a navy, either. What the North did have—on paper, anyway—was its infamous proclamation of a blockade. Just a few days after Fort Sumter and after his call for 75,000 soldiers, Lincoln declared a blockade of the ports of all the seceded states. The objectives: Keep the South from receiving war material from abroad, keep it from exporting its goods (primarily cotton), and bottle up any ships the South might send to prey on Union merchant ships.

Did Y'all Know?

Seven of the seceded states had quickly set up their own navies before the Confederacy was formed. "Mosquito Fleet" was the name given to North Carolina's state navy.

All easier said than done. When the blockade was announced, the Union navy had fewer than 50 ships in the water. Divide 3,500 miles of coast by 50 ships, and you can see that the blockade was, at first, a joke. It didn't stay that way long, however, because the Union knew that it needed more ships in a hurry. It had the funds and the resources to build more ships than the South did, as the South was painfully aware.

Happily, the Confederacy had a capable secretary of the navy, Stephen Mallory, who had served on the Naval Affairs Committee in his U.S. Senate days (he represented Florida in the Senate). Mallory faced the obvious: The South needed warships, ships that could evade ("run") the blockade, and "commerce raiders" to harass Union shipping (which would require attention from the Union navy, thus drawing their ships away from the blockade).

Mallory hadn't much to work with at first. The Confederacy had 12 small ships and about 300 officers who had resigned from the Union navy. As of October 1861, there were a grand total of 3,674 enlisted men in the navy, plus the Confederate Marines, totaling 539. The Confederate Navy would never be huge. Confederate boys were rushing to join the army, not the navy. If numbers weren't the answer to Mallory's problems, perhaps technology was.

The Ironclad Obsession

Mallory was always looking for a "sea monster" that would terrify the U.S. Navy. He knew that the French and British had produced battleships with thin armor. Mallory raised an obvious question: What if a warship had *heavy* armor? Couldn't it become the "Terror of the Seas," destroying or frightening off every wooden ship that belonged to the Union?

When the U.S. Navy evacuated its naval yard in Norfolk, Virginia, it burned everything. But among the ruins and wreckage were the hull and engines of the U.S.S. *Merrimack*, which quickly got a name change: the C.S.S. *Virginia*. Mallory's clever naval designers armed the ship with 10 heavy guns, plus an iron ram (weighing 1,500 pounds) on the bow. It rode low—real low—in the water. It was plated all over with laminated iron, 4 inches thick. It was 275 feet long, 39 feet wide, and weighed 3,200 tons.

On March 9, 1862, Lincoln and his cabinet got some shocking news: The Rebels had an ironclad ship. Edwin Stanton, the always-fretful secretary of war, ranted that the Rebel ironclad "would destroy every vessel in the service," and would "disperse Congress, then destroy the Capitol and public buildings." Mallory would have been proud: The ironclad ship that was supposed to cause panic in the North was doing just that.

Voices from Then

I regard the possession of an iron armored ship as a matter of the first necessity …. Inequality of numbers may be compensated by invulnerability, and thus not only does economy but naval success dictate the wisdom and expediency of fighting with iron against wood.

—Navy Secretary Stephen Mallory, May 9, 1861

Franklin Buchanan, a Maryland-born naval officer and the first head of the U.S. Naval Academy, had offered his services to the Confederacy. Stephen Mallory made him an adviser, then later named him flag officer in command of defense of the James River. (A little geographical reminder: The wide James River would take you from Chesapeake Bay to the capital, Richmond. Obviously, it was a high priority for the Confederacy to keep Union ships out of the James River.)

Buchanan made the newly iron-plated *Virginia* his flagship. On March 8, 1862, he set out to attack Union ships in Hampton Roads. (This odd name refers to the area in Virginia where the James, Elizabeth, and other wide rivers flow into the Chesapeake Bay. The cities of Norfolk, Portsmouth, and Hampton face Hampton Roads.) Buchanan's target was the Union ship *Cumberland*. The two ships exchanged fire, then the *Virginia* rammed it. The *Cumberland* was sunk. Buchanan then attacked the *Congress*. Its captain so feared being rammed by the *Virginia* that he ran his ship aground to avoid it.

Did Y'all Know?

John Mercer Brooke of the Confederate Navy was involved with converting the *Merrimack* into the *Virginia*. More importantly, he designed the Brooke rifle, a cast-iron cannon manufactured at Confederate iron works. The Rebels were proud of the Yankee-pounding Brooke rifles, since they were Confederate-designed and Confederate-made.

Buchanan didn't let up. The *Virginia* pounded the *Congress* with shot until it caught fire.

Mallory's dream of a Yankee-killing sea monster had come to life. The news spread quickly, and Southerners rejoiced. After the dismal military news of February 1862, here was good news from the naval front. Unfortunately, in the *Virginia-Cumberland* battle, Buchanan was wounded. This meant he was out of commission for the most famous naval battle of the war, and one of the most famous of all time.

The Battle: Clunker vs. Clunker

It happened on the next day. Buchanan turned command of the *Virginia* over to Lieutenant Catesby Jones. Jones and everyone else in the Confederacy knew that the Union hadn't been sitting on its hands. It was producing its own ironclad ship, the *Monitor*. Inevitably the two had to meet. When Jones and his crew awakened on the morning of March 9, 1862, they didn't know the *Monitor* had arrived overnight. (The light from the burning Union ship *Congress* helped the *Monitor* find its way.) Jones had to change plans quickly: Instead of attacking the other wooden Union ships as planned, he had to do battle with another ironclad.

The famous four-hour battle—two clunky pieces of metal firing shots at each other—was a draw. What ended the fight was a shot fired at the *Monitor*'s pilothouse. The captain was temporarily blinded, and the *Monitor* pulled away. The *Virginia* was low on ammunition and the tide was falling, so it returned to the navy yard at Norfolk. Neither ironclad had seriously damaged the other. The confrontation has gone down in history because it was the first real battle between two heavily armored warships. The era of wooden warships was over. The Union's sunken *Cumberland* and *Congress* were testimony to that.

The *Virginia* itself didn't last long. The Confederates had to evacuate Norfolk in May 1862, and much as they would have liked to keep the sea monster in

Voices from Then

Ironclads definitely weren't pretty. Some Confederates referred to the Union's *Monitor* as "that Yankee cheesebox on a raft." However, the "cheesebox" had something that would revolutionize warfare: a revolving turret.

Go See It!

Some of the relics of the *Virginia*, including an anchor, can be seen at the Museum of the Confederacy in Richmond. If you want a good look at a Confederate ironclad, you can see the C.S.S. *Neuse* at the Caswell State Historic Site in Kinston, North Carolina.

operation, the ironclad, with its 22-foot draft, could not be taken up the shallower James River. Rather than leave the ship for the Union to use against them, the Rebs set fire to her.

But ironclad fever was still burning. The *Virginia* was, you might say, a "working prototype." Mallory believed that design for ironclads could be improved. The *Virginia* drew 22 feet of water, making it unsuitable for shallow river waters. Couldn't someone design a shallow-draft ironclad—and in the process make the ship easier to maneuver?

Necessity is sometimes the mother of cleverness. Confederate ironclads became smaller, shallower, faster, and better armored. There was a *Virginia II* and *Columbia*, both major improvements on the original *Virginia*. Mallory's dream was "to traverse the entire coast of the United States and encounter, with a fair prospect of success, their entire navy." While he first thought of ironclads as part of an offense, he shifted the emphasis to defense, particularly of the James River (meaning defense of the capital at Richmond).

Mallory was pleased with the ironclads, but he was constantly looking around for other naval novelties. One thing must have crossed his mind: With the ironclads sitting so low in the water, what about a ship that was completely *under* the water?

The Hunley Machine

"Confederate submarines" sounds like a plot device from the old *Wild Wild West* TV series. But in fact there were Confederate submarines, and modern navies can thank Confederate Secretary of the Navy Stephen Mallory and some clever inventors for moving the technology forward.

Word was reaching the Union that the Rebels had—or would soon have—an "infernal machine" that could travel underwater and sink Union ships without ever being detected. In the preradar age, this was genuinely frightening. As a piece of psychological warfare, the submarine was doing damage even before it existed.

The first Confederate *submarine*, appropriately named the *Pioneer*, did what many experimental ships did: It sank. But the famous *Hunley* had better luck. Named for its primary financial backer, H. L. Hunley of New Orleans, the sub was the brainchild of inventor J. R. McClintock. He, Hunley, and other backers experimented with subs in Louisiana's Lake Pontchartrain. When New Orleans fell to the Federals, the group changed its base to Mobile, Alabama. The *H. L. Hunley* was 40 feet long, 4 feet deep, and not quite 4 feet wide. It was powered by a propeller, which in turn was powered by hand cranks—muscles, in other words. Eight men powered the cranks, and a ninth man was the captain and the ship's "eyes." The sub had no periscope but did have a "conning tower" just barely above the water. (This, happily, also allowed the men to breathe.)

Something this simple couldn't fire a projectile. The idea was to arm the sub with a spar torpedo—that is, an explosive attached at the end of a long shaft projecting from the sub. It sounds primitive to us, but in the 1860s it caused terror. General Beauregard, by this time placed in charge of the defenses of Charleston, heard of the submarine and insisted it be brought to that city. Some local men manned the sub—and sank it. When the men were found, their faces and bodies showed they had died in intense agony. The locals were horrified.

Did Y'all Know? _____

Since submarine hadn't entered the American vocabulary yet, many people, North and South, referred to it as the "newfangled boat."

Hunley and his gang traveled to Charleston to train a new crew. Unfortunately, he and the crew all perished in the sub, too. "Experimental ship" was coming to mean "death ship." Alarmed, Beauregard tried to cease further experiments with the *Hunley*, but some of its backers (the ones still living, that is) were determined to make it work.

Did Y'all Know? _____

The long-submerged *Hunley* got resurrected in the year 2000, and as this book goes to press, archaeologists and others are examining the remains (including the eight crew members) in painstaking detail. Doubtless the sub will find a home eventually in a museum.

Persistence finally paid off on February 17, 1864. The *Hunley* sank the U.S.S. *Housatonic* in Charleston harbor. It happened sneakily and suddenly, as the Confederacy had hoped it would. Shortly after 8 P.M., an officer on the deck of the *Housatonic* spotted what looked like a log floating toward the ship. He yelled out a warning, but too late. The torpedo attached to the *Hunley* exploded and lifted the Union ship completely out of the water. In the morning some of the crew were found alive in the rigging in the ship. Needless to say, the survivors talked loud and long about this amazing and fearsome "stealth ship."

The *Hunley* had sunk its first—and last—ship. Years later the sub and crew were found—under the hull of the *Housatonic*. But for all the Union navy knew, the *Hunley* was still out prowling the waters, a danger to every Union ship on the seas.

Many Confederates' lives had been lost, along with the sub itself—and only one Union ship sunk for all that trouble. Still, the Confederacy had struck a psychological blow against the Union—and revolutionized naval warfare in the process.

Rains and His "Infernal Machines"

One of the most influential men in the Confederate Navy was an army man, Gen. Gabriel Rains of North Carolina. Rains fit the usual army pattern: West Point grad, Mexican War vet, then Confederate officer. Commanding troops in Virginia, Rains had a brainstorm: Plant shells with percussion caps on the road where the Federals would pass. These caused some destruction, as was intended. They also caused an outpouring of wrath, as people in both North and South bewailed the "barbarity" of using booby traps in war. Many officers, perhaps most, believed it was both uncivilized and ungentlemanly. Southern officers believed the South, even if it was outnumbered by the North, shouldn't stoop to using such dirty tricks.

Rains disagreed. Like Stephen Mallory in the Navy Department, he thought the Confederacy should use whatever means it could to convince the Federals to leave the South alone. George W. Randolph, the Confederacy's third secretary of war, called Rains to Richmond to serve in the War Department—and experiment with explosives.

Jefferson Davis didn't warm to Rains's ideas—not at first, anyway. The courtly, civilized Davis wished the war could be kept on an honorable plane. But then, it wasn't really fair anyway, with the South being outnumbered and all, … right? Rains confronted Davis with some logic: Every new weapon had, when it was first introduced, been described as barbaric. In time, every "barbaric" weapon became an accepted part of warfare. Davis had to agree.

Rains's services were needed more by the navy than the army. With the South short on ships and the Union blockade causing so many problems, Southern navy men hit upon a plan: Plant explosives in Southern harbors to blow up Union ships. These would be called "mines" today, but in the 1860s they were "torpedoes." Rains took the responsibility for placing them in the harbors of Mobile, Charleston, and Savannah. (Obviously, Confederates would know the locations of the mines so as to avoid them.)

These "infernal machines," as many called them, were clever and diverse. Floating torpedoes were turned loose to drift with the currents of rivers. Anchored torpedoes stayed submerged and stationary. There were "coal torpedoes," painted black and shaped like

---

Go See It!

At Vicksburg National Military Park in Mississippi, you can see the remains of the U.S.S. *Cairo*, an ironclad sunk by a torpedo planted in the Yazoo River. It was the first ship sunk by the Confederacy's torpedoes. A total of 37 Union ships, including 9 ironclads, were sunk by Confederate torpedoes.

lumps of coal, and sneakily placed in a Union ship's fuel bin. When it was thrown onto the ship's fire, the inevitable happened.

Part of the challenge—and fun (if that word is appropriate)—of torpedo making was that the Confederates could use lots of old cast-off materials—beer kegs, cans, oil boilers, things that normally would have ended up in the garbage heaps. The basic principle was simple: Pack a hollow container with explosives and float it in the water. The tricky part was detonating it, but the Rebs had several solutions: contact fuses, clocks, and sparks that could be controlled from the shore.

Despite many people's misgivings about such "dirty" warfare, it was effective. After the war ended, U.S. Navy Secretary Gideon Welles stated that the Confederacy had done the Union navy more damage with its torpedoes than with its ships.

Go, Rams!

If you've seen movies like *Ben-Hur* or *Cleopatra*, you probably know what a ram ship was: a large warship armed with a "ram" (long spike, that is), designed to poke a lethal hole in the enemy's ship. The ancient concept got resurrected in the 1860s, the difference being that the old ram ships were powered by oars and sweating slaves, while the rams of the 1860s were powered by steam. The famous *Virginia* was a ram as well as an ironclad.

A kind of ram fever gripped both North and South, with the South in a big hurry to build more ram ships. Not all the rams were built from scratch. Plenty of paddle-wheel riverboats were fitted with rams on their prows. Since they weren't built sturdily enough to carry large cannons, the ram-fitted riverboats relied on the ram as the offensive weapon. For defense, the Confederates showed some cleverness. Some of the riverboats became "cottonclads," using bales of cotton as their exterior armor. Others added an extra layer of wood, or a thin layer of metal (the "tinclads").

Some of the South's rams managed to do some serious damage. The *Palmetto State* and *Chicora* made a surprise attack on the Union blockade vessels off Charleston. The fearsome *Tennessee* was a major player in the Battle of Mobile Bay. Commanded at the time by Franklin Buchanan, the Confederacy's biggest ironclad was hopelessly outnumbered (17 to 1) by David Farragut's Union ships, but the *Tennessee* put up a brave fight. One of Farragut's ships was sunk—not by Buchanan's ships, but courtesy of the Confederate torpedoes in the bay.

Go, Raiders!

Raphael Semmes, a Maryland-born navy man, had many talents. He was a Mexican War vet, a lawyer, and author of a popular book (*Service Afloat and Ashore During the War with Mexico*). Thanks to his years of naval experience, he knew the Southern coast like the back of his hand. Ironically, he would spend most of the Civil War far away from Confederacy waters. Semmes gained world renown as the South's greatest plunderer of Yankee merchant ships.

Semmes grew up on a tobacco plantation in Maryland and was sailing boats into the Potomac River from early childhood. The Maryland boy settled in the gulf port city of Mobile, Alabama, and when the state seceded, he went with it, resigning from the U.S. Navy. Old Beeswax could see that the tiny Confederate Navy was no match for the Union's. But perhaps it could at least make the Union Navy's job more difficult. The

> **Did Y'all Know?**
>
> "Old Beeswax" was Semmes's nickname, and any picture of the Confederacy's most famous sea hawk can tell you why. Semmes was noted for his upturned (thanks to beeswax) mustache.

Confederate government gave Semmes a task he relished: "Do the enemy's commerce the greatest injury in the shortest time." In short, hurt the North by attacking and destroying its merchant ships (and seizing their cargoes, of course). He did.

The Confederacy had to have many of its ships built abroad, mostly in England. Britain prohibited the building of warships for other nations, so Confederate agents wisely contracted for English shipbuilders to construct "merchant vessels" (wink) with every intention of using them to attack Union ships. The sleek *290* slipped out of Liverpool harbor in July 1862 and became famous as the C.S.S. *Alabama*, Semmes's *commerce raider*. In less than two years of cruising the world's oceans, Semmes and his crew captured 65 Yankee ships, with a value of about $6.5 million. Northern merchants feared Semmes, the infamous "Terror of the Seas," and there is no doubt that he seriously hurt Yankee trading.

Due to the Union blockade, Semmes couldn't send the captured ships back to Southern ports, so he generally burned them—but not always. Sometimes he took them to neutral ports. On one occasion he arrived in a Cuban port with seven Union ships in tow as trophies. He captured the *Conrad*, armed it, and turned it into another commerce raider, the *Tuscaloosa*. (Note how the Alabama resident bestowed Alabama names on his ships.)

> **RebeLingo**
>
> The Confederate ships known as **commerce raiders** were also called "cruisers."

The owners of nearly 1,000 U.S. merchant ships began a "flight from the flag," registering their ships in foreign countries so they could escape Semmes's detection by *not* flying the U.S. flag. Supposedly the commerce raiders helped to raise marine insurance rates by 900 percent.

Did Y'all Know?

The infamous *Alabama* had very few actual Confederates among its crew. Most of the men were foreigners, and mostly from the roguish element. Semmes had to maintain strict discipline over this motley crew that he called his "precious set of rascals."

The *Alabama* met its doom in the English Channel, off the coast of Cherbourg, France, on June 19, 1864, when it battled the U.S.S. *Kearsarge*. The Union ship wore a kind of chain-mail armor, and after the one-hour battle the gallant *Alabama* sank to the bottom of the sea. A huge crowd had gathered on the cliffs of northern France to watch the fateful battle. The crowd included French master artist Edouard Manét, who immortalized the battle on canvas. The Yankee sailors were pleased at sinking the legendary raider, but they were so impressed with Semmes and his gritty crew that they refused to cheer as the *Alabama* went down. Semmes, who had a theatrical touch, threw his sword into the sea and was picked up by an English yacht, whose skipper garnered an official thanks from the Confederate Congress.

Despite all the publicity given to Semmes and other commerce raiders, they had no real effect on weakening the blockade, nor on nudging the Union to negotiate for peace. But Semmes and his like did manage to do the Union some harm, and their exploits reminded the world that a nation of farmers could do some amazing things at sea.

We'll save the subject (an exciting one) of blockade running—and how the blockade affected the lives of both Confederate soldiers and civilians—for Chapter 20.

The Least You Need to Know

- With an inadequate navy, the Confederacy was willing to try various naval innovations, notably ironclad warships.

- The *Monitor-Virginia* battle of the ironclads spelled the end of wooden warships.

- The Confederacy experimented with submarines, ram ships, and naval mines.

- Commerce raiders, notably the *Alabama* commanded by Raphael Semmes, caused serious harm to Union shipping around the world.

Part 4

Politics, Power, and Pettiness

In Richmond, President Jefferson Davis had expected neither to walk on streets of gold, nor to lie on beds of roses. If he had any such exalted expectations, he wouldn't have survived. He had expected labor, and he found it, and did it, and made the best of it.

Politics is not always pretty, nor does it always attract the noblest souls in a society. The Confederacy was fortunate in having a handful of the better sort. It also had its petty-souled prima donnas more focused on their reputations than on the public good. Somehow this motley mix of political saints, sinners, and in-betweeners had to work together to establish a new nation—and fight a war at the same time. President, cabinet, Congress, governors, and diplomats—all fought their own sorts of battles while the soldiers were fighting theirs.

Chapter 17

Yeah, Still Obsessed with States' Rights

In This Chapter

◆ Congress's new anti- and pro- parties

◆ "Imaginary" Congressional districts

◆ Secret sessions with knives and fists

◆ Two "state kings" and their pettiness

If you don't know the names of many Confederate politicians, don't be surprised. In the Old South, men took more pride in their performance on the battlefield than the political field. (The two fields were connected, of course. Jefferson Davis had been a Mexican War hero, which gave him some fame, so Mississippi sent him to Congress, leading to a long political career.) There was always a bias in favor of men who had gone to battle and roughed it, while politicians ate well, slept in fancy hotels, wore fine clothes, and savored the sound of their own voices.

Still, politics is a necessary evil, and so are politicians. And the Confederacy had to have a central legislature. Since it was populated by men obsessed with states' rights, the state versus nation tug-of-war made for some interesting political battles. We will meet some big-time prima donnas, some in the national capital, some in the state capitals.

The Great Divides

The Confederacy modeled its Congress on the old one, with a Senate and a House of Representatives, with most of the old rules applying—and many of the same old faces. There were no political parties in the usual sense. Its members had been, in their U.S. days, Democrats or Whigs. (No Republicans, of course!) Those labels never were applied in the Confederacy.

Did Y'all Know?

The offices of the *Richmond Whig* newspaper were a favorite gathering place for congressmen who opposed the Davis administration. The paper was aggressively anti-Davis throughout the war.

But parties, or factions, exist whether they are given labels or not. Assemble a large group together in one place, and it is certain the group will divide into two or more factions. These did not have names, but we can call them what they were: pro-Davis and anti-Davis.

Congressmen had to engage in a balancing act, keeping their home voters happy while trying to keep the entire nation afloat. The president had to focus on the national picture, so inevitably he and the more local-minded congressmen locked horns.

In a nutshell: The South didn't have the material resources to beat the North in the war. The Confederacy needed more men for its armies, so Davis grudgingly signed legislation for conscription (draft, that is), which many congressmen supported while others groaned. The nation needed supplies for its armies, so Davis grudgingly signed legislation for confiscation (impressment), which caused more groaning. It needed revenue, so it imposed new taxes and raised old ones (more groaning). It needed to curtail the activities of Unionists who were aiding and abetting the enemy, so Davis grudgingly had to suspend (very rarely) habeas corpus and impose martial law on occasion (more groaning and even some shouting). None of this was pleasant for Davis, the Congress, or the millions of citizens of the Confederate States of America.

On the positive side, Confederate congressmen didn't vote along party lines. That is, their votes were not affected by that question that still carries such weight in the U.S. Congress: "Will it make my party happy?" The men in the Richmond Congress actually voted their conscience, or to please their constituents, or both—but not to please the party bosses, for there were none.

Meet the Boys

In the 4 years of the Confederacy's life, 267 men served in its Congress. Slightly less than a third of them were former members of the U.S. Congress, and about two thirds had been state legislators. About 10 percent had no previous political experience. Roughly a tenth (27) served continuously the entire four years. There were a few more Whigs than Democrats, even though the old labels were no longer used. Lawyers far outnumbered planters.

All 11 seceded states had representation, as did the two "sort-of" Confederate states, Kentucky and Missouri. (Remember that these two had both held secession conventions and elected pro-Confederate governors, who never had full authority in those states.) The five Indian nations (Cherokees, Chickasaws, Creeks, Choctaws, and Seminoles) had nonvoting delegates, as did the Arizona and New Mexico territories.

Each state had two senators and the same number of representatives as in the U.S. Congress. The same election procedures were followed. Soldiers could vote absentee, as could refugees. Many Democrats and secessionists (or men who were both) were often elected to the First Congress, but as the war dragged on and the population became disenchanted, former Unionists trickled into Congress as well.

One of the curiosities of the Congress was that with every passing day, more congressmen represented *imaginary districts* (also called "phantom districts" or "shadow districts")—areas occupied by the Union, that is. In these areas, the laws of the Confederacy no longer applied, of course. The Confederacy continued to lose territory to the Union throughout the war, and by the last session of Congress (November 1864), there were more congressmen from imaginary districts than from Confederate-held districts.

Congressmen from imaginary districts were, as you might imagine, happier to be in Richmond than at home. Even so, they had to keep their constituents' needs in mind as they worked on legislation. Obviously they were under pressure to pass any legislation that would help get the Yankees off their turf.

> **RebeLingo**
>
> **Imaginary districts**, also called phantom districts, were Confederate Congressional districts that had been occupied by Union troops. As the war progressed, there were more and more of these.

> **Did Y'all Know?**
>
> The Provisional Congress met between February 4, 1861, and February 17, 1862.
>
> The First Congress met from February 18, 1862, until December 7, 1863.
>
> The Second Congress met from May 2, 1864, until March 18, 1865.

Put Up Your Dukes

Politics could be violent in those days. In a lengthy debate in the Senate, Ben Hill of Georgia threw an inkstand at William Yancey, cutting him very slightly on the cheek, and leading to an unsightly mix of blood and ink. When Yancey chose to ignore this, Hill rushed at him with a chair, but some other senators held him back. Yancey actually died not long afterward, and a few of his fans said Hill had caused his death, which was ridiculous. It wasn't the first altercation Yancey engaged in. He had squabbled with James Phelan of Mississippi, and journalists wouldn't even report this, fearing for their own safety.

This was nothing new among politicians. (The U.S. Congress at this time was just as rowdy.) Tempers flared, most men carried weapons, and with no cameras rolling, blood sometimes flowed. Henry Foote of Tennessee, the most vocal Davis-hater in the House, was a noted brawler. Even minor officials of the Congress were subject to brawling. Two House clerks shot it out on Capital Square, one murdering the other.

Drunkenness and brawling go together, of course. In a day when alcohol was medication as well as a beverage of pleasure, moderate drinking was hardly even noticed. But at times members of Congress were visibly drunk. Former U.S. Sen. James Hammond wrote to Robert M. T. Hunter in 1863: "Some malign influence seems to preside over your councils. Pardon me, is the majority always drunk?" He was probably exaggerating, but we can't be sure how much. Nor can we be sure why there were several times when the House couldn't transact business because of a lack of a quorum. Where were the congressmen? Didn't they take the nation's business seriously enough to at least try showing up?

The Scapegoat Gallery

If you listen to talk radio today, you're probably aware that many people love to rant about the failings of politicians. Certainly there was much to complain about during the Confederacy. As the war progressed and the Confederacy's situation worsened, it was standard practice to deride the Congress. Considering that many of the congressmen enjoyed doing the same to the president, perhaps this was payback.

When the First Congress was just settling down to work, Richmond was threatened by George McClellan's troops moving up the Virginia Peninsula. Congress adjourned itself—leading practically every newspaper in the Confederacy to yell "Cowards!" The body somewhat redeemed itself in 1863, when Union cavalry threatened Richmond and some congressmen actually volunteered for local defense.

Voices from Then

Congress contains material which but for the very small number of men of sense in it, would precipitate the country into untold evils. Indeed, we are afraid they will do so anyway .... What good can be expected from such a body? What hope can the People entertain from the legislation of servants who have impudently assumed to be their masters?

—An Athens, Georgia, newspaper, January 1864

Newspaper editors are not politicians. They aren't elected, and they don't have to do their work in collaboration with hundreds of other folks. Thus it is easy to editorialize and criticize. And, frankly, it's more fun to read fault-finding than praise. Such is human nature. The Southern people had gripes, life wasn't always good, and congressmen made enough mistakes to be good targets for criticism.

Still, the Congress was neither as lazy nor incompetent as the papers claimed. Facing some monumental problems, they did surprisingly well. The much-hated Conscription Acts offended many, but they were necessary to fill the ranks of the army. (The only other option: surrender to the Union.) Taxes were resented, naturally, but the nation was in an emergency situation. The confiscation of farm products for use by the army was widely resented too, but again, the Confederacy was fighting for its life.

We Do Not Approve

Jefferson Davis had an admirable quality that got him in trouble: He was loyal to his friends. When he appointed someone to an office, he didn't shove that person aside just because someone complained about his performance. His basic attitude was right: Give the person a chance to prove himself, and don't be swayed by the inevitable gripers out there.

Admirable, but only to a point. Davis was correct in assuming that some of his enemies would find fault with anyone he appointed. But in fact, he did keep a few people in office who were simply incompetent. One whom we've mentioned before was the Commissary General Lucius Northrop, whose ineptitude and crabbiness alienated everyone he worked with. Congressmen howled for his dismissal, but Davis stood by him. He stood by his Cabinet appointees also, notably his friend Judah Benjamin. When people howled for Benjamin's dismissal as secretary of war, Davis accepted his resignation—then made him secretary of state (a slot where, happily, he proved more competent). Then, of course, there were the generals. It wasn't Davis's fault that the

Union had more soldiers. Nor was it his fault that good generals were hard to find. It was definitely his fault that he stood by a controversial failure like Braxton Bragg (see Chapter 25), who should have been sacked long before he finally resigned. This stubborn refusal to listen to advice was one reason many of his enemies thought Davis had the makings of a tyrant.

We Love You, Jeff

In his four years as president, Jefferson Davis vetoed 39 Congressional bills. Congress only overrode one veto. (Davis always took time to explain why he vetoed.) If that sounds like he had a working majority in Congress, it's because he did. Generally speaking, the pro-Davis party outnumbered the anti-Davis folks—at least, it did for the first two years of the Confederacy.

Davis had a handful of faithful supporters. Calling them "yes men" wouldn't be quite fair, for none of them was mindless enough to simply rubber-stamp every proposal of the president. In the Senate, Davis's most loyal men were Ben Hill and Howell Cobb, both of Georgia, Robert M. T. Hunter of Virginia, Clement C. Clay of Alabama, and James Phelan of Davis's home state of Mississippi. You might remember that it was Cobb who presided over the Montgomery convention that formed the Confederacy.

The experienced statesman had been a Georgia governor and James Buchanan's secretary of the treasury. He presided over the original Confederate Congress and, to the regret of many, laid aside his political career for a military one, heading the 16th Georgia Infantry and later becoming a major general. He and his brother Thomas both opted for the traditional Southern route of proving one's true worth by commanding armies. A lovely tradition, but one that kept some good men out of the political arena.

Ben Hill was called "Hill the Faithful" by Davis. Aside from backing Davis on most policies, Hill became Davis's unofficial ambassador to Georgia, where Gov. Joe Brown and Vice President Alexander Stephens spewed their anti-Richmond propaganda constantly. Hill was pushed to run against Brown, a states' rights fanatic, for governor, but feared Brown was too popular to defeat. (Incidentally, at age 39, Hill was the youngest senator.)

> **Voices from Then**
>
> Davis to the new Congress in January 1863: "The fate of the Confederacy especially devolves on you … to sustain in the people a just confidence in the government of their choice."

> **Did Y'all Know?**
>
> The Confederacy never did have a supreme court. Sen. Ben Hill of Georgia pushed for one, but Yancey, Wigfall, and other senators worked against it, fearing that Davis would pack the court with his supporters.

In the House, Jabez Curry of Alabama and Ethelbert Barksdale of Mississippi were loyal to Davis. Curry chaired the Commerce Committee and worked to monitor the Confederacy's finances (which couldn't have been a pleasant task). Like a few other Congressmen, his pro-Davis stance irked his constituents enough that, in 1863, he was not reelected.

Barksdale, a newspaper editor, had been among the Southern delegates who walked out of the 1860 Democratic Convention, splitting the party into Southern and Northern branches (see Chapter 5). While he claimed to be as gung-ho for states' rights as any other Southerner, he believed that in wartime, emergency measures had to be taken. He introduced a measure in Congress allowing Davis to suspend habeas corpus and impose martial law, according to his judgment. The bill's aim was to enforce the draft and to suppress Unionist

Go See It!
Although Jabez Curry isn't a household name, you'll find a statue of him (representing Alabama) in the Capitol's Statuary Hall in Washington. Alabama honored him there for his postwar work in public education, not for his brief service to the Confederacy.

activities in various regions. The bill was defeated. (Everyone in Congress knew good and well that Lincoln suspended habeas corpus as he saw fit, without getting Congress's approval.) The Confederate Congress did give Davis some limited power to suspend habeas corpus in areas threatened by invasion. In 1864, when things looked somewhat desperate, he was given power to suspend habeas corpus in order to arrest deserters, people harboring deserters, or those engaged in unlawful trading with the enemy.

Some of Davis's supporters genuinely liked the man, but their attachment to his policies wasn't all personal. You might say his supporters were the political realists of the Confederacy, willing to sacrifice some civil liberties that they would have insisted upon in peacetime. They didn't like the draft, impressment, increased taxes, or suspension of habeas corpus, but they went along with them as temporary emergency measures. Opposed to the realists were the idealists, so obsessed with states' rights and so fearful of anything that looked tyrannical that they would sink the Confederacy rather than allow Davis to become a despot—which never entered his mind, of course.

The Sulking Gnome in Georgia

Alexander Stephens, "Little Aleck," former U.S. congressman from Georgia, was the vice president, and not terribly happy about it. The vice president's official duties were minimal: Preside over the Senate and, in case of a tie vote there, break the tie.

In 1861, he did make a few speeches to drum up support for the nation. Unofficially, he could have served as a close adviser to the president. But he was seldom asked, and the vain little man resented his intellectual powers not being put to use.

Alexander Stephens (1812–1883), "Little Aleck," the Confederacy's only vice president, who spent much of his energy criticizing Jefferson Davis and the Richmond government.

(Georgia Division of Archives and History)

The scrawny little bachelor lawyer—whose only close relations were with his half-brother, Linton, and his old dog, Rio—was an intellectual, living in a mental universe where abstractions were more real than human beings. In this universe, liberty was real, and so was despotism. While almost all Southerners believed in states' rights, Stephens was not merely a believer but a fanatic. In his gloomy view of the world, every human being was a potential tyrant (which might be true), and Jefferson Davis definitely wanted to be one (*not* true).

Clearly he was filled with a great deal of envy. Stephens had always been obsessively ambitious, and one obvious reason he detested Davis was that he thought he would have made a better president. In his long idle hours of pouting, he worked out in his head the details of his own presidential administration, should Davis die or be removed.

Stephens opted to do his pouting and criticizing at his Georgia home instead of in Richmond. During 1863 and 1864, Stephens was away from the Senate for a year and a half, with Robert M. T. Hunter of Virginia serving as president pro tem of the Senate. Some of Stephens's friends begged him to return to Richmond, but he preferred not to—but he wouldn't resign, either.

> **Did Y'all Know?**
>
> Stephens on himself: "I have in my life been one of the most miserable beings, it seems to me, that walked the earth—subject to occasional fits of depression that seemed well-nigh bordering on despair. Without enjoyment, without pleasure, without hope, and without sympathy from the world."

Tucked away with his books and dog in Georgia, the absentee vice president kept in touch with two other Davis-haters of Georgia, Gov. Joe Brown (more about him later in this chapter) and Robert Toombs. Toombs, you might recall, had been on the short list for Confederate president. He got passed over for Davis, and Davis gave him the consolation prize of secretary of state, which Toombs held for only a few months. Stephens, Brown, and Toombs were all by nature ambitious, vain, and good

> **Did Y'all Know?**
>
> While sulking in Georgia, Stephens denounced the draft in a letter made public in September 1862. In another public letter, he said Davis had no right to impose martial law, even in an emergency.

with words (meaning they could criticize eloquently). All had (so they thought) a beef against the Davis administration, and during the life of the Confederacy they didn't keep quiet.

Stephens was too vain to sulk permanently in Georgia. He would resurface a couple of more times, and would actually prove to be of some help to the Confederate cause.

The Executive's Executives

Like the United States, the Confederacy had three branches of government—executive, legislative, and judicial. The legislative (Congress) has been dealt with. The judicial existed only on paper, for although the Confederate Constitution provided for a Supreme Court, none was ever created. (The individual states had their own courts, of course.)

That leaves the executive branch—Davis and his cabinet. The cabinet posts were secretary of state, secretary of the treasury, attorney general, secretary of war, secretary of the navy, and postmaster general. We looked at the navy secretary in Chapter 16 and will look at the state secretaries, treasury secretaries, and postmaster general in later chapters. Davis had five different men in the attorney general slot, an interesting position, since its holder had to balance the national interests against the interests of the state courts. In some ways the attorney general had to play the role the Supreme Court would have played.

Perhaps more interesting (and demanding) than that was the work of the secretary of war. Six different men held that post, and a very awkward spot it was, considering Davis himself had been U.S. secretary of war and was more inclined to manage the war department himself than to delegate too much authority to the secretary. Most of the war secretaries were unimpressive (including George W. Randolph, who was a grandson of Thomas Jefferson). The man who served longest as secretary of war was a sickly civilian, James Seddon of Virginia. Despite his poor health, Seddon was hard-working and efficient, and his courtly manner helped him in his role as intermediary between the president and the griping generals. Like every other cabinet member, poor Seddon faced the usual problem: complaints from governors and other state officials that the national government was not respecting states' rights. He and every other cabinet member grew accustomed to criticism from congressmen, but Davis proved to be loyal to his appointees.

States' Men: The (Sometimes) Cooperative Governors

Politicians who maintain themselves in office cannot be total idiots. All of the governors in the Confederacy had brains enough to see that states' rights might, occasionally, have to take a back seat to national authority. The Civil War was, obviously, a national emergency that required all the states to join together for the purposes of fielding armies, clothing and feeding the soldiers, and distributing the Confederacy's meager resources around the new nation.

Most of the governors were extremely cooperative with the Confederate government. They understood that if the Davis government fell, so would the whole South (governors included). A pattern quickly emerged in the Confederacy: Richmond would announce a policy (the draft, for example), the governors would denounce it on behalf of states' rights—then, having made the right noises to satisfy their states, they would cooperate with Richmond.

But a couple of the governors saw the Confederacy as their chance to be kings in their own states, with Jeff Davis as a sort of far-off emperor with very limited power. These "Southern kinglets" were a constant thorn in Richmond's side, and their stubbornness, selfishness, and blind devotion to states' rights helped bring the Confederacy down. One historian has written that the Confederacy's epitaph might be "Died of States' Rights."

Good Ole Zebulon

One governor who was semicooperative was North Carolina's Zebulon Vance, a former lawyer and newspaper editor and a popular "good ole boy" character. When Vance ran for governor, he wooed the many voters who were dissatisfied with the Confederacy. Even so, in his inaugural address, Vance pledged his support of the Confederate cause. But Vance was a strong believer in states' rights, as Richmond was to learn.

North Carolina, the last state to secede, supplied the Confederacy with more soldiers than any other state. Vance never lost sight of this, nor did he lose sight of the attention that was lavished on the neighboring state of Virginia. (North Carolinians had a long tradition of considering Virginians to be snooty.) In Vance's view of things, North Carolina officers weren't being promoted as rapidly as those of other states. A former Whig and Unionist, he claimed President Davis favored Democrats. He fired off catty letters to Davis and to Secretary of War James Seddon, and the two fired back. Things got so hostile that at one point Davis threatened to break off communication altogether.

Vance was criticized for his hoarding of clothing. In 1864, North Carolina had 40 textile factories (about half as many as the other Confederate states combined). He had no intention of all those factories' output aiding the Confederate war effort. The state's warehouses held 92,000 uniforms in reserve, plus blankets and large quantities of leather. In the meantime, thousands of Rebel soldiers were marching barefoot and clad in rags. Vance had taken states' rights to an extreme.

Naturally, he opposed the Confederacy's draft laws at every turn. Vance insisted that petty local officials like justices of the peace be exempt from the draft. After all, he said, they were needed at home. (Not true. The Confederate Army needed them more.) Despite all this, Vance was, in his own way, pro-Confederate to the very end. If he was zealous for states' rights, he was less so than the real fanatic, Brown of Georgia.

> **Go See It!**
>
> If you're in D.C., you'll find a statue of Zebulon Vance in the Capitol's Statuary Hall. North Carolina apparently thought highly of their wartime governor. You can visit the Zebulon Vance Birthplace State Historic Site northeast of Asheville.

> **Voices from Then**
>
> Experience has taught me to expect of Governor Vance unjust constructions of my conduct.
> —Jefferson Davis

Bad, Bad Joseph Brown

Joseph E. Brown was Georgia's governor during the entire life of the Confederacy, so he had four full years to obstruct, gripe, and otherwise do everything possible to irk Richmond. He did it all in the name of states' rights, and on behalf of the citizens of Georgia. If you know anything about human nature, you can bet he did it all on behalf of Joe Brown, who liked the idea of himself as King of Georgia, beholden to no one else, especially Jefferson Davis.

Georgia had rich farmland, some developing industries, and a large population. Brown intended to see that those resources served Georgia, not the Confederacy. As far as he was concerned, thumbing his nose at Davis's government came just as easily as thumbing his nose at Lincoln's.

> **Did Y'all Know?**
>
> In his younger days, Brown's political enemies sometimes called him "the Ploughboy," since he was from the yeoman class, not the planter class. Naturally he turned this to his advantage, using it to appeal to the yeoman voters.

Following the Fort Sumter incident, thousands of Georgia boys volunteered for service. Weapons were scarce then, and Brown worked to keep Georgia soldiers from carrying weapons outside the state. He never got past the idea that Georgia regiments were at the service of Georgia, not the whole Confederacy.

Like Zeb Vance, Brown did show some genuine concern for his own people, including the soldiers. To get needed clothing and other supplies for "his boys," he sent purchasing agents to other states and abroad. When taxes increased during the war (as they did everywhere in the South), Brown tried to lighten the burden on the poor and middle-class folk and shift the burden to the wealthy. Georgia had a welfare system to aid the families of yeoman soldiers. (With the main breadwinner and laborer off fighting, farm families with no slaves suffered terribly during the war.)

No one could fault Vance or Brown for having their states' interest at heart. What else would any governor do? But Brown could never grasp the obvious: If the Confederacy didn't survive, the whole South would suffer, Georgians included.

Master Obstructionist

Naturally, Brown reacted with horror to the Confederate draft. He claimed it was "at war with all the principles for the support of which Georgia entered into the revolution." Left to his own devices, he might not have let a single Georgia soldier serve outside the state. But the Georgia Supreme Court sided with the Confederacy: The draft was in to stay, like it or not. Brown was forced to do what all other Southern states did: Enlist very young and very old men to serve as home defense. He also did what Vance did in North Carolina, insisting on hundreds of draft exemptions for "essential" state employees. He created new state offices—all exempt from the draft.

Brown could be incredibly petty. When Davis declared a fast day for the Confederacy, Brown wouldn't observe it in Georgia. Instead, he announced his own *state* fast day—a week later. He announced that the people of Georgia had much more to fear from the "military despotism" of Richmond than from "subjugation by the enemy."

The governor had a highly placed friend: Vice President Stephens, who spent much of the war sulking in Georgia. Brown, Stephens, and Bob Toombs formed the nucleus of an anti-Davis party in Georgia. If Brown thought Georgia's yeoman farmers would join him in his contempt for the Richmond government, he was right.

The fateful year 1864 put Brown to the supreme test. He was the head man in the state when the blue demons, General Sherman's Federal hordes, made their long, destructive march from Atlanta to Savannah. (More about that devastation in Chapter 26.) When Atlanta fell to the Federals, Brown put the men in the Georgia militia, called *Brown's Ten Thousand*, on furlough. Why? So they wouldn't come under Confederate control. (Groan!) Then, stupidly, Brown charged the Confederacy with "abandoning Georgia."

> **RebeLingo**
>
> **Brown's Ten Thousand** was the name given to the Georgia militia. They were also known as **Joe Brown's Pets.** Brown went to great lengths to see that these state defenders were not pressed into the service of the Confederacy.

Was Brown treasonous enough to cut a deal with General Sherman? Sherman thought so. He sent word to both Stephens and Brown to meet him in Atlanta to discuss terms. Sherman's offer: If Georgia would withdraw from the war, he would keep his troops on the main roads and pay for whatever they consumed. Brown and Stephens were not as treasonous as Sherman thought. Neither would meet with him. But Brown hadn't turned pro-Confederate. As late as February 1865, he was calling for a Constitutional amendment that would strip Davis of his powers as commander in chief.

Worth noting: Brown's and Vance's actions were generally approved by their home states. Both of them constantly received letters from soldiers and civilians, complaining about their states' needs being neglected by the Confederate government.

The Least You Need to Know

- The Congress was mainly divided into pro-Davis and anti-Davis factions, but no actual political parties.

- The war forced the Richmond government to impose a draft, impressment, and new taxes, which drew accusations from some congressmen that Davis was a tyrant.

- Davis had some loyal supporters who saw the war as a national emergency that required giving extensive powers to the president.

- Confederate governors mostly cooperated with Richmond, but Zebulon Vance of North Carolina and Joseph Brown of Georgia were noted obstructionists.

Rebel Innocents Abroad

In This Chapter

- ◆ The first nondiplomatic diplomats
- ◆ The world-shaking *Trent* incident
- ◆ Under-the-table purchases
- ◆ Lots of promises, lots of waiting

In the world's eyes, was the Confederacy a nation—or just a bunch of rogue states trying to break away from the legitimate government of the United States? That question never really got answered during the entire course of the Civil War. The nations of the world watched, waited, and drove the Confederate government insane with hints that they *might* recognize the new nation … maybe. The U.S. government took pains to see to it that Britain, France, and other nations stayed out of the war as much as possible.

This story of the Confederacy's foreign relations is amusing, and also a little sad. You get the impression at times that the Confederate government was expecting Europe to appear on the scene as a kind of fairy godmother, making everything right. That myth of Europe as deliverer took a long time in dying, just like the related myth of King Cotton. Still, while

Europe never delivered the South from all its troubles, it did engage in some useful under-the-table transactions that aided the South immensely.

New Kid on the Block

Time for another revisiting of 1776; in their minds, the Confederates revisited it constantly. They recalled that in the American Revolution, nations abroad aided the colonists in their struggle for independence. Great Britain had been the enemy, of course, but the colonists got valuable aid from France. Perhaps that could happen again. Perhaps Great Britain would aid the South, savoring a chance to give the United States a poke in the eye.

Judah Benjamin (1811–1884), former U.S. senator from Louisiana, and holder of several Confederate cabinet posts, most notably secretary of state, giving him oversight of the new nation's foreign relations.

(Florida State Archives)

In its foreign relations, the South had three objectives: Get other nations to recognize the independence of the Confederacy, get foreign aid to break the Union blockade, and secure foreign loans. Overseeing the operations was Davis's longtime confidante, Judah P. Benjamin, who had garnered nothing but criticism when he was secretary of war, but who did a pretty decent job as secretary of state. Benjamin had represented Louisiana in the U.S. Senate, and he and Davis were old pals from their Senate days. Davis in his post-war days claimed that Benjamin was the most accomplished states- man he ever knew. Even so, Benjamin irked many people, who never knew how to inter- pret his peculiar, constant half-smile.

> **Voices from Then**
>
> In his famous epic poem about the Civil War, *John Brown's Body*, poet Stephen Vincent Benét described Benjamin in this way:
>
> Judah P. Benjamin, the dapper Jew
> Seal-sleek, black-eyed, lawyer and epicure,
> Able, well-hated, face alive with life.

Although it clearly had less than the North, by world standards the Confederacy was a rela- tively rich country. It possessed a long coastline with excellent harbors, rich farmland, and vast mineral resources. It also had an organized gov- ernment, well-defined borders, and a homo- genous people. It certainly had more assets and more stability than some of the new Latin American nations that seemed constantly on the verge of another revolution.

In short, there was no reason the Confederate States of America couldn't have taken a legitimate place on the world stage, respected by other nations. This would have happened—*if* there had been peace, *if* the North had not been determined to force it back into the Union, *if* there had been no blockade hindering trade and travel. We will never know what would have happened if those *ifs* had not been such obstacles.

King Cotton, Revisited

We have already looked at the Confederacy's misguided notion of "cotton diplomacy." But the South had a few other cards it could play in the diplomatic game. One was eliminating the middleman. In the past, Southern products made their way to Europe via Yankee middlemen. Plus, there was that nasty matter of the United States' high tariffs. (The U.S. Congress passed yet another high tariff act right after the South- erners departed.) The Confederacy could promise the nations of Europe a low tariff on exports, and direct dealing with Southern producers. In the process, the Confederacy and Europe could deal an economic blow to the United States, which most European nations, England especially, were happy to do.

England, with its hundreds of textile mills, needed cotton—but the bumper cotton crop of 1860 had already been sold and warehoused. The Confederacy chose to embargo cotton, hoping to cause a cotton famine in England, and thus encourage the

" " **Voices from Then**

We point to that little attenu-
ated cotton thread, which a child
can break, but which nevertheless can hang the world.
—Sen. Ben Hill of Georgia,
regarding King Cotton

Cotton can be made to sustain
our government, support our
army, supply our people, and
secure our independence.
—The *Montgomery Daily Post*

English to rally to the Southern cause. Nothing of
the kind happened. The English had plenty of cotton
stashed away. It turns out that the cotton embargo
was incredibly stupid. The first year of the war, when
the Union blockade was barely effective, would
have been the perfect time to sell lots of cotton to
Europe. The effect on the South's economy would
have been phenomenal.

The English did, however, need something else
more desperately than cotton: wheat. A failure of
England's wheat crop in 1861 and 1862 meant the
English were buying wheat from … the United
States. For the time being, the English needed the
North's crops more than the South's.

The First Wave of Diplomats

In the 1860s, no one held the title "ambassador." If you represented a nation abroad
you were a minister (for example, the U.S. minister to France). Since the Confederacy was not, in the world's eyes, a legitimate nation yet, it never really had ministers. The men it sent abroad were agents or commissioners, doing everything that
ministers did, except that they often had to endure snubs and unofficial meetings with
government officials. They didn't usually get the red-carpet treatment given to regular diplomats.

Because the United States was a powerful nation and was making it clear that the
Southern states couldn't legally secede, the world's nations had to handle Confederate
agents carefully. If they were treated *too* nicely, the United States might be angered,
leading to economic sanctions or war. If they were treated badly, there might be consequences later if the Confederacy finally did achieve independence.

The Confederacy wasn't blessed with the tactful, suave type needed in diplomacy. It
had some fine orators, but the type of person who can impress visitors to the U.S.
Senate is not the same type who can charm a roomful of foreign officials. The first
wave of Confederate agents sent abroad were definitely not the right choices. One
was fire-eater William L. Yancey of Alabama, who had helped create the Confederacy
but hadn't been given any kind of post as a reward for his labors.

Yancey was getting his pat on the head from the Davis administration, and it was
the only official post the fire-eater would ever hold on behalf of the Richmond

government. He was certainly not qualified for diplomacy. He was a honey-tongued orator, but that wasn't what was needed in dealing with English officials.

Pierre Rost of Louisiana had been born in France, had served in Napoleon Bonaparte's army, and could speak French, so he was sent to (surprise!) France, to the court of Emperor Napoleon III. The third agent, A. Dudley Mann of Virginia, actually did have some diplomatic experience with the United States. The three faced a problem all Confederate agents in Europe would face: The U.S. diplomats worked against them at every turn. (The main obstacle was Charles Francis Adams, U.S. minister to Great Britain and son of John Quincy Adams.)

Yancey returned to the South in March 1862, thoroughly disgusted with the British. Pierre Rost was sent to Spain, but had no luck in turning that country to the Confederate side.

Another War with Britain?

Nothing would have pleased the Confederacy more than having the United States at loggerheads—or, even better, war—with Britain or France. This came darn near close to happening.

The Confederacy's second wave of diplomats was composed of James Mason of Virginia and John Slidell of Louisiana. Mason was to go to London, Slidell to Paris. Like everyone else leaving the Confederacy during the war, they had to slip past the Union blockade. They did so on an English mail ship, the *Trent*. On November 8, 1861, the ship was stopped by a U.S. Navy ship, the *San Jacinto*, which began the incident by firing shots across the *Trent*'s bow. The U.S. boarding party was not exactly given a warm welcome by the English crew and its mostly Southern passengers. Slidell had his wife and daughters with him and was literally torn from the grasp of one of his daughters. Mason and Slidell were removed and taken prisoner to Fort Warren in Boston.

> **Did Y'all Know?**
>
> Founding Father George Mason, James's famous grandfather, had refused to approve the U.S. Constitution because it permitted slavery. James, of course, owned slaves.

Captain Charles Wilkes, commander of the *San Jacinto*, became a hero in the North, since he captured the two "traitors," Mason and Slidell. Britain saw it differently: Seizing an unarmed mail ship was *not* a heroic act, whatever the North believed. Technically, Wilkes had done something unthinkable—forced a peaceful British ship to stop, then seized two of its passengers. The British were outraged. The government dispatched 8,000 British soldiers to Canada, waiting to see what would happen between Britain and the United States. Britain's prime minister fired off a nasty letter to the Lincoln administration.

The U.S. Secretary of State William Seward knew that the last thing the United States needed was another war. So, officially, the U.S. government disavowed what Captain Wilkes had done. Mason and Slidell were released and arrived in England in January 1862. War had been prevented, but it was still an embarrassing incident for the United States, and the Confederacy was ecstatic.

> ### Voices from Then
>
> It was, perhaps, the best thing that could have happened.
>
> —Confederate Secretary of State Judah Benjamin, on the Union's capture of Slidell and Mason aboard the *Trent*

But the diplomats themselves didn't accomplish much when they arrived. While serving in the U.S. Senate, Mason had written the Fugitive Slave Act (part of the Compromise of 1850), which endeared him to Southerners, but not to the English, whom everyone knew to be strongly anti-slavery. (A quick reminder: In 1833, the English government had passed a law mandating the freeing of all slaves over a period of seven years.) Mason never got on well with the English, who, among other things, objected to his tobacco chewing.

Mason had been instructed to do what the first wave of diplomats had done: Try to persuade the British that the Union blockade wasn't legitimate, since it was totally ineffective. The Confederate agents carried lists of the more than 400 ships that had evaded the blockade. The problem with this argument was the blockade was growing more effective with each passing day.

All the Confederate diplomats were pressed to make it clear to foreign governments that the South was only fighting for its independence—*not* to preserve slavery. (The flip side—the North was not fighting to destroy slavery—was an important part of this message, too.) The North, so the Confederate agents said, was turning into a despot, with Lincoln running roughshod over civil and states' rights.

Swiss Rebel in London

One of the Confederacy's most effective men abroad was Swiss-born Henry Hotze, who had served on the staff of a newspaper in Mobile, Alabama. The Confederacy sent him to London in late 1861, where he proved to be such a talented writer that several London newspapers allowed him to write for them—more specifically, to write pro-Confederate, anti-Union articles. It wasn't such a hard task, actually, because the majority of English papers tended to be pro-Confederate already.

Hotze had two tasks: one, to be the South's chief propaganda man in England, and two, to keep the Confederacy informed of English public opinion. Hotze reported that the English as a whole would have been happy to see the United States broken up into two nations, and also would have been happy to trade with the South. On the negative side, no one wanted war with the United States, and most of the English were strongly anti-slavery. (Having outlawed slavery themselves just 30 years earlier, the English were "newly righteous" about this issue.) Hotze observed that the English upper classes generally were pro-South. This wasn't news. For years, Englishmen traveling in the United States spoke well of Southern planter aristocracy. (Obviously, the English folk who could afford to travel abroad were the upper crust, not the lower classes. And, naturally, they hobnobbed with the South's elite, not with the plain folk.)

> **Did Y'all Know?** _____
>
> Hotze had a kind of subagent for Ireland, which was seeing many of its young men immigrate to join the Union army. The Rev. John Bannon spread propaganda about the ill treatment that Catholics received in the United States. He didn't have to exaggerate much.

Hotze is best remembered for his own newspaper, a weekly which was launched in May 1862. It was *The Index: A Weekly Journal of Politics, Literature, and News*. We talk of a liberal bias in the media today, but in the 1800s, *every* newspaper had a bias of some kind, with no attempt at objective journalism. The aim of *The Index* was, of course, to make the South look good and the North look bad. Many of the contributors were pro-Confederate writers at other newspapers. Hotze's paper didn't have a huge circulation, but it did reach the influence shapers in society. It was essential that the South have a publication like *The Index*, since otherwise all the news of America came from Northern newspapers.

John and Nappy III

John Slidell did finally get to France, where his family was well treated by Emperor Napoleon III. The nephew of the greater (and shorter) Napoleon Bonaparte, Napoleon III believed that France was superior to England in every way, and yet in regard to the Confederacy, his position was always "wait and see what England does." Slidell and others reminded him, of course, that France had aided the American colonies in their war of liberation, so couldn't they please aid the Confederacy now? Napoleon always appeared to be on the verge of officially recognizing the Confederacy—almost, but not quite.

While playing the waiting game with the emperor of France, Slidell wasn't sitting on his hands. He negotiated a loan with the Paris banking firm of Emile Erlanger and

Company, which the Confederate Congress approved in January 1863. The so-called Erlanger loan was basically a scheme of high-risk speculation in cotton. In the shorter term, the scheme worked, and it is estimated that the Confederacy netted around $7 million from the sale of Erlanger's cotton bonds. The security for the loan was, of course, cotton. (If cotton wasn't king, it did sometimes carry some clout on the world stage.) The Erlanger loan was only one of many examples of private foreign firms accepting Confederate business, regardless of their nations' official attitude toward the South.

> **Did Y'all Know?** _____
>
> Napoleon III had spent some time in the United States, having been deported there in 1836 at the command of his rival, the French king Louis Philippe.

Them Other Countries

Great Britain and France were definitely the leading powers in Europe at this stage, which is why they got most of the Confederacy's attention. Russia was a huge country but had never been a major trading partner for the South, so it wasn't considered important. Curiously, for a nation that never had a history of democracy or liberty, Russia proclaimed itself to be strongly anti-slavery. No nation was more blatantly anti-Confederate than Russia, where most peasants lived in conditions much worse than Southern slaves. Jefferson Davis sent Lucius Q. C. Lamar as commissioner to Russia, via England and France, but he never got to Russia, as by this time Davis decided to wash his hands of Europe. (No love was lost on either side.)

> **RebeLingo** _____
>
> **Bounty troops** was the name Rebels used to refer to the German and Irish men recruited by the Union to fight. The Union recruited these men not only at U.S. ports but in their home countries. Southerners deeply resented these soldiers, who had not even been in the country long enough to be considered Americans.

Germany as a nation did not exist in those days; instead, there were several small German-speaking nations in the territory we now call Germany. Germans on the whole were even more anti-slavery than the English working classes. Nearby Poland showed some signs of pro-Confederate feeling, even sending a commission to Richmond, but nothing came of it.

Confederate agent A. Dudley Mann was sent to the court of the world's smallest nation, the Vatican. Mann was to meet with someone who had little political power, but much clout: the pope, Pius IX. (Mann reported he was treated much more pleasantly there than in the other courts of Europe. His audience with the pope lasted 40 minutes—which was pretty long.) Like every other Confederate, Mann was aware of a key source of Union soldiers: Ireland. The Union shamelessly recruited *bounty troops* from new Irish immigrants (who were almost all Catholic, of course) to the North.

The main thing Mann got for his labors in the Vatican was a letter from Pius IX in which he addressed Jefferson Davis as "President of the Confederate States of America." For Mann, and for many other Confederates, this was like a small morsel thrown to a starving dog. *At last, a nation has recognized the Confederacy!* But no other nation, including the United States, interpreted it that way.

Everybody Loves a Winner

Slidell and every other Confederate agent knew the importance of timing. If the South had just won a battle, then the agents could press for recognition. If the North had just won, they were quiet. This was natural. Neither France nor England wanted to put itself in the position of backing a loser. This is why, for four years, the agents played this tiresome waiting game, because France and England had to wait and see whether the South might actually win its independence. The aim of the Confederate agents was, of course, to gain recognition from Europe, get Europe's aid in breaking the blockade, and make independence more likely. You can see why this was a frustrating game to play. Europe was saying, "We will recognize you if you win," and the South was saying, "Help us win, then!"

One of the biggest names in British politics in this period was William Gladstone. At the time of the Civil War, Gladstone was chancellor of the exchequer (roughly equivalent to secretary of the treasury). A devout Christian and a spellbinding speaker, Gladstone made a pro-Confederate speech on October 7, 1862, which raised the South's hopes. Without saying anything anti-Union, Gladstone stated that "Jefferson Davis and other leaders of the South have made an army; they are making, it appears, a navy; and they have made what is more than either—they have made a nation .... We may anticipate with certainty the success of the Southern states so far as regards their separation from the North."

The South was elated that someone of Gladstone's stature could make such a statement. But if they thought this signaled great things to come, they were wrong. The British government continued in its wait-and-see course.

Meanwhile, the Cash Registers Ring

The Erlanger loan, mentioned previously, was one of many transactions taking place between the Confederacy and private firms abroad. Jefferson Davis, Judah Benjamin, and the Richmond government were eager for the official recognition of England and France, but in the meantime the Confederacy had several agents at work, plying their trade with private companies eager to make money from South or North or both.

Caleb Huse, born in Massachusetts, was a former West Point instructor who resigned his U.S. Army commission and sided with the South. The Davis administration sent him off to Liverpool, England, which he made his base as he traveled around Europe. His job: to purchase weapons and equipment for the Confederate armies. He found plenty of firms in France and Austria that were more than willing to supply the South.

James Bulloch of Georgia was a former U.S. Navy man who offered his services to Navy Secretary Stephen Mallory. Bulloch shipped off to England, with the tall order of purchasing ships. He arranged the building of some of the most notorious commerce raiders, including the *Alabama*. Since Britain was technically neutral in the war, Bulloch was always careful to see that warships and commerce raiders built in England were *not* equipped with weaponry until after they left British ports. Bulloch had a young nephew, Theodore Roosevelt, who would later become quite famous.

Huse, Bulloch, and the various other Confederate purchasers abroad had to operate in a kind of cloak-and-dagger atmosphere. Technically, neither Britain nor France was supposed to build warships or supply weaponry to the Confederacy. The Union had its own agents abroad sniffing out such things, constantly snooping around the dockyards of Liverpool to learn what ship-in-progress might be destined for the Confederacy. Seward, the Union's secretary of state, monitored such things closely, and he was forever dropping veiled threats of war if the nations of Europe aided the South in any way. Nevertheless, ships, weapons, and many other items produced in Europe made their way into Confederate hands, whether Seward approved or not.

The Least You Need to Know

- The Confederacy desperately sought recognition and aid from the nations of Europe, especially Britain and France.

- Confederate diplomats were hampered by their unofficial status, the influence of U.S. diplomats, and their own lack of tact.

- Britain and France were both home to many influential Confederate sympathizers, but both nations feared offending the United States.

- Confederate agents managed to secure a colossal loan from France, as well as purchasing ships, weapons, and other materials from Britain and France.

Part 5

Faith, Hope, and Poverty: Civilian Life Goes On

The subject of this book is the Confederacy, not the Civil War—not that you can really separate the two. From the firing on Fort Sumter in April 1861 to the surrenders (plural) in 1865, the people of the Confederacy could not (unless they were sleeping) forget their country was at war. The familiar patterns of civilian life got changed, often dramatically. For those who survived, the experiences made for rich remembering.

In this part, we'll take a close-up look at life on the Southern home front. Life did go on—but no aspect of it was unchanged. People faced forms of government coercion (such as the draft) they'd never known before. They faced shortages of darn near every daily necessity (and, needless to say, luxuries). They came to find the phrase "sound as a dollar" truly laughable.

Enjoy this part, for it has as much drama (and comedy) as any of the war's battle stories.

19

Drafting, Impressing, and Other Coercion

In This Chapter

- ◆ The dying away of "Rah-rah, go team!"
- ◆ Conscripts, draftees … whatever
- ◆ The Twenty-Slave Law, substitution, and other beefs
- ◆ A big bevy of deserters
- ◆ Pressmen and other unpopular things

Freedom from a busybody government was one of the prime motivations behind the forming of the Confederacy. Unfortunately, for the new nation to stabilize itself and, incidentally, wage a war for its freedom, it had to (gulp) do things to interfere with its citizens' freedom. The Confederate government in Richmond learned pretty quickly that the burst of patriotic zeal in 1861 died away fast. So the South had to resort to something totally unprecedented in American history: a military draft.

If you were living in the Confederacy in 1862, chances are you or someone close to you would be subject to the draft. Even if you weren't, you might have to stand by and see some of your property "impressed" for government use. Southerners of all persuasions learned to cope with government interference—by meek submission, whining, laughing, or, sometimes, overt aggression.

Where Have All the Soldiers Gone?

You should recall that, following the firing on Fort Sumter in April 1861, there was a rush of men to enlist in the Southern armies. Men "j'ined up," either because of patriotism, a sense of adventure, boredom, pressure from females, or any combination of the above. Most didn't expect a long war, although some of the wiser men—Jefferson Davis and Robert E. Lee, for example—fully expected a fairly lengthy conflict. But the Rebel victory at Manassas in summer 1861 helped feed the illusion that the Yanks would get whipped good and go home—short and sweet. As the months passed by, the South could see this wasn't going to be the case.

The original volunteers had signed up for 12 months. Late in 1861, Jefferson Davis and his third secretary of war, George W. Randolph, toyed with an unpleasant but seemingly necessary option: a draft. Neither man was stupid enough to believe that the states would be happy about it. Wasn't the Confederacy founded so as to *minimize* government interference in people's lives? But war had created a national emergency. Something had to be done to keep volunteers where they were and to add new men to the ranks.

On April 16, 1862, the Confederate Congress passed the Conscription Act. (No one knew it at the time, but it would later be known as the *First* Conscription Act.) Subject to the draft: all white males between the ages of 18 and 35. (Note that this not only excluded slaves but also free blacks as well. Interestingly, some free blacks did volunteer for the army. Some of these were very light-skinned men who passed as whites.) Draftees would sign on for three years, unless, of course, the war ended sooner. Volunteers already in the ranks suddenly found themselves committed to three years instead of one. As a bit of consolation, they were given 60-day furloughs. Men subject to the draft could, of course, volunteer before being conscripted. This would save them from the shame of

Did Y'all Know?

The South had 1.1 million whites males between the ages of 15 and 40, while the North had 4 million. Immigration added to the North's supply during the war years, while there was practically no immigration to the South.

Voices from Then

I tremble to think of the consequences that may befall us next spring when all our twelve-month's men may claim their discharge.

—Robert E. Lee

being "a dang conscript." Also, if they volunteered, they could ask to serve in a particular unit, meaning they could join up with friends or relatives already in the ranks. Volunteers, unlike conscripts, could vote for their officers.

Worth noting: The Confederate government never lost sight of the importance of states. Draftees were assigned to units from their own states. Also worth noting: The South never experienced bloody draft riots like those the Union endured after the United States instituted a draft in March 1863. New York, noted at the time for its hatred of Lincoln, was the scene of three days of draft riots in July 1863, days in which blacks were lynched, police beaten, and more than 70 people killed.

Exceptions, and Some Heavy-Duty Whining

Southerners took one consolation from the Conscription Act: They knew that the president and the Congress weren't happy about it. They saw it for what it was, an emergency measure. And it was fair. If you were an able-bodied white male between the ages of 18 and 35, off you went to the war.

Unless, of course, you fell into the *exempt* categories.

Davis and the Congress knew that having every able-bodied man in the army would mean that certain vital industries would be without manpower. So, a mere five days after the Conscription Act passed, it was amended, with a list of exempt occupations that were (supposedly) crucial to the war effort. The list included government officials, railroad workers, newspaper printers, miners, factory workers, telegraphers, mail carriers, ministers, teachers (if they taught at least 20 students), druggists, and a few other categories.

RebeLingo

Twenty-Negro Law, or Twenty-Slave Law was a provision of the Confederacy's April 1862 draft law that exempted the owner or overseer of 20 or more slaves. Opponents claimed the law favored the wealthy.

There was some logic in the list of exemptions. But one exempt category caused the maximum amount of griping: the so-called *Twenty-Negro Law,* also known as the Overseer Clause. Essentially, the law said that a plantation could exempt one white male for every 20 slaves. The idea was that plantation slaves would not work or, even worse, might revolt if white males weren't around to keep them in line. Southerners had feared slave revolts—"servile insurrections"—since the time of the bloody Nat Turner revolt in 1831. No wonder Congress declared that the Twenty-Negro Law was "to secure the proper police of the country."

The Twenty-Negro Law was logical—and infuriating. To nonslaveholding Southerners, it was an abomination. The rich men had gotten them into this war—and now were exempting their precious overseers (or themselves) from fighting. The frequently repeated phrase "a rich man's war and a poor man's fight" was inevitably linked with the Twenty-Negro Law. In reality, relatively few men were exempted because of it—only 201 in Georgia and 120 in North Carolina, for example.

Hating the "Bombproofs"

We already noted that not every Southerner was filled with patriotic fervor for the Rebel cause. Some were Unionists, some frankly didn't care one way or the other, some were pro-South but cowardly. Since the Confederacy had exempted national and state employees from the draft, there was a swift rush to sign on as a government clerk, even if the pay was low. As you might imagine, soldiers in the ranks had a mighty low opinion of government pencil pushers, men they sneeringly referred to as "bombproofs."

Did Y'all Know?

Since druggists were exempt, draft dodgers would set up makeshift "drugstores" with a few bottles of pills and patent medicines, castor oil, and so on. The South suddenly found itself with a lot more "druggists" than were actually needed.

More irritating to soldiers, and to the families of soldiers, was the practice of *substitution*. The law allowed a man—known as the "principal"—to hire a substitute to take his place in the army. Congress allowed this loophole for what it thought was a good reason: Wealthy men involved in industry could continue their vital work. But in fact, it simply became a way for the lazy-wealthy to stay out of the war. You can hear the cry again: "a rich man's war and a poor man's fight." Griping against substitution was loud, and Congress finally abolished it in December 1863.

If the principals were less than noble, the substitutes were often worse. Since they were getting paid (by the principals, that is), the craftier substitutes could make a career out of joining up, deserting, then joining up again in another locality.

Draft, Phase II

A mere five months after Act I, Congress passed its Second Conscription Act (September 27, 1862). The Richmond government had learned to its displeasure that many Southern men were clever when it came to avoiding military service. There were thousands of substitutes around, as well as the many "druggists" and other crafty types. Worse, the men in the ranks were being killed off. So many bullets, so few men.

The Second Conscription Act raised the upper age limit to 45. And with a new act came a new list of exemptions. It included some that might strike us as silly—shoemakers, for example. But in fact, shoes were desperately needed in the Confederacy (particularly for the soldiers, who were often barefoot). Also exempted were farmers—to be specific, one man for every 500 head of cattle or sheep, or 250 horses or mules. As you can figure from the numbers, this discriminated in favor of wealthy farmers, and was viewed as another slap in the face of the plain folk.

Government medical examiners faced many potential draftees with real or faked ailments. Men who were in the bloom of health suddenly, after the draft act was passed, found themselves bewailing their rheumatism, gout, dyspepsia (the generic name for digestive ailments), epilepsy, or other complaints.

Voices from Then

Humorist Charles Henry Smith, writing as the character "Bill Arp," claimed that the draft "developed more rheumatics and chronics than was thought possible."

The Second Conscription Act still left plenty of room for loopholes. In fact, Congress passed the act in response to grassroots griping about the first act. The second act did not stop the griping, since all it did was raise the draft age—and, more importantly, extended the long list of exemptions.

Speaking of draft age: The Third Conscription Act, passed February 17, 1864, extended the draft age from 17 to 50. It also eliminated about half of the exemptions—rather late in the game, as some observers saw it.

Just Deserts

How many men actually served in the Confederate Army? The historians are still debating this, but a reasonably accurate figure is about 900,000. Of these, roughly 300,000 were drafted. The volunteers were highly suspicious of conscripts, and with good reason: Draftees had made it clear they didn't wish to serve. They were soldiers only because they were forced into it. And, more importantly, when the opportunity came, many of them deserted.

There were probably about 50,000 substitutes altogether, and military officials estimated that about nine tenths of the deserters came from this group. This surprised no one. The substitutes were purely bounty hunters, eager for a fast buck and (big surprise) a sneaky dash out of the army at their first chance.

Of the other deserters, conscripts (draftees, that is) formed a large part. For whatever reason, they had wanted no part of the fight. Following a battle, with so many of their comrades dead, wounded, or missing, it was fairly easy to skedaddle, particularly if they were near a woodsy, mountainous region with lots of hiding places—and, even better, with more of their own kind as companions. Some of these men just wanted to be out of the army, but some became bitterly anti-Confederate. In areas like northern Alabama and the mountains of Tennessee, North Carolina, and Virginia, deserters banded together, turning into cutthroat fugitives who preyed on loyal Confederates.

Voices from Then

Following the defeat at Antietam (Sharpsburg), Maryland, in September 1862, Robert E. Lee told President Davis that deserters "were the main cause of retiring from Maryland." Deserters and stragglers had reduced Lee's army by almost half.

Did Y'all Know?

Jefferson Davis was grieved at the many deserters, but he rarely had deserters executed. Davis claimed that "the poorest use that could be made of a soldier was to shoot him." Some said Davis was too lenient on deserters.

Deserters weren't all a bunch of lazy slobs, of course. Many a farmer-soldier was led to desert by pleading letters from home, his wife lamenting the lack of food or money and, worse, the crops in the field—or *lack* of crops, due to the husband's absence. ("Plow furlough" was slang for deserting in order to return home and tend one's farm.) Plenty of good, noble-hearted Southern men made the painful decision to desert their regiment and hightail it home, believing it was their first duty to feed and clothe their wives and children. Some of these men later returned to the ranks, and some didn't.

Rebel soldiers captured by the Union could be given the option of swearing allegiance to the United States and fighting in its army. Rebels who did so were called "galvanized Yankees." There were also Rebel deserters who, of their own accord, became galvanized Yankees. Some were men who had been Unionist from the beginning, while others became more anti-Confederate as they saw the South losing the war.

Go Ahead, Impress Me

What was impressment all about? At the root of it was the South's lack of resources. Thanks to the Union blockade of Southern ports, and to the South's shortage of industry, the Confederate government found itself lacking in various supplies. Ironically, to get those supplies it had to turn to its citizens—who were themselves suffering from various shortages. The government believed—correctly—that the less patriotic Southerners would have to be coerced into contributing to the war effort.

The most patriotic ones were already pitching in. The others wouldn't pitch until the government's *pressmen* breathed down their necks.

On March 26, 1863, Congress passed the Act to Regulate Impressments—more commonly known as the Impressment Act. As you might gather from the world *regulate* in the name of the act, the law didn't initiate impressment, but merely regulated it. In fact, long before the act of 1863, the armies and the state governments were already seizing private property for government use. This included livestock, cotton, tobacco, sugar, produce, wagons, machinery, and so on—in other words, all things vital to people involved in farming.

RebeLingo

Pressmen were the government agents who impressed food, horses, wagons, and so on for government use.

Was this a case of the government simply stealing from its own people? No, though it seemed that way to many people. Citizens were to be paid for what was taken. That was the good news. The bad news was that the government's payment was usually less than the normal market value. When the war ended in 1865, one estimate says that the Confederate government owed its citizens $500 million for the property it had seized.

One purpose of the Impressment Act of 1863 was fairness. The government had its list of prices to be paid for particular items, thus preventing local agents from charging whatever they liked (and skimming off for themselves, of course). Local agents traveled around and scoped out supplies of farmers, merchants, and others. Agent and owner would collaborate in assessing the value, and the owner would be paid, either in Confederate money or with a certificate promising payment later.

There was relatively little griping about impressment when the war first began. Most people regarded it as an emergency measure, necessary so long as the war was on. But by mid-war, out-of-control inflation meant that if your property was impressed, not only would you be paid a price below market value, but you would be paid in money that was losing its value by the day. People began to despise the pressmen.

Drafting Slaves—Sort Of

Rich people don't suffer more during hard times, but they do squawk the loudest, and they have the ears of politicians and newspaper owners. Among the wealthy during the Civil War, one of the biggest beefs was having to have their slaves drafted—or, more accurately, *impressed*—into government service.

This was inevitable. The government had a labor shortage, and the slaves represented a huge human resource. While it wasn't until the very end of the war that the Confederacy considered making slaves into soldiers, from the very beginning slaves were used by the army for building fortifications and as cooks and drivers. The Impressment Act of 1863 applied to slaves as well as to other property used for government purposes. As with impressment of property (and remember, slaves were considered to be property), the government was expected to reimburse owners for the use of their slaves.

Did Y'all Know? _____

Free blacks weren't drafted, but in February 1864 Congress passed a law making free black males between the ages of 18 and 50 subject to service in war factories, building fortifications, and military hospitals—at the same pay as soldiers. White Southerners had a real fear of putting firearms into the hands of blacks.

Happily for the planters, there were limits on slave impressment. No more than a fifth of a planter's slaves could be impressed. Gangs of impressed slaves were to be taken proportionately from the planters in a given region (meaning that agents couldn't impress 20 slaves from Planter Jones and none from neighboring Planter Smith—they had to be fair). Even so, planters complained that their slaves were returned to them in worse condition than when they left, and some slaves who left their home plantations with tools didn't return with them. (Did the slaves lose the tools, or did the government take them? Planters suspected the government.)

The Least You Need to Know

- Facing a shortage of men in the army, the Confederacy resorted to the first military draft in America, beginning in April 1862.

- Due to the stigma attached to being conscripted, many men volunteered, and conscripts were generally looked down on.

- A long list of draft exemptions, including men who oversaw more than 20 slaves, caused widespread griping about the war being "a rich man's war and a poor man's fight."

- Draft dodgers used various techniques, such as faking ailments, but the practice most resented by citizens was the hiring of substitutes, which only the wealthy could afford.

- The government could "impress" civilian property for official use, including slaves as well as livestock, produce, wagons, and machinery.

Chapter 20

Confederate Money, and Other Consumer Burdens

In This Chapter

◆ Herr Memminger, the crank on the money machine

◆ Coffee substitutes, wooden shoes, and other clever inventions

◆ The heroic (and greedy) blockade runners

◆ A few smart (and some very dumb) economic policies

◆ The horror of a (gasp!) 1 percent income tax

◆ Dodging bullets to get the mail delivered on time

Say the word *finance* and some people start yawning. It certainly wasn't boring in the Confederacy—money matters caused riots, and the changing value of Confederate money was constantly on people's minds. The central government pursued a policy that governments still follow today: Print lots of worthless paper money, even if that wrecks the economy (which it did).

Nothing boring in this chapter. We'll look at the nation's treasury secretaries, who faced a hopeless task. We'll look at those two-legged reptiles called speculators, who made themselves rich at the expense of their suffering neighbors. And we'll look at how the average Reb coped with shortages of … well, darn near everything. You may find yourself admiring these tough people and asking, *How the heck did they survive this?*

Rebel Finance (and You Won't Get Bored)

You may have heard that Confederate money is much more valuable now than it was when the Confederacy existed. It's true. Collectors value these historical scraps of paper. By the time the Civil War ended, the citizens of the Confederacy were painfully aware that their so-called dollars had more value as paper than as money. (And, by the way, if someone ever tries to sell you Confederate *coins*, don't fall for it. The Confederacy only issued paper money, not coins.)

> **Did Y'all Know?**
>
> Ten of the Confederate states issued their own paper money. When collectors talk about buying and selling Confederate money, it includes these state notes as well as notes issued by the central government in Richmond.

The fall in the value of money didn't happen overnight, of course. In early 1862, the Confederate dollar hadn't devalued much, and prices hadn't changed that much (except for a few favorite items, such as coffee). The Confederacy had inherited from the United States a generally sound system of money. It hadn't inherited much else—above all, not much *gold*, which in those days was the standard for all paper money. The U.S. mint in New Orleans was in Confederate hands only a year, for after spring 1862 the Federals held New Orleans. With no metal for minting coins, the Confederacy did the obvious thing: continued to accept U.S. coins. (Coins last a lot longer than paper money, obviously.) In those days, U.S. coins went up to the value of $10. The Confederacy also allowed English, French, Spanish, and Mexican coins to serve as legal tender. There was an estimated $20 million in U.S. coins in the Confederacy, which people hoarded. They assumed—correctly—that those coins would hold their value even if the Confederate paper money didn't. They also used Confederate postage stamps as coin substitutes.

Shinplasters were small paper notes, from 5 to 50 cents, issued illegally by merchants, railroads, saloons, butchers, bakers, candlestick makers, and so on. An Atlanta paper said that shinplasters "hop out upon us as thick as the frogs and lice of Egypt and are almost as great a nuisance."

For the average Southerner, banking went on as usual, with one crucial difference: You couldn't get hard money, only paper money. This didn't shock anyone at first, but as time passed and inflation ran amuck, the reality sank in: The paper money has no gold behind it.

The Taxman Cometh

At the head of the Southern money machine was the secretary of the treasury—Christopher Memminger, born in Germany, but a lawyer in South Carolina when that state seceded. He had the personality of a damp sponge, and not much imagination either. He could have used it in his position, for the new nation was seriously lacking in most resources. Memminger's financial experience was limited to being a director of a Charleston bank and serving on his state assembly's finance committee. This didn't prepare him to manage the finances of a new nation—and one at war, to boot.

Taxes stink—but how do you run a government without them? In 1861, Southerners (and many Americans) believed they were overtaxed. By our standards today, those people lived in a tax paradise. But think back to the American Revolution: One of its root causes was taxation. (Remember the old slogan, "Taxation without representation is treason"?) The colonists believed they were overtaxed, and in its early years the U.S. government really worked hard not to overtax citizens (and states and counties did the same).

All this means that Southerners didn't wish to find themselves in a new nation with *more* taxes than the old one had. But there was a problem: They were at war, and wars cost money. The government had to tax something, but what?

Did Y'all Know? _____

Part of the April 1863 tax package was a "license tax" placed on various occupations.

Memminger, who was grouchy and generally disliked, did have a grip on reality: He believed the government would have to impose heavy taxes if the nation was to survive. (In theory, it would reduce those taxes once the war was over.) By 1863, two years into the war, the president and the Congress had to agree. On April 24, 1863, Congress passed a comprehensive tax package. It placed an 8 percent tax on rice, sugar, tobacco, liquor, flour, and wool. And—horrors!—there was an income tax, a whopping 1 percent on incomes up to $1,500, 2 percent after that. (Sounds heavenly to us, but to people who had never had their income taxed, it wasn't pleasant.)

Many of the taxes were "tax in kind"—meaning you pay the government in the item itself, not in money. This made sense in the situation of money losing its value. In effect, it meant the government was doing what consumers were doing among themselves—bartering (accepting goods instead of money, that is). The tax in kind was imposed on all agricultural commodities—corn, wheat, cotton, tobacco, sugar, and so on. Farmers, particularly the poorer ones, hated this, naturally.

The Big, Magic Inflation Machine

Taxation, much as the people may have griped about it, wasn't what kept the Confederate machine running. Paper money did—or, rather, was supposed to. The South's printing presses spewed out over a billion and a half dollars in money—more than three times the amount of greenbacks printed in the North in the same period. It wasn't just the national government printing money, but also states—and even cities, railroads, and insurance companies.

> **Voices from Then**
>
> Make money cheap and you make men cheap.
>
> —Texas senator Louis Wigfall

Economics is a boring (and often unpleasant) topic for many people. But most people do understand a basic economic fact: If you print lots of paper money without gold or silver to back it up, the value of the money continually goes down. That is what *inflation* is. And the Confederacy faced inflation like the United States had never seen before.

In 1861, the inflation was a minor nuisance. But by mid-war—1863—inflation was too big to ignore. From May through August of 1863, the value of Confederate money fell more than during the first two years of the war. At the time of Gettysburg (July 1863), four Confederate dollars equaled one U.S. dollar. (Inflation affected everyone. Beggars switched their line from "Give me a penny" to "Give me a dollar.")

Pricewise, the cities were much worse off than the boondocks. Corn might be $2 a bushel in rural South Carolina and $20 a bushel in Charleston. Richmond, the capital, definitely had the highest cost of living of any Southern city. Regarding a Richmond bakery's loaves of bread selling for $1, $2, and $3 apiece, one author wrote,

> **Voices from Then**
>
> I have just procured leather for our negroes' shoes by exchanging tallow for it. I am now bargaining with a factory to exchange pork and lard with them for yarn and for thread to weave homespun for myself and daughters—a pound of lard paying for a yard of cloth. They will not sell their cloth for money.
>
> —Mistress of a Georgia plantation

"The first is only visible by microscopic aid, the second can be discerned with the naked eye, and the third can be seen with outline and shape distinct." A soldier in Richmond in 1863 wrote, "It would cost about fifty dollars to get tight here." It wasn't just booze that was expensive—in 1864 a cup of coffee in some Richmond establishments was $5. Some basic food staples in Richmond, late in 1863: potatoes, $9 a bushel; butter, $4 a pound; eggs, $3 a dozen; a man's suit, $1,500; a gallon of whiskey, $100. Toward the end of the war, a soldier's monthly pay wouldn't buy a pound of bacon.

You might remember from your high school economics class that barter is older than money. That is, long before people used money for financial transactions, they simply swapped things. I have a pound of bacon, you have a barrel of flour, we trade. A pretty usable system, and one that humans always fall back on when money isn't reliable.

The people of the Confederacy did a *lot* of bartering. The busy Tredegar Iron Works in Richmond swapped ironware to planters for food products. Like various other employers, it sometimes paid its workers in goods instead of money. (They didn't mind.) Doctors, editors, and professional men accepted pay in produce. It made sense—you can't eat or wear paper money.

Victory Gardens, and Other Government Programs

Dixie was "de land of cotton"—but remember that the Confederacy chose to with-hold its cotton from the European nations, hoping to create a cotton famine there. This would (they thought) move those nations to come to the Confederacy's aid. That misguided policy didn't work, so the nation faced an awkward problem: lots of cotton, but how do we convert it into cold hard cash? One answer was blockade running. Another answer was crop diversification. Confederates were finding they couldn't make a meal of their "white gold."

All Southern farms, whatever their size, had always raised food crops—not necessarily to sell, but for the families' own use. The war made food crops even more crucial. So citizens were asked (not ordered) by the government to reduce their cotton and plant more food crops. Vigilance committees acted to "encourage" this. One committee asked Georgia statesman-general Robert Toombs to reduce his cotton acreage, and naturally he defied it. (No national government pushing him around, by golly.) When volunteering didn't work, states passed laws, often called *two-bale laws*, requiring the reduction. Cotton production went from 4.5 million bales in 1861 to 300,000 in 1864. Arthur Fremantle, the English traveler, noted that in 1863 in Texas, only one third of cotton land was now planted with cotton, the rest in corn.

The government had been right about one thing: The United States definitely missed its supply of Southern cotton. Needless to say, when the Yanks occupied an area of the South, they were quick to seize bales of cotton. Alas, part of the wastefulness of war is destruction of one's own property—to keep it from falling into the enemy's hands, that is. Many a Southern farmer shed tears as he set fire to his cotton to prevent the Yanks from having it. It

RebeLingo

The **two-bale laws** passed in some Confederate states prohibited any farmer from planting more than two bales of cotton per field hand. This was to encourage farmers to plant more food crops instead of cotton.

made sense, of course—since it would be gone anyway, better to destroy it than have it benefit the Federals.

> **Voices from Then** _____
>
> The planter class had a prejudice against keeping hogs, believing it wasn't digni-fied. (After all, blacks and poor whites kept hogs.) A Macon, Georgia, newspaper:
>
> It is one of the enigmas of the planting race that it hates to raise hogs, which are the first article of prime necessity. Planters had rather raise a pound of cotton at three cents a pound than a pound of bacon at a dollar.

Rebel civilians could benefit the war effort in more positive ways. The country was at war, and soldiers needed gunpowder. A necessity for making gunpowder was niter, so the South had to develop niter beds, or "nitriaries." Pits two feet deep were filled with carcasses, manure, compost, and human waste. Mixed occasionally, the putrid stuff would yield niter after 18 months. Stray dogs usually provided the carcasses.

Soldiers also need lead (for bullets, obviously), and this was in short supply. The lead shortage led the government to ask people to contribute pipes, window weights, roof-ing, and common utensils. In need of copper, the government raided stills (illegal moonshine distilleries, that is), though their owners sometimes killed the confiscators as they had killed Federal "revenooers" in the past.

The matters just mentioned here were voluntary—the government *suggesting* certain courses of action. Runaway inflation led many citizens to beg the government to in-tervene in the economy—specifically, to impose price controls. Strictly speaking, the Confederate government never did—Jefferson Davis feared being called a "tyrant" who directed the nation's economy from Richmond.

Reptiles and Bottom-Feeders

Among the Confederate citizens was a kind of traitor, one who deserved no respect at all: the speculator. He was the person who purchased a commodity, held it, and sold it for a much higher price. Yes, in business circles today, the practice is widely accepted and people make fortunes doing it. But it wasn't standard practice in the America of the 1860s. And in the Confederacy, with its spiraling inflation and the shortage of so many things, it was downright cruel. Simply put, speculators saw an opportunity to make themselves rich by taking advantage of their nation's poverty.

The basic tactic of speculation worked this way: Buy and hoard a particular commod-ity (salt, for example) in a given community, spread the word that there is a shortage, then sell that item at a ridiculous price. A basic rule of business applied: It takes money to make money. Thus, the speculators tended to be people who already had money to spare.

They had no shame at all. Some would enter a community, claim to be Confederate government agents, and buy commodities at a good price (good for them, that is; not good for the sellers). Word of this spread, but not before speculators had made off like bandits. States and cities passed laws against hoarding and price gouging, but the laws were almost impossible to enforce.

Did Y'all Know?

In the novel *Gone with the Wind*, Rhett Butler is a speculator—something the movie doesn't mention, for the producers feared audiences would despise him.

That Blasted Blockade—and Its Evaders

Southerners despised the speculators, but they really hated the Union navy and its blockade. When, on April 19, 1861, Lincoln first declared the blockade of all ports in the seceded states, people in both North and South snickered. Exactly how did Lincoln plan to enforce this, since the Union barely had enough navy ships to patrol its own coasts, much less the South's? When Lincoln proclaimed the blockade, the Union had a grand total of 69 ships on the water.

Gideon Welles, the U.S. secretary of the navy, had zero naval experience, but he was no fool; he did the obvious thing and set to work building up the Union navy. The Union built ships (which aren't built overnight, of course) and chartered private ships as a temporary measure. By the time the war ended in spring 1865, there were over 500 Union ships involved in the blockade. So *blockade running* was fairly easy in 1861, but pretty darn hard in 1865.

According to one reasonable estimate, about 1 in 10 blockade runners were captured in 1861, about 1 in 8 in 1862, about 1 in 4 in 1863, and 1 in 2 in 1864. This averages out to about 1 in 6 ships during the course of the war. In all, about 600 ships were involved in running the Union blockade.

Gone with the Wind's Rhett Butler was fictional, but he represented dozens of real men who engaged in the adventurous—and occasionally

RebeLingo

Blockade running meant avoiding the Union's attempts to prevent water transport into and out of Southern ports. Blockade runners referred to the ships that did this, and to the crews that ran those ships.

dangerous—business of running the blockade. Rhett, like many real blockade runners, was a rather selfish character who made a nice profit for his labor and (only incidentally) aided the Confederate cause. (It is safe to say that blockade runners were the highest-paid men in Confederate service.) He also earned the undying gratitude of spoiled Southerners like Scarlett O'Hara, who resented having to do without their fancy clothes, brandy, cigars, and other "necessities." If they had to rely on roguish, greedy, foreign ship captains to obtain their pet items, so be it.

On the more patriotic side of things, plenty of essential items made their way past the blockade. On the export side, Southern cotton did manage to find its way to foreign markets. It helped pay for the vitally important items that were imported: arms, medicine, salt, and so on.

But the Confederate government and the army had to face one unpleasant fact: The blockade runners were more greedy than patriotic, and somehow (blame it on human nature) silk, which turned a high profit, had a way of getting to Richmond, while less profitable medicine for the soldiers often didn't.

Did Y'all Know?

During the course of the war, blockade runners brought in 330,000 arms for the Confederacy's Ordnance Bureau.

If you were the owner or captain of a blockade-running ship, you had to ask yourself the obvious question: Do I do my patriotic duty and bring in guns and medicine and other necessities, or do I supply spoiled civilians with luxury items? The answer wasn't always exclusively one or the other. Many a blockade runner had cargoes of guns *and* silk (silk being more profitable). But the Confederate government learned early on that not all ship captains were true-blue patriots. Nor were the many Scarlett O'Haras, who either didn't know or didn't care that their precious luxuries occupied cargo space that was needed for items more essential than French perfume, champagne, and lace. (Worth noting: A majority of the blockade-running crew members were foreign, so the glorious cause of the Confederacy wasn't that big a concern for them anyway.)

The runners themselves faced a serious problem: With each passing month, the Union army and navy were capturing more land—and more ports. Not only had the Union built more ships to enforce its blockade, but as more Southern ports were captured, the Union could concentrate more ships on fewer ports. Putting it another way, the blockade runners had more Union ships to avoid and fewer places to dock. (A few mice, not many mouse holes, and a lot of cats.)

Makin' Do and Smilin' Through

The Union blockade was never a 100 percent success, but it worked well enough to assure that there was a shortage of darn near everything in the Confederacy. If the blockade wasn't enough, there were the speculators creating false shortages and high prices, plus the government and its reckless printing of paper money and … well, all in all, everything was working to deprive the people of both luxuries and necessities. By the end of the war, some people had learned that things they thought were necessities really weren't. The word "Confederate" took on the meaning of "substitute"—as in "Confederate coffee" or "Confederate sugar." With so many necessities in short supply, Confederates got very clever about finding substitutes.

We've noted already that one "necessity" that was quickly in short supply was coffee. Strictly speaking, humans don't need coffee to survive—plain water would be the best beverage of all, in terms of body health. But Southerners dearly loved their coffee (has anything changed?), and they detested the many loathsome substitutes for it. They certainly tried every option—various roots, ground-up peas or beans, burnt corn, whatever. None of these even remotely *tasted* like real coffee, nor had that delightful smell, but desperate Southerners seemed to be aiming for at least the *look* of coffee. (None of the substitutes provided that familiar caffeine jolt, alas.)

Did Y'all Know?

Some of the food substitutes were just plain bizarre. Perhaps the weirdest: gunpowder as a substitute for salt. (Maybe they wanted their meals to go over with a bang.)

Salt is even more vital than coffee. It is absolutely essential to human life. In a sense, the people of the 1860s needed it even more that we do, because it was the primary means of preserving and storing meat. The Confederacy had some salt works in Virginia, Florida, Louisiana, and other locales, but most of the prewar supply had come from the Caribbean islands, and the blockade cut off most of that. Naturally the price rose sky-high. Just before the war, a bushel of salt could be had for $1.25. By the end off 1862, it was $30. Rebels didn't live without salt—strictly speaking, no humans can—but they paid dearly for it.

The mere task of writing things down was an ordeal. There was a severe shortage of both paper and ink. Ink, at least, lent itself to substitutes: shoe polish, elderberries, green persimmons, pomegranate rind, dogwood and magnolia bark, ground-up pine needles. A favorite, and one easily gotten, was poke juice—that is, the dark purple juice of the berries of the common pokeweed. People "recycled" all forms of paper, using old envelopes, scraps, even wallpaper for writing material.

What about clothing? Slaves and the poorer whites were accustomed to wearing homespun clothing—plain but durable. As the war progressed, many Southerners who had purchased most of their fine clothes from Northern or European clothiers found themselves dressed in homespun. No one was too pleased at this, but it is human nature to try to make a virtue of necessity. Southern girls who had prided themselves on dressing well changed their attitude. So what if the Yankee girls are wearing the latest fashions? Big deal. We Southern lasses are dressing plainly, but at least we have our independence from the hated North.

Shoes were a chronic shortage for the army (with the sad spectacle of skinny soldiers marching barefoot), but civilians felt the pinch as well. There was a leather shortage, and in those days all shoes were made of leather—until people in desperation found they could make shoes of old carpet strips or burlap bags or (Dutch-style) out of wood. Better than these leather substitutes were squirrel skins and (in Florida and Louisiana) alligator hides.

Probably the shortage causing the most literal aches was the lack of medicine. The North took pains to see that no medicines reached the South, and that included bandages, anesthetics, and surgical instruments. Some of these made their way through the blockade, but the lion's share went to the army, which was right, but this meant civilians had to make do with home remedies and folk medicine. Dr. Francis Porcher's 1863 guide, *Resources of the Southern Fields and Forests*, might be laughable by today's medical standards, but it did help many Southern families muddle through.

And people did muddle through, and sometimes laughed. They could mock their lack of food and alcohol by holding "starvation parties" and "coldwater parties." They could snicker at the writings of Charles Henry Smith, who wrote as the simple but wise bumpkin Bill Arp. The people of the Confederacy proved how tough, and buoyant, human beings could be.

Changing Heads, Not That It Mattered

Christopher Memminger impressed most people as crabby and abrupt, and he was widely hated by 1864, when he took a lot of the blame for the South's economic plight. A man who had been his friend and adviser was George Trenholm, another Charleston man, and probably one of the richest men in the Confederacy. Under much public pressure, Memminger resigned in June 1864, and Trenholm took his place. He didn't know it, but he had less than a year to try to salvage the Treasury Department. It was an impossible task, but he did his best, even donating $200,000 of his own money to the treasury.

When Trenholm took over the Treasury Department, the country was bankrupt. It was in debt to everyone—the soldiers (in pay, that is), various cities and towns (for rent of government buildings, hospitals, depots, etc.), and so on. One estimate puts the debt at $500 million—tiny by our standards, but a mind-boggling sum in those days.

Voices from Then

I took my money in the market basket and brought home the purchases in my pocketbook.

—A popular street saying in Richmond

George Trenholm couldn't have saved the South's economy by himself, even had he been treasury secretary from the very beginning. The factors involved in the Confederacy's demise were way beyond the control of any individual—factors like the blockade, lack of industry, war with a nation that had more men and supplies, civilians who could be both patriotic and selfish … the list goes on.

Got Mail?

In the 1860s, the primary means of long-distance communication was through the mail. Postmaster General John Reagan of Texas had to get clever in the mundane matters of procuring stamps and delivering letters.

June 1, 1861, was the "divorce date," when Southern post offices officially came under Confederate control. Until that time, South and North continued to exchange mail, and Southerners continued using U.S. stamps. After June 1, the South suddenly (though temporarily) found itself with no stamps. For more than four months, postmasters had to make do with hand stamps.

Did Y'all Know?

The United States has always had the rule that no living person is depicted on its stamps. The Confederacy broke that custom when it printed stamps with the face of Jefferson Davis. Other faces on Confederate stamps: George Washington, Thomas Jefferson, Andrew Jackson, and John C. Calhoun—all Southerners and slaveholders.

The very first Confederate stamp went on sale in Richmond on October 16, 1861, and within a month it was in use throughout the country. It was green and bore the face of Jefferson Davis. Saying it was "green" should be taken with a grain of salt. Throughout its existence, the Confederacy always had problems with the quality of the inks used on its stamps. Its best stamps were printed in Britain, not in the Confederacy. (Many of the stamps printed in Britain never made it to the South. The Union blockaders captured many and dumped them in the ocean.)

The U.S. Post Office hadn't been self-supporting since it began in 1789. The Confederacy decided early on that its postal service would pay its own way. It was supposed to be on its own by March 1863, and that required postal rate hikes that, in those days, seemed astronomical. At the beginning, in February 1861, the price to mail a letter in the United States was 3 cents. The Confederacy hiked that to 5 cents (horrors!), then in 1862 raised it to 10 cents. Sounds laughable to us, but a penny would buy you more in those days, and a 10-cent stamp seemed monstrous. Besides raising rates, Reagan cut costs by cutting back on deliveries, and he cut the number of employees by half.

People griped constantly about the mail service. Items arrived slowly or never arrived at all. Some of the cattier newspaper editors claimed that two out of three letters were lost, which was certainly not true. People who had the money entrusted their mail to a private firm, the Southern Express Company. Some people suggested discontinuing the postal service altogether and turning all the mail over to Southern Express, but Congress never voted to do this. With so many men away at war and others working in government offices, the mail was often handled by boys and old men who, frankly, were not the brightest bulbs in the box.

It wasn't Reagan's fault if the Union tore up rail lines or otherwise disrupted service. Union soldiers seemed to take fiendish pleasure in burning down Southern post offices, knowing it disrupted the lives of civilians. He couldn't control the fact that other nations would not accept mail with Confederate stamps. Neither would the United States. Confederate mail to the United States had to go through a private express company. To send mail abroad, Confederates had to hope they could get their letter or package aboard a blockade runner and that it would pass through the blockade. Assuming it did, it would have to have suitable postage affixed abroad. None of this was done for free, naturally.

Did Y'all Know?

The one time the Confederate Congress overrode a Davis veto was regarding a mail matter. Congress had passed a bill allowing newspapers to be sent free to the war front (for the benefit of the soldiers, obviously). Davis said no, the Congress said yes; the Congress got its way.

Homesick soldiers desperately wanted to stay in touch with their families, and vice versa. High rates and erratic service made this difficult. Congress debated the possibility of letting soldiers send and receive mail for free. Davis understood the sentiment, but vetoed such measures. As a kind of compromise, soldiers were allowed to send letters postage due (meaning the recipient paid) if they would write their company and regiment names on the envelopes.

The fall of Vicksburg in July 1863 practically divided the Confederacy in half, since the Federals controlled the Mississippi River. But mail service between the two halves of the nation did not end. Reagan arranged for rowboats loaded with mail to cross the river at night, thus avoiding Union patrol boats.

Did Y'all Know?

One clever soul in Virginia used a kite to carry letters across the Potomac River into Maryland.

With all its problems, the post office managed to operate in the black. One thing that helped was that many people used stamps as petty cash. The Confederacy never issued its own coins, and as U.S. coins grew scarce, stamps filled the gaps.

Though Reagan did a decent job, critics claimed his obsession with balancing his budget made him sacrifice service. Soldiers and their families aching for news of each other depended on the mail, and the mail wasn't always there. Today, with so many ways of communicating, it's difficult for us to grasp the effect of unpredictable mail service on Southern morale.

I Will Survive

We shouldn't be too surprised that the Confederate government did some dumb things—such as causing runaway inflation by printing so much paper money. What should surprise us is that the people somehow muddled through—giving up both luxuries and necessities, finding substitutes, getting by on boring food, wearing worn-out clothing, dealing with money that changed in value practically by the hour … the Yankees experienced nothing like this, which is why they puzzled (a generation later, and beyond) about how Southerners couldn't "let go" of the war.

The Least You Need to Know

♦ Finding itself lacking in gold and silver, the Treasury Department pursued an inflationary policy of printing lots of paper money.

♦ Southerners groaned about new taxes, including an income tax (low by our standards) and an even more hated "tax in kind."

♦ Costs of everything soared during the war, more so in the cities than in rural areas, and many people resorted to the barter system.

◆ Blockade runners were more greedy than patriotic, but they did bring needed supplies to the Confederacy.

◆ People showed cleverness and patience in devising substitutes for everyday items such as coffee, sugar, shoes, and ink.

◆ The Confederate post office was self-supporting throughout the Civil War, but people complained about erratic service and the high cost of stamps.

Chapter 21

A Friend in the Highest Place

In This Chapter

- ◆ Those reverend Rebels
- ◆ Yankee church vandals
- ◆ Praying for *which* president?
- ◆ The Fighting Bishop
- ◆ Davis's days of prayer and fasting

In the U.S. elections of 1862 and 1864, the Republican Party had a catchy slogan to use against the Democrats: "The party of Dixie, Davis, and the Devil." The Democrats were (if you believed the slogan) the party of all evil things, so play it safe and vote Republican (which, by implication, was *God's* party). Most Rebels, of course, believed God was on *their* side.

Christianity, as you might guess, was a vital part of Confederate life, becoming even more so as thousands of soldiers died and civilian life became more and more confused. Ministers found themselves dispensing to people that most precious gift: hope.

Reverend Rebels

Very few Christians in the 1860s were pacifists, so there were no radical anti-war clergymen making headlines as they did a century later when protesting American involvement in Vietnam. The lion's share of Southern clergymen were pro-Confederate, and most were convinced that God wanted the South to win its independence.

Voices from Then

Soldiers of the South, be firm, be courageous, be faithful to your God, your country, and yourselves, and you shall be invincible. In such a cause, victory is not with the greatest number, nor the heaviest artillery, but with the good, the pure, the true, the noble, the brave. We look to your valor, under the blessing of God, for the triumphs of the future.

—From a sermon of Presbyterian pastor J. W. Tucker in May 1862

It didn't occur to most Southerners—certainly not at the beginning of the war—that they might be on the *losing* side. After all, they weren't doing anything wrong. They were being invaded, so naturally their men went forth to fight in defense of their homes. The Bible told them slavery was all right, and the Constitution guaranteed their right to property and the right of each state to make its own laws. Besides that, the North was full of radicals and agitators, chief among them those troublesome abolitionists who dared to call themselves Christians. Southerners hadn't forgotten that abolitionist-terrorist John Brown chopped people to pieces in the name of God.

Did Y'all Know?

Southerners liked to point out that the U.S. Constitution never refers to God, while the Preamble to the Confederate Constitution calls upon "the favor and guidance of Almighty God."

Southern ministers generally supported the Confederacy's view of politics. States were right to secede, the Union had become too oppressive, slavery was sanctioned by God, and so on. But the ministers added another element to the Southern struggle for independence: The Northern churches, they believed, had grown too radical, too concerned with social reform and not concerned enough with evangelism and Bible study. In short, South versus North equaled conservative versus liberal, evangelical Christianity versus social gospel.

Southerners remembered—as did many Northerners—that the original Revolution had its roots in a key idea of the Bible: a chosen people, fleeing corruption and tyranny for a promised land of republican liberty. In the Old Testament, the "chosen" was Israel, fleeing the tyranny of Egypt. In 1776, it was the American colonists, fleeing the tyranny of England. In 1861, it was the Confederacy, fleeing the political tyranny—and the religious apostasy—of the Republican-dominated United States. The "chosen people," the "righteous remnant"—powerful ideas in the Bible, with a powerful hold on American politics.

Though the Confederacy lost the war, the South retained its conservative Christianity—still has it, in fact. Even today, many evangelicals still study the *Systematic Theology* written by Presbyterian pastor Robert L. Dabney—who happened to be a friend and staffer of Stonewall Jackson. After the war, Dabney was blatantly "unreconstructed," and he would probably be pleased to know that the Southern evangelicalism of the 1860s is very much alive.

While harsh comments about Jefferson Davis and the Confederate government filled the newspapers, the clergy as a whole were pro-Davis and, even in the darkest days of the war, sermons tended to be optimistic and very pro-Confederate. The Southern ministers' role as spiritual cheerleaders during the war cannot be overestimated. Of the two primary opinion-shapers of the day—newspapermen and clergymen—the clergy were definitely more pro-Davis.

Praise One Day, Plead the Next

Victory in battle was, of course, an occasion for people to praise God. After the first real victory at Manassas (July 1861), the Confederate Congress officially resolved "that we recognize the hand of the Most High God, the King of Kings and Lord of Lords, in the glorious victory with which He hath crowned our arms at Manassas." This was to become a pattern throughout the war: Praise the Lord of hosts when the Southern armies triumphed.

But they didn't always win. The month of dismal failures, "Black February" 1862, caused some to wonder what God's purpose was. The loss of Roanoke Island, Forts Henry and Donelson in Tennessee, then the fall of Nashville.

> **Voices from Then**
>
> Pray constantly, my brethren, for eyes to see beyond the present moment, for eyes to see the grander purpose of the Almighty. Pray for the moving of the Spirit in your hearts and minds, to illuminate the gloom on these darkest of days.
>
> —From a sermon of Lutheran pastor Stefan Schulz of North Carolina

Why had God allowed the greater part of the state of Tennessee to fall into the Yankees' hands? Southerners asked themselves that age-old question: *What did we do to deserve this?*

Some of them turned to the Book of Job in the Old Testament. Did poor Job suffer because he had been bad? Not at all. His afflictions were a kind of testing, and faithful Job passed the test. He endured, and kept praising God, even when he didn't understand his present predicaments.

RebeLingo

Croakers was the term commonly used in the Confederacy to refer to chronic complainers.

The devout Thomas "Stonewall" Jackson claimed his favorite Bible verse was Romans 8:28: "We know that all things work together for good to them that love God." Now there was a Bible passage to see you through good times and bad, and to give the *croakers* something to think about. Keep believing, don't get discouraged, accept the bad with the good. God moves in mysterious ways.

Losses on the battlefield and deprivation on the home front did lead some people to ask a painful question: Are we being punished for slavery, as the Yankees have said? Some people (including pastors) answered with a loud "No!" Others said, "No, but …" There was a feeling among many Southerners, including some slaveholders, that perhaps they hadn't treated their slaves well enough. Both before and during the war, many Southern pastors had preached on the necessity of treating slaves as God's creatures. While the Confederacy was under siege, many pastors suggested changes in the rules governing slaves. They suggested that slave marriages be recognized as legal, that slaves be allowed to learn to read and write, and that slave families be kept together whenever possible.

Scattering the Flocks

Not all the Southern ministers were at home with their churches. Hundreds of them joined up with the army, either as chaplains or as regular soldiers. This left many churches pastorless, particularly in rural areas where several "circuit" churches might share one minister. Few churches actually closed down, but many found their services either suspended or irregular. Sunday schools met less often as well.

Several famous battles were fought in the vicinity of churches, including Antietam and Shiloh (which took its name from the small church at the site). Any church within a mile of a battle was likely to be turned into a field hospital, with all the blood and gore that entailed. Not quite as messy but equally degrading, Southern churches

might be taken over by occupying
Federals and used as stables for horses.
And sometimes the Union soldiers could
be plain malicious. Many a Southern
church had its stained glass windows broken and its walls and pews vandalized by
the Federals. Some of the graffiti was downright obscene. When Sherman's troops
marched through Georgia and South Carolina,
they sometimes tore down wooden churches
and used the timbers to build sleeping huts,
which they abandoned in a few days.

> **Did Y'all Know?** _____
>
> Some Union soldiers didn't
> even hesitate to vandalize
> George Washington's church.
> The Pohick Episcopal Church in
> Lorton, Virginia, built on a site
> Washington himself selected,
> was vandalized by the Federals
> and used as a stable.

Such abusive treatment had the positive effect of uniting churches. Prior to the war, ministers could be brutal in denouncing how other denominations were wrong in their beliefs and practices. Christians fussed over such matters as the proper way to baptize (was it necessary to immerse?), how often Communion should be taken (every Sunday? four times a year?), whether ministers should wear robes, and so on. These trivialities faded into the background as churches of all denominations faced some common enemies—Yankees, death, vandalism, famine, and all the senseless waste of war. There was a kind of nondenominational Christianity shaped by common sorrows.

Praying for Which President?

In the Episcopal churches of America, praying for the president was (and still is) a required part of Sunday worship. Obviously, there was a new problem to deal with: Could Episcopal ministers in the seceded states be expected to pray for Abraham Lincoln?

Recall from Chapter 5 that the Episcopalians didn't split prior to the war as the Baptists and Methodists did. But that matter of praying for the president … well, there seemed to be no way to sweep that under the rug. So, without all the anger and hissing and name-calling that the Baptists and Methodists experienced, the Southern Episcopalians scheduled a conference in October 1861, in which they formed the Protestant Episcopal Church in the Confederate States of America. No nastiness, just a peaceful separation, which was ended almost immediately after the Civil War ended. Both sections used the same Book of Common Prayer as their guide to worship, so in the part of the ritual mentioning "the president," Northerners prayed for Lincoln, Southerners for Davis.

Did Y'all Know?

Union general William Tecumseh Sherman was skeptical about religion and didn't particularly care if Southerners in occupied areas prayed for the Confederate president: "Jeff Davis and the Devil both need it," Sherman said.

When Federal troops occupied an area, they took a great interest in the Episcopal worship service. Ridiculous as it sounds to us, Union officers could be very harsh to Episcopal ministers who attempted to pray for "our president, Jefferson Davis." Some ministers knuckled under and, grudgingly, offered up a prayer for Lincoln. Some others thought they could simply omit the prayer altogether, but in one Episcopal church in Virginia the minister was arrested for doing this. In a church in Arkansas, a Union officer realized the minister had omitted the prayer, so he yelled out "Stop, sir!" and insisted on reading the prayer himself. In a few churches, women showed their contempt for the Union and Lincoln by walking out of the service when the prayer was read.

The Episcopalians were the only denomination *required* to pray for the president. Almost all other churches *chose* to, of course. But when the Federals occupied an area, they monitored worship services carefully, waiting to leap on pastors who dared to pray for Jeff Davis or the Confederacy. Those sacred parts of the Constitution—free speech and free exercise of religion—were not applied by the Union to the conquered parts of the South.

One other item about the Episcopalians: One of their bishops, Leonidas Polk of Louisiana, was also a Confederate general. Polk, a West Point graduate, gave up a military career to become a minister—then, in 1861, offered the Confederacy his military services. Northerners mocked the "Bishop-General," but Southerners were pleased that a high-ranking church official was also a high-ranking general.

Presidential Piety

Put yourself in Jefferson Davis's shoes. You have to deal, every single day, with petty, egomaniacal politicians. You have to read and hear the complaints—many of them valid, many of them silly—of people all across the Confederacy. You see your every word and deed cursed and ridiculed in the newspapers. You have to oversee a war in which the enemy has vastly more men and material than you. Your wife and houseful of children need your attention, too. Your health, which has never been all that good, gets even worse under stress.

Now ask yourself: Under such circumstances, would you likely become less religious—or more? You can probably guess that the Confederate president became *more* religious with each passing day.

Davis had always acted according to Christian morality, as he understood it. What changed during the war was not his moral standards, but the *emotional* element of religion. The thing that lies at the root of every religion—feeling confused and helpless and needy in a threatening world—suddenly enlarged. He was finding that there were chasms in his soul which could be filled only by faith. In May 1862, Davis was baptized and confirmed in the Episcopal church.

His critics scoffed. It was a "foxhole conversion," they said, and probably insincere—a public relations move, designed to convince pious Southerners that their president was a good man. But from everything we know of Davis, his joining the church was totally sincere. He, like most other Southerners, realized he was not master of his own fate and needed to rely on a higher power.

Fairly early in the war, even before he joined the church, Davis announced national days of prayer and fasting. Christians gathered together in their churches to hear their pastors preach on sin and repentance. For some, this was an opportunity to enumerate the sins of the Yankees. But in most congregations, preachers spoke out against the Southern people's own transgressions. These included, as you might expect, swearing, Sabbath breaking, drunkenness, and infidelity. But there were also the prevalent sins of greed and selfishness, seen in the many people engaged in speculation, hoarding, overcharging customers, and using the war as an excuse for all manner of shady dealings. Pastors were painfully aware that while war brought the community together, it also allowed corruption and avarice to flourish.

> **Go See It!**
>
> St. Paul's Episcopal Church is at Grace and Ninth Streets in Richmond, Virginia, within a block of the state capitol. This is the church that Jefferson Davis and his family attended, and practically everything in the church is a memorial, many of them connected with the Confederacy.

Davis proclaimed nine national days of prayer and fasting during his tenure. He was probably aware that, aside from their spiritual value, they were good for morale, as is any activity in which people all across a nation are doing the same thing at the same time. While there were some gallows-humor jokes about fasting when so many people were hungry anyway, people understood the basic purpose of a fast: self-denial, contributing what you might have consumed to someone who has nothing. Many churches and charitable groups collected money and food to give to the really destitute.

Summing up: Christianity was alive and well in the Confederacy, despite the many obstacles that the war presented to the normal routines of the churches. Southern pastors were faithful supporters of the cause, and there is no doubt that as a group they worked harder than anyone to keep Southern morale high. Like all trials and tribulations, the war served to deepen faith.

The Least You Need to Know

- ◆ Southern ministers as a whole were enthusiastic supporters of the Confederate cause.

- ◆ Military defeats and other trials led many to seek consolation in the Bible and in the belief that the Southern cause was right.

- ◆ In Union-occupied areas, churches were often vandalized by the soldiers, and ministers were harassed for any anti-Union messages.

- ◆ Jefferson Davis's own faith was deepened during the war, and he proclaimed several national days of prayer and fasting.

Chapter 22

Morale Builders: A Handful of Heroes

In This Chapter

♦ Stonewall the martyr

♦ Jeb—centaur, dragoon, cavalier

♦ Forrest—wizard and devil

♦ Rebel spies

Even in an age before movie stars, recording artists, and sports celebrities, people had their idols. In the Confederacy, the idols tended to be (big surprise) military heroes—specifically, those who won battles over the detested Yankees. If the heroes could do daring things (such as capturing a Union general's personal belongings), so much the better. In a way, the Rebels of the 1860s were no different from us today: They liked to be entertained, and stories of tough-fighting generals, crafty spies, and hard-riding cavalrymen were very entertaining.

As a nation in the making, the Confederate States of America had a definite need for heroes and saints, for bigger-than-life figures who would make Southerners proud to be free and independent. It had such characters in abundance, and they still fascinate people today.

Heroes, Local and National

Your author recalls his fourth-grade Alabama history textbook, *Know Alabama*, which had a chapter on "The Gallant Pelham," a handsome young Alabama lad who made a name for himself as an artilleryman in Virginia. Pelham died in action, and girls in Virginia and Alabama mourned for the blond hero. A hundred years later, Pelham was still being praised in school textbooks.

Every Confederate state had its John Pelhams: courageous, handsome boys (most of them single) who felt the call of patriotism—and who knew that the surest way to win the love of women and the admiration of men was to show bravery under fire. While the South had its share of army deserters and shirkers (not to mention greedy speculators and windbag politicians), it had its "knights," too, men so bold and brave that all the romantic talk about Southern cavaliers wasn't mere legend. Some of the exploits got stretched in the telling, yet there were some honest-to-goodness heroes behind the myths.

The Last Cavalier

The Virginia-born James Ewell Brown Stuart—"Jeb," always—was a mama's boy who seems to have dedicated his life to pleasing women—platonically, of course. He made a boyhood vow to Mama Stuart never to touch liquor (a common vow to mamas in those days), and he never did. While he was totally faithful to his wife, Flora, he sucked up female attention like a sponge. His jangling golden spurs and his red silk-lined cape impressed soldiers in both armies, but Jeb's main aim seems to have been to impress the ladies. He succeeded, and they showered him with tokens of their affection (such as twining roses around his horse's bridle).

Stuart carried a French saber and wore gauntlets reaching almost to his elbows. His hat with its famous black plume and his cape lined in red silk were known all across the South. His saddle straddled a bright red blanket. Some admirers gave him two Setters, whom he named Nip and Tuck. His band of merry cavalrymen included the banjo-picking Joe Sweeney (known for his comic parody

> **Did Y'all Know?**
>
> In his prewar days, Stuart had encountered abolitionist-terrorist John Brown in Kansas. In 1859, when Brown and his band holed up in the Federal arsenal at Harper's Ferry, it was Stuart who was able to identify Brown—who, at the time, was using the clever alias "Mr. Smith."

songs, not for soldiering) and some other colorful characters, all proud to be part of the entourage of the near-legendary Jeb.

Jeb relished his role as the "Jolly Centaur," the great cavalry hero of the South. His troops somehow managed to make a complete circle—undetected—around the troops of Union general McClellan (the famous "Ride Around McClellan"). Much has been written about this exploit in June 1862. Stuart and about 1,200 cavalrymen were on a scouting mission, scoping out the Union troops of "Little Mac," George McClellan. In 5 days, the Stuart band rode 100 miles around Little Mac's army of more than 100,000. The Ride Around McClellan provided Robert E. Lee with information about the Union flank. It also boosted Southern morale, for the ride somehow made the huge blue-clad army seem not so threatening. And it provided the Confederacy with a new hero.

Another brassy deed was his capture of the personal effects of egomaniac Gen. John Pope. Like the Ride Around McClellan, this was a great morale booster for the Confederates. On another occasion, Stuart's men captured the trunk of a Union officer. It contained letters from the officer's wife *and* from his mistress. Stuart saw a chance to be moral and impish at the same time: He mailed the mistress's letters off to the wife. On another occasion, the Jolly Centaur had one of his men send a telegraph message to a Union officer, complaining about the quality of the mules he had just captured from the Union.

Always the chatty, laughing, back-slapping people person, Jeb somehow became a close friend of tight-lipped, reticent Stonewall Jackson. Perhaps opposites attract. One night, after a long day of riding, Stuart crawled into bed (with his spurs still on) beside the sleeping Jackson. In the morning, Jackson appeared at breakfast rubbing his scratched calves. He requested that if Stuart ever slept with him again, would he please not "ride him around like a horse all night." (Oh, those cavalrymen.) When Jackson was mortally wounded after his smashing victory at Chancellorsville, Stuart was given temporary command of Jackson's forces.

> **Go See It!**
>
> Just south of a shopping mall on U.S. Highway 1, north of Richmond, Virginia, you will see a roadside marker indicating the spot where the famous Jeb Stuart was mortally shot.

Like several Confederate generals, Stuart died young. He had once stated that "All I ask of fate is that I may be killed leading a cavalry charge." He got his wish—sort of. In fact, the shot that killed him at Yellow Tavern, Richmond, was fired by a Union soldier *on foot*. After being mortally wounded, the ever-spunky Stuart said, "I had rather die than be whipped." A fighter to the end, he ordered his men, "Go back! Go back and do your duty, as I have done mine, and our country will be safe. Go back! Go back!"

As he lay dying in Richmond, Jeb received numerous visitors, including President Jefferson Davis. The pious Episcopal mama's boy died singing "Rock of Ages" with his devoted men. His last words: "I am going fast now. I am resigned. God's will be done." The fatherly Robert E. Lee grieved at Stuart's death, noting that "he never brought me a piece of false information." Lee, who had been head of West Point while Stuart was there and who called Stuart "the eyes of the army," later claimed that "I can scarcely think of him without weeping." Stuart was only 31 when he died.

The Gritty, Profane Wizard of the Saddle

If Stuart had a cavalry counterpart in the western Confederacy, it was probably the "Wizard of the Saddle," Nathan Bedford Forrest. Both men were tough, fearless fighters. They didn't have much else in common, though. Stuart was of the Virginia plantation aristocracy, West Point–trained, devout, jolly, and ever concerned about his looks. Forrest was of the plain-folk class, with no formal military training, no religion (until his old age, anyway), and not the slightest concern about his appearance. Nonetheless, he was, like Stuart, an amazing character, so much so that after the war, Union general Sherman referred to Forrest as "the most remarkable man our Civil War produced." And, oddly, for someone who was only semiliterate, he was also one of the most quoted.

Nathan Bedford Forrest (1821–1877), "Wizard of the Saddle," who enlisted as a private at age 40 and became the best-known cavalry general in the Army of Tennessee.

(Tennessee State Library and Archives)

Forrest's middle name was appropriate, coming from his backwoods birthplace, Bedford County, Tennessee. He personified the ornery, hard-working, backwoods farmers who far outnumbered the high-bred plantation aristos like Lee and Stuart.

Did Y'all Know?

Forrest was, at best, only half-literate. On paper he referred to the Yankees as "suns of biches."

Forrest's father died when Nathan was only 16, and Nathan became head of the family and chief provider for a large brood. Nathan managed to make a small fortune in a lucrative (and dubious) business—buying and selling slaves.

When war broke out, 40-year-old Forrest enlisted as a private. With no military training whatsoever, he rose to the rank of lieutenant general in three years. The Confederate Army was packed with West Point graduates ("P'inters," as he called them, mostly in disgust), but Forrest made his military reputation with sheer gutsiness. The backwoods boy took an unromantic view of war: "War means fightin' and fightin' means killin'." Forrest knew something about killing, since he claimed at the war's end that he had personally killed more men than any other American gen-

Did Y'all Know?

Forrest had no patience with army officers who thought that manual labor was beneath them. When a lieutenant wouldn't help to row a boat, Forrest slapped him so hard he fell into the river. The men pulled him back into the boat, and Forrest told him he would either row or be drowned.

eral. (This included one of his own subordinates, whom he killed in a brawl.) Though he gained fame as the Wizard of the Saddle, his horses knew something about killing, too. Forrest had 29 horses shot from under him. The men he called his Critter Company idolized the valorous man with martial fire in his blood. He once told his soldiers, "Men, if you will do as I say I will always lead you to victory."

"That devil Forrest," as he was dubbed by his Yankee opponents, galloped to fame in the western regions of the Confederacy, far from the better-known battlefields of Virginia. His doings didn't go unnoticed, though, and Union general William T. Sherman sent a message to Secretary of War Stanton: "There will never be peace in Tennessee until Forrest is dead." In one noted cavalry battle, Forrest prevailed with 3,500 men against the Union's 8,000. Forrest had gone on record as saying, "Get there firstest with the mostest," but he proved that having the mostest wasn't always necessary.

Voices from Then

War means fightin' and fightin' means killin'.

Forward, men, and mix with 'em.

The way to whip an enemy is to git 'em skeered, and then keep the skeer on 'em.

Shoot at everything blue and keep up the skeer.

Charge, give 'em hell, and when they fall back, keep on charging and giving 'em hell.

In a rout like this, ten men are equal to a thousand.

I did not come here to make half a job of it.

Men, if you will do as I say I will always lead you to victory.

Give him hell, Captain Morton—as hot as you've got it, too.

If they'd give me enough men, we could whip old Sherman off the face of the earth!

I ain't no graduate of West P'int, never rubbed my back up agin any college.

I will share the fate of my men.

—The quotable Nathan Bedford Forrest

In his official farewell to his Critter Company at the war's end, Forrest truthfully told his men, "I have never on the field of battle sent you where I was unwilling to go myself." Historians still ponder Forrest and wonder how the Confederacy might have fared if there had been more generals like him. Perhaps the South, so much dominated by its planter class, had underestimated its tough, tenacious yeoman farmers.

Incidentally, the novel (though not the movie) *Forrest Gump* reveals on its first page that the main character was named for Nathan Bedford Forrest.

Again, the Aggressive, Peculiar Jackson

A soldier who served under General Nathan Bedford Forrest claimed that "the commonest soldier under his eye became a hero." The same soldier said that Forrest's "commission as general was not only signed by Jefferson Davis, but by the Almighty as well, and his soldiers knew it." Soldiers who served under "Old Jack"—"Old Blue Light"—"Stonewall"—Gen. Thomas J. Jackson—said the same thing. They also observed something else that was true of both Forrest and Jackson: Some commanders inspire courage and zeal on the battlefield, but a select few can even conquer fatigue. Veterans of Jackson's brigades looked back on the war years and wondered, "Did we really march that far and fight that hard—with so little food and so little hope?" Jackson gave them hope, and he showed a genuine concern about the food as well.

Like Forrest, Jackson was from the plain-folk class (Jackson being slightly higher on the economic scale), both from that tough Scottish-Irish stock that settled the South's mountains and hill country. Both were plainspoken, no-nonsense types, with Jackson more genteel and definitely less profane than the razor-tongued Forrest. Though Jackson was a West Point man (a type Forrest usually disliked), both men shared the same philosophy of war: "Always mystify, mislead, and surprise the enemy" (Jackson's words). His battle plans he carried only in his own head, a source of endless frustration to other officers. He once stated that "If my hat knew my plans, I would burn it." No doubt Forrest would have approved of Jackson's words, "Attack at once, and furiously!"

> **Go See It!**
>
> Stonewall's famous horse, Little Sorrel, is stuffed and preserved at the Virginia Military Institute's Museum in Lexington, Virginia. His own name for the horse was Fancy, and he had originally planned to give it to his wife, but grew so fond of it he kept it.

Unlike his friend Jeb Stuart, Jackson could never play the role of elegant cavalier. He clomped around in oversized boots (his feet were huge), rode a horse barely larger than a pony, and kept his cap pulled down so far that his eyes were barely visible. Still, those blue eyes had an almost demonic (or was that heavenly?) way of flashing when he was fired up.

As a God-fearing man, Jackson claimed never to seek glory for himself. It came anyway, and he wasn't comfortable with it. His friend Jeb Stuart loved getting gifts from admirers; Jackson had more of an "aw shucks" attitude. He wrote his wife, Anna, telling her to disregard the press coverage of his victories: "Don't trouble yourself about representations that are made of me. These things are earthly and transitory. There are real and glorious blessings for us beyond this life." He once caught a captured Yankee soldier plucking hairs out of his horse's tail. Jackson asked him why, and the soldier doffed his hat and said respectfully, "General, each one of those hairs is worth a dollar in New York." Jackson blushed.

Jackson had handled his troops well at Sharpsburg in Maryland (more about that tragic battle in Chapter 23), and in December 1862 he led the right wing of the army to a smashing victory at Fredericksburg, Virginia. His troops wintered on the Rappahannock River, and the devoted husband got to spend some time with his beloved Anna ("my sunshine"). In late April 1863, his domestic bliss was cut short by the news that 134,000 Federals were crossing the river, led by the handsome, daring, and loose-living Gen. Joe Hooker. (One observer claimed that Hooker's headquarters was "a combination of barroom and brothel.") Was this some sort of divine morality play—the pious Lee and Jackson versus the boozy, womanizing Hooker?

The Martyr "Crosses the River"

Lee and Jackson faced Hooker at Chancellorsville, Virginia, the first week of May 1863. (There was no actual *ville* at Chancellorsville—no town or city, that is. It was merely a road junction with the large Chancellor mansion and its outbuildings.) Before the battle Hooker predicted—wrongly—"God Almighty will not be able to prevent the destruction of the Rebel army."

> ### Go See It!
>
> A must-see for Civil War buffs is the multisite Fredericksburg and Spotsylvania National Military Park, one of the sites being the Chancellorsville battlefield. The sites cover a large area west of Fredericksburg, Virginia; all are worth a visit. One of the sites contains the Stonewall Jackson Shrine, the small outbuilding where he died. It is maintained to look as it did at the moment he passed on.

Apparently God did. The battle was a severe blow for the Union, with 17,000 casualties. Everyone blamed Hooker for the loss. The blame lay in a brilliant maneuver, Lee facing Hooker's front, with Jackson making a flank movement toward Hooker's right, attacking from the rear. On May 2, he completed his flank march around the Union right. The Rebs had whipped a force twice their size.

But the day ended tragically. At twilight, some of Jackson's own men mistakenly fired on him. Two in his party were killed, and he was wounded in three places. One of Jackson's stretcher-bearers was shot (this time by Union fire), and Jackson was dropped—landing on his severely wounded left arm. The arm had to be amputated and was buried reverently. (Ironically, the one time in his life he ever requested liquor was after his wounding—when there was none available.) His wife brought their infant daughter Julia to his deathbed, and Jackson, floating in and out of delirium, stroked her head with his one remaining hand and said, "Sweet one! Little comforter!"

Jackson's wounds weren't that severe, and many men survived amputations. But in this preantibiotic world, all sorts of infections could afflict a wounded man. Pneumonia set in. The devout Presbyterian lingered a few days, then died (as he wished) on a Sunday—May 10, 1863. His final words—"Let us cross over the river and rest under the shade of the trees"—have been some of the most quoted words of the Civil War era. Stonewall—"Old Jack"—was only 39.

> **Voices from Then**
>
> Even in his dying delirium, Jackson thought of his men: "Tell Major Hawks to send forward provisions to the men."

The Confederacy went into deep mourning. Not long after Jackson's death, someone found Jefferson Davis staring blankly into space. Davis said, "You must forgive me. I am still staggering from a dreadful blow. I cannot think." Robert E. Lee wept over Jackson, lamenting that Jackson had lost his left arm (literally), while Lee had lost his right arm (his best general, that is). Stuart, who temporarily assumed Jackson's command, said that "the good and great Jackson was the dearest friend I had." Less than two months later, at the fateful Battle of Gettysburg, the entire Confederacy was asking the question, "What if Jackson had been there …?"

Virginia is thick with Stonewall Jackson monuments (including one in a black church), and he was one of three Confederates (along with Davis and Lee) immortalized in the colossal sculpture at Stone Mountain, Georgia. The orphan boy from western Virginia continues to inspire, puzzle, and fascinate people the world over.

A Bevy of Rebel Spooks

The Confederacy had some notable spies—and some overrated ones, too. The very theatrical Belle Boyd of Virginia made a postwar career of lecturing on her spying exploits—which she exaggerated considerably. Still, the horse-faced woman known as "La Belle Rebelle" and the "Secesh Cleopatra" did do the Confederacy some good, possessing the knack for wheedling information out of Union soldiers.

Women, you might recall, played a key role in recruiting for the Confederate Army. ("What? You won't fight for the South, you coward? Why, then, I won't marry you!") They also played the serious role of maintaining hearth and home while the menfolk were away. But some women, Belle Boyd among them, just had to play a more active, and dangerous, role in the war. For the most romantic and adventurous, spying was a natural calling.

Recall from an earlier chapter that at the first major battle of the war (Manassas, Virginia, in July 1861), the Confederate troops had been telegraphed vital information about Union movements. It came from Rose Greenhow, who was every bit as theatrical as Belle Boyd, and probably more effective in the Confederate cause. The widow of a Federal worker, Rose was a charming Washington hostess with friends in high places. Continuing to live in D.C. after the war commenced, she wheedled information out of federal officials and passed it on to Richmond via her "little birds," mostly lower-class girls and young women who were thrilled to be involved in spying.

Did Y'all Know?

Both Belle Boyd and Rose Greenhow were confined at the Old Capitol Prison— formerly the Old Capitol Boarding House, where Greenhow had grown up. In an earlier time, it was many congressmen's home away from home. During the war it housed many spies and others suspected of working for the Confederacy.

Her nemesis was the Union's chief spy catcher, Scottish-born Allan Pinkerton, who tried his darndest to find evidence Rose was spying for the Confederacy. She was put in prison for a time, which the Confederacy held up as an example of how Lincoln had no respect for habeas corpus. Eventually, the Union sent her south. She was the toast of Richmond, then went to Europe as a Confederate diplomat. In one of the war's most dramatic pursuit stories, she returned from Europe with thousands of dollars in gold for the Confederate treasury, but off the North Carolina coast her ship was chased by a Union vessel. Fearing capture, "Rebel Rose" insisted on being let down in a small boat. It capsized, and Rose drowned—weighted down with all the gold she had.

The Least You Need to Know

- Cavalry general Jeb Stuart fascinated the South with his warmth, fine dress, daring, and piety.

- Backwoods-born Nathan Bedford Forrest rose from private to general with no military background and a great deal of grit.

- The quirky Stonewall Jackson, killed by friendly fire at Chancellorsville in 1863, was widely mourned, probably the greatest one-man loss the nation experienced.

Part 6

War, Total War, and Terrorism

The first year of the war, 1861, didn't give much hint of what was to come. The Confederates were pleased with their July victory at Manassas, and there followed a lull, during which the Yankee war machine was assembled and refined. Things would get nastier in 1862, and the old rules about "civilized" warfare would be cast aside by Union generals like William Tecumseh Sherman and Phil Sheridan. The horrors that were visited upon civilians would be remembered by Southerners for generations. What many of them endured was not war but terrorism. Some of the terrorists were pro-Union guerrillas, but others were regular Union army men, brutalizing people who had once been their fellow citizens.

All was not gloom and bloodshed and deprivation. If nothing else, a badly outnumbered Rebel army proved it was made of pretty tough material (and ditto for Southern civilians). That army's exploits still inspire people today, as did the fortitude of civilians. Sorry to give away the ending, but the South lost. Then the defeated Rebs had to endure another 12 years of hell in what became known as Reconstruction.

Chapter 23

1862: The "Beast," Maryland, and More

In This Chapter

- ◆ The too-nice-to-be-nasty McClellan
- ◆ The beer-bellied, cross-eyed Beast of New Orleans
- ◆ Pope, the hindquarters-headquarters man
- ◆ Rebs on Union soil (wow!)

This chapter will remind you of something you may have noticed already: One of the Confederacy's biggest advantages for the war's first two years was that the North, with all its manpower, couldn't seem to find a really tough general to head its armies.

We'll meet a couple of Union generals who deeply offended Southerners through their treatment of civilians. And we'll see more of the civilized— but timid—George McClellan, "Little Mac," who faced off with the Rebels in the bloodiest one-day battle of the war.

The Unvillainous Little Mac

The original Evil Yankee Villain for the Confederacy was, of course, Abraham Lincoln. But Lincoln himself wasn't personally invading the South, shooting at Rebel soldiers, invading their homes, and trampling on their rights. The dirty work was left to those whom Confederates called "Lincoln's hirelings." Some of these hirelings proved to be much nastier characters than the despised Lincoln.

Year one of the war, 1861, was relatively civilized. The only major battle was at Manassas in Virginia, where the green Southern troops beat the green Northern troops, which (alas!) left many Southerners wandering around in a fool's paradise, assuming (or praying) that the war would end quickly, with the South an independent nation.

But Lincoln was more pro-Union than the Rebs could possibly imagine. He fully intended to bring Southerners back into the Union, whether they liked it or not. (Most didn't.) But to do this required military men who were as determined as he was. One who failed in that was George McClellan, who was simply too slow and indecisive to whip the Rebels. Southerners never really hated McClellan.

McClellan, who knew many of the Southern generals from his West Point and Mexican War days, was personally liked by most of them. Yes, he was vain and bratty at times (ditto for many other generals), but he held to a concept of war that was passing away quicker than any of them realized. For Mac, chivalry wasn't dead. This view he shared with many Southerners. War, he believed, ought to be guided by certain basic principles, a key one being that civilians ought to be respected—and left alone—as much as possible. Let the opposing armies decide the outcome of a war.

Voices from Then

This rebellion has assumed the character of war; as such it should be regarded, and it should be conducted upon the highest principles known to Christian civilization. In prosecuting the war, all private property and unarmed persons should be strictly protected .... All private property taken for military use should be paid or receipted for; pillage and waste should be treated as high crimes; all unnecessary trespass sternly prohibited, and offensive demeanor by the military toward citizens promptly rebuked.

—Union general George McClellan to Abraham Lincoln

Little Mac had an ego, but he still had morals. When the war ended, some asked Robert E. Lee who was the best Union general, and Lee replied without hesitation, "McClellan, by all odds."

But the North didn't stick to the old notion of war for long, and by 1862 we get some glimpses of how the Yankees might treat Confederate civilians.

Beastly Times in N'awlins

In 1862, a plum prize fell into the Union's lap: the South's largest city, sprawling, cosmopolitan New Orleans. Founded by the French, the quaint old city had boatloads of charm and pride—and business as well, being the South's busiest port by far. No one doubted that the Union wanted the city. If it was inevitable that the North would win the war (the jury is still out on that one), it was inevitable they would capture New Orleans. *But so early in the war?* How did it happen?

The city, with wide Lake Pontchartrain on its north and the wide and muddy Mississippi River on its south, was defended (so everyone thought) by Forts Jackson and St. Philip, about 75 miles downriver. The Union's Southern-born naval man David Farragut and Gen. Benjamin F. Butler led an amphibious assault on the forts and New Orleans in April 1862. On May 1, Butler's New England boys occupied a very unwelcoming Southern city.

> **Go See It!**
>
> The U.S. mint in New Orleans' French Quarter was the Confederacy's only mint. Located at 400 Esplanade Avenue, it is now a museum.

Ten thousand Confederates fled New Orleans, torching 15,000 bales of cotton, a dozen large ships, and several steamboats. One New Orleans woman emptied her chamber pot on Farragut as he passed beneath her balcony. He was lucky in that, unlike Butler (who stayed, governed the city, and was despised), he left New Orleans soon after its capture.

The Beast in the Tinklepot

In the days before flush toilets, people relieved themselves outdoors (in privies, also called outhouses) or indoors (in containers called chamber pots, tinklepots, slopjars, and so on). One of the favorite stories of civilian life in the Confederacy is that some Southerners had the face of Gen. Ben Butler painted on the bottoms of their tinklepots. Among the Union generals, Butler was the first bogeymen of Confederates.

Butler was an easy man to hate. He was physically unattractive—bald, cross-eyed, and pot-bellied. Like most political generals, Butler loved the show of soldiering. He had a gorgeous uniform bedecked with rich gold embroidery. One observer noted that he "looked around with a sort of triumphant gaze, as if to assure himself that the bystanders were duly impressed." Someone called Butler a mere politician "who could strut sitting down."

Butler was in the army for one reason only: to climb up the military ladder as high as he could. He had to look tough in governing occupied New Orleans, and tough he was. He knew how to hit the locals where it hurt. In this booze-loving city, he ordered the distilleries and breweries closed. (N'awlins without alcohol—horrors!) He deeply offended the locals by executing William Mumford, a popular gambler who had the nerve to take down the flag from the U.S. mint building. He imprisoned Mayor Monroe—who had made his anti-Yankee sentiments known—for the duration of the war. He forced teachers to swear allegiance to the Union, he controlled the newspapers (no freedom of the press in occupied areas!), and he prohibited ministers from expressing pro-Confederate sentiments in sermons.

> **Voices from Then**
>
> In her famous Civil War diary, Mary Chesnut referred to Butler as "this hideous cross-eyed beast." During the war years, Southerners could get a laugh by telling a child to "do a Butler," which meant the child would cross his or her eyes.

Butler's Beastly Order

"Beast" Butler prohibited anyone from singing the popular Confederate song "The Bonnie Blue Flag" in public. When the threat of a $25 fine for doing so was not effective, Butler changed the punishment to imprisonment. One person who sang the song in public and got away with it was visiting actor John Wilkes Booth, a noted Southern sympathizer. (What might have happened if Booth had been sitting in prison instead of hatching an assassination plot against Lincoln?) The city's many music publishers were prohibited from publishing or selling "secession music."

> **Go See It!**
>
> If you visit New Orleans, you will inevitably visit Jackson Square in the French Quarter. As you look at the large equestrian statue of Andrew Jackson there, note the inscription on the base: "The Union Must and Shall Be Preserved." The inscription was placed there by order of Ben "Beast" Butler.

But Butler's chief offense to the Southerners of the time was his contempt for Southern womanhood—as they saw it. Southerners prided themselves on treating all woman as ladies. Women, in turn, responded to courtesy by behaving as, well, ladies. But Butler wasn't finding them very ladylike. He wasn't stupid enough to expect proud New Orleans women to *like* the Yankee soldiers patrolling their streets. But he expected them to show a minimum of respect.

Many did not. Union soldiers were spit on, had tinklepots emptied on their heads, were hissed at, laughed at, and cursed. Some of this was general hatred for their conquerors, while some of it was intended as a slap at Beast. The women couldn't get rid of him, but they could at least mock his authority by disrespecting his soldiers.

Beast responded with his General Order No. 28, generally known as the Woman's Order, issued on May 15, 1862 (yes, a mere two weeks after Butler took office). In a nutshell, the order said this: If you women insult Union soldiers, we will treat you like whores.

Voices from Then

As the officers and soldiers of the United States have been subjected to repeated insults from the women (calling themselves ladies) of New Orleans, in return for the most scrupulous non-interference and courtesy on our part, it is ordered that hereafter when any female shall, by word, gesture, or movement, insult or show contempt for any officer or soldier of the United States, she shall be regarded and held liable to be treated as a woman of the town plying her avocation.

—Major General Butler, General Orders No. 28, May 15, 1862

Did the order have an effect? Oh, yes, and immediately. Insults to Union soldiers became quite rare. A few women defied the order, and some ended up in prison. One woman spent three months in jail for laughing out loud when the funeral procession of a Union officer passed her house.

If the Woman's Order mostly stifled the women, it loosened the tongues, and pens, of Southern men. Most were horrified. Treating Southern women as "women of the town"? Horrors! What did the Yankees expect when they conquered Southern cities—love and respect? President Davis denounced Butler (the man who had once proposed him as Democratic presidential candidate) as "a felon, an outlaw, a common enemy of mankind," who would, if captured, be hanged immediately. Even people in Europe were horrified by the Woman's Order. Beast was practically a one-man propaganda machine for the South. Under a great deal of pressure, Lincoln removed Butler from his post.

The South never completely forgot Beast Butler in its postwar days, but it had much nastier Yankees than him to recollect. Butler was essentially a small-minded, greedy, corrupt politician—but there were to be other Union generals much more deserving of the nickname "the Beast."

Headquarters and Hindquarters

The Union faced its old problem: Who could lead the Northern armies to victory in Virginia, when the South had such luminaries as Lee and Jackson? McClellan, small man with a humongous ego, had boasted he could do the job, but failed. Abraham Lincoln, in the days before Grant and Sherman began to shine, was vexed and perplexed: Who was the Union's man of the hour? Who could conquer Virginia?

Maybe John Pope? He had a reputation for being a loud-mouthed braggart, but Lincoln's choices were few. Lincoln thought (or hoped) that Pope had grit, so he made him commander of the new Army of Virginia, moving the sluggish McClellan elsewhere. Little Mac bided his time, hoping Pope would suffer defeat and humiliation.

Pope had a theatrical streak, which some people found offensive. He wrote dispatches from his "Headquarters in the Saddle." (Wits North and South made cracks about the general who put his "headquarters where his hindquarters ought to be.") To his new command, the Army of Virginia, Pope bragged, "I have come to you from the West, where we have always seen the back of our enemies." This rankled many of the Eastern soldiers. (Confederate General Dick Ewell responded, "By God, he'll never see the backs of my men. Their pants are out at the rear, and the sight would paralyze this western bully.") Pope's dispatch ended with this quotable: "Success and glory are in the advance, disaster and shame lurk in the rear." Ah, such optimism.

A New Villain in Virginia

Encamped in Virginia, Pope published a series of draconian rules governing the conduct of civilians in his path—rules threatening wholesale imprisonments as well as executions. One example: If any Union soldier was fired upon from a house, the house would be razed to the ground and the inhabitants sent to military prisons. There was no precedent for this vile treatment of civilians, but mostly this was typical Pope bluster, and there were few actual punishments. Nonetheless, the order provoked Virginia-loving Robert E. Lee to inform his generals that this barbarian Pope would have to be "suppressed."

> **Did Y'all Know?**
>
> Pope, against his will, supplied the makings of a grand Confederate feast. On August 27, 1862, the Rebels captured vast stores of Union supplies at Manassas Junction. Decades later, soldiers still remembered the bonanza—a hundred freight cars loaded with ammo, medicine, shoes, pants, underwear, saddles, plus food and drink of every kind—beer, wine, whiskey, meat (50,000 pounds of bacon alone), coffee (wow!), flour, cheese, oysters, and candy. Underfed and underclothed Rebs had a party (and also disobeyed Stonewall Jackson's order to pour out all the whiskey).

Pope got "suppressed" by Lee. The second battle at Manassas (August 29 and 30, 1862) in northern Virginia was the test. Was Pope all vaunting bluster, or a real fighter? Answer: bluster. Pope lost 14,000 out of 80,000 men, Lee lost 9,000 out of 54,000. As the defeated Union army straggled back toward Washington, people began to skedaddle, fearing a Confederate invasion. Outbound trains were packed. The South was elated, the North mortified.

Pope was relieved of command and assigned to the Northwest to curb the Indians. What McClellan and his fan club had hoped and (no doubt) prayed for came to pass: Pope failed, and on September 2, 1862, Lincoln recalled Little Mac—new loser replaced by old loser. The Union troops were relieved to be rid of Pope and back with Mac. The battle had made Southerners think Lee was invincible. They were likewise pleased that Little Mac, the Virginia Creeper, was back in command of the Union boys in blue.

Pope's General Order No. 5 was remembered by Virginians. The general directed that Union soldiers could live off the "surplus" of Virginia's farms. Virginia civilians who could prove they were loyal to the Union would be given vouchers for their goods, but Confederates would not. In effect, Pope's order authorized Yankee soldiers to steal from Confederates' homes and farms. Here was the beginning of Union "foraging," which led to incalculable harm to Southern families in later days of the war.

"Foraging" to fill an empty belly is one thing, but some of the Union soldiers took to destroying crops and plundering houses. When families reacted by trying to defend their property, Union soldiers sometimes burned the houses and shot or axed the livestock. Worse things would follow later in the war.

Maryland, Whose Maryland?

Ah, dear old Maryland, the slave state that sympathized with the Confederacy and probably would have joined it—had it not been for its pro-Union governor and (much more importantly) for the swift action of Abraham Lincoln, who wasn't about to let Washington, D.C., find itself an island surrounded by Rebel territory. He had to throw a number of pro-secession Marylanders in jail to keep the state under the Union thumb, and he got plenty of criticism in the South (and North as well) for forgetting all about habeas corpus. Lincoln's effectiveness in keeping Maryland in the Union was based on acts that were unconstitutional and illegal. For these acts the South called him a tyrant and despot. Many Northerners did the same.

Did Y'all Know?

During the war, the Federal government closely supervised state and local elections in Maryland, pulling strings to see that only loyal Unionists were elected to office. (Most of the more outspoken pro-secession Marylanders were in jail anyway.)

Remember from an earlier chapter that Maryland's state song, the beloved "Maryland, My Maryland," was written after the bloody Baltimore riots, when local pro-secession folk locked horns with Union soldiers marching through town. The song laments the "despot's heel," but it didn't matter during the war, because the despot's heel stayed exactly where it was (on Maryland's neck).

Was the state of Maryland all that important? In terms of morale, maybe it was. It was one Union state that (so everyone believed) would gladly have been *out* of the Union. So "liberating" it and joining it up with the Confederacy would be a sign to the world that the Confederacy was anti-tyranny and pro-freedom. Please remember this: The South did not think of itself as "invading" Maryland. They were entering a slave state that was, much against its will, still in the Union.

Aside from that, by summer 1862 the South was tiring of its defensive war with the Union. Jefferson Davis had made it clear to the world that the South wanted nothing—except to be left alone. Thus, the Rebel armies had the mission of protecting Southern fields and homes from the Yankee invaders. Most Southern men who joined the army had this goal in mind. It all sounded very noble. The only problem was, it wasn't working. This defensive war was dragging on. It was time to try something new—such as a bold offense.

The Bold Patriarch, Marse Robert

"Marse Robert," the great Lee, had smashed the braggart Union general, John Pope, at Second Manassas in August 1862. Lee remembered *First* Manassas—a Confederate victory, but one that (very stupidly) had not been followed up, which was the loss of a great opportunity. He had no desire to see *Second* Manassas go to waste in the same way.

Lee decided (with Davis's approval) to "shift the burden of military occupation from Confederate to Federal soil." On September 7, his troops crossed the Potomac River from Virginia to Maryland and entered the town of Frederick. His hopes: Impress the wavering nations of Europe (which, as we noted already, always dragged their feet about recognizing the Confederacy), influence the upcoming U.S. elections (November 1862), and recruit Maryland boys for the army. He officially announced to the citizens of Maryland that he was there to protect their rights and liberties.

> **Voices from Then**
>
> They were the dirtiest men I ever saw, a most ragged, lean, and hungry set of wolves. Yet there was about them a dash that the Northern men lacked.
>
> —A resident of Frederick, Maryland, on the Confederate troops passing through

The underfed, badly clothed Rebel soldiers definitely made an impression on any Marylanders who saw them. The Johnny Rebs were actually in an up mood as they went north, loudly singing "Maryland, My Maryland" and hopeful about the victories that would be theirs under "Uncle Robert."

Lee's Army of Northern Virginia faced a familiar opponent: McClellan.

Patriotic Marylanders?

The Southern people as a whole approved of Lee's plan for entering Maryland—they wanted to strike at the enemy and were tired of merely playing defense. Maryland was, so the Rebs believed, strongly "secesh," eager to extend a warm welcome to the "liberators" from south of the Potomac. Was this a dream, reality, or somewhere in between?

Mostly a dream. Maryland men didn't rush to join the Confederates. But individual "secesh" citizens did shower attention (and food) on the soldiers. The Rebel boys must have thought they had died and gone to heaven—bread with butter, chicken, sweets, real honest-to-God coffee (mercy!). Many of the men experienced something novel: full bellies.

Lee, believing strongly in civilized warfare, made it quite clear that the Rebel soldiers

> **Did Y'all Know?**
>
> When the Rebs entered Maryland, Stonewall Jackson was ambulance-ridden, having been thrown by a powerful gray mare that an admirer had given him. Lee, too, was in an ambulance, both his hands in splints. Were these omens of how the Rebs would fare in Maryland?

would *not* steal from Maryland civilians. The South had already gotten a taste of Union soldiers foraging and living off the land. If the Yankees were a bunch of barbarian invaders, he would show the world that Confederate men were not.

Maryland witnessed a rare thing: the stern Jackson showing a sense of humor. The famous general was surrounded by women who begged for a souvenir—a lock of his hair, perhaps, or a button from his coat? Jackson, who never felt comfortable with fans, said, "Really, ladies, this is the first time I was ever surrounded by the enemy!"

The War's Most Famous Cigars

The brief sojourn at Frederick, Maryland, was a lark, a spree before one of the war's nastiest encounters, the battle known to Confederates as Sharpsburg, to Yankees as Antietam. That infamous battle will forever be connected with some unknown Confederate officer who left behind him three cigars wrapped in a piece of paper.

This wasn't just any piece of paper. It was a copy of Special Order No. 191—Lee's plan for the Maryland campaign. An officer on the staff of Gen. Daniel Harvey Hill had left the cigars—and the famous "Lost Order"—behind at the Rebel encampment outside Frederick. A Union private found the cigars and paper, and rejoiced over getting free cigars. Wondering if the paper might have some importance, he passed it on up the chain of command, until finally it reached a jubilant George McClellan. Little Mac had been advancing slowly, not having a clue what Lee's next move would be. Suddenly he knew. The cautious Mac had something that might actually inspire him to be audacious.

Did Y'all Know?

We know who found the Lost Order, and we know some officer or aide under Gen. D. H. Hill lost it. But *which one?* This will not surprise you: No one ever came forward to admit losing the order.

Lee's plan was itself audacious. He was dividing up his forces on enemy territory. He had counted on McClellan being his usual slow-to-act self, so the plan was actually pretty smart. But who would have predicted the plans falling into Mac's hands? Lee's ultimate plan—moving on beyond Maryland into Pennsylvania—would be thwarted by the wised-up (and very lucky) McClellan.

Ignorant of what Mac had found, Lee sent Jackson's forces off to Harper's Ferry (remember, the site of John Brown's raid), where they captured the Union garrison and made off like bandits with thousands of rifles, ammo, and (hallelujah!) food supplies. Jeb Stuart's men, scouting through Maryland, made a horrible discovery: Lee's plans had fallen into Mac's hands.

Sharpsburg, Antietam, That Very Bloody Place

Jackson's well-fed Rebs didn't linger long at Harper's Ferry. Two of his divisions crossed the Potomac again after a night march. They and the other Confederates were concentrating near the little town of Sharpsburg. Nearby was Antietam Creek (hence the two different names for the battle).

McClellan had over 80,000 men with him. Lee had only 50,000, and some of these had remained at Harper's Ferry, while Jackson's newly arrived men were sleeping from exhaustion after marching all night. But Mac didn't attack that day, September 16, 1862. He did the usual McClellan thing: hesitated. In the meantime, Jackson's men rested, and the other Rebel troops arrived from Harper's Ferry. Almost the entire Army of Northern Virginia was concentrated in one spot.

> **Go See It!**
>
> The site of the war's bloodiest one-day battle is, of course, a must-see. Antietam National Battlefield is on SR 34/65 in Maryland, not far from the Potomac River.

On September 17, all hell broke loose in a bloodletting that had never been seen on American soil. It made Shiloh, the gore-fest of April, seem small by comparison. At day's end, over 23,000 men were killed, wounded, or missing. (The Union lost more men than the Confederacy, but percentage-wise the Rebs lost more.) Doing the math, at Sharpsburg men fell at the rate of about 2,000 per hour.

Maryland, My Aftermath

The history books record Sharpsburg as a Union victory because Lee ordered his men back to Virginia. But, strictly in terms of numbers and losses (and pints of blood, perhaps), it was a draw. If it dimmed Lee's reputation, it didn't do much to polish McClellan's halo. Technically, he had driven Lee's army from Union soil, but he had still behaved hesitantly, which was pretty bizarre, considering what a godsend the Lost Order was (and considering his army had vastly superior numbers).

The Rebs had performed well even though badly outnumbered. But the Johnny Rebs had seen thousands of their comrades die on Maryland soil. South of the Potomac, there were thousands of new widows and fatherless children. It was best that they didn't see the mass graves that the dead soldiers were piled into.

We can't help but pause here and consider one of history's great what-ifs. What if the Lost Order hadn't been found by McClellan? Before the order was found, he was being his usual dilly-dallying self, which Lee had counted on. Had the order not been found, Lee, Jackson, and the other Confederate generals might have pressed on to Pennsylvania, menaced Washington, and … who knows?

Christ in the Camp

We saw in an earlier chapter that Johnny Rebs both played and prayed. And sometimes their play took forms that conflicted with praying—such as drunkenness, gambling, swearing, and whoring. Officers in both armies knew there was a thin line between innocent recreation and demoralization.

Voices from Then

Any history of this army which omits an account of the wonderful influence of religion upon it—which fails to tell how the courage, discipline, and morale was influenced by the humble piety and evangelical zeal of many of its officers and men—would be incomplete and unsatisfactory.

—J. William Jones, chaplain in the Army of Northern Virginia

But a religious revival swept the Army of Northern Virginia in the long fall of 1862. What brought this about? Probably a combination of things. Many of the boys had been away from their families since the war began. They had seen comrades killed and dismembered. They had listened to the wails of the dying. It was impossible to keep heaven (and hell) off their minds.

Their most notable leaders certainly had their minds on eternity. Lee and Jackson were devout, and both men were notoriously steady under pressure, convinced the Almighty watched over them. Jeb Stuart, his spurs jingling, his face ever-smiling, was also a good Christian boy. Men in this army inevitably had to turn their thoughts to religion now and then.

Chaplains in Lee's army that fall were impressed with the changes. Perhaps their accounts of the revival exaggerate things a bit, but even allowing for exaggeration, we can believe that many of the Johnny Rebs gave up (if only temporarily) their familiar vices. Some soldiers constructed log chapels for preaching services, splitting tree trunks lengthwise into benches. Lee, Jackson, and others often attended the services, which made a deep impression on the soldiers. Considering how many of them would die before the war's end, it was well they had the consolation of being ready to meet their Maker. It is estimated that probably 10 percent of Lee's soldiers were converted during the religious revivals.

Who Will Be Big Man Blue?

After Sharpsburg, Lincoln wanted Mac to pursue Lee, beating the already battered gray soldiers to a pulp, ending the war. McClellan didn't, believing (as always) that

Lee's army was greatly superior in number. The sluggish little general had disappointed Lincoln for the last time. In a few weeks he was removed from command—for good.

McDowell, McClellan, Pope, McClellan again … who now? In November 1862, the Union turned to the bald man with the fancy facial foliage, Ambrose Burnside. He was a refreshing change in at least one respect: He was totally lacking in ego. He frankly did not want command of the Army of the Potomac, saying he wasn't up to it. He would soon prove he had been right.

Midway between D.C. and Richmond, Fredericksburg on the Rappahannock River is one of Virginia's prettiest little towns, rich in historic sites. Regrettably, some of those sites are associated with a key battle there in December 1862.

By late November 1862, Burnside's Army of the Potomac had encamped on the east bank of the Rappahannock. Numerically, the army was awesome: 130,000 men. The goal: Defeat Lee's army and march on to Richmond.

The Rebs had a much smaller force than Burnside—a mere 75,000 men, and about 300 cannons. But they held a fine position: Marye's Heights, a high ridge. It was as close to being an impregnable position as the Rebs would ever have. And, in spite of the earlier losses in Maryland, the Army of Northern Virginia was at its peak, both in numbers and in spirit. As an additional morale booster, Stonewall Jackson looked handsome in a new gold-braided dress coat, a gift from jaunty Jeb Stuart.

> **RebeLingo**
>
> **Chicken guts** was the name the common soldiers used to refer to the gold braid seen on generals' coats.

Burnside ordered an attack on December 13. It wasn't pretty. He kept hurling his Union troops at the heights, and they dropped like flies, bodies piling up on the frozen ground. The Union suffered over 12,000 casualties, the Rebs only about 5,000. Two days later, in a torrential rainstorm, the Yanks retreated across the river.

Militarily, the battle had accomplished nothing, but it did raise Southern morale and vex the Yankees. In fact, the battle had gone so well that Lee ordered one of his more famous quotes amidst the shooting: "It is well that war is so terrible—else we should grow too fond of it." But some people at the time, and later, thought Lee had missed a grand opportunity: He could have pursued the Federals, dealt another blow, and ended the war.

Meanwhile, the Poor Civilians

We noted that Lee and the Army of Northern Virginia crossed the Potomac River with "civilized" intentions, with Lee warning the men not to steal or otherwise harass civilians. Burnside likewise was a civilized man, but not all of his soldiers were. Many of them took special delight in harming these "barbarian" Southerners.

When Burnside's Federals approached Fredericksburg that fall, the locals got an ultimatum: Surrender the city to them, or in 16 hours it would be shelled. They surrendered, as Lee advised them to do. (The town had no military value whatsoever, by the way.) Aware that two huge armies were at their doorsteps, the people moved out—at night, and in a snowstorm. Some boarded trains to Richmond, others headed off in carriages or wagons to nearby towns or friends in the country.

Two days before the actual battle, the Yankee cannoneers had a brilliant idea: Get some target practice, using the now-vacant houses of Fredericksburg. True, the town had, in theory, been evacuated. But the locals weren't pleased to learn that, after the humiliation of evacuating, their homes were destroyed.

For Southern civilians, much worse things would follow.

The Least You Need to Know

- In the early months of the war, Union general George McClellan still held to traditional notions of "civilized" warfare, which required leaving civilians alone.

- Ben Butler, the Union's military governor of occupied New Orleans, was one of the earliest villains in the war, a man Confederates enjoyed hating for his treatment of civilians.

- John Pope, a Union general operating in Virginia, instituted some anti-civilian measures that horrified Southerners.

- Tired of fighting only on the defensive, Lee took his army into Maryland, but lost thousands of men at the bloody Battle of Sharpsburg.

Chapter 24

1863: Year of the Two 'Burgs

In This Chapter

◆ A race to hold the river

◆ Grant, Sherman, and rehearsals in nastiness

◆ Hell on earth (also known as Vicksburg)

◆ Mr. Lee's Pennsylvania excursion

◆ The address: Gettysburg

If the person on the street knows the name of only one Civil War battle, it's probably Gettysburg. It's also the one the historians have given the most attention, and perhaps the one that still causes the most debates. In this chapter we'll take a close-up look at the battle, and also ask the question, "Was Gettysburg really *that* important?" (A preview of the answer: It was important, but …)

You might say 1863 was the Year of the Two 'Burgs. Gettysburg has gotten lots of coverage, but the other "burg" that year was just as important (some would say more important), and that was the riverside town of Vicksburg, Mississippi. Open your brain up good and wide, because you're going to get a lot of detail in this chapter, and a lot of big names like Lee, Grant, Meade, and Sherman (and even some ill-fated Confederate generals like Pickett and Pemberton).

Union River Rats

In early May 1863, Lee's Army of Northern Virginia proved it could kick Yankee butt, defeating Joe Hooker soundly at the Battle of Chancellorsville. But in the evening after the Chancellorsville victory, mighty Stonewall Jackson was fatally wounded—by Confederate fire (see Chapter 22). The South went into mourning, and while it wept, it also shifted its gaze westward, to the Mississippi River.

Go See It!
If you visit Vicksburg, you might enjoy a tour of the home Cedar Grove at 2300 Washington Street. The house, like most other Vicksburg homes from the period, was damaged by Union shells. This one has an in-house reminder of the war: a Union cannonball embedded in the parlor wall.

Back at the very beginning of the war, the Union's old Gen. Winfield Scott put forward his "boa constrictor plan" (which got renamed the "anaconda plan"). Part of that plan was to choke the life out of the Confederacy by taking control of its main water route, the wide, muddy Mississippi River. In April 1862, the South's main port on that river, New Orleans, fell to the Federals. In June, further up the river they captured the busy port of Memphis, Tennessee. The "biggies" along the river were falling, and one remaining biggie that got serious attention was the bustling city of Vicksburg on bluffs above the river. In November 1862, the Yanks launched their Vicksburg Campaign.

Just as some Southerners fought for the Union, a few Yanks fought for the Confederacy. One of the higher-placed ones was Gen. John C. Pemberton, a reserved, dignified Pennsylvania man who had made Southern friends in his West Point days and (even more important) married a Virginia woman. Siding with the Confederacy meant sacrifice: His well-to-do family had disinherited him. Jefferson Davis liked and respected Pemberton and had no doubts about his loyalties. Frankly, though, defending Vicksburg was a task too big for this man of moderate ability.

The task of conquering Vicksburg fell to that short, quiet, cigar-addicted rising star, Ulysses S. Grant. His Federals had to rely on supply lines coming from Tennessee and Kentucky, and the South's cavalry wizard, Nathan Bedford Forrest, used his fast-moving men to harass and delay the Federals at every turn.

The period of mid-October through mid-December 1862 is called the First Vicksburg Campaign. It was a failure, as Grant found, because his men were deep into enemy territory.

Plan B, Which Worked

Forrest and Earl Van Dorn (the general who was later killed by a jealous husband's bullet) were formidable opponents for Grant. Obviously, the overland route to Vicksburg wouldn't work. The river wasn't proving too kind to the Union, either. Vicksburg's artillery had managed to fend off more than one Union gunboat attack.

Grant's new plan: Go south of Vicksburg and march north. This involved ferrying his troops to the west bank of the river and marching them south. (Happily for him, Rebel troops in the Trans-Mississippi Department—the soldiers west of the Mississippi River, that is— were occupied elsewhere.) Once the Union troops were south of Vicksburg, they were transported back across the river (to the east bank, the same side as Vicksburg).

> **Did Y'all Know?**
>
> U. S. Grant sent a curious item out on the Mississippi River to draw the fire of the Vicksburg artillery batteries: a dummy gunboat made of logs and barrels. It worked.

Before trying to capture Vicksburg, though, the Yanks made an eventful side trip—marching through Mississippi to capture the state capital, Jackson. In doing so, the men "lived off the land"—doing to Mississippi what Sherman would later do (more destructively) to Georgia.

> **Go See It!**
>
> If you're in Jackson, Mississippi, you can see the Confederates' trenches at Battlefield Park.

Mississippi farmers, rich and poor, had to watch soldiers take their fruit, vegetables, and chickens—while the livestock was sometimes killed outright, not to feed the troops, but simply for the pleasure of making war on Southern civilians.

The task of turning Jackson into rubble fell to William Tecumseh Sherman, of whom we will hear much more later. The redheaded general known as "Cump" to his friends understood the value of Jackson. As a state capital, its loss would be a belly blow to Southern morale. It was also a railway center, meaning it had some military value and had to be "reduced." Not only were military supplies destroyed (which is understandable in wartime), but also untold amounts of civilian property. Even churches were vandalized. Such destruction was unauthorized—but also unpunished. Sherman attributed it to "bad rum" his troops had drunk.

Turn Eden into a Living Hell

Vicksburg today is a fairly small town, graced with some lovely old homes that are worth touring. During the Civil War it was the Gibraltar of the Confederacy, the state's second-largest city and the biggest Mississippi River city after Memphis and New Orleans. Cotton planters from the surrounding lands floated their white gold down the smaller rivers to Vicksburg, and from there it went (in happier times) to points north and south. The city's wharves were thick with riverboats hauling cargo and humans hither and yon. With Memphis and New Orleans in Federal hands, Vicksburg was even more important: It was the main link between the Confederacy's east and west. If captured by the Union, not only would the Federals have almost total control of the river, but the South would be split in half. Abraham Lincoln referred to Vicksburg as "the key" and affirmed that "the war can never be brought to a close until that key is in our pocket."

Go See It!

Vicksburg National Military Park on U.S. Highway 80 is a fascinating place for learning about the siege and the related battles. The national cemetery that is part of the park is fascinating in itself, with some truly awesome memorials (more like temples, actually).

On May 19 and 22, the Yanks made two attacks on Vicksburg. Both failed. The city was guarded well by artillery batteries on the high bluffs. So Grant reverted to the time-honored tactic of the siege. If you can't capture a city, starve it out. To do this, the Federals constructed a 12-mile line around the city's east (land) side. By mid-June, about 75,000 Federals were present.

The lovely, prosperous town turned into a living hell. The Union had 220 guns firing on the city. Having to endure (and dodge) constant shelling, the locals cowered in their basements. Some even dug caves into the hillsides. (Rich folk like their comforts. Some of the caves were furnished with carpets and brocaded chairs.) Assuming they could avoid the Union's projectiles, they couldn't avoid the inevitable: starvation due to a quickly dwindling food supply. When the normal meats of the table were all gone, locals turned to mules—and rats, cats, and dogs as well. (Vicksburg was the one case of mule meat being made the *official* ration for the soldiers.) Survivors of the siege recalled later that mule meat was tough, but preferable to starvation. Desperate people fought over scraps of food, painfully aware that the blue-clad Yanks surrounding the city were well fed as well as well armed. The Rebel soldiers existed (barely) on one-quarter rations. It was summer, and the hot, humid city wasn't a pleasant place to starve in. The noise from artillery, including *Whistling Dick*, was maddening. One soldier wrote in his diary that the constant firing of Union cannons was like the pounding of hammers on shingles—right in one's ear. Those foolish enough to raise their heads above the trenches risked not only cannon fire but also the bullets of the ever-present Federal sharpshooters.

The siege lasted throughout June, in a state well described by Confederate veteran and newspaperman Alexander Abrams:

> Vicksburg was in a deplorable condition. There was scarcely a building but what had been struck by the enemy's shells, while many were entirely demolished. The city had the appearance of a half-ruined pile of buildings, and on every street unmistakable signs of the fearful bombardment it had undergone, presented themselves to the observer.

Pemberton had to wave the white flag. He did, on July 4. He was mobbed as he left Vicksburg, widely hated by the Rebs, and the Confederate government took some heat for having put the defenses of Vicksburg into the hands of a Yankee.

If the Vicksburg civilians thought the nightmare was over, they were wrong. Again, I can't resist quoting someone who was present at the time, Alexander Abrams:

> After the enemy's forces had stacked their arms, they scattered over the city, and then commenced a scene of pillage and destruction which beggars all description. Houses and stores were broken open, and their contents appropriated by the plunderers. The amount of money and property stolen in this way was enormous, and the Yankee soldiers appeared to glory in their vandalism …. Every place that they could possibly enter without fear of resistance was broken open and robbed. The enemy seemed to glory in their course, and on one occasion, in reply to a remonstrance on the part of a gentleman whose residence they had broken open, they said, 'We have fought hard enough to capture Vicksburg, and now we have got it, we intend to plunder every house in the damned rebel city.'

Four days after the surrender of Vicksburg, Port Hudson on the river also fell. The Mississippi was now completely under Federal control. As Lincoln phrased it, "The Father of Waters goes unvexed to the sea." After Vicksburg fell, individual Confederates could cross the river, but troops and supplies could not. The Confederacy had been cut in half, and the Union had the entire river to use as a supply route.

The Pennsylvania Polka

The siege of Vicksburg didn't go unnoticed by the rest of the Confederacy. Barely recovered from the loss of Stonewall Jackson, the Rebs held their breath, wondering what would befall them if they lost Vicksburg. Its loss wasn't certain, and the generals and politicians fretted over the available options.

Did Y'all Know? _____

Stonewall Jackson was, strictly speaking, irreplaceable. But technically, his corps command was given to Richard Ewell, "Old Bald Head," famous for his hooked nose, lisp, profanity, temper, and late marriage to the widow Lizinka Brown, whom he wedded just before Gettysburg. Even after they married he continued to refer to her as "Mrs. Brown."

Back in Virginia, Lee chose to repeat what he had done the previous year: Take the war to the North. Perhaps then the long stalemate would end—and maybe the war, too. A Rebel army doing serious damage in the North could raise Southern morale and lower the North's, and take everyone's mind off what was happening at Vicksburg.

Regarding Vicksburg, Jefferson Davis and his generals had considered several options, one of which was bringing some of Lee's army to the West, applying some heat to Grant's army. Lee preferred pushing into Pennsylvania and capturing some Northern cities, perhaps Philadelphia, Baltimore, or (the prize) Washington. He believed this would push the Northerners to negotiate a peace. (Remember, Vicksburg wasn't a done deal yet.)

Lee's plan prevailed, which means Jefferson Davis, the man who swore he wouldn't lose Vicksburg, approved it. The historians still debate the wisdom of it, but, of course, we have no way of knowing how the alternatives might have worked. At any rate, on June 3, 1863, the Army of Northern Virginia began its second excursion onto Northern soil. On Pennsylvania's well-maintained roads, the men marched in columns of four. Considering the devastation they had witnessed in their own land, they couldn't help but be impressed by the neat farms. Fields of grain, orchards heavy with almost-ripe fruit, fat cattle and sheep grazing peacefully … it all must have brought back memories of happier days in their homeland.

Lee repeated his order of the previous year: no preying upon civilians or their property. Again, he did this because he had morals and because it was good public relations to the larger world. If vandals like Sherman and Grant could let their men commit atrocities on civilians, *his* soldiers wouldn't.

At least some of the Pennsylvanians wished the gray-clads luck, urging them to press on to Washington and whip the "baboon" Lincoln. As had happened in Maryland the previous year, many people came out to get a glimpse of the fabled Lee and his skinny, ill-clad troops. Responding to the occasional sneering and jeering, some of the Rebs hollered back, "We don't wear our good clothes to go hog-killing."

Lee's army had vexed several Union generals. Hooker, defeated at Chancellorsville, had resigned. Who would Lincoln pick as his wonder boy to lead the Army of the Potomac?

Stumbling Into History

At 3 o'clock one fateful summer morning, Union general George G. Meade got a rude awakening: A courier asked him if he would accept command of the Army of the Potomac, at the request of President Lincoln. Meade's reply is classic: "I have been tried and condemned without a hearing, and I suppose I shall have to go to execution." This was June 28, 1863—three days before the best-known battle of the Civil War.

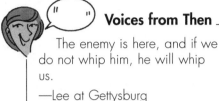

Voices from Then

The enemy is here, and if we do not whip him, he will whip us.

—Lee at Gettysburg

He and Lee had no idea of the other's whereabouts. Lee's "eyes," the cavalry under jaunty Jeb Stuart, seemed to have disappeared. Stuart, Lee found out later, had been busy, capturing 150 Union supply wagons. Fine work, except that his adventure slowed him down so much that he didn't arrive at Gettysburg till the second day of the three-day battle. A clearly peeved Lee greeted him with, "Well, General Stuart, you are here at last." (It was probably the closest Lee ever came to cussing out an officer.)

Lee was hoping for The Biggie, a decide-it-all battle on a grand scale. In fact, one of the great battles of history was almost an accident, two huge armies practically bumping into each other. When it finally got underway it stretched out over three days, July 1–3, 1863. On the first day the Rebels drove the Union troops through the small town of Gettysburg. The armies then took positions on ridges that faced each other, the lower ground in between. On the second day, it was Lee's aim to envelop the Yankees by attacks on their left and right. General "Bald Dick" Ewell took the right, but James Longstreet was too late to take the left. Ewell renewed his assault on the morning of the third day, but his men were driven off the ridge.

On this last day was the famous assault on the main body of Meade's army, led by the division under Gen. George Pickett. Pickett, with the curled beard, had a theatrical streak, hollering at his troops, "Up, men, and to your posts! Don't forget today that you are from old Virginia!" The Union artillery opened up. A few of the Rebs broke into Union lines, but they were shot or captured. Little was left of Pickett's division. (More than a century later, Civil War buffs still love to discuss the ill-fated Pickett's Charge.) Some people still puzzle that Pickett somehow emerged without a scratch while almost his entire division became casualties in less than an hour.

Lincoln had ordered the Yanks not to let the Rebs escape. On July 5, Lee and the Army of Northern Virginia began their withdrawal, in a torrential rain. They had to pause several days at the Potomac River, which had been swollen by the rains. Had Meade chosen to pursue Lee, he would have found the Rebs with their backs to the river. To his credit, Meade never did claim Gettysburg as a Union victory. He claimed he had kept Lee from the objective of destroying the Union army.

Blood had flowed in buckets. The Confederate losses: 3,900 killed, 18,000 wounded, 5,400 missing. The Union: 3,100 killed, 14,500 wounded, 5,300 missing. It was definitely the most costly battle of the war. Americans had never witnessed such a bloodletting. And the Confederacy had never lost so many officers in one place.

Then, Monday Morning Quarterbacking

Lee, so much the master of his emotions, couldn't quite contain them at Gettysburg: "All my fault!" and "Too bad! Too bad!" Later, he sent his resignation to Davis: "I therefore, in all sincerity, request Your Excellency to take measures to supply my place …. No one is more aware than myself of my inability for the duties of my position …. I have no complaints to make of anyone but myself." (Typical Lee—no blaming of subordinates or circumstances.) Davis didn't accept. He needed Lee too much.

Voices from Then

After Vicksburg and Gettysburg, Confederate ordnance chief Josiah Gorgas wrote in his diary, "Today absolute ruin seems our portion. The Confederacy totters to its destruction."

Lee rarely ever referred to the battle in later years. Once, though, he let his guard down, saying, "If I had had Stonewall Jackson with me, so far as I can see, I should have won the battle of Gettysburg." Many Southerners thought so in 1863, and later, as well.

Did Y'all Know?

The defeats at Vicksburg and Gettysburg were both followed by numerous desertions among the Rebs. Virginia roads were crowded with disgusted soldiers headed home after the loss in Pennsylvania. In some cases, when authorities stopped and asked to see their furlough papers, the soldiers would pat their rifles and say, "This is my furlough."

Most of the Confederate generals at Gettysburg gave major attention to the battle in their memoirs. Ewell, like Lee, didn't dwell on it, though he did say that it took "a dozen blunders to lose Gettysburg" and admitted he had committed "a good many of them." Most of the other generals at Gettysburg wrote memoirs excusing themselves and blaming others.

Despite all the blood spilled at Gettysburg, there was something civilized about the whole affair. Lee had been mostly successful in preventing his Rebs from stealing from the civilians. Lee and Meade had been friends before the war, and though Meade was a little younger, both were from the old school, respectful of civilians, modest, and dignified.

Lee lost a lot of men at Gettysburg and his reputation was dimmed, but no territory was lost. Even if the Confederates had won at Gettysburg, what would have happened? The North would still have been elated over the capture of Vicksburg. Certainly it was unlikely that the North would have considered ending the war just because the Rebs had won at Gettysburg. If the Rebs had won in Pennsylvania, *and* the siege of Vicksburg had been lifted, then the South would have had bragging rights. As it was, the North won both, and at the same moment.

As a loss, Gettysburg was more mental than real. The amazing "Uncle Robert" Lee had been defeated in his second (and last) venture into the North. He could fight hard, and with underfed men, but he couldn't win on Northern soil. The world took note. Years later, British statesman Winston Churchill penned his famous *History of the English-Speaking Peoples* and lavished praise on the Confederates in general, Lee in particular. Churchill claimed that at Gettysburg, Lee "had lost only two guns, and the war." An exaggeration? Maybe. But sometimes perception is reality. Churchill continued: "By the end of 1863 all illusions had vanished. The South knew they had lost the war, and would be conquered and flattened. It is one of the enduring glories of the American nation that this made no difference to the Confederate resistance …. The departure of hope left only the resolve to perish arms in hand."

The Least You Need to Know

- The Union army worked hard to capture Vicksburg, the well-defended Mississippi city on the river.

- Union general Sherman reduced the Mississippi capital, Jackson, to rubble and harassed numerous civilians.

- During late May and all of June 1863, the Federals besieged Vicksburg, shelling the city constantly and starving out the people.

- Robert E. Lee took the Army of Northern Virginia into Pennsylvania, hoping to defeat the Union's Army of the Potomac in a decisive battle.

- The three-day Battle of Gettysburg (July 1 to July 3, 1863) caused the most casualties of any Civil War battle, though its importance has been overrated.

Chapter 25

The Wild, Wild (and Forgotten) West

In This Chapter

♦ Rebel Texas

♦ More very bloody border battles

♦ General Headache, Braxton Bragg

♦ The land of Kirby Smithdom

Can you name a Civil War battle in Texas or Arkansas? How about a famous general in the western Confederacy? No? The western Confederacy has been sadly neglected in studies of the Civil War. Granted, there were fewer key battles in the West, and the Confederacy's best-known generals were mostly in the East. But the West was still a wild place during the war.

It's time to highlight some key people and events in that sprawling section of territory that was known as Kirby Smithdom during the war years. It's also time for another look at those much-disputed border states, Kentucky and Missouri.

God Bless Texas

Texas was the Confederacy's largest state, though it didn't have the largest population. There were a few major cities (Austin, San Antonio, Galveston, and Fort Worth), but mostly the vast state was sparsely populated. In the eastern section, the big crop was the Confederacy's white gold, cotton. Further west, cattle were the main source of income. (Texas led the nation in beef production, with about 3.5 million cattle.)

Texas's famous governor, the near-legendary Sam Houston, lost his post because he wouldn't accept the state's secession. Houston was strongly pro-Union, as were thousands of other Texans, but the state's many farmers felt emotional ties to the Deep South. Texas, you might recall, was its own country for a while, the Republic of Texas. Texans had an independent streak, thought of Texas as a very special place (they still do), and weren't slow to fight if they thought their rights were being stepped on.

> **Voices from Then** _____
>
> They were representative men from all portions of the state—young, impetuous, fresh, full of energy, and fire—men of action—men who, when they first heard the shrill shriek of battle, as it came from the far-off coast of South Carolina, at once ceased to argue with themselves, or with their neighbors, as to the why-fores and where-fores. They were all imbued with one purpose, to fight for "Dixie."
>
> —Nicholas Davis, chaplain of Hood's Texas Brigade

The frontier soldiers from Texas tended to be cocky about their fighting ability. They had good reason to be. They fought well most of the time. Three regiments in particular served with distinction in the Army of Northern Virginia, and some of the hard-bitten veterans were present when Lee surrendered at Appomattox in April 1865. These three regiments made up a unit that is familiar to military historians: Hood's Texas Brigade. Organized in Virginia in November 1861, the brigade was made up of the 1st, 4th, and 5th Texas Infantry, plus the 18th Georgia Infantry. The brigade took its name from Gen. John Bell Hood, who had at first been commander of the 4th Texas. The men fought like tigers in many crucial Virginia battles, notably Gaines' Mill (June 27, 1862). They performed well in several other major battles, including Gettysburg.

But there were far more of the Texas boys in the Army of Tennessee, charged with defending that vital space between the Appalachian Mountains and the Mississippi River. Remember that Albert Sidney Johnston, the gallant general who was killed at the 1862 Battle of Shiloh in Tennessee, had earlier been an officer in the Republic of Texas. Johnston was Kentucky-born, but called himself a Texan, and Texans still consider him one of their own.

> **Go See It!**
>
> You can see Albert Sidney Johnston's impressive tomb at the Texas State Cemetery in Austin.

Like Johnston, Tennessee-born Ben McCulloch had served in the army of the Republic of Texas (and in the Republic's legislature as well). McCulloch had originally moved to Texas at the urging of his Tennessee buddy Davy Crockett (yes, the guy who died at the Alamo). McCulloch had led a unit of Texas Rangers during the Mexican War, and at the time Texas joined the Confederacy, he was serving as a U.S. marshal. He resigned that post and soon found himself a general in the Confederate Army.

Like many other high-ranking Confederates, McCulloch preferred his own distinct getup to a regulation uniform. It was his custom to wear a black velvet suit. That is what he wore on March 7, 1862, when a Federal sharpshooter fatally wounded him at the Battle of Elkhorn Tavern (also called Pea Ridge) in Arkansas. If you know nothing about that fateful (but neglected) battle, keep reading.

So, Who Rules Missouri?

Missouri, you'll recall, had rival pro-Union and pro-Confederate governors. The state sent men to the Confederate Congress, but Missouri was never "fully" Confederate. Neither South nor North wished to give up the state without some serious bloodshed. There was plenty to go around.

On August 10, 1861, the first major battle in the western Confederacy occurred at Wilson's Creek, Missouri. Yanks faced Rebels at a site southwest of Springfield. The Yanks were led by red-bearded Nathaniel Lyon, the Rebs by chubby former governor Sterling "Pap" Price and black-velvet-clad Ben McCulloch. Lyon was killed that day, the first Union general to die in the Civil War. In the five-hour battle, the Union men lost—not surprising, since this was the rare battle in which the Rebels outnumbered the Yanks. (It was, incidentally, a far bloodier battle than the more famous First Manassas.)

Did Y'all Know?

Not only was Nathaniel Lyon the first Union general killed in the Civil War, but he was among the very few who were openly anti-slavery.

Did Y'all Know? _____

Wilson's Creek was the preferred Union name for the battle, while the Rebels more often referred to it as Oak Hills, or Springfield.

Coming less than a month after Manassas, the victory at Wilson's Creek gave another boost to Southern morale. For a brief few months the Confederates could believe that they were triumphant in both East and West. But the Rebel victory served to harden the North's resolve to control Missouri.

The Ladies' Man and the Cherokees

The Yanks were optimistic after the Confederacy lost Forts Donelson and Henry (and much of Tennessee) in early 1862. The Union had renewed hopes it could control all of Missouri. Missouri furnished 20,000 Confederate soldiers and 100,000 Union soldiers.

Opposing this plan was the colorful character Earl Van Dorn, the dapper, bushy-mustachioed ladies' man who had gained fame in Texas as a fighter against the Comanches. The Confederacy made him a major general with command of the vast area known as the Trans-Mississippi Department—essentially, all the territory west of the Mississippi River, which included Texas, Arkansas, and parts of Louisiana. It also included Missouri—*if* the Confederacy could maintain control of it, that is.

Go See It!

Pea Ridge National Military Park is in northwestern Arkansas, not far from the Missouri border. At the park you can see the Elkhorn Tavern, with the set of antlers for which it is named. (Too bad the National Park Service chose to name the park for the *Union* name of the battle. Isn't Elkhorn Tavern a nicer name than Pea Ridge?) Incidentally, Pea Ridge was the only major Civil War battle in which the Confederacy's Indian troops played a key role.

Van Dorn wasn't lacking in grit. Discretion was another matter. The general was fond of women, and some of them happened to be married to other men. He also liked to drink, which got him into trouble more than once.

Rebel troops under Price and McCulloch had been driven from Missouri. Van Dorn ordered them back, accompanied by the Cherokee Indian troops commanded by Albert Pike. Inevitably these forces would lock horns with the Yanks. They did, on May 7 and 8, 1862, at a site called Elkhorn Tavern by the Confederates, Pea Ridge by the Federals. Ailing at the time, Van Dorn had to issue his battle orders from an ambulance wagon. Though the Rebels outnumbered the Yanks (about 16,000 to 12,000), and though each side lost about 1,300 men, the Union was victorious. As noted previously, the velvet-clad McCulloch was among the casualties.

For another two years, the Union was in control of Missouri. Worse, it also controlled some sections of northern Arkansas. Coming soon after the losses of Forts Donelson and Henry, the defeat at Elkhorn Tavern was another blow to Southern morale.

Union morale was boosted, and not just because the blue boys won the battle: The North found a great piece of propaganda, thanks to the fact (or rumor) that the Indians fighting for the Confederacy had scalped some of the dead Union soldiers. The Northern press was thick with accusations of barbarity and savagery, and some Southerners were embarrassed at having the Indians on their side.

Union control of Missouri meant the Federals had a base for launching military campaigns into Arkansas. In 1863, pressure from Union troops forced the state's government to flee from the capital (Little Rock) and establish as a new capital the town of Washington. Early in 1864, Arkansas Unionists from 23 counties met together in Little Rock, put together a new (and Unionist) state constitution, and set up their own pro-Union government. For the duration of the war, Arkansas had a Union government and a Confederate government—divided, roughly speaking, by the Arkansas River.

Missouri, the "Show Me Blood" State

So far we've talked about the *official* armies of the North and South. Every Confederate state—and the border states as well—had its share of unofficial warfare. We're talking about guerrillas, and nowhere were they worse than the disputed state of Missouri. Some very violent people—some pro-South, some pro-North—were literally cutting each others' throats.

Both Missouri and Kansas were home to the pro-Union guerrilla fighters known as Jayhawkers, whose pro-Confederate counterparts were known as Bushwhackers. Newspaper publisher Horace Greeley popularized the term "border ruffians," which applied to both groups. He might have done better to refer to both as "trash" and "scumbags" and "sociopaths," for that's what most of them were.

The Civil War, like any war, had its psychopath fringe. There were lowlifes in the border states who had no noble ideals about preserving the Union or fighting for Southern rights, but the war gave them a motivation to do nasty things in the name of patriotism. Thus the Jayhawkers called themselves pro-Union and anti-slavery, and they may have believed they were, but mainly they were thieves and murderers, with the war giving them an excuse to do harm to people they didn't like.

Most of them were, like the Bushwhackers, drawn from the dregs of society. However, one "respectable" Jayhawker (in name if not in actions) was James Lane, the "Grim Chieftain" who represented Kansas in Congress. Lane is probably one of the sleaziest characters ever to disgrace the Capitol's halls (which is saying quite a lot). Lane led a band into Missouri in fall 1861, slaughtering as they went, burning Confederates' homes and barns, torching crops, and stealing slaves and livestock. (Always a volatile character, Lane committed suicide in 1866, which must have pleased his numerous enemies.)

The most infamous guerrilla incident of the war was actually an attempt to destroy James Lane. This was the raid on Lawrence, Kansas, on August 21, 1863, perpetrated by William C. Quantrill's Bushwhacker gang. The wily Lane escaped with his life (clad in his nightshirt, he hid in a cornfield), but 150 others didn't, and much of the pro-Union town was burned.

Probably the best-known (and perhaps most violent) Jayhawker was Charles "Doc" Jennison, a New York–born horse thief, who found that the war gave him an excuse to steal (from Confederates, of course) and play the Union hero at the same time. Doc collected a motley crew of anti-slavery advocates and the most thuggish of criminals, men who had no scruples about committing theft, arson, rape, and murder on people they called "rebel scum." Jennison's trademark: He sliced off the ears of his victims.

Notions such as chivalry and Christian principles never entered the ruffians' minds. In their view of things, war was a delightful barbarism, and they seemed to take pleasure in following no rules (which is why most weren't in the regular armies). For them the war was not so much a war as a feud—one side committing atrocities, the other side committing more atrocities in return.

The Bloody, Border, Bluegrass State

Like Missouri, the other slave state that was "sort of" in the Confederacy, Kentucky, saw its share of bloodshed, much of it during the early months of the war. Remember that Kentucky had hoped to remain neutral in the war (while holding on to its slaves, naturally), but this wasn't to be. Both Union and Confederacy wished to recruit soldiers in the state (all told, Kentucky supplied about 35,000 Confederate soldiers and about 75,000 Union soldiers), and it wasn't long before a very eager Rebel general brought neutrality to an end.

The "Fighting Bishop," Leonidas Polk, was a West Point grad, Episcopal bishop, and the first Confederate invader of Kentucky. On September 3, 1861, General Polk led Confederate troops from Tennessee into Kentucky, capturing the Mississippi River ports of Columbus and Hickman. A little-known (at the time) Union general, Ulysses S. Grant, then seized Paducah, Kentucky, on the Ohio River. Kentucky's state militia came to life—and began siding either with the Union or Confederacy. (Bye-bye, neutrality.)

Polk and Grant collided at the Battle of Belmont (Missouri, across the river from Columbus, Kentucky), on November 7, 1861. Columbus was an important site (as Polk knew when he captured it), the Gibraltar of the West along the mighty Mississippi. The battle was, in a real sense, the first battle in the war's western campaign.

Polk met with Grant under a flag of truce afterward to discuss exchange of prisoners. Polk reported later that he wished to discuss "the principles on which I thought the war should be conducted; denounced all barbarity, vandalism, plundering, and all that, and got him [Grant] to say that he would join in putting it down." The war was still in its early stages, West Point men still respected each other (an old boys' network), and Polk could assume (temporarily) that the war would be "civilized."

> ### Go See It!
> Columbus-Belmont Battlefield State Park on SR 58 in Kentucky, has the massive chain the Confederates stretched across the Mississippi River to halt Union boats. You can see the chain, its six-ton anchor, and other relics at the park's museum.

Enter the "General Problem," Bragg

When the Civil War began, Braxton Bragg of North Carolina was high on the Confederacy's "Most Likely to Succeed" list. Why? Part of the early Bragg legend involved his Mexican War service. Supposedly the young Bragg had helped win a key battle when he obeyed the order of Gen. Zachary Taylor: "A little more grape, Captain Bragg." ("Grape" was grapeshot, the iron balls that were standard ammo.) The often-repeated "grape story" had a special place in the heart of Jefferson Davis, whose first wife was Zachary Taylor's daughter.

Bragg commanded a corps at the fateful Battle of Shiloh (see Chapter 15). Albert Sidney Johnston, Bragg's commander at the time, was mortally wounded on the Shiloh battlefield. This created an opening in the chain of command. The logical choice was Beauregard, the little egomaniac from Louisiana, whom the president had come to dislike. Conveniently, Beauregard took sick leave. Davis then made Bragg a full general (four stars) and put him in command of the Western Department, and Bragg thought another invasion of Kentucky would be wise. The campaign in late summer 1862 started optimistically. Moving north from Tennessee, Gen. Edmund

Kirby Smith (more about him shortly) entered Kentucky and won the Battle of Richmond. A few days later the Rebel troops occupied the state capital, Frankfort.

The Rebs appeared to be doing well in Kentucky. Bragg went to Frankfort to be present at the inauguration of Richard Hawes, the governor—*Confederate* governor, that is. Briefly, it seemed, Kentucky was going to have a full-fledged pro-Confederate government. This was on October 4, 1862. But within mere hours of the inauguration, Bragg and Hawes both had to retreat from Frankfort, thanks to the Union forces commanded by Gen. Don Carlos Buell. The new governor was delivering his inaugural address when the boom of Federal guns interrupted rudely. Poor Hawes never had the opportunity to function as governor. And who did he blame? Bragg.

Four days later, Bragg and Buell went head to head at the Battle of Perryville in central Kentucky. Bragg's 17,000 Rebels defeated Buell's 22,000 Yanks. If that sounds enormous, it was—definitely the biggest (and bloodiest) battle fought on Kentucky soil. It should have been even bloodier, for everyone expected Bragg's troops to push on and thoroughly smash the Federals.

But no. To the supreme irritation of his own boys, Bragg chose to retreat. After winning a victory—or at least a half-victory—the Rebel soldiers headed back to Tennessee, abandoning Kentucky to the Union. A grand opportunity had been lost. The Confederacy wouldn't get another chance to push all the way to the Ohio River.

On their long march back to Tennessee, the soldiers began hating their commander. They could tolerate his strictness, but not his halfheartedness (or indecisiveness, or whatever it was). Confederate soldiers proved they could fight well under stern commanders, such as Stonewall Jackson. But there was kind of an unspoken agreement: *Work us hard, general, but let us fight to win.* Bragg worked them hard, but he wouldn't let them win.

Bragg had a long list of physical ailments (such as killer migraines), which affected his mental state, and vice versa. We will see a little more, shortly, about General Bragg, the man one newspaper described as having an "iron hand, iron heart, and wooden head."

Incidentally, it was shortly after the Battle of Perryville that the western troops under Bragg's command were given their famous name, the Army of Tennessee.

> **Go See It!**
>
> Perryville Battlefield State Historic Site is on SR 1920 in Kentucky. If you visit on the weekend closest to October 8, you can witness a reenactment of the famous battle.

> **Voices from Then**
>
> Considering all his problems with his generals, the fractious Bragg paid an appropriate compliment: "History will award the main honor where it is due—to the private soldier."

Gen. Smith, of Kirby Smithdom

Florida-born Edmund Kirby Smith's army career is a familiar story in these pages: He graduated from West Point and served with distinction in the Mexican War. (His West Point classmates knew him as "Seminole," since he hailed from Florida.) When the South seceded, Smith followed his home state out of the Union. His loyalty to the Confederate Army took him away from Florida for most of the war—a good thing in terms of seeing parts of the American wilderness, but a bad thing, given his sentimental attachment to Florida.

Edmund Kirby Smith (1824–1893), who became military head of "Kirby Smithdom," all the Confederate territory west of the Mississippi River.

(Florida State Archives)

The Florida man was a respected general, also noted for his devoutness. (As with Robert E. Lee, another Episcopal saint, Smith seasoned his letters both personal and official with references to "the Almighty" and "Providence.") On more than one occasion (usually when the war was going badly) he considered abandoning the soldier's life and becoming an Episcopal minister, but always believed himself unworthy. One of these times was following the ill-fated invasion of Kentucky, when the perplexing, frustrating Braxton Bragg, Smith's commander at the time, chose to retreat after the almost-victory at Perryville.

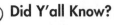

Kentucky had proven to be at best a waste and at worst a disaster. Smith came out of the ordeal looking better than Bragg did, and he was promoted to lieutenant general (three stars, that is). Quicker than anyone would have guessed, the general found himself wielding more earthly power in the Confederacy than anyone else except Jefferson Davis himself.

How did the western Confederacy become "Kirby Smithdom"? To begin with, Smith had sparkled at the First Battle of Manassas, leading to fame and promotion, and he served out the war's early years in Virginia, Tennessee, and Kentucky. Then in February 1863 came a fateful order from the Confederate government in Richmond: "The command of Lieut. Gen. E. Kirby Smith is extended so as to embrace the Trans-Mississippi Department." In brief, Smith was the head military honcho of everything west of the Mississippi—Texas, Arkansas, and some of Louisiana. Wow. And if this seemed like a grand assignment at the time, it became even more impressive—and burdensome—following the fall of Vicksburg in July 1863. With Vicksburg in Federal hands, the entire Mississippi River was under Federal control. It was as if the mighty river had become a boundary between Confederacy and Kirby Smithdom.

Alas, most of the best fighting men from the region were shedding their blood in Virginia, Tennessee, and Georgia. Smith observed that "the aged, the infirm, and the lukewarm constitute the mass of the population that remains." Nonetheless, he was the Big Man of the western Confederacy, pretty much left on his own, not a task he enjoyed. He summed up his situation nicely: "It is no bed of roses." Kirby Smithdom faced not only Union attack but also marauding bands of deserters and bushwhackers, Comanche and Kiowa Indians raiding white settlements, plus the burden of feeding and sheltering hordes of women and children fleeing from the eastern Confederacy.

Smith was no dictator. The governors and legislatures in Texas, Arkansas, and Louisiana continued to function; ditto for the various counties and towns in the region. Smith was the area's highest-ranking Confederate official, and he tried to respect, and work with, local officials. In summer of 1863, governors and other state officials in the Trans-Mississippi met together, agreed to try to coordinate things, and expressed a vote of confidence in Smith. The governors made it clear, however, that they would swiftly arrest him if he ever considered surrendering the Trans-Mississippi armies to the Union. As it turned out, he was one of the last generals to surrender.

Stay Away, You Feds

In spring of 1864, Union troops under Nathaniel Banks and Frederick Steele pushed forward in what was known as the Red River Campaign. The goal: to capture Louisiana's capital city of Shreveport. (Baton Rouge, Louisiana's capital, had been occupied by the Federals in 1862, so the Confederates had to move the state's government to Opelousas, then Shreveport.) Shreveport also happened to be the headquarters for General Kirby Smith. To fend off the Federals, Smith sent a feisty character: Richard Taylor, son of president Zachary Taylor. (Recall that Jefferson Davis's first wife was Zachary Taylor's daughter. Thus Richard Taylor was brother-in-law of the Confederate president.)

> **Go See It!**
>
> Southeast of Mansfield, Louisiana, on Highway 175, you can visit the Mansfield State Historic Site, which has some relics from the famous battle where Dick Taylor and his Rebels repulsed the larger Union force of Nathaniel Banks.

With fewer than 9,000 men, Taylor managed to defeat a Union force of 20,000 on April 8, 1864, at the Battle of Mansfield. (More multiple naming: The battle is also referred to as Pleasant Grove, or Sabine Cross Roads.) There was little actual fighting in Louisiana for the rest of the war. Western Louisiana remained in Confederate hands, while the Federals controlled the east, including Baton Rouge and New Orleans. Union general Banks had been thwarted in his objective of planting the U.S. flag in Texas. Taylor had proven to everyone's satisfaction that the troops of the Trans-Mississippi Department could fight well under a competent general.

Tribes and Borders

Once Vicksburg had fallen and the Mississippi River was in Union hands (July 1863), communication with the Richmond government was difficult for Smith. Davis and his cabinet had their hands full, frankly, and the last thing they could do was spare men, or supplies, to aid the western Confederacy. There was a flip side to this: By the fall of 1863, the West had pretty much stopped contributing anything to the Confederate government. Virginia was no longer much help to Texas, nor Texas to Virginia.

The West had plenty of its own problems to keep it occupied. North of Texas, the various tribes in the Indian Territory (it's Oklahoma today) fell into their traditional patterns: fighting each other, and harassing whites along the Texas border. So the state's northern and western borders required policing. Ditto for the southern border with Mexico. Texas set up a State Military Board and created a new Texas Frontier Regiment.

Isolated from the east, Texas, Arkansas, and western Louisiana found themselves cut off from needed supplies. Yet, as travelers through the region noticed, Confederate soldiers in the district appeared better fed and better clothed than the ragged Rebel scarecrows in Virginia and Tennessee. Somehow Kirby Smithdom managed to scrape through the war's final two years, making do with such tactics as putting state prisoners in Huntsville, Texas, to work making textiles.

Texas took advantage of its border with Mexico. Through the Mexican port of Matamoros (across the Rio Grande from Brownsville, Texas), about 300,000 bales of cotton left Texas—bound for either England or New York. (Most Yankee merchants had no scruples about illegally buying and selling Confederate cotton.) After July 1863, the Union may have prevented Confederate goods from crossing the Mississippi River, but they had no such luck patrolling the Rio Grande.

A steady stream of refugees from the eastern Confederacy reminded Texans that they were fortunate to be far from the scene of the Union's "total war" policy. The crops and livestock of the West were largely unmolested by the Federals, and Union "bummers" didn't ransack western homes, stealing silver and other valuables. With no Union troops nearby, there was less chance of slaves running away to Union lines. So, for the most part, war was not hell in Kirby Smithdom. It was, however, no picnic.

The Least You Need to Know

- The sprawling state of Texas provided the Confederacy with some excellent fighting men and generals.

- Colorful general Earl Van Dorn tried but failed to secure Missouri for the Confederacy.

- Guerrilla fighting was probably worst in Missouri, with its border ruffians.

- Indecisive general Braxton Bragg led a promising invasion of the neutral state of Kentucky—then angered his men and generals by retreating.

- General Edmund Kirby Smith was practically the military ruler of the Trans-Mississippi Confederacy after the fall of Vicksburg in July 1863.

Tennessee Waltz, Georgia Wail

In This Chapter

- ◆ Sherman, that "war is hell" guy
- ◆ The relief at the relief of Bragg
- ◆ "Retreatin' Joe" out, "Reckless Hood" in
- ◆ Battles in the clouds, and other scenic spots
- ◆ Total war on civilians (or just plain terrorism)

If you think terrorism is relatively new, think again. It was practiced in the 1860s, and one of its chief practitioners was a redheaded Union general named Sherman. For several generations, that name conjured up horrible images for Southern families. Sherman threw aside the old idea of civilized warfare and decided that since "war is hell" (his famous words), it is best to make it very hot and get it over with. His famous March to the Sea through Georgia proved he took his own words seriously.

This chapter looks at the uncivil war on civilians, but also at the luckless Army of Tennessee, which seemed to be cursed with bad commanders and tough opponents. We'll see that 1864 was a rough year for both Tennessee and Georgia—and, as always, bad luck makes good stories.

New Year's Slaughter

Middle Tennessee was a major concern in 1862, for the Yanks already held the capital, Nashville, and they showed every sign of wanting to push further south, capturing more of Tennessee, then on to Georgia. Their commander in Tennessee was sandy-haired, beak-nosed General William Rosecrans, "Old Rosey," a devout Catholic who loved to discuss theology and to curse. Rosecrans commanded what was called the Army of the Cumberland. The day after Christmas 1862, half that army advanced from Nashville, where they would face Braxton Bragg near the town of Murfrees-boro. Rosecrans had about 47,000, Bragg about 38,000. The two forces met on December 31.

Go See It!

The battle was called Murfreesboro by the Confederates, Stone's River by the Federals. Near Murfreesboro, Tennessee, on U.S. 41, you can visit the Stone's River National Battlefield, which, as it happens, has the nation's oldest Civil War monument, erected in 1863. Note at the battlefield that the Union dead were buried in individual marked graves. The Confederate dead were buried in a mass grave nearby at the town's Evergreen Cemetery.

As usual for him, Bragg at first attacked furiously. The battle seemed to be going in the Rebels' favor. At the end of the last day of 1862, Bragg was sure the new year would begin with a great Rebel victory. As it turned out, the three-day battle was a draw. (Actually, it was a two-day battle spread out over three days. There was fighting on December 31 and January 2, but not on January 1—supposedly because the devout Rosecrans didn't wish to fight on a Sunday.)

The men of the Army of Tennessee had fought well. But then the general did the typical Bragg thing: withdrew. (To give the man credit, he was urged to do so by his subordinate generals.) Bragg believed, incorrectly, that Rosecrans had received reinforcements. Since Old Rosey held the field, he declared it a Union victory. It wasn't, and both sides had major casualties. Rosey had 1,700 dead, 7,800 wounded, 3,700 missing. Bragg's losses: 1,300 dead, 7,900 wounded, 1,000 missing. For a drawn battle, it drew a lot of blood. Murfreesboro didn't accomplish much for the Union side, since Rosecrans chose not to pursue Bragg. But it was another blot on Bragg's much-blotted record, and the common soldiers began to hate him even more. On the positive side, Old Rosey's Army of the Cumberland had been so badly damaged that it was practically helpless for another six months.

In the spring and summer of 1863, a religious revival swept the Army of Tennessee. The war was wearisome, men were underfed and badly clothed, and many of them turned to God, since their earthly leaders (Bragg, in particular) were so disappointing. Among the many converts, interestingly, was Bragg himself. Would his newfound faith help him win battles—or get along with his own generals? Read on.

Chattanooga, Chickamauga, and Other Colorful Names

Our nation's biggest Civil War park, Chickamauga and Chattanooga, has over 8,000 acres, spread out over sites in two states, Tennessee and Georgia. Several fateful battles took place there in the fall of 1863, most of them ending in Confederate defeats. While these haven't gotten the attention of the big headline makers of 1863 (Gettysburg and Vicksburg), they deserve to be studied more.

In 1863, the Federals still held Nashville, while the Rebels had a base at Chattanooga on the Tennessee-Georgia line. Chattanooga was spread out among several high hills at the strategic bend in the wide Tennessee River. Known as the Gateway City, Chattanooga was a key railway center, and clearly the Yanks wanted it. The man in charge of taking it was Old Rosey. The man in his way was, again, Braxton Bragg.

Their two armies locked horns September 19 and 20, 1863, just south of Chattanooga at Chickamauga Creek in Georgia. (The name Chickamauga meant, to the Indians, "river of death.") Bragg had the superior numbers (an advantage the Rebs rarely had in Civil War battles), and Chickamauga was his greatest victory. But it was a costly one. The Rebs had 2,300 dead, 14,700 wounded, 1,500 missing. The Union losses: 1,600 dead, 9,700 wounded, 4,700 missing.

Bragg won—but, as usual, failed to follow it up. After Chickamauga, his subordinates had circulated a round-robin letter urging Bragg's removal. Jefferson Davis showed up at Bragg's headquarters and asked the commanders—with Bragg present—if the Army of Tennessee should have a new commander. They all said yes, but Davis postponed any action. He had much patience with Bragg, the man everyone else loved to hate.

Did Y'all Know?

Among the Rebel casualties at Chickamauga was Gen. Ben Hardin Helm—whose wife happened to be the sister of Mrs. Abraham Lincoln. It caused some murmuring in Washington when the First Lady put on mourning clothes for a Confederate general.

The Union's Army of the Cumberland retreated back to Chattanooga, so the Rebs still had the task of taking the city. Bragg decided to do to Chattanooga what the Yanks had done to Vicksburg: Starve it out. The Rebels cut all rail lines to Chattanooga, halted river traffic on the Tennessee, and destroyed wagon trains bringing supplies to the Federals.

Old Rosey's reputation was ruined at Chickamauga, and Lincoln replaced him with George Thomas, the "Rock of Chickamauga" who had saved Rosecrans's army from complete destruction. (Thomas, was a Virginia soldier who scandalized his family by fighting for the Union during the Civil War.) So Thomas was in command of the Army of the Cumberland, and his chief was a formidable character: Ulysses S. Grant. Knowing the Federals at Chattanooga were in danger of being starved out, Grant approved an operation called the "Cracker Line," bringing in supplies by river from Alabama.

Called to Grant's aid was Joe Hooker, who hadn't fared well against Robert E. Lee in Virginia. Hooker did better in Tennessee. His Union troops faced off with Bragg's in what was called the "Battle Above the Clouds," officially the Battle of Lookout Mountain, where Hooker's men charged up the mountain through dense fog and mist. The date was November 24, 1863.

The following day brought another Union victory. Bragg faced a Union general we have already met and will hear more of shortly: Sherman. Bragg held Missionary Ridge. The blue boys of Sherman and Thomas charged the ridge, and Rebels fled in panic. Missionary Ridge, a seemingly impregnable position, had been captured.

Bragg, whipped and disgusted, retreated to Georgia. Rebel soldiers were whipped and disgusted, too. When Bragg passed by, some would shout out, "Bully for Bragg, he's hell on retreat!" On December 1, 1863, Bragg asked to be relieved from command. Davis accepted the resignation, then in February 1864 called the failed general to Richmond and made him his military adviser. The griping, Davis-hating Joe Johnston was made commander of the Army of Tennessee in Bragg's place. The name "Army of Tennessee" had become a sad joke. By the end of 1863, almost all of Tennessee was held by the Union. It was only a matter of time before the Yankees pressed on into Georgia.

Move Over, Scarlett

Atlanta in 1864 wasn't the hectic, humming, traffic-snarled, urban-suburban sprawling mass of today. It was pretty small, a fairly new town, not even the state capital at the time (Milledgeville was). When the Civil War began, the city had fewer than 10,000 people but was important as a railway center (four railroads converged there). The war had increased its importance, not only for rail transportation but for war industries as well—steam engines and railway cars, for example. With the cities of New Orleans, Memphis, Nashville, Vicksburg, and Chattanooga occupied by the Union, Atlanta was the Confederacy's most important transportation center, outside of Richmond.

As early as 1862 the Yankees had made some attempts on Atlanta. The "Great Locomotive Chase" occurred on April 12, 1862, when the Union's James Andrews and his men dressed as civilians and hijacked the *General* (a locomotive, that is) while the other passengers were enjoying a meal break. Along the railways, the Andrews band cut telegraph lines and threw railroad ties on the tracks, hoping to derail their pursuers. But their main goal, burning railroad bridges, was thwarted because of recent heavy rains. Rebels pursued the Yanks on a handcar, then on the *Texas*, and captured them near Chattanooga. Andrews and his band were taken to Atlanta, tried, and hanged as spies.

> **Did Y'all Know?**
>
> The Andrews locomotive raid provided the plot for one of the best silent movies ever made, Buster Keaton's comedy *The General*, and also a Disney movie, *The Great Locomotive Chase*.

> **Voices from Then**
>
> There has been no such army since the days of Julius Caesar.
>
> —Joe Johnston, speaking of Sherman's troops

Andrews's aim had been to destroy the Western and Atlantic Railroad. That task would fall to someone much more famous than Andrews, a guy named Sherman.

In March 1864, Ulysses S. Grant was named general in chief of all the Union armies. Grant had a simple plan: He would concentrate his attention on the Army of Northern Virginia commanded by Robert E. Lee. Sherman would concentrate on the Army of Tennessee commanded by Joe Johnston. By applying pressure in both Virginia and Georgia, the Union forces could prevent the two Rebel commanders from sending each other reinforcements.

Sherman had about 100,000 men (which he called "one of the best armies in the world"). Johnston had far fewer—perhaps 53,000. On May 7, Sherman began what is called the Atlanta Campaign. The early battles in the campaign took place between Chattanooga and Atlanta. Among these was the Battle of Resaca, May 14 to May 15, a Confederate victory, though one that involved Johnston retreating. (He maintained his reputation as "Retreatin' Joe"—but then, facing such superior numbers, what else could he have done?)

On June 27, Johnston and Sherman faced off again at Kennesaw Mountain, and it was probably Sherman's worst-fought battle. Sherman lost more than 2,000 men, four times what the Rebs lost. For a few days, Johnston had managed to delay Sherman's march to Atlanta. The Northern newspapers, which had never been too kind to Sherman in the past, skewered him for his performance at Kennesaw.

Johnston had won at Kennesaw, but he still kept retreating farther south. Jefferson Davis was exasperated. On July 17, the Confederate president did something historians discuss to this day: He replaced Johnston with John Bell Hood as commander of the Army of Tennessee. Davis had changed horses in midstream. What would happen?

Hood, the Young and the Reckless

Hood was much younger than Johnston, only 33 at the time he took over Johnston's command. He was known as a bold fighter, and for Davis in his desperate situation, that must have seemed an appealing alternative to Retreatin' Joe Johnston.

John Bell Hood (1831–1879), a tough fighter who had no luck against the superior forces of Union generals like Sherman.

(Tennessee State Library and Archives)

Before he lost his right leg and the use of his left arm, the Kentucky-born Hood was considered quite a catch. He was 6-foot-2, with sad blue eyes, thick blond beard, blondish red hair, broad shoulders, and a lovely voice. He was no pampered pretty boy, however—he lost the use of an arm at Gettysburg and had a leg amputated after Chickamauga. The man with a double handicap was offered a civil post after the amputation of his leg, but he refused. "No bombproof place for me," he said.

Did Y'all Know? _____

At age 33, Hood became the eighth, and last, of the Confederacy's full (four-star) generals.

Hood graduated from the Point while Robert E. Lee was superintendent there, and Lee was fond of him. Hood had the same philosophy of war as Lee: Destroy, don't merely defeat. Lee claimed that Hood's Texas Brigade were the fiercest and most dependable troops in the Army of Northern Virginia.

The gritty general with one leg and a useless arm in a sling had to be strapped to his saddle, but he was raring for a fight. He got his wish, and within three days of being made commander. He took the offensive on July 20 at Peachtree Creek, 3 miles north of Atlanta. The Rebs lost. Two days later he lost the Battle of Atlanta. Within 11 days of taking command of the Army of Tennessee, Hood lost nearly as many men as Johnston had lost in 74 days of battle and retreat.

Go See It!

The Atlanta History Center at West Paces Ferry Road has a permanent exhibit on the city during the Civil War. The city's Grant Park (note the name) is near the site of the Battle of Atlanta and has the famous Cyclorama, a 360-degree painting of the battle, with sound and light effects. In the same building is the *Texas,* the engine used to pursue the Yankees in the Great Locomotive Chase.

Union troops entered Atlanta on September 2, 1864. You might be familiar with this thanks to *Gone with the Wind,* where Scarlett and Melanie (who, inconveniently, happens to be in labor) are told to evacuate the city. The city's houses were used to quarter the Yankee troops, while Atlanta's women, children, old men, and sick folk trudged the countryside.

When they departed Atlanta on November 15, 1864, they burned the city—1,800 buildings, in fact. On that date began a march that Southerners never forgot or forgave.

It was one week after Abraham Lincoln had been reelected U.S. president. Confederates had hoped and prayed his Democratic opponent—none other than Lincoln's failed general, George McClellan—would win and, perhaps, negotiate a peace with the South (since the Democrats were perceived as the "peace party"). But in November 1864, not only was the hated Republican Lincoln reelected, but his party increased its majorities in both House and Senate. The Rebs knew Lincoln would push the war to its bitter end—and his party's South-haters in the Congress could make the war's aftermath a living hell.

If the Union elections didn't make Rebels howl, Sherman certainly did.

The Devil Went Down to Georgia

As the war progressed, it became more and more uncivilized, with the Union troops showing less and less respect for civilians. It had begun as war fought among gentlemen, with the dignified Beauregard observing all the courtesies as he subdued Fort Sumter. Somewhere between Fort Sumter and Sherman's march through Georgia, a major change had occurred. It was no longer war, but total war—or terrorism.

Military historian Caleb Carr, in a interview published in the *St. Petersburg Times*, February 3, 2002, gave his definition of the word: "Terrorism is violence and warfare waged deliberately against civilians for the purpose of affecting their political loyalties and hopefully of forcing them to get their political leaders to change their policies." Carr went on to say that Gen. William Tecumseh Sherman, Union hero of the Civil War, was a terrorist.

Was he? The South didn't know the word *terrorist*, but they certainly knew the concept. From 1864 on, for generations after, Southerners couldn't say the name Sherman without spitting. Even Southerners who lived nowhere near the line of

RebeLingo

March to the Sea refers to the march of Sherman's troops from Atlanta to Savannah. Sherman's army split into 2 wings, which marched as far as 50 miles apart, covering about 15 miles per day.

Sherman's march had heard of the horrors perpetrated on civilians. If the South could have chosen a picture to illustrate the phrase *damn Yankee*, it would have been Sherman's portrait.

You might recall from Chapter 24 that Sherman got some practice in Mississippi in 1863, with his men burning and looting the capital city of Jackson. His men had also delighted in looting Jefferson Davis's own plantation, Brierfield, carrying off Davis's books and purebred horses. That was only a warm-up for what would happen in Georgia.

Departing from a smoldering Atlanta, Sherman had a definite goal: Savannah near the Atlantic coast, where he would link up with the Union navy. How would his thousands of blue-clad soldiers be supplied on their *March to the Sea?* They would live off the land—something Southern civilians had endured before, but never to such a degree. Sherman, calculating soul that he was, had access to the Georgia census records of 1860. His troops' route through the state wasn't chosen at random. From the census records he could judge which Georgia counties were richest agriculturally. His men would march accordingly.

Burning Through the South

The Yankee foragers or *bummers*, as they were called, knew more than just their route. They knew which farms' men were away at war, how much booty could be had at each plantation, everything. They had no intention of just finding food to eat. As Mammy said to Scarlett in *Gone with the Wind*, "They took everything, honey." Food supplies vanished, of course—not just fruits and vegetables, but any meats stored in smokehouses, plus chickens, turkeys, cows, and hogs. The Southerners expected this. What horrified the people was the outright theft—jewelry, silver, china, crystal, candles and lamps, anything that could be carried away, even clothing. Many a Yankee wife or sweetheart received gifts that had been stolen from Georgia homes. (Clothes were very personal items, and Confederate women long remembered their favorite dresses and hats being stolen by blue-coated Yankee men.) To make the demoralized, frightened Southerners feel even more insecure, the bummers took any guns they could find.

RebeLingo

The infamous **bummers** were Federal soldiers under Gen. William T. Sherman, who, in the Carolinas and Georgia, gave them orders to forage for supplies—meaning take food and other necessities from Southern homes. They turned into outright **vandals** and thieves, stealing jewels and other valuables, burning homes, and slaughtering livestock.

Besides theft was the wanton vandalism—burning books, slashing paintings, destroying family records (even Bibles), smashing pianos and clocks. Featherbeds were sometimes ripped open and the feathers scattered. Some soldiers in their dirty boots enjoyed trampling on fine linens. The women who screamed out their protests heard a phrase the Yankees used quite often: "Rebels have no rights!"

The civilians resorted to various tricks, of course. On plantations, clothing might be concealed in the slave cabins. (Yankees caught on to this pretty fast, and occasionally a slave would deliberately give away the hiding place.) Silver and china were buried, and so were hams and lard in tins. Chimneys, wells, and cisterns served as hiding places. The farther the Yanks marched, the cleverer the Southerners became—but the Yanks quickly caught on.

Yankee vandalism wasn't limited to inanimate objects. What livestock the Yanks couldn't take with them, they killed. To save ammunition to use on men, Sherman's men sabered pigs and poleaxed horses and mules between the ears. Dogs were often killed, because (so the Yankees said) they were used to track down fugitive slaves. On one plantation alone more than 100 horses were slaughtered.

Gone with the Wind might have you believe that only the plantation aristocrats got looted, but this wasn't so. The plain folk did, too—and so did slaves. Yankee soldiers actually looted slave cabins. The spectacle of the "liberating" soldiers stealing the possessions of poor blacks made a deep impression on all who witnessed it.

Sherman excused the atrocities, claiming it was all necessary: "To make war we must and will harden our hearts." And why not? Besides liberating the slaves, the Union soldiers had their chance to hurt wealthy Southerners (who, after all, were cruel slave owners) and poor ones (who, so they had always been told, were ignorant, illiterate barbarians, barely better than animals). Taking this attitude, Sherman's men did an estimated $100 million worth of property damage—a figure in 1864 dollars, by the way.

Sherman took the position that making war on civilians was necessary. It had to be done (so he said) to end the war. True? Not at all. His men (who were well fed even before they started their march through Georgia) outnumbered and outgunned the poorly fed, demoralized Army of Tennessee. In spite of his one loss at Kennesaw, Sherman knew his troops could and would whip the Army of Tennessee soon enough. Defeating the Johnston-Hood army quickly and decisively would have ended the war quicker and caused less bitterness among Southern civilians.

Lincoln hadn't forgotten the original goal of the war: Preserve the Union. But Sherman certainly had. His actions guaranteed that if the South was forced back into the Union, its people would despise the North … and they did.

Merry Christmas, Mr. Lincoln

The infamous March to the Sea began on November 16. One of its goals had been the destruction of Southern railroads. Sherman's men became experts at the task. They built bonfires with the wooden railroad ties, then heated the rails and twisted them into spirals around trees and telegraph poles. (The twisted rails entered the Southern vocabulary as "Sherman's neckties" or "Sherman's hairpins.") More than 250 miles of railway were demolished.

Meanwhile, the Army of Tennessee still existed, barely. One problem it faced: Hood, its commander, had no idea where Sherman was headed. Macon? Augusta? No Confederate knew. Anxious to accomplish something, somewhere, Hood headed the Army of Tennessee north again, hoping to recapture Tennessee. So Sherman's army was practically unopposed as it cut its path through Georgia.

A logical question arises: Why didn't the world rise up in righteous anger against Sherman at the time? Simple answer: The world didn't know. For practically a month, the world at large only knew that Sherman's army was somewhere in Georgia. Sherman wanted it that way. Not even Lincoln or Grant knew his location.

Did Y'all Know?

Sherman's troops—and Yankee troops in general—took great delight in destroying Southerners' cotton gins. To the Yanks, gins symbolized the "cotton kingdom" they were working to subdue.

On December 17, Sherman called on Confederate general William Hardee to surrender Savannah, Georgia's largest city.

Hardee wasn't stupid enough to think he could hold the city against such superior numbers. By night he shuttled his troops across a pontoon bridge into South Carolina. The Yankee troops occupied Savannah on December 21. A triumphant Sherman telegraphed Lincoln, telling him that Savannah was his "Christmas present."

Sherman had ended his notorious March to the Sea—but he had more damage to do, in another Confederate state that, in his view, hadn't suffered nearly enough. More about that in the next chapter.

Ending the Tennessee Waltz

The gallant, reckless John Hood had hoped to retreat from Georgia into Tennessee and get Sherman to pursue him there. Always thinking boldly (some would say "stupidly"), Hood hoped to retake Tennessee, then Kentucky, then link up with Lee in Virginia. Sherman chose to proceed on through Georgia, but he sent part of his army after Hood. While his Union boys were "making Georgia howl" (as Sherman put it), Union men in Tennessee were devastating Hood's army.

On November 30, 1864, Yank and Reb encountered each other south of Nashville near the town of Franklin. In 5 hours of fierce fighting,

Go See It!

Franklin, Tennessee, has the Carnton Plantation on SR 431, which saw some of the bloody action of the Battle of Franklin. Part of the property is a Confederate cemetery. The Carter House on U.S. 31 also commemorates the battle.

more than 6,000 Confederates died (the Union lost 2,000). The Battle of Franklin is often called the "Battle of the Generals" because six generals were mortally wounded there, including the feisty Irish-born Patrick Cleburne and the South Carolina gent with the striking name States Rights Gist. Six other generals were wounded or captured. Many Civil War buffs claim Franklin as the most underrated battle of the war.

Hood marched his men north to Nashville and laid siege to the Union-held city. This was foolish: He had about 25,000 men, while the Union's George Thomas (who had been one of Hood's instructors at West Point) had 60,000. Thomas attacked, and with fury. The Battle of Nashville, December 15, 1864, was a debacle for the Rebels. Northern newspapers declared that Thomas, the "Rock of Chickamauga," was now the "Sledge of Nashville."

Poor Hood requested to be relieved of command. What remained of his Army of Tennessee drifted back southward. Because of the bitterly cold ground, those who were barefoot turned their hats into foot wrappings. They were singing their new (and bitter) parody of the old song "The Yellow Rose of Texas":

> You may talk about your Beauregard
> And sing of General Lee,
> But the gallant Hood of Texas
> Played hell in Tennessee.

Alas, 1864 hadn't been kind to Tennessee or Georgia. The Army of Tennessee hadn't fared well, either. Bragg, Joe Johnston, Hood … the western Confederacy was rough on its generals. Or, more accurately, the Union generals in the western Confederacy were tough opponents. And at least one of those generals—Sherman—was a terrorist to boot.

The Least You Need to Know

- After losing several key Tennessee battles, General Braxton Bragg resigned—and was made Jefferson Davis's military adviser.

- Bragg's replacement, Joe Johnston, constantly retreated before Sherman's Union army, so Johnston was replaced with young, reckless John Hood.

- Union troops under Sherman burned Atlanta, then marched 300 miles to Savannah, terrorizing Georgia civilians and destroying more than $100 million worth of property.

- General John Hood's rash plans to recapture Tennessee failed completely and Hood resigned, with the Army of Tennessee barely a remnant.

27

Virginia Rendezvous, and the Ending(s)

In This Chapter

- ◆ The Secession State gets some action (finally)
- ◆ Sheridan, the dwarf terrorist
- ◆ The Petersburg siege, and that gaping hole in the ground
- ◆ The actor Booth in his most dramatic role
- ◆ Lee surrenders, Johnston surrenders, and so on

If you've been paying attention, you may have noticed that South Carolina, the first state to secede, hasn't been mentioned much since the war began. In fact, following Fort Sumter, the state had seen little military action. True, the civilians suffered shortages and deprivation as all parts of the Confederacy did. But somehow the Secession State had mostly escaped bloodshed and destruction. That was about to change dramatically.

Union general William Tecumseh Sherman boasted he could "make Georgia howl"—and did. Everyone fully expected that after reaching Savannah (his 1864 "Christmas present" to Lincoln), Sherman would then ship his army of vandals off to Virginia to link up with Grant's army as it pressed on Richmond. But Sherman wanted to apply his total-war strategy to the Carolinas—to the home of secession, South Carolina, in particular. Logically, he would want to punish proud old Charleston for being "Secession City."

The Terrorist Turns North

His men were itching for this. The blue-clads had apparently enjoyed making life a living hell for Georgia civilians, but Georgia was only a warm-up for South Carolina. Once the blue boys were across the Savannah River, they made South Carolina howl even louder than Georgia. The Carolina civilians wept and protested as the soldiers in blue made off with food, livestock, clothing, jewelry, silver, and linen. Their protests provoked the typical Yankee response: "Rebels have no rights."

> **" " Voices from Then**
>
> The whole army is burning with an insatiable desire to wreak vengeance upon South Carolina. I almost tremble at her fate, but feel she deserves all that is in store for her.
>
> —William Tecumseh Sherman

Let's backtrack a bit: Fort Sumter near Charleston was captured by the Confederates in April 1861 and held for the rest of the war. Few pieces of property have ever been defended so expensively. The fort had symbolic value, and the Federals desperately wanted it back. Union shells fell on the fort's walls for month after month. The constant pounding changed it from a brick masonry fort with vertical walls to a large earthwork, with the Rebels dumping sand and dirt on the sides as the bricks became loosened. (Dirt is amazingly hard to destroy.)

The man in charge of defending Charleston, and Fort Sumter, was the Confederacy's first hero, the short, vain P. G. T. Beauregard, famed for both Sumter and First Manassas. The president sent Bory to defend Charleston, and the snooty egomaniac fit in well with the proud locals. The people were pleased at having the Sumter hero among them.

The Yanks desperately wanted the city (as well as Fort Sumter), and they had managed to capture some other forts nearby. At one of them was planted a powerhouse artillery piece known as the Swamp Angel. From sandy Morris Island, the Swamp Angel could fire 200-pound shells into Charleston—5 miles away. Some banks and hospitals in the lower city were evacuated. Some locals chose to stay on at home, setting tubs of water throughout the houses (in case the shells caused a fire). Many complained that the shells' screaming woke them at night. Fortunately, the Swamp Angel burst after firing only 36 rounds. Beauregard had his faults, but he was chivalrous, and this shelling of Charleston went against his idea of civilized war. He, the

Charlestonians, and every other Southerner saw such destruction of civilians and their property as barbarous.

But the really serious devastation was being done elsewhere by Sherman's troops, cutting a destructive path from Savannah to Columbia, the capital. By February, Columbia was in his hands. The city went up in flames on February 17, probably because of drunk Union soldiers. After the war, Sherman wrote, "Though I never ordered it, and never wished it, I have never shed any tears over the event, because I believe that it hastened what we all fought for, the end of the war."

The noted Southern author William Gilmore Simms happened to be in Columbia when it was sacked by the Yankees, and he left a painfully picturesque description of it:

> Humiliation spreads her ashes over our homes and garments, and the universal wreck exhibits only one common aspect of despair. Stores were broken open within the first hour after their arrival, and gold, silver, jewels, and liquors eagerly sought. Woe to him who carried a watch with a gold chain pendant, or who wore a choice hat, or overcoat, or boots or shoes. He was stripped in the twinkling of an eye.

The vandals moved on to North Carolina, where Sherman's men took fiendish pleasure in literally "setting the woods on fire"—that is, burning the huge pines used for making turpentine. Yankee soldiers had only to light a match to the notched trunks of pines, and the sap would catch fire, turning the tall trees into torches.

At Fayetteville, Sherman naturally destroyed the Confederate arsenal—along with a lot of nonmilitary property as well. And he ordered away the "twenty to thirty thousand useless mouths," the "black sheep" who followed (and hindered) his blue soldiers. Union terrorists didn't wish to be hampered by the thousands of grateful black people who saw the blue-clad soldiers as "liberators."

Go See It!

The State House (capitol, that is) in downtown Columbia, South Carolina, is a beautiful and historic building. On its outside walls are bronze stars—marking the scars made by Union cannons. The building was still incomplete when Sherman shelled it. Across the street, Trinity Cathedral has the grave of Gen. Wade Hampton, who is also commemorated with a large bronze statue on the capitol grounds.

Two Ornery Cusses in Virginia

It's worth mentioning again: Richmond, the Confederacy's capital, is a mere 100 miles from Washington. Why, for heaven's sake, had the Yankees not been able to capture it? From the Wilderness to Petersburg, the Union's Army of the Potomac had lost more men than the 60,000 Lee had when the campaign began. At the time, after so much war and bloodshed, Richmond seemed as untakable as it was in 1861. But it would be taken, because Grant had a stubbornness and willingness to fight that George McClellan, "Little Mac," simply didn't have.

The Union had someone else besides Grant. It had a runty little black-haired Irish fellow named Philip Sheridan, a cavalry general who shared Sherman's enthusiasm for total war on Southern civilians.

Grant had made "Little Phil" Sheridan commander of all cavalry in the Army of the Potomac. Little Phil reorganized the cavalry and sent them to battles at the Wilderness, Spotsylvania, and Cold Harbor. They were notorious for severing vital communication lines around Richmond, sending fear through the Confederate capital.

Opposing the profane Sheridan was the profane Jubal "Old Jube" Early, the gray-bearded, tobacco-spitting Virginia lawyer who Robert E. Lee jokingly referred to as his "bad old man." Old Jube, cranky, stoop-shouldered, with a longtime mistress and four out-of-wedlock children, was a tough fighter, and aside from his performance at Gettysburg, had a fine record.

Voices from Then

Jubal Early once swore that he wished the Yankees were all dead. Robert E. Lee chided him and said, no, he only wished they would all go home and leave the South alone. Early, out of Lee's earshot, snarled, "I not only wish them all dead but I wish them all in hell!" On another occasion, Early called some Federal cavalrymen "you God-damned Blue-butts!"

Promoted to lieutenant general in May 1864, Early was given a major task: Threaten Baltimore and Washington, the aim being to divert Grant's troops from Richmond—a game of "whose capital is in the most jeopardy?" With his small but spunky Army of the Valley—never more than 14,000 men—Early raided Maryland, collecting $220,000 in tribute from the towns of Frederick and Hagerstown. Then, on July 11, his troops threatened to enter D.C.

In the almost-raid on Washington, some of Jube's sharpshooters took aim at a tall figure in a high hat on the parapets of Fort Stevens—but they missed Lincoln. One man was shot dead 3 feet from the president. Early told one officer, "We haven't taken Washington, but we've scared Abe Lincoln like hell!"

Old Jube was incensed at the Federals' destruction of property around his hometown of Lynchburg. He got vengeance on July 30 and 31, 1864: Under orders from Early, the town of Chambersburg, Pennsylvania, was told to fork over $100,000 in gold or $300,000 in greenbacks as recompense for the Union destruction of Virginia property—otherwise the town would be "laid in ashes in retaliation." The citizens refused to pay up, so the Rebs torched a warehouse, the courthouse, and town hall, and much of the town was burnt. Damages amounted to about $1.5 million. Early considered it just.

Alas, Early's Washington and Pennsylvania raids were to bring hellacious retribution on the South, the Shenandoah Valley in particular. Grant made Sheridan the commander of the Army of the Shenandoah in August 1864, with orders to move the Confederates south and destroy

any supplies that would aid them. Grant ordered him to "eat out Virginia clear and clean … so that crows flying over it will have to carry their provender with them." Little Phil obeyed, in spades. Southerners had good reason to despise him, for he laid waste the Shenandoah Valley—Virginia's "breadbasket"—with the same demonic thoroughness that Sherman applied in Georgia.

Sheridan believed that cutting Virginia's supply of foodstuffs would help end the war swiftly. He cheerfully rattled off how he destroyed over 2,000 barns and 70 mills, as well as seizing livestock and grain for his own troops. If any of the locals dared to shoot at a Union soldier, Sheridan made sure the shooter was hanged. The farmers of the valley watched in horror as their burning barns lit up the night skies. Many of the farmers were pacifist Mennonites, but this didn't faze Sheridan's destroyers. They also didn't seem to care that it was fall and the Southerners would face a long, hungry winter. One Virginia officer wrote that "the government of Satan and Lincoln sent Phil Sheridan to campaign in the Valley of Virginia." Shenandoah residents referred to it for years as "the Burning."

Facing pugnacious, foul-mouthed Confederate general Jubal Early's troops at Cedar Creek, Virginia, Sheridan turned a near defeat into a victory, aided by the fact that Early's men got distracted looting a Federal baggage train. (Funny how hungry men can be so easily distracted.) Little Phil rode to the front to rally his troops, waving his cap and hollering, "We'll get a twist on these people yet! We'll raise them out of their boots before the day is over!" They did.

News of Sheridan's defeat of gutsy Old Jube sent Northern cities into ecstasies—parades, fireworks, the whole nine yards. A popular poem, "Sheridan's Ride," was read from platforms all over the Union—a great boon to Lincoln in his reelection bid. Lincoln was pleased mightily.

Early was criticized for losing the Shenandoah Valley to the Federals. Whether anyone else could have prevented the loss is doubtful. (The famed "Defender of the Valley," Stonewall Jackson, was long dead.) The fertile valley was a smoldering ruin. The Federals could turn all their attention to that vexing old problem: Richmond.

Petersburg, South of Richmond

In late August 1864, Ulysses S. Grant, the "Great Hammerer," had been hammering away toward Richmond since May—yet he was no closer to Richmond than McClellan had been in 1862. In spite of losing more than 80,000 men, Grant still had double what Lee had. But he didn't have Richmond—yet. Many Rebels (and Yanks as well) must have wondered if Richmond had a whole flock of guardian angels.

Grant saw that the key to Richmond was Petersburg on the Appomattox River, about 20 miles south of the capital. It was a transportation hub, with five railroads and nine wagon roads converging there. With Petersburg captured, Richmond would be cut off from supplies from the Southern heartland and from the coast as well. If Petersburg fell, inevitably Richmond would fall. But Petersburg was no pushover. It took the Union army from June 1864 to April 1865 to subdue it.

Did Y'all Know?

Lasting from June 15, 1864, to April 3, 1865, the Petersburg campaign under Lee was the longest sustained defensive operation of the war. Casualties were high—28,000 for the Confederacy, a whopping 42,000 for the Union. Although the North lost more men, it could afford to.

One of the most bizarre episodes of the war occurred in July 1864, what is known as the Crater incident. A Pennsylvania officer had a novel idea: Dig a tunnel under the Rebels' artillery and blow it up. For more than a month the soldier-miners worked at the 580-foot shaft under the Rebel fortifications, then set in place 320 kegs of powder—8,000 pounds of it. When the powder was ignited at 4:40 on the morning of July 30, it produced an immense column of debris, smoke, and flame. Two South Carolina regiments were hurled aloft, resulting in 300 killed or seriously wounded. For the Yanks, so far so good. But, stupidly, the Yankee soldiers who charged in after the explosion jumped into the Crater instead of forming around it, and the surviving Rebs turned their artillery on them. Grenades were thrown in, and heads, arms, and legs sailed through the air. The Union lost 3,700 men, the Rebs only 1,500. The famous Crater, still there in Petersburg, was 170 feet long, 80 feet wide, and 30 feet deep. Grant called it a "stupendous failure," but certainly it was one of the most colorful—and gory—events of the war.

In the meantime, though the Crater incident was a Union failure, both the Yanks and Rebs were literally digging in at Petersburg, preparing for a long entrenchment—and a long siege. Grant knew that the saintly Lee was an aggressive fighting man—and not an easy man to defeat on the battlefields. So capturing Petersburg—and eventually Richmond—would require another tactic: the siege, which had worked so well in Vicksburg, Mississippi, in 1863. Lee's already underfed soldiers would eventually be starved out.

> ### Go See It!
>
> If you are in the Richmond area, the Petersburg National Battlefield on SR 36 is a must-see. You can view the famous crater, which, covered over with grass, looks much more serene than it did on July 30, 1864. Petersburg also has the Siege Museum at 15 W. Bank Street.

Bars and Stripes Forever

We pause here to look at one of the most unpleasant aspects of the war, the military prisons. Yes, there is a connection between those prisons and the Union's great hero. Grant is remembered as the hero of the Union, the Great Hammerer, the Unconditional Surrender guy. But he had his critics in the North, some of whom saw him as a "butcher" who didn't seem to mind wasting the lives of thousands of Union men.

But in fact, Grant's usual question after a Union victory in battle was "How many prisoners?" He seemed concerned that the enemy had been captured, not maimed or killed. You might say he did *not* have a "take no prisoners" mentality.

Thousands of Yankees were languishing (and almost starving) in Southern prisons, while thousands of Rebs pined away (and often froze) in the North. Andersonville, the unsanitary, hellishly overcrowded prison camp in Georgia, is the most remembered military prison of the Civil War, but it was actually fairly typical. No military prison, North or South, was a country club, and Rebel soldiers in Northern prisons not only faced crowding and inadequate food, but cold winters that their already-weak bodies could hardly bear.

> ### Did Y'all Know?
>
> What single color of clothing were Confederate prisoners in the North allowed to receive from family and friends? Only gray. As with prison uniforms today, a standard color ensured that escapees could be easily spotted.

After the war, Southern soldiers talked bluntly of the various "hells" they endured—the Yankee prisons, that is. Perhaps the worst was New York state's Elmira Prison. From July 1864 to

July 1865, 3,000 out of 12,000 Elmira prisoners died from disease, exposure, or malnutrition. The overcrowding, inadequate rations, and poor sanitation were all endorsed by Edwin Stanton, Lincoln's waspish, vindictive secretary of war, as retaliation for what Union men were enduring. Stanton told Lincoln that Union prisoners were "undergoing ferocious barbarity or the more horrible death of starvation," so "precisely the same rations and treatment should be practiced to the Rebels in our hands." Originally Elmira prison was said to have a maximum capacity of 5,000—but it swelled to over 10,000.

Throughout the war, thousands of prisoners were "exchanged"—that is, North and South would frequently swap prisoners and return them to their units (if their health permitted, that is). Exchanges were "like for like"—for example, three Union captains for three Rebel captains. It was, in most people's view, a humane system—but Ulysses S. Grant brought it to a halt in April 1864.

Voices from Then

Ulysses S. Grant on prisoner exchange: "Every man we hold, when released on parole, becomes an active soldier against us. If we hold those caught, they amount to no more than dead men."

Grant thought he could shorten the war by keeping Reb soldiers in prison—even if that meant keeping Yankee soldiers in Southern prisons. In the meantime, both North and South wailed—with justification—about the horrors their brave boys were enduring in prison camps.

Here's a tidbit worth remembering: After the war, Rebel veterans showed no shame about having served time in Union prisons. Certainly it increased their bitterness toward the "damn Yankees."

That Actor, and His Most Dramatic Role

While Sherman was marching destructively through the Carolinas, and while Grant was working to starve out Lee's army in Virginia, a handsome, dapper little actor was hatching one of the most famous plots in history.

John Wilkes Booth was 1 of the 10 children of a noted English actor, Junius Brutus Booth. John, born in Maryland, made his acting debut in Baltimore, and gained fame for his beautiful speaking voice, his athleticism, and his hypnotic eyes. Southern aristocrats adored him, and he identified completely with the South and its society. He believed slavery was right, "the greatest gift God ever bestowed upon a favored nation." (He had been present at the hanging of abolitionist John Brown and heartily approved of it.) He utterly despised the "low-born" U.S. president, who he believed was a tyrant wanting to be king.

Lincoln's reelection in November 1864 sent Booth into a frenzy. He hatched a crack-pot scheme: Kidnap Lincoln and carry him off to Richmond, where he would serve as the ransom for all the Confederate prisoners of war. From the underbelly of Washington and Baltimore he recruited a gang of Lincoln-haters, all of them losers and misfits. They studied floor plans of the White House and began stalking the president. One thing in their favor: Lincoln was notoriously careless about his personal safety.

We will return to the actor Booth shortly.

Slaves as Rebel Soldiers?

The Confederacy had passed several draft laws, yet the war dragged on, and more Southern men joined the lists of the dead and wounded, and more men deserted. Where to get more men? What about making soldiers of ...?

The Irish-born Patrick Cleburne had been one of the six generals fatally wounded at Franklin, Tennessee, the Battle of the Generals. Cleburne had proposed a novel idea to the Confederate government: arm the slaves and have them fight for the South. At the time he died (November 1864) the notion was mocked. But within a few months, with dire straits looking more dire, the idea got resurrected. In fact, by Christmas 1864, Jefferson Davis was giving serious thought to Cleburne's notion.

The proposal was to arm the slaves and give them their freedom if they fought for the Confederacy. Why not? After all, when the Yankees occupied areas of the South, they aggressively recruited slaves as Union soldiers. So in January 1865, the honorable Robert E. Lee himself gave the plan his stamp of approval, if arming the slaves was "accompanied by a well-digested plan of gradual and general emancipation."

> **Voices from Then**
>
> It is the enemy's avowed policy to convert the able-bodied men among them [the slaves] into soldiers, and to emancipate all. Therefore we must decide whether slavery shall be distinguished by our enemies and the slaves be used against us, or use them ourselves at the risk of the effects which may be produced upon our social institutions.
>
> —Robert E. Lee, January 1865

An obvious question occurs to us today: Would slaves fight for the Confederacy? The answer is definitely, yes—not all, certainly, but many would have. Some had been telling their masters from the very beginning that they would gladly fight for the South—but, as we already noted, whites were very reluctant to place firearms in the hands of slaves. (What if they went on a killing spree?) But things were desperate.

So, near the bitter end—they didn't know it was near the end, of course—the Confederate Congress passed a law that no Southerner could have imagined in 1861: a draft of slave men. But the new draft law made no mention at all of emancipation. It didn't matter, for the law never had a chance to go into effect.

Sherman, Once More

Sherman and Union vandals got some welcome news in North Carolina: Wilmington, the last major Confederate port, had fallen to the Yanks. Union troops were being landed at Wilmington and would march inland to join Sherman's band.

Hindering their progress—but barely—was what remained of the Army of Tennessee. With the ill-fated General John Hood gone, Davis replaced him with the ill-fated Joe Johnston—and, second in command to Johnston, General Beauregard. Here were the two generals who hated Davis the most—in their last assignment, keeping Sherman's horde out of Virginia. Joining them was the notable failure Braxton Bragg, who had served for months as Davis's military adviser in Richmond. The army also had Wade Hampton, D. H. Hill, William Hardee, and … well, many other notables. There was something pathetic about an army of 20,000—and so many generals (mostly failures) commanding it.

By now the South—civilians as well as soldiers—had been ground into the dirt. Much of the land was occupied by the Union, the blockade was almost 100 percent effective at this point, prices were sky-high, and the money barely worth the paper it was printed on. You may well wonder why the soldiers of the South even bothered to fight anymore. Call it pride, stupidity, stubbornness, whatever. They still believed, curious as it may seem to us, in something called *honor*. They believed you could still have it, even if you could count all your ribs and hadn't bathed with soap in six months.

The Political Nonsolution

Jefferson Davis and Abraham Lincoln both spent the war hoping they could negotiate a settlement. This had as much chance as a snowball in Key West, for the simple reason that Davis believed there were two nations and Lincoln believed there was only one. Neither would budge on this, but in February 1865 there was one last try.

The so-called Hampton Roads Peace Conference was held February 3, 1865. The Confederacy sent Vice President Alexander Stephens, Sen. Robert M. T. Hunter, and Judge John Campbell. They met with Lincoln and his secretary of state, William

Seward, aboard a steamer in Hampton Roads, the waterway between Norfolk and Hampton, Virginia.

Stephens, "Little Aleck," asked Lincoln and Seward a sensible question: "Is there no way of putting an end to the present trouble?" The answer, alas, was a resounding "No!" Davis insisted there were two nations, Lincoln insisted there was one. So, no deal.

Perhaps it was just as well. The Confederates knew that the U.S. Congress wasn't nearly as generous as Lincoln was. If the Confederacy had willingly reentered the Union, there was no guarantee that a vindictive Congress wouldn't trample on Lincoln's good intentions.

Jefferson Davis got some propaganda value out of the failed conference. Three days after it, he delivered a speech in Richmond, denouncing the Lincoln administration and its foolish demand that a free people (the Rebs, that is) would willingly lay down their arms and their liberties. Stephens, who by this time utterly despised Davis, admitted the speech was superb. And the crowd loved it. Even with the nation at the end of its rope, it could still applaud its president. The Congress passed a resolution affirming its "unalterable determination" to continue the war.

Funny Name, Appomattox

Jefferson Davis was, as Confederate president, the commander in chief of the armed forces. He was a Mexican War hero and former U.S. secretary of war, and he believed himself quite adept as a military strategist. Many didn't agree, and as the war progressed, Davis took much of the blame for the South's losses. His many enemies in Congress frequently suggested appointing a general in chief. Davis finally did, on January 23, 1865—and it was Robert E. Lee, who else? Neither knew it at the time, but Lee would serve barely two months as general in chief. (When you hear someone say that Lee was head of the Confederate Army, be aware that this wasn't true until January 1865. Prior to that, he was only the commander of the Army of Northern Virginia.)

If this "promotion" pleased Lee, it was lost in the exasperation over the Confederacy's situation. Lee toyed with the idea of abandoning Richmond and moving his army south to join up with Joe Johnston's army in North Carolina. There was a slim chance they could strike a blow at Sherman before Sherman's forces could join Grant's.

Here we pause to ask an obvious question: Did capturing Richmond mean the North would win the war? Not necessarily. After all, in the War of 1812 the British captured Washington, and the Americans later regained it. But Davis saw a lot of symbolic value in Richmond. No, he would not abandon it—not willingly, anyway.

Petersburg, after a long siege, finally fell to the Yanks. Richmond would be next to go. On Sunday, April 2, 1865, Jefferson Davis was seated in St. Paul's Episcopal Church. A messenger discreetly brought him a message from Lee: "I think it is absolutely necessary that we should abandon our position tonight." Davis quietly walked out, and every eye in the church was on him. The news spread like wildfire: Evacuate. The government hurriedly packed up records and what was left of the treasury.

> **Voices from Then**
>
> There is nothing for me to do but to go and see General Grant, and I would rather die a thousand deaths.
>
> —Robert E. Lee

The departing Rebel soldiers set fire to the arsenals (to keep the Yanks from getting them). The exploding artillery shells set fire to other buildings. Richmond's many lowlifes took advantage of the confusion, pillaging whatever was left behind in stores and warehouses. At 8 o'clock the next morning the first of the Union troops arrived, and they attempted to stop the spread of the flames. The following day there was a new president in Richmond, a tall, lanky, bearded man named Abraham Lincoln. He treated himself to a tour of the house where "that t'other feller," as he called Jefferson Davis, had lived.

Lee's ill-fed Army of Northern Virginia fought one last battle, Sayler's Creek, in Virginia on April 6. The following day, under a flag of truce, Robert E. Lee and Ulysses S. Grant began to exchange letters regarding surrender.

Some of Lee's subordinates begged him not to surrender. One general suggested disbanding the army so it could "scatter like rabbits and partridges in the bushes," then reassemble later—either as a true army, or as guerrilla fighters. Lee feared such men, already on the verge of starvation, would become "mere bands of marauders." So Lee chose, as he put it himself, "to go to General Grant and surrender myself and take the consequences of my acts."

> **Go See It!**
>
> About 90 miles west of Richmond, Appomattox Court House National Historical Park is on SR 24 in Appomattox County, Virginia. The original Wilmer McLean house where Lee surrendered to Grant is long gone, but there is a reconstruction on the site, and the park includes 27 buildings in their 1865 appearance. If you go in the summer, you can witness the living-history programs.

The date was April 9, 1865—Palm Sunday, which the Christian society of that day definitely noticed. The place was a tiny village known as Appomattox Court House. The gray-haired but handsome Lee dressed in his finest gray uniform—in fact, his *only* uniform, for his others were lost during the retreat from Richmond. Grant, dumpy and seedy-looking as always, had a blue uniform spattered with mud. Shortly after noon, the two generals met in the home of Wilmer McLean—a man who had relocated to Appomattox because he had lived in Manassas and tired of all the fighting in that area.

According to Grant's terms, Lee's men would be paroled, provided they swore not to take up arms against the United States again. Arms and artillery would be turned over to the United States, but officers could retain their side arms. Each man could return home and be undisturbed. Lee, thoughtful soul that he was, asked that the cavalrymen be allowed to retain their horses, which would be needed for farm work. He also asked for something more urgent: food for his starving men. Grant said yes.

Voices from Then

> After four years of arduous service, marked by unsurpassed courage and fortitude, the Army of Northern Virginia has been compelled to yield to overwhelming numbers and resources …. I have determined to avoid the useless sacrifice of those whose past services have endeared them to their countrymen …. I earnestly pray that a merciful God may extend to you His blessing and protection …. I bid you an affectionate farewell.
>
> —Robert E. Lee's farewell to the Army of Northern Virginia, April 10, 1865

Lee emerging from the McLean house was, to put it mildly, quite dramatic. Though he was still the self-controlled man, Lee struck his fist into his palm several times. The scrawny Rebels broke ranks and crowded around Uncle Robert just to touch him or even his horse. The triumphant Union soldiers could have spoiled the moment by cheering or firing their guns, but Grant wouldn't allow it. Soon after, the Rebs stacked their arms and furled their battle flags. The ill-clad, underfed, scrappy Army of Northern Virginia was no more.

The Endings, Plural

Strictly speaking, the Civil War didn't end at Appomattox, nor did the Confederacy. Lee hadn't surrendered the entire Confederate Army, nor did his surrender mean anything politically. He had only surrendered the Army of Northern Virginia. Other armies were in the field, and so was the president.

Davis and his cabinet had moved their capital to Danville, Virginia, then on to Greensboro, North Carolina, putting them nearer the Army of Tennessee under Joe Johnston, who didn't learn until April 16 that Lee had surrendered a week earlier.

In between, something quite shocking had occurred, something that would affect the South for years to come: The U.S. president had been assassinated.

Following Lee's surrender at Appomattox, John Wilkes Booth altered his earlier plan: Instead of kidnapping Lincoln, he would kill him, along with Vice President Andrew Johnson and Secretary of State William Seward. (As it turned out, the accomplice who was to kill Johnson got cold feet, and the man who tried to kill Seward only injured him.) Now, about that night at the theater: Suffice it to say that actor Booth was a familiar face at Ford's Theatre, knew its floor plans, and had no trouble slipping into it that fateful night, Good Friday, April 14, 1865.

Did Y'all Know?

The Federal government, paranoid after the shooting, jailed the entire cast of *Our American Cousin*, suspecting they might have known of the plot. Booth's gentle sister Asia was also jailed for a while. Brother Edwin announced he would take a long sabbatical from the American stage.

The play that night, a comedy, *Our American Cousin*, was one that Booth knew by heart. While actor Harry Hawk was speaking his lines on stage, actor Booth opened the door to Lincoln's theater box and shot him with a derringer in the back of the head. When Booth leaped from the box, his spur caught in a flag. When he crash-landed on the stage, his left shinbone broke just above the ankle. Booth called out the state motto of Virginia: *Sic semper tyrannis*— "Thus always to tyrants." The assassin then hobbled off, leaving Ford's by its back door, and galloped away on his horse.

Booth kept a diary, and thanks to it, we have some idea of what ran through his mind in those frantic days after Lincoln's death. He expressed surprise that he wasn't hailed as a hero—even most diehard Confederates were horrified at the shooting—but was being hunted down like a dog. "Our country owed all our troubles to him [Lincoln], and God simply made me the instrument of his punishment …. God, try and forgive me, and bless my mother."

A certain doctor (his name was Mudd), a Southern sympathizer, set Booth's broken leg and made him a pair of crude crutches. Booth holed up in a tobacco barn in Virginia, where the Feds found him. His accomplice Davy Herold came out with his hands up, but Booth, carrying two guns, yelled out, "Well, my brave boys, you can prepare a stretcher for me." The Feds set the barn on fire to smoke him out, and one man shot Booth. After being dragged from the burning barn, he gasped, "Tell my mother … tell my mother that I died for my country." His body, sewn up in a bag, was brought to Secretary of War Stanton, who feared that Rebels might try to carry it off. The paranoid Stanton had Booth buried in secret under the floor at the Washington Arsenal.

Were Southerners happy over the assassination? A few were, and probably a few toasts were drunk and guns fired off. But once the news sunk in, it was clear that this didn't bode well for the South. The South haters in Washington would punish the entire Confederacy for Booth's foolish act. Aside from that, most people of the time thought of assassination as barbaric—something that "can't happen here." But it had happened, and the Republicans in Washington were licking their chops over the propaganda value of the assassination. Conveniently for them, Booth had removed the generous Lincoln, the man who had promised leniency to the South.

Down in North Carolina, Joe Johnston was preparing to surrender to Sherman. The redheaded terrorist, the commander of soldiers who loved to use the phrase "Rebels have no rights," had ordered his men to cease their destruction of private property right after he heard of Lee's surrender.

On April 26, Johnston formally surrendered to Sherman at the Bennett House near Durham, North Carolina. The surrender terms were the same as those offered to Lee. At Johnston's side was the Confederacy's last secretary of war, John Breckinridge. As a Kentucky man, Breckinridge was pleased that Sherman offered him and Johnston some bourbon. But, later during the negotiation, Sherman took another drink and offered none to the Confederates. Breckinridge later told Johnston that Sherman was "a hog" for not offering them another drink. Many Southern civilians thought Sherman was far worse than a hog.

The Army of Northern Virginia had surrendered, then the Army of Tennessee. What was left? Dick Taylor, son of late president Zachary Taylor, surrendered his troops in the Deep South, and on May 26, 1865, Edmund Kirby Smith surrendered the Army of the Trans-Mississippi. The last Confederate general to surrender his command was Cherokee Indian leader Stand Watie, who surrendered on June 23 in the Indian Territory (now Oklahoma).

Done—but not quite. The Confederate president and his Cabinet were still a "government on wheels." We will finish that story in the following chapter. Old Edmund Ruffin, the silver-haired Virginia plantation patriarch, the fire-eater who had been present at John Brown's hanging, at Fort Sumter, and at First Manassas, returned to a home that had been looted and vandalized by the Yankees. Having no desire to live in a Yankee-dominated South, the aged gentleman shot himself on June 17, 1865. His children told his grandchildren, "The Yankees killed your grandfather." In some odd sense, it was true.

If you feel a little sad after reading this chapter, you should. The Confederate States of America had suffered, not a little, but a lot. All its people—white and black and red, slaveholders and slaveless, Unionists and secessionists and in-betweeners—all endured hardship. Except for a handful of speculators, blockade runners, and outright thieves, most Southerners were poorer in April 1865 than they were four years earlier. Many were completely ruined. The one group that you might expect to be happy—the thousands of slaves—were happy, sort of, but also puzzled and more than a little frightened, for some had learned quickly that their Yankee "liberators" weren't especially kind or trustworthy. They really hadn't the vaguest idea of what their freedom would involve. They, like the South's whites, were living in a world turned upside down.

Up in Massachusetts, a shy poet named Emily Dickinson spent the war years penning one poem after another, on a wide variety of subjects. You would never guess from those poems that her country was involved in a bloody war. But there were no Southern writers in this period who failed to write about the war and its effects. There were no sheltered lives in the Confederacy.

The Least You Need to Know

- ◆ General Sherman's Union troops caused major devastation in the Carolinas, particularly the South Carolina capital city of Columbia.

- ◆ In Virginia's Shenandoah Valley, the Union's General Sheridan also did major damage, though hindered by the South's spunky Jubal Early.

- ◆ Ulysses S. Grant's long siege of Petersburg, Virginia, finally led to the evacuation of the capital, Richmond.

- ◆ Pro-Southern actor John Wilkes Booth assassinated Abraham Lincoln, an act which would have grave consequences for the South.

- ◆ Robert E. Lee surrendered his army at Appomattox, Virginia, in April 1865, and within a few weeks all other Confederate generals surrendered, ending the four-year Civil War.

Chapter 28

Unhappy Aftermath

In This Chapter

- ◆ St. Andrew (Johnson) the Merciful
- ◆ The dead-horse kickers in Congress
- ◆ Carpetbaggers, scalawags, and other not-so-nice folk
- ◆ The dreaded "K" word
- ◆ Being bitter and reconstructed

The Confederacy ended … or did it? After the Confederate generals' surrenders in spring 1865, and after the eventual capture of Jefferson Davis, it seemed all was lost. Rebels had spent (or wasted, rather) four years, and now they were back where they started—or, rather, worse off than before, for now they had no representation in Congress, no slaves, and a lot of devastation to clean up.

On the positive side, the war was over. On the negative side, there were still plenty of vindictive Northerners who didn't think the Rebels had been punished adequately. The South had lots of enemies in high places (the Congress, the cabinet). Former Rebels had to endure Reconstruction. They had to endure a Northern minority that wanted to completely quash the Southern spirit. It didn't happen. The South did change—but not in the ways the Reconstructers hoped.

Call it spirit, or gumption—or stubbornness.

The Land of Houseless Chimneys

Northerners in the South after the Civil War made the tasteless observation that there were a lot of chimneys around with no houses attached to them. In some places, entire towns had turned into "Chimneyvilles." When a house burns, a chimney will be the one thing left standing. And as Yankee troops passed through, they were, as some Rebels put it, "a mite careless with fire and powder." Decades after the war had ended, some of the houseless chimneys were referred to as "Sherman's sentinels."

There were very few areas in which buildings didn't go up in flames—not to mention theft or slaughter of livestock, burning of crops in the fields or storage, pillaging of homes, and … well, we've touched on the damage already. As you've probably guessed, war is very wasteful. The real waste was the human property. Consider a few numbers:

Confederate Casualties in the Civil War

Casualties	Numbers (Approximate)
Died of Disease	140,000
Died in Prison	26,000
Killed in Action	54,000
Died of Wounds	40,000
Nonmortally Wounded	226,000

That last number is important. Thousands of soldiers (Yanks as well as Rebels, of course) spent the rest of their lives blind or handicapped or disfigured. Many historians have done dollar estimates on the property damage done during the war. No one has figured out how to place a dollar value on the people who died, or who spent the remainder of their days living with a disability.

Much of the South had been invaded—a feeling that most Americans of that time (and our own) never experienced. Whatever the South's failings were (and there were some, notably slavery), you couldn't argue that invasion of one's home turf is a light punishment.

Civilians and soldiers both knew what it was like to eat boring food—or no food at all. As one descendant of Confederates recently stated, few Yankees in 1865 had been forced to make a meal of chicken-head soup. Rich and poor in the South had shared the great bonding experience, adversity. More was to come.

Many Northerners didn't think the South had suffered enough. The Radical Republicans in Washington weren't about to let such traitors as Jefferson Davis, his cabinet, or the Southern governors slip by without a wrist-slapping.

> **Voices from Then**
>
> De massa had three boys go to war. But dere wuzn't one to come home. All the chillun he had wuz killed. Massa, he los' all his money an de house soon begin droppin' away to nothin'. Us niggers one by one left' de ole place.
>
> —William Colbert, a former slave from an Alabama plantation

Chaining Mr. Jeff

Many high-ranking Confederates skedaddled after the war ended. Governors, cabinet members, and prominent members of the Congress all feared the worst, so there was a swift exodus to Canada, Mexico, Brazil, and Europe. Probably as many as 10,000 went into exile.

One who didn't was Jefferson Davis himself. Having fled Richmond and moved south with part of his cabinet, he was captured on May 9, 1865, surrendering with the words "God's will be done."

The North was ecstatic. The head Rebel was caught. To give the cartoonists something to work with, the rumor was that Davis had tried to escape dressed as a woman. Apparently the Union soldiers who captured him told everyone that Davis had been wearing a shawl (which was true), so the newspapers had a field day with "Jeff Davis in drag" (which wasn't true). A song started making the rounds: "We'll Hang Jeff Davis from a Sour Apple Tree."

At Fort Monroe in Virginia, Davis was thrown into a damp, gloomy cell, with his legs shackled, literally chaining him down. The chains were there only five days, for word of this humiliation got out, and even Northerners thought it was a bit extreme.

In his cell he had no privacy whatsoever, having to perform his bodily functions in full view of his guards. (There was one guard inside the cell, two outside.) He had to drink from a wooden horse bucket. In the cell that was too dark by day, things were too bright at night, because a lamp was kept burning in the cell all night. The U.S. president was Tennessean Andrew Johnson. He and Davis had known each other from their Congressional days, and they didn't like each other. Davis had once made a slightly snooty remark about Johnson's vocation (he was a tailor), and Johnson never forgot it. Besides that, Johnson had always detested the way Southern politics was dominated by wealthy planters like Davis.

> **Voices from Then**
>
> When I look at the husband of my youth, now beatified by such holy resignation, slowly dying away from his little ones to whom I could offer no higher examples, or better guide, I feel it is a bitter cup and doubt if my Father wills that we should drink it.
>
> —From a letter of Varina Davis to Dr. John Craven

Johnson made a few remarks after the war ended about "hanging the traitors." It was Johnson's style to bluster a lot and soften up later. Keeping Davis in a cold, damp prison cell for a while had to be done to keep the more vindictive Yanks happy. But Johnson was no sadist. He saw Davis as a fellow Southerner and a basically decent man, and he had no intention of hanging him. He allowed Dr. John Craven, who was looking after the ailing Davis, to smuggle out Davis's prison journal. Tidied up by an editor, the journal was published as *The Prison Life of Jefferson Davis*. If Johnson thought the book would cause Northerners to let up in their hatred for Davis, he was quite correct.

One unlikely supporter of Davis was newspaper publisher Horace Greeley. Throughout the war, Greeley had beaten the anti-South drum loudly. Either from a sense of guilt or the pleasure of something different, he went to bat for Davis. His *New York Tribune* insisted that Davis be released or tried. Public opinion was definitely shifting that way.

Davis left Fort Monroe on May 11, 1867. He had been in prison two years. He was taken up the James River to Richmond. The civil court there released him on $100,000 bail. The money for bail had been raised by, among others, Horace Greeley and (surprisingly) abolitionist leader Gerrit Smith. Davis received a warm letter from Robert E. Lee: "Your release has lifted a load from my heart which I have not words to tell."

That very night, Davis and his family departed for Canada. They lived there, and in England, for several years. Davis finally did return to the United States in 1877, settling in Mississippi and penning his memoirs. When he died in 1889, he had outlived Northern hatred, and his funeral was attended by thousands. Former Confederates had finally come to honor their one president, and Northerners had come to respect him immensely.

Der Fall Guy

In the aftermath of the war's end and Lincoln's assassination, it was clear there had to be a fall guy—or several. One of the most prominent was already dead: John Wilkes Booth. So were his fellow conspirators, who were all hanged at the Old Capitol Prison in Washington on July 7, 1865.

Before their execution, all were thoroughly grilled as to their connections (if any) to the Confederate government. Stanton and other Federal South-haters had hoped the conspirators would implicate Jefferson Davis and other top Confederates, but this didn't occur. This frustrated Stanton, but it certainly boosted public sympathy for Davis.

Did Y'all Know? _____

One alternative scapegoat was Adm. Raphael Semmes, commander of the infamous Rebel commerce raider *Alabama*, which had preyed on Yankee ships across the globe. Semmes was brought to trial in 1865, charged with piracy and treason. All charges were eventually dropped. The man that Northerners despised as a glorified pirate made a living for a while by thrilling audiences with his lecture, "The Cruise of the *Alabama*."

But some Confederate official had to die. The easiest man to hate was Heinrich Wirz, usually known as Henry Wirz. Born in Switzerland, Wirz had come to America in his 20s, joined the Confederate Army, and in 1864 was made commandant (head man, that is) of the prisoner-of-war camp in Andersonville, Georgia. While its horrible conditions weren't that different from other military prisons North and South, it somehow became the focus of the North's anger. Wirz, with his thick German accent and brusque manner, didn't help his own cause any.

The Andersonville trial was a sad joke. No one doubted that Wirz would be convicted. (The charge was "impairing the health and destroying the lives of prisoners." Using that charge, most prison commandants North and South would have been executed.) It was mostly a show trial, with the ending already scripted. Wirz was hanged at Old Capitol Prison on November 10, 1865. He was the only Confederate ever executed for his crimes.

Speak Loud, but Carry No Stick

Andrew Johnson, we already noted, had endeared himself to the North by threatening to hang all the Rebels. We also noted he had no intention of doing it (politics is a strange business). He was a Southerner and knew the Southland—his own home—had suffered enough.

Poor Andy, the former tailor of Greeneville, Tennessee, was not in a pleasant position. On the one hand, he couldn't seem too soft on the Rebels. On the other hand, he couldn't let his cabinet boss him around, which they gladly would have done. Seward and, worst of all, Stanton probably would not have objected to mass executions of all Confederates. But not all Northerners were as vindictive as they were, fortunately.

In May 1865, Johnson issued his first amnesty proclamation. Former soldiers under the rank of colonel, sailors under the rank of lieutenant, and people with taxable property valued at $20,000 or less could apply for individual pardons. Thousands did. (Typical Johnson—he held out a while before pardoning the wealthier Southerners.)

Feeling magnanimous, he ordered the governor of North Carolina (appointed by him) to call a convention for the purpose of establishing a state government. To qualify for voting for delegates to the convention, you had to have taken the amnesty oath (swearing your loyalty to the United States) and have been eligible to vote before the state seceded.

Throughout June and July 1865, Johnson applied the same principle to the other Confederate states. He was feeling cocky because, as it happened, Congress wasn't to meet until December. Before then, all the Confederate states (except Texas) had formed constitutions and elected governors. Almost all the states' legislatures had ratified the Thirteenth Amendment (the one abolishing slavery).

They had also revoked (as ordered) their secession ordinances. Playing by Johnson's rules, they had already elected senators and representatives.

Sounds great, doesn't it? Johnson was giving the people a chance to pull themselves out of the wreckage and start governing themselves again. And why not? He shared Lincoln's idea that the Confederate states had never really been out of the Union. The Confederacy and the Civil War were just part of a family feud that had ended.

When the Republican-dominated Congress dragged itself to Washington in December 1865, it had an entirely different view of things.

Sado-Republicans with Thumbscrews

In the Radical Republicans' eyes, Johnson was letting the South return to just what it had been before. Granted, slavery was no longer legal. But the North feared the South hadn't changed its attitude toward blacks (true—why would the war have changed it?).

They believed the Southern states had ratified the Thirteenth Amendment because they
had no choice (true), not because they
believed slavery had been wrong (definitely
true).

So the Congress brought Johnson's efforts to a
screeching halt. The newly elected Southern
senators and congressmen (they were called the
"Confederate Brigadiers," and among them was
former vice president Alexander Stephens)
could not take their seats. Legally Congress
could do this, and the president could do nothing about it. Congress appointed a Joint
Committee of 15 members to handle
Reconstruction. That committee was to be a
thorn in Johnson's flesh (and in the South's) for
a long time.

RebeLingo

Reconstruction refers to
the period following the Civil
War (1865–77), and to the
attempt during that period to
reunite the former Confederate
states with the Union. **Presidential Reconstruction** refers to the
mild and lenient actions taken by
Andrew Johnson. **Congressional
Reconstruction** refers to the vindictive anti-South actions of the
Republican-dominated Congress.

The Southern states had brought some of this Congressional wrath on themselves.
Between Johnson's amnesty and the session of Congress, the new state governments
in the South had passed the very restrictive Black Codes. Laws varied from one state
to another, but they all had in common one goal: to restrict the movements of the
newly freed blacks. Some of the laws restricted them to certain jobs (farming or
domestic service), some prohibited them from carrying weapons, and some denied
them the right to own land.

The Black Codes' vagrancy laws made it legal to arrest jobless people hanging out on
the streets—and most of the newly freed blacks were jobless, naturally. The bottom
line: Blacks might be free, but the laws made them second-class citizens.

Racist? Yep. The Rebels' justified such laws by saying that the freed slaves were (even
Northerners agreed) a problem, because most of them didn't know what to do with
themselves now that their food, clothing, and shelter were no longer supplied by the
masters.

The Black Codes were the whites' reaction to a situation that seemed like chaos to
them.

The Republican-dominated Congress passed its Reconstruction Acts in 1867. The
"Rebel states" were placed under military government, strict rules kept most whites
from being eligible to vote, blacks were to be registered to vote, and (most importantly) the president's powers were curtailed—a lot. Having the South under military

Did Y'all Know? _____

From 1865 to 1867, the Northern states of Connecticut, Kansas, Minnesota, Ohio, and Wisconsin had nixed proposals to give blacks the vote. Note the irony: Northern states could still decide whether blacks could vote, while the Congress would not allow Southern states to make that decision for themselves.

rule was a bitter pill. Southerners had spent four years detesting the men in blue uniforms—and now they could no longer even shoot at them! Military occupation meant that blue-clad soldiers could boss and heckle white Southerners on a daily basis. Congress's so-called Military Bill divided the former Confederacy into five "military districts." Technically the Southern states, as political units, didn't even exist. This was quite an insult to people who took their loyalty to their states very seriously.

Aside from the soldiers, there were the infamous Yankee "carpetbaggers." (Some of these were former boys in blue themselves.) Supposedly their name came from their carrying their belongings in one cheap piece of hand luggage. Most were political and financial opportunists, the sort who wanted to register blacks to vote so as to get them on the Republican side. The sort who found lots of shady financial opportunities in the economically ravaged region.

Just as hated, maybe more so, were the "scalawags," Southerners who cooperated with the carpetbaggers. They were seen as turncoats, traitors, sell-outs to the hated Yankees and the freed blacks. One of the most prominent of these was Georgia governor Joe Brown, who had been such a thorn in Jefferson Davis's flesh. Brown loved holding office, so seeing that the Republicans held power in his state, he joined them (drawing a lot of boos and hisses from former Confederates, naturally).

Convinced Against Their Will

The Thirteenth Amendment made slavery illegal, but it probably didn't change very many people's attitude toward blacks. (This was true of Northerners as well as Southerners.) Former masters could no longer give orders to slaves, but mental patterns don't change because a law does. Most Southerners still thought of blacks as inferiors.

Southerners knew that blacks in most Northern states couldn't vote. The hypocrisy was pretty blatant. Something else stung Southerners, too: They had been listening for 30 years to abolitionists preach about how slavery had degraded blacks. Now, suddenly those "degraded" people were to be given the right to vote and hold office. Did it make sense? (A quick reminder here: In the South, black *men* were being registered to vote. Women, whatever their race, did not vote at this time in American history.)

Some moderate Northerners in Congress suggested giving the vote to blacks who could read the Constitution. But the Radical Republicans preferred blacks they could easily sway, so illiterate was fine. As blacks were registered to vote (under the watchful eyes of Federal soldiers), in some areas they outnumbered white voters. So when, in 1868, six Southern states finally qualified to send men to Congress, these men were (surprise!) Republicans—and some were black. This caused some blushing in the North, where many whites claimed they were embarrassed at the presence of black senators and congressmen.

Did Y'all Know?

During Reconstruction, there were two black senators and 14 congressmen. Interestingly, both black senators were from Jefferson Davis's home state, Mississippi.

The Reconstruction-era governments in the South were notoriously corrupt. White Southerners were paying taxes (high ones), not being allowed to vote, and forced to watch state officials (scalawags, Northerners, and freed blacks) dipping their hands into the public treasury. Judges and legislators grew fat off bribes, and if one got caught, odds are that the court or the *carpetbagger* governor would pardon him. It was a low point in American political life.

Reconstruction had a powerful effect on the South: it united it. The war itself didn't really unite the South. There was too much bickering about states' rights, constant griping about Davis, desertions from the army, and so on. But the postwar years, with military occupation and Congressional Reconstruction, did unite white Southerners. Hate can unite people. And the South had more hate for the North after the war than during it. Fighting an enemy is bad enough, but living under the conqueror is worse.

RebeLingo

Carpetbagger in the Reconstruction period referred, as we already noted, to Northerners coming South to help (or exploit) the blacks and to exploit (but not help) the whites. The word still gets used today in political circles. It refers to someone elected to office from a district that is not really their home.

The (Gulp!) K Word

Alas, we can't consider Reconstruction without talking about the Ku Klux Klan. The group was born out of a sense of desperation. Oddly, it didn't begin with any serious purpose. In Pulaski, Tennessee, in late 1865, six Confederate veterans organized a kind of prankish club, scaring freed blacks by riding by night and wearing hoods and robes. It dawned on them that fear might be a useful tool in the political war against blacks and carpetbaggers. So in 1867 it organized formally, calling itself the Invisible Empire of the South, made of up local *dens*. The head was the Grand Wizard, and some members had such titles as *hydras, furies, goblins,* and *nighthawks*. (Apparently, the prankster element never completely vanished.)

Did Y'all Know? _____

The Klan is mentioned several times in the novel *Gone with the Wind,* but when the popular book was made into a movie, the producers thought it wise to omit any reference to the controversial group.

If you're curious about the wizard title, it came into use when the group put forward Gen. Nathan Bedford Forrest, the Wizard of the Saddle, as its first head.

The hoods and robes did intimidate many blacks (Klansmen sometimes padded their horses' hooves for added stealth), and although most blacks and carpetbaggers knew the hooded horsemen weren't actual ghosts, the act was pretty intimidating. It wasn't just the look, of course, that intimidated.

They posted placards, warning their targets to act right or leave the community. Even worse, they whipped and sometimes lynched their victims, usually by hanging. Blacks weren't their only targets—they murdered carpetbaggers, too. The main idea: Keep the enemy on his toes constantly, make him afraid, make carpetbaggers want to head north, make blacks fearful of voting.

Human beings are afraid of the unseen. This was the fear the Klan used so well. They operated in stealth. Carpetbaggers and blacks were never sure just how many whites belonged to the Klan. Were the Klansmen's number overestimated—or underestimated? No one knew. Secrecy made them strong.

Their secrecy made them an elusive prey. Whenever suspected Klansmen were arrested, local whites protested, and when the suspects were released, they were hailed as heroes. Because of the group's anonymity, we have no way of knowing how many whites participated. We also have no way of measuring how much influence the Klan had on ending Reconstruction. About the only proper answer is "some" (and, probably "a lot").

Northerners of a Different Breed

Not all Northerners were Radical Republicans (and not all Republicans were Radicals). The entire North had never been deeply anti-South, and there were plenty of people in the North who believed that the South had suffered enough. There was a slim hope, in 1868, that a sensible Northern Democrat might win the presidency. Since the great war hero, Ulysses S. Grant, was the Republican candidate, it seemed liked a *very* slim hope.

Definitely *not* in the race was Andrew Johnson. He was, you probably recall, the first president to be impeached. In a nutshell: Johnson was detested by the Radical Republicans, who impeached him for firing his disloyal secretary of war, Edwin Stanton (the most radical Radical in the Cabinet). When the Senate voted to con-vict or acquit, Johnson squeaked through by one vote.

The Radical Republicans hated Johnson, partly because he was a Southerner himself (and a Democrat!), partly because he stood in the way of their plans for the South. He would leave office in March 1869, and the Radicals expected Grant to be their puppet man.

> **Did Y'all Know?** _____
>
> Politics makes strange bed-fellows. One of Horatio Seymour's campaign managers in the 1868 election was William Rosecrans—the Union general who had been such a formidable foe in Tennessee. Old Rosey apparently wasn't an admirer of his fellow general, Grant.

The Democrats' man in 1868 was Horatio Seymour of New York. He and the Democrats campaigned on a platform of ending the Radical Republicans' domination over the South. The Democrats were not saying this to win ex-Rebels' votes—because in 1868 there weren't many of those. Scalawags, carpetbaggers, and blacks weren't going to vote Democratic, so Seymour was trying to appeal to the more gen-erous among the Yankees. There were Yankees who had friends and relatives in the South, and they couldn't help but hear that things were unpleasant there.

Many Northerners were aware that there was one issue that wouldn't go away: states' rights. Reconstruction had shown that Congress would gladly trample on the rights of states to govern themselves. States' rights were still valued by many Americans, not just Southerners. Northerners couldn't help but notice that Congress was forcing Southern states to register black voters (which was ironic, since Northern states still could still decide that for themselves).

Grant won in 1868, but not by much. He got a little over 52 percent of the popular vote, Seymour got a little over 47 percent. Without black votes in the South, Grant wouldn't have won. As a kind of consolation prize for the South, lame-duck president Andrew Johnson issued another amnesty proclamation on Christmas Day, 1868. With a few exceptions, former Confederates were given an unconditional pardon.

In, or Really In?

If you scan the following table, you'll see two sets of dates. In the first column are the years the former Confederate states were readmitted to the United States—that is, they had satisfied Congress's requirements, one of which was registering blacks to vote. You'll notice that several of the states were readmitted in 1868—just in time to allow the blacks in those states to vote (for Grant, naturally).

When the Southern states were readmitted, they (the registered voters, that is) could elect senators and congressmen. Since most former Confederates still couldn't vote, these elected representatives were carpetbaggers, scalawags, or blacks. Put another way, the majority of Southern whites hadn't voted for their states' representatives in Congress. More important, they didn't like these men, for they believed that they were actively working against the interests of most Southern whites.

The second column in the table shows the dates that, for former Confederates, really counted. These are the dates of "redemption," the dates when Southern whites were *redeemed* from being under domination of carpetbaggers and blacks. Southern states were redeemed when a majority of former Confederates were able to vote and elect their own candidates to state and federal office.

Dates of Readmission and Home Rule of Former Confederate States

State	Date Readmitted	Date "Redeemed"
Alabama	1868	1874
Arkansas	1868	1874
Florida	1868	1877
Georgia	1870	1871
Louisiana	1868	1877
Mississippi	1870	1876
North Carolina	1868	1870
South Carolina	1868	1876
Tennessee	1866	1869
Texas	1870	1873
Virginia	1870	1869

For all the Southern states, 1874 was a crucial year: In the fall elections, Democrats regained control of Congress for the first time since before the Civil War (even though Grant, the Republican, was reelected in 1872). Southerners still living in unredeemed states were optimistic.

The complete redemption, as it was called—and the end of Reconstruction—came about in an odd way. A Union veteran, Rutherford Hayes of Ohio, was the Republican candidate for president in 1876. Hayes won—or did he? The vote was close. Democrat Sam Tilden of New York probably won the popular vote. (He carried the South.) But Republicans claimed they had carried three Southern states and won the electoral vote. A commission was set up to decide the issue. By one vote, the commission gave the presidency to Hayes.

Since there were threats of a violent reaction if Hayes won, he took office handing out some consolation prizes for the South.

He would remove Federal troops from the South. He would appoint a Democrat to his cabinet. He would promote internal improvements in the South. He would "restore efficient local government" to the South. "Rutherfraud" Hayes was a Republican (blech!), but under the circumstances, white Southerners breathed a collective sigh.

Reconstruction was over. The bitterness was not. Southerners had endured four years of a bloody war, followed by an even longer period of Federal military occupation. They had witnessed a government attempt to take a mostly illiterate group of people and give them the vote, guiding them to vote for the party in power in Washington. White Southerners believed they were hated by Yankees and hated by the freed slaves. They hated back.

RebeLingo

Redeemed means that home rule was restored—that is, the state's government was again under the domination of native whites.

Unreconstructed refers to former Confederates who made it clear that the Civil War and Reconstruction hadn't convinced them they were wrong about blacks, Yankees, secession, or the Federal government.

Voices from Then

I don't want no pardon
For what I was and am,
And I won't be reconstructed,
And I do not give a damn.
—Postwar song, "The Good Old Rebel"

A good illustration of the "unreconstructed" attitude was Robert Toombs, former Confederate general and cabinet member. Unlike many other high-ranking Confederates, Toombs never held elected office again because he would never ask for a pardon from the Federal government. Supposedly his remark on the subject was, "Pardon for what? I haven't pardoned you all yet!"

For Southern white children born during and just after the war, 1877 was their first year of peace and freedom, with no fear of war or Yankee occupation.

If Republicans in the 1860s and 1870s had been trying to turn Southerners against their party for 100 years, they were successful. The party, from its very beginnings, made no attempt to reach out to Southerners. The war intervened, and Lincoln being the "Black Republican" president, Southerners had no reason to change their mind about the party. Then came Reconstruction, with the Republicans in Congress trying to remake the South (they failed), which included getting all the newly freed blacks to vote Republican. Reconstruction had been a one-party tyranny. It helped to create a one-party South, a situation that didn't change for 100 years.

The Least You Need to Know

- ◆ Andrew Johnson tried to get the South back into the Union quickly, allowing the states to send men to Congress.

- ◆ Radical Republicans in Congress undid Johnson's work, insisting that former Confederates were still denying rights to blacks.

- ◆ Southern whites resented the new political power held by Northern carpetbaggers, Southern Unionist scalawags, and the newly freed blacks, and one tactic for fighting back was the Ku Klux Klan.

- ◆ Former Confederates eventually regained control of their state governments, in the process known as redemption.

29

Still Rebels After All These Years

In This Chapter

- ◆ Memorializing the South's heroes
- ◆ The heritage vs. racism debate
- ◆ Reenacting the past

While former Rebs were undergoing Reconstruction (and hating it), some other emotions beside Yankee-hate were growing. Southerners were getting sentimental over "the Lost Cause." Sure, they had lost the war. Meaning what? That the Yankees had been right? Heaven forbid! No, the South had lost because the North had more men and more resources—not because of any moral superiority. A few ex-Confederates might throw in their lot with the carpetbaggers, but most Rebels stayed Rebels in their hearts—and passed the Lost Cause religion on to later generations.

Reb Memories

So they created monuments—some on paper, some in marble and bronze. Former Rebels wrote their memoirs, and Northern publishers had no

Is it a Lost Cause now?
Never! A thousand times no!
Truth crushed to the earth will rise
again! Can never die!
—Jefferson Davis, in a speech in
the 1880s

qualms about publishing them. Generals wrote them, hoping to "set the record straight" (and justify their own actions, of course). Relatives and friends of the great dead (like Jackson and Stuart) memorialized the heroes in a flood of books and magazine articles. Both the president and vice president produced their own two-volume histories of the Confederacy. And authors like Father Abram Ryan, the "Poet-Priest of the Confederacy," memorialized the Lost Cause in popular, sentimental poems like "The Conquered Banner" and "The Sword of Robert E. Lee."

And once the Rebs began to pull themselves together financially, they could afford to do what the Yankees were already doing—erect marble and bronze monuments to their heroes. Over time, the former capital, Richmond, turned into "Monument Central," with its impressive statues in the Capitol and on the city's famed Monument Avenue. Organizations like the United Confederate Veterans and the United Daughters of the Confederacy were active in setting up monuments—not only the grand ones, but the more modest ones that still grace many Southern courthouse lawns, often a simple statue of a generic Johnny Reb. The Biggy (literally) is Georgia's Stone Mountain, outside Atlanta, with its nine-story-tall granite carving of Lee, Davis, and Jackson, finally completed in 1970. Even today, groups like the Sons of Confederate Veterans set up gravestones for Rebels who had to be hurriedly buried in mass graves during wartime.

Survivors of the war eventually died off, but the affection for books about the Lost Cause lived on. Margaret Mitchell published *Gone with the Wind* in 1936, and it was neither the first nor last best-seller about the Old South. In recent years we have seen such popular and critical successes as *The Killer Angels* and *Cold Mountain*, and if people are tiring of such novels, the bookstores aren't aware of it. (And certainly there is no corresponding interest for, say, Ohio or Michigan during the Civil War. For most readers, "Civil War fiction" means "Southern fiction.")

Margaret Mitchell's classic novel became probably the best-loved movie of all time, the 1939 masterpiece that still pleases audiences worldwide. And movie buffs generally agree that one of the best silent movies ever made was *The Birth of a Nation*, the 1915 epic showing the war and Reconstruction from a Southern point of view. And probably the best silent comedy, in many people's view, was Buster Keaton's 1926 gem, *The General*, with Keaton as a spunky Rebel railroad engineer chasing down Yankee saboteurs. Mere coincidence, that some of the most beloved movies of all happened to be about the Confederacy? Or is there some lingering affection for the

Lost Cause, some feeling that the South was a spunky little David who, this time, got whipped by Goliath—making David all the more sympathetic for fighting the good fight in spite of the odds? Obviously, audiences—and not all them of Southern, certainly—feel the appeal of this "defeated David" theme.

Non-PC in the PC World

When Confederate veterans aged, they gathered at reunions, often proudly unfurling the Southern Cross, the famous (and infamous) Confederate battle flag. Affection for the flag (and the Lost Cause) never died out, of course, but the flag got a new (and controversial) lease on life in the 1960s, when it came to be associated with segregation, and with anti-integration governors like George Wallace of Alabama and Lester Maddox of Georgia. Sadly, the flag that in years past had symbolized an affection for one's Southern roots began to symbolize racism and backwardness.

Does the Southern Cross today symbolize heritage, or hate? That question is at the root of the recent controversies mentioned in the introduction to this book, squabbles over flying the flag over the state capitol (South Carolina) or having it as part of the state flag (Georgia and Mississippi). "Heritage and history," say the flag's defenders. "Bigotry and racism," say the opponents. The same disagreement explains why a Richmond city park mural showing Lee aroused such a fuss, and why some museums have taken heat over merely displaying Confederate money (some of it showing happy slaves working in the fields). And the same forces are at work whenever a high school band is banned from playing "Dixie."

> **Did Y'all Know?** _____
>
> In 2001, the state of Mississippi opted to let the voters decide whether they preferred a new state flag or the old one with its Rebel battle flag in the corner. By a 2 to 1 margin, voters went for the old version.

Pettiness, or healthy disagreement? Both sides might do well to give each other the benefit of the doubt. No doubt some of the people flying the Rebel flag are racists. But not all are—definitely. In a culture with so little concern for history, interest in the Civil War and the Confederacy is a healthy thing. Textbooks can reduce history to "isms"—racism, sexism, etc. History is more complicated than that, and much more interesting, too. If the politically correct crowd really values tolerance, it ought to learn to tolerate neo-Confederates.

Rebs in a Rootless World

"Dixie" begins with this line: "I wish I was in the land of cotton/Old times there are not forgotten." Maybe that is part of the draw: In the twenty-first century, too many people feel rootless. This is why they spend endless hours digging up facts on their genealogies.

Maybe this is the attraction of the Old South—or of the South in general. With the exception of slavery, the Old South was more appealing in many ways than the old North. People are moving in droves to the "Sun Belt," and it has to be more than just the climate drawing them. People just like the South. And for those who move South, they have to learn to tolerate—or like—Southern folks' fascination with the old times.

Richmond, Virginia, with its summer heat and humidity—and happy reenactors in their authentic wool period clothing.

(Photo by the author)

The most visible manifestation of this fascination is, of course, the reenactment phenomenon. Thousands of suburban dads (and quite a few moms, too) are willing to turn themselves into "weekend Rebels," donning authentic wool uniforms (and wool undies, to boot) and braving summer heat and humidity to participate in encampments or even full-scale battle reenactments. Some take the hobby so seriously that while they are in their period dress, they adopt an actual character (often an ancestor) and limit their conversation to things an actual soldier would have discussed. Some people find it all rather silly, but they sometimes change their minds after visiting an encampment or watching a mock battle. While there

RebeLingo

A "farb" is a reenactor who doesn't try hard for the authentic look and materials of a Civil War soldier. "Farb" is short for "far-be-it-from-authentic." Serious reenactors strive for clothing and equipment that would perfectly match the real items.

are reenactors all over the United States, it won't be a surprise that there are more in the South, and more in gray uniforms than in blue.

Heroes Wanted

Stone Mountain in Georgia has a carving of the "Confederate Trinity," Lee, Jackson, and Davis. These three—Lee and Jackson even more so than Davis—have a grip on the imaginations and affections that none of the Union biggies ever had. (We're excluding Lincoln, obviously. There are Lincoln-admirers all over the world.) The North appreciated the generalship of Grant and Sherman, and D.C. boasts statues of all the best-known Union generals. But no Union soldier has had the legions of admirers that Lee and Jackson have had. British statesman-author Winston Churchill (who, you might recall, had an American mother) described Robert E. Lee as "one of the noblest Americans who ever lived, and one of the greatest captains known to the annals of war." Churchill had no such praise for the Union generals.

If you can look at the Civil War objectively, you have to say, "Well, sure the North won—usually the world's Goliaths do beat the Davids." When David loses, you still have to admire his spunk. Whatever the merits of Lincoln, Grant, Sherman, McClellan, Meade, Sheridan, or whoever, Civil War buffs face this obvious fact: The North held most of the cards in this game, and the South didn't. The Rebs fought on anyway.

When Robert E. Lee decided, painfully, to surrender his army to Grant at Appomattox, one of the officers asked him what history would make of his surrender. Lee sadly replied, "They will not understand how we were overwhelmed by numbers." But on that point, Lee was wrong. Even Grant admitted that Lee was never really "defeated" but simply "overwhelmed."

Americans like underdogs. You might say that by losing the war, the Confederacy won its place in the world's affections. When Jefferson Davis told his nation that they had "unconquered and unconquerable hearts," he was quite right.

The Least You Need to Know

- The grip the Confederacy has on the South *and* the North is evident in the number of popular movies and books about it.

- Detractors of Confederate heritage charge that it is racist and bigoted; proponents claim it is an important part of their heritage and should not be forgotten.

- People from all over the country engage in Civil War reenactments, with more as Confederates than as Yankees.

Index

states (Confederate States),
admission to U.S., 319-322
Stephens, Alexander
anti-Davis supporters,
183-185
appointed as vice president
to Davis, 68
Stone Mountain memorials,
324
Stone's River National
Battlefield, 282
Stowe, Harriet Beecher
abolitionists, 26-27
Stuart, James Ewell Brown,
234-236
substitution inventions,
219-220
substitution practices
(military drafts), 206
Sumter, Charles, 27-28
supply shortages
available soldiers, 95-96
coffee famine, 135-136
dyes, 137-138
food shortages, 94-95,
133-136
forging, 134
rations, 134
suggestions of Lucius B.
Northrop, 136
impressment
Impressment Act, 209
pressmen, 208-209
slaves, 209-210
medical supplies, 137-139
soaps, 137
submarines, 169
substitution inventions, 96,
219-220
Swamp Angel, 294

T

Taney, Roger, Dred Scott
case, 30
Tariff of Abominations, 20

tariffs
1832 Tariff Act, 20
high tariff acts, 19-21
Tariff of Abominations, 20
taxes, one percent income tax,
213
Tennessee
Army of Tennessee, 302
Bragg, General Braxton,
282-283
Chickamauga battle,
283-284
Hood, General John,
291-292
Rosecrans, General
William, 282-283
secession movement, 85-86
Texas
Confederate refugees, 278
Hood's Texas Brigade,
270-271
Houston, Governor Sam,
270
secession movement, 60
State Military Board, 279
Texas Frontier Regiment,
279-280
Third Conscription Act, 207
Thirteenth Amendment, 62,
316-317
tigers, 139
Toombs, Robert
Confederate president
candidates, 66
Montgomery convention,
66
torpedoes, 171-172
transportation problems, 94
Treasury Department
Memminger, Christopher,
213, 220-221
Trenholm, George,
220-221
Trenholm, George, 220-221
Trent incident, 195
Trinity Cathedral, 295
Turner, Nat, 25
Twenty-Negro Law, 205-206
two-bale laws, 215-216

U

unconstructed Confederate
states, 321
unicamerals, 99
uniforms
butternuts, 138
militias, 117
Rebel soldiers, 121-122
regulations following
Battle of Manassas,
131-132
shortage of gray dyes,
137-138
Union
after war feelings towards
South, 310-311
Arkansas establishment of
government, 273
Atlanta, Andrews, James,
285
Battle of Manassas,
127-132
McDowell, Irvin, 127
rally of Confederate
troops, 129-130
Rebel yell cries, 129
regulations on uniforms
and battle flags,
131-132
blockade
blockade runners,
217-218
effects on Confederate
supply shortages,
219-220
Burnside, Ambrose,
256-258
capture of New Orleans,
247-250
Constitutional Union
Party, 52
end of the war, 305-308
Grant, General Ulysses S.,
285-288
invasion of Maryland by
Robert E. Lee, 252-256
memorials, 323-325

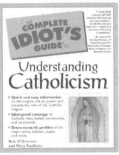

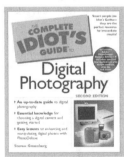
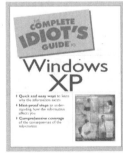